EROS AND THE SHATTERING GAZE

# EROS AND THE SHATTERING GAZE

## Transcending Narcissism

Kenneth A. Kimmel

*Eros and the Shattering Gaze*
*Transcending Narcissism*

Copyright © 2011 by Kenneth A. Kimmel
First Edition
ISBN 978-1-926715-49-0 Paperback

Published simultaneously in Canada and the United States of America by Fisher King Press. For information on obtaining permission for use of material from this work, submit a written request to: permissions@fisherkingpress.com

Fisher King Press
PO Box 222321
Carmel, CA 93922
www.fisherkingpress.com
info@fisherkingpress.com
+1-831-238-7799

Every effort has been made to trace all copyright holders; however, if any have been overlooked, the author will be pleased to make the necessary arrangements at the first opportunity.

# CONTENTS

*To Shawn and Sara,*
*My deepest gratitude and love*

# ACKNOWLEDGMENTS

While many have given generously of their time and shown me great support during these many years, there are two individuals without whose help this book would not have come to be. My gratitude goes beyond any words I can muster here.

To Ladson Hinton, for his ongoing presence, hearty discourses, and warm encouragement throughout these ten years of research, my humble thanks. He opened my eyes to wide-ranging questions through the opportune bread crumbs he dropped along the path, and he never failed to critique those lofty passages of mine, in need of embodied earth.

Deepest thanks go to Shierry Nicholsen, whose encouraging and unshakable dedication to the text came at a time when mine was failing, and who, through countless espressos and wisecracking sanded the manuscript's remaining grit while reigning in my tendencies (not completely) towards an antique, romantic style of writing.

My gratitude extends as well to each of the following individuals: Sigrid Asmus, whose careful editing tamed my exuberant ramblings and brought the full weight and structure of the Chicago Manual to bear upon me; Andrew Samuels, whose generosity of spirit and tenacious encouragement, despite the disappointments, helped the manuscript find its home at Fisher King; John Beebe, through keen eye and elegant language helped identify and deepen many key areas throughout the manuscript; Ann Belford Ulanov, whose presence and support early on in the process, and whose contemplation upon the 'burn wound of Eros' guided me to the Ecstasy of Saint Teresa; Susan Persson, who offered early encouragement, taught me a very useful writing exercise from which creative bursts of prose could emerge, summarizing the close of each section of the book; John Haule helped to whittle down the 'mountain of ideas' comprising an early version of Chapter Eleven; Sara Kimmel taught me that sometimes, three crisp sentences are better than one long one.

Thanks go as well to Mel Mathews, Publisher of Fisher King Press, whose generosity and kindness are matched only by his skill and the integrity of his word. The support from family, friends, and colleagues have meant so much to me and I wish to take this moment to thank them all.

Last and most importantly, I offer my deepest appreciation and gratitude to my patients—past and present—for their willingness to share their stories that fill these many pages. They are the real teachers.

# INTRODUCTION

*I want to be able to fly. I want to hover around you like a*
*winged Cupid in attendance on his Goddess.[1]*

From *The Golden Ass* by Apuleius. Lucius here pleads with his lover, a witch's apprentice, to steal a magical potion so that he can be transformed into a god. Instead, he is given the form of an ass and must submit himself to an existence as a loathsome beast of burden.

We live in a time and culture predisposed toward life at the surface. Ours is a society that privileges eternal youth and beauty, consumer-driven instant gratification, and narcissistic preoccupation with self-centeredness, not self reflection. Like Narcissus we often look no deeper than the reflection in the mirror, seeing only skin-deep beauty, never daring to know our own—nor the other's, inner depths.

Contemporary thought has attempted to respond to this cultural climate that, in the words of Stephen Frosh, "[fights] against the deepening of relationships [and love], against feeling real."[2] Psychoanalysis, analytical psychology, and philosophy have addressed the contemporary individual's crises of the heart, separation from authenticity, and repudiation of the other. They offer a variety of viewpoints on the problem of narcissism, from its ontological and healthy conformations to its pathological forms, and its grandiose illusions leading to growth or to defense.

Jacques Lacan's notion of the mirror stage helps us to understand the essential alienation inherent in narcissism and its search for perfection in an idealized image of another. Lacan describes a moment in infancy when the six-month-old child "recognizes" himself in the mirror and falsely identifies the reflection as an image of the unified wholeness and mastery he does not in fact possess. In that moment, the infant, with his smiling mother's assent, is lured into an illusion of false certainty and omnipotence that splits him off from his fragmented body/self with its accompanying experiences of terror and uncertainty.

Lacan's conception of the mirror sequence describes the way a mental construction of a perfect, alienating identity can originate, separating the infant from his own insufficient self image. The *I* itself that takes form here is an artificial representation, a self split between its idealized mirror image and the raw truth of human existence.[3] It is not difficult to imagine, then, how this narcissistic ideal can be later projected onto objects of desire who mirror this ideal.

Narcissism is not limited to the psychology of individuals. American culture, politics, and its recent national wounding uncannily mirror these narcissistic phenomena. The Patriot Act and the War on Terror can be seen as unconscious fantasies enacted upon the world stage. In this post-September 11 world many individuals err on the side of security and rigid borders, thereby sacrificing freedom, relationality, and dimensionality. Nor is narcissism merely a contemporary phenomenon. Literature and history provide ample illustrations of the historical and cultural contexts underlying the problem of narcissism and the way it is transcended.

The essence of narcissism is the repudiation of the other in its differences. Sometimes this takes the form of appropriating the other under the guise of romantic love, and sometimes it takes the form of casting out the other to protect the vulnerable self. In these pages I attempt to present a *theory of the transcendence of narcissism*, in which the humble capacity to love comes about through the surrender of the self to the shattering truth of the other.

•  •  •  •  •

Western culture's most ancient tale of love, "Psyche and Amor," which forms part of Apuleius' *The Golden Ass*, will introduce us to these dynamics. The story features a leading man—*Amor*, the very personification of Love—whose amorous desires are so embedded in narcissism that he never dares to reveal himself to the object of his passion. The couple, Psyche and Amor, remains suspended in a dark fusion removed from life until Psyche has finally had enough; the illusion is pierced and shattered, and loss ensues. Emerging from his state of wounding, Amor comes in a new way to the side of his beloved, the mortal human Psyche, his act signifying the inner "awakening of the sleeping soul through love," as James Hillman puts it.[4] How many hundreds of modern romantic dramas follow in the train of the Tale of Psyche and Amor, telling the story of the selfish or hardened man who uses everyone, then loses everything, but then finds a woman from whom he learns how to love?

More than a millennium later, the tales of medieval courtly romances portray the fate of lovers whose longing for oneness can be realized not on earth but only in their sacrificial death and reunion in Heaven. These are tragedies portraying an idealized longing for true love that can never be sustained in our flawed human condition.

The blissful fantasy of everlasting union merely conceals the face of narcissism. This romantic ideal privileges the allure of the lovers' paradise over the enduring struggles in human relationships in all their vicissitudes. These are the romantic fantasies of a happily-ever-after ending, illusions ultimately deriving from childhood experiences. Time and again, lovers plunge blindly into brief enthrallments that are doomed to failure, yet hold fast to their unquestioned, cherished beliefs, and to a faith in an idyllic innocence that is inevitably shattered. Young lovers blindly enter marriage with the fantasy that romantic love will endure forever. But predictably, when the burning fires of first love's desires have cooled to warm embers, many men devalue the apparently known quantity at home and look to a passionate love affair with a mysterious other, in which to be absorbed. For the narcissist this process signals the avoidance of human relationship in its fullness, rife with difficulties, limitations, and ethical responsibilities, in favor of the grandiose illusion of ecstatic oneness and freedom from all pain.

Ultimately the narcissistic avoidance of the difficulties of life arises in response to a primal experience—the inevitable wounding and loss suffered in the earliest infant-mother relationship. Thus narcissistic dynamics are deeply impacted by the experience of trauma. Psychological wounds too devastating to bear are reflexively partitioned and buried, while simultaneously, reactionary wars of retaliation against one's pain are staged in order to provide safeguards from disavowed shame and profound vulnerabilities. Throughout life grandiose fantasies in all their forms will magically supplant the experience of unbearable vulnerability, literally obliterating it.

These clinical themes are richly amplified by cultural signifiers found in the myths and mysteries of antiquity and from the medieval Tales of Courtly Love through the literature of the mystics and Romantics, to Gothic horror stories and modern romances from contemporary popular culture. These provide the historical and cultural contexts for the contemporary problem of narcissism as well as its transcendence.

As we will see, Levinas's postmodern philosophy describes the way the encounter with the ineffable Face of the Other shocks and deconstructs the sameness and narcissism within eros, freeing the subject to assume an enduring responsibility for the other from which new and transcendent capacities to love may be envisioned.

• • • • •

My theory of the transcendence of narcissism is based on the work of two men: C. G. Jung and the philosopher Emmanuel Levinas. Jung's theory of the *complexes* (see the Glossary for italicized terms) illuminates two vital concepts that are threaded throughout this book: the ego's primitive identification with the negative or overly positive aspects of the Mother, and the relationship of the *puer aeternus*, the eternal boy, with his split-off counterpart, the *senex*, the old man. We can see how these complexes come about by observing the characters in Apuleius' *The Golden Ass*, which contains the immortal "Tale of Psyche and Amor." The path through which they are overcome leads from the romantic, narcissistic, predatory preoccupations of what I call the *mother-bound man* to the wound that shatters the isolation of his standpoint. Through the work of the *transcendent function* this shattering may culminate in the emergence of empathic dimensions of emotion and a humble yet still masculine standpoint.

One of the ways this book contributes to the development of contemporary analytic psychology is through the cross-fertilization of Jungian and contemporary psychoanalytic ideas. For instance, I argue that narcissistic defenses arise not after the development of the complexes, but prior to them. The puer aeternus psychology described by Jung comes into being in reaction to the narcissistic defenses that have appropriated the infant's most archaic, unsignifiable complex—the mother. These narcissistic defenses encapsulate the infant's ego, protecting it from experiences reminiscent of its original loss of maternal containing. Another original area of contribution may be found in my analysis of the Grail Legend, where I view von Eschenbach's *Parzival* through the lens of eros development in its dual guise, as both a narcissistic and wounding process and one that is relational and healing.

The work of the French philosopher Emmanuel Levinas provides the second major source for my theory of how narcissism may be transcended. A traumatic encounter with an utterly unknowable, transcendent *Other*[5]—sometimes initiated by analytical work or psychotherapy—may violently shatter the narcissistic illusions that maintain, among other things, the individual's endless, romantically driven projections and erotic fantasies. There is therefore a painful, even violent, yet redemptive potential to the wounding. Levinas's postmodern philosophy is essential to an understanding of this kind of encounter with the Other by a subject; he too emphasizes its capacity to decenter the ego's "solipsism"— the belief that the self is the only reality and the only thing that we can be certain of. Levinas attempts to describe this shift from an ego-centered view of the universe as something that defies understanding or category. All religious experience perhaps stems from such a primordial awareness. His ethical philosophy, informed by the Holocaust in which his entire family was murdered, centers upon the "relation of infinite responsibility to the other person."[6] Levinas provides a profound insight into the dangers of how individuals can be so easily subsumed in the vision of a tyrannical utopia which he often refers to as a "totality."

To Levinas, the Other is unknowable, ineffable, ungraspable, tormenting, enigmatic, infinite, irreducible, sacred. Its mere trace can only be glimpsed interpersonally or *intersubjectively*—a term defining a psychological experience created between individuals. The Other does not originate in the psyche. It is infinite, already there, before subject or object exists, and our subjective awareness of it comes through the primacy of its impact upon us. It transcends subjective being, defies our concepts or categories, and cannot be engulfed or appropriated by ego consciousness.[7]

As Levinas would say, the trace of the Other is glimpsed in the irreducible "face of the human other," who is revealed in (her) vulnerability, sacredness, and nakedness.[8] In Levinas's ethical view, one's responsibility emerges from the trauma he feels for the useless suffering and destitution of the one now standing before him. He is taken hostage to the guilt of surviving when the other is stricken. He is even compelled to wish to substitute himself for the other, to put himself in (her) place—but it is too late. This is the torment of which Levinas speaks—the unavoidable responsibility to the other invoked by the shattering Other. It is impossible to evade this summons, which accuses one and even leads him to wonder just how much truth he can bear.

In moving from the ethics of human justice and compassion to personal psychology, one can observe how the traumatic impact of the Other destabilizes and shatters the ego's narcissism, awakening the subject from his slumber. Such a violent blow often appears to the ego in forms that are dark and shadowy, or that threaten to obliterate its fixed orientation and need for certainty, its wish for everything to remain the same. For Levinas, the ego's need to appropriate alterity—the other's difference—and to reduce it to sameness is the origin of all violence: narcissism *is* violence. In those cases where the shattering encounter is successfully navigated, a restructuring of a man's core of being occurs. An inner cohesion develops that enables him as an ethical subject to bear love's separations, uncertainties, longing, as well as its closeness.

Here I propose a significant revisioning of Jung's concept of the enigmatic Self, conceptualizing it as an idea akin to Levinas's unknowable Other, where both, I contend, transcend subjective being and the boundaries of the psyche. I argue that this revised understanding of the Self provides the basis for what I have previously described as a unifying theory of the transcendence of narcissism.

* * * * *

This book is concerned with *men's* problems with love due to narcissism. While some of these difficulties are common to women as well, I will leave the exploration of the woman's perspective to another. Similarly, I write primarily about heterosexual relationships, but many of these ideas can also be applied to homosexual relationships.

At the same time, though it focuses on narcissism in individual men, the book is not intended to be a textbook on the clinical theory and treatment of narcissism. Rather it is meant to bring to light the prevalence of narcissism in our culture and the possibilities for its transcendence. It does so through stories—stories old and new, epic and personal, fictional and historic. They include vignettes from my over thirty years of clinical experience as well as examples from a variety of cultural and historical sources, beginning with Apuleius and other Greek, Roman, and Biblical material and continuing through medieval romances to contemporary culture. Permission has been given in all case vignettes and each patient's identity has been carefully disguised. Some case vignettes are composites. I have found films to be particularly helpful in illustrating the forms narcissism takes in contemporary love relations.

* * * * *

The book consists of three parts, preceded by a Prologue that follows this introduction. The Prologue summarizes Apuleius' story for those unfamiliar with it; the retelling of the tale is followed by the description of what I term the *Eros template*—that is, those narcissistic qualities illuminated in the character of Eros, or Amor, in his relationships to his mother, Venus, and to his lover, Psyche.[9] Apuleius' work offers important glimpses into the reversal of narcissistic states in men, and in doing so also provides the metaphorical entry points for the three parts of this book.

Part One is entitled, "Narcissism in the Romantic: The Mother, Her Son, His Lover." These chapters depict how romantic and erotic desire for the instant but transient pleasures found in the lovers' fusion enacts men's earliest longing to return to the fantasy of a lost maternal paradise. The primitive development of these defensive and destructive forms of narcissism maintains and insulates men throughout life against the perceived threat of retraumatization that emotional depths or mutual relationships could initiate. Their desire seeks its ideal object through projections that *colonize* the individuality of the other, as the other is used for the colonizer's own completion. This creates an inflated state of fusion in the couple.

Part Two, "The Predator Beneath the Lover," shows how this fragile wholeness ultimately collapses. The object is discarded and devalued, leading to reactive attempts to restore the lost union through colonization and manipulation of a new object. As an alternative the subject withdraws into narcissistic encapsulation. Narcissism's disavowal of the other's human distinctiveness and mutuality in relationships can be viewed as a tyrannical maintenance of *sameness* that results in the annihilation of otherness. These obstacles to loving are portrayed in Ovid's myth of "Narcissus and Echo," where we see the tragic isolation of the person hopelessly ensnared at the surface of existence. He lives in desperate fear of contact, both with other humans and with his own internal depths. The existence of the other (Echo) is negated through a false sense of superiority. Part Two will enlarge upon these Ovidian themes.

In Part Three, "The Shattering Gaze," we encounter the traumatic *gaze of the Other*, who is unknowable and transcendent. It may shatter the individual's narcissistic omnipotence, whether it comes through unforeseen and unbearable tragedy, loss, or in the naked truth of revelations that seem too devastating or shameful to bear. Following this encounter, a resilient, emotional depth may evolve in a man, signifying the greater psychic cohesion needed to endure love and loss.

The Endnotes that follow the completion of each chapter contain a wealth of additional material too extensive to be included in the body of the book.

It is my hope that this work will appeal across theoretical lines and bridge the differences between diverse schools of thought. Therefore, a number of terms from analytical psychology, psychoanalysis, and philosophy, have been defined in the Glossary provided at the end of the book. These terms are italicized in the text. Through the Glossary those readers unfamiliar with ideas from different theoretical traditions and disciplines will gain a deeper understanding of this broad and inclusive area of study.

## Notes

1 Apuleius, *The Transformations of Lucius otherwise known as The Golden Ass.* Translated by Robert Graves (NY: Noonday Press, 1951), 42.

2 Stephen Frosh, "Melancholy Without the Other," in *Studies in Gender and Sexuality* 7(4) (2006): 368.

3 Jacques Lacan, "The Mirror Stage as Formative of the *I* Function," in *Ecrits*, translated by Bruce Fink (New York: Norton, 2006), 78.

4 James Hillman, *The Myth of Analysis* (Evanston, IL: Northwestern University Press, 1972), 55.

5 The term "Other" stemmed from the philosophy of Hegel's dialectic and gained contemporary relevance primarily from the work of Jacques Lacan and Emmanuel Levinas. Lacan doesn't see the Other in an infinite or transcendent way as Levinas does. Rather, he identifies the Other with the world of the Symbolic, which encompasses the cultural, social and linguistic networks into which the person is born, and from which subjectivity comes into being. The two men are similar in a general way, in that both privilege an 'otherness' that is already there at the origins of the subject, and from which the subject emerges. That is, for both, the 'self' is not an entity that is present from the beginnings of development. See Simon Critchley, *Ethics, Politics, Subjectivity* (New York: Verso Press, 1999), 198-216. See also Suzanne Barnard, "Diachrony, *Tuche*, and the Ethical Subject in Levinas and Lacan," in *Psychology for the Other*, edited by Edwin E. Gant & Richard N. Williams (Pittsburg: Duquesne University Press, 2002), 160-181.

6 Simon Critchley, "Introduction," in *The Cambridge Companion to Levinas*, edited by Simon Critchley and Robert Bernasconi (Cambridge, UK: Cambridge University Press, 2002), 6.

7 Jung may have had a similar idea of the Other in mind in his conception of the *Self* as ineffable and different from the ego, in a way that transcends even the psyche and is an infinite mystery disclosing itself only gradually over time. See the Glossary.

8 Adriaan Peperzak, *To the Other: An Introduction to the Philosophy of Emmanuel Levinas* (West Lafayette, IN: Purdue University Press, 1993), 89, 161.

9 My rendering and commentary is but one in a long line of previous and noted endeavors. Why have so many depth psychologists delved into the subject, and tried their hand at bringing new meaning to the myth, almost in the way that serious actors must all take a stab at Shakespeare? Simply put, we are all intrigued by a story that features as its star Psyche, the namesake of the profession to which we have all tethered ourselves. There must be some profound meaning we may yet discover in the relationship between Love and Psyche. For some examples see Erich Neumann, *Amor and Psyche*; Marie-Louise von Franz, *The Golden Ass of Apuleius*; Robert Johnson, *She*; James Hillman, *Myth of Analysis*; Donald Kalsched, *The Inner World of Trauma*; Polly Young-Eisendrath, *Women and Desire*.

# PROLOGUE

*The Transformations of Lucius, otherwise known as The Golden Ass,*
*by Lucius Apuleius*[1]

In this story a nobleman of high standing, who bears the same name as the author of the *Golden Ass*—Lucius—sets out on a journey to visit his *mother's homeland* in Thessaly, a place famed for its sorcery, black magic, witchcraft, and occult phenomena. It is a lawless land, filled with roving bands of cutthroat thieves and bandits. Lucius, whose name means "the light one," seeks to be enveloped and enchanted by occult forces and the dark side of the ancient mother goddess, the realm of the *dark feminine*. It is She who secretly brings about transformation and the new life that springs from death, though rarely without great pain. Once arrived, Lucius manages to seduce the slave girl who is the servant in the home where he is staying, hoping he may persuade her to reveal the secrets of her mistress, who is secretly a witch of enormous powers. In effect, this woman serves the goddess of the underworld, who has the power to transform men into beasts. After many pleasurable nights with the slave-girl, however, the arrogant visitor is still craving for more. He is filled with grand ideas of wielding great magical powers that he has no idea how to control. As Apuleius writes, he wants to be like a god, "a winged Cupid standing opposite her, Venus."[2] His plan backfires. Instead of finding himself transformed into a love god and taking flight, his grandiosity suffers a compensatory deflation and he is changed into an ass, a lowly beast of burden.

His lover, who stole the witch's magic ointment that transformed Lucius, reassures him that the antidote to his predicament is simple: he need only chew on *roses*; these will transform him back to human form. But the solution is not simple: roses are not in bloom during this part of the year. Lucius remains in animal form throughout the duration of the novel, suffering mightily over several seasons. He regains his human form only through the grace of the Goddess Isis. But that is a later story.

The author Apuleius was an intellectual, a man somewhat removed from an earthy existence, and seemingly more concerned with aesthetics and beauty.[3] von Franz writes, "Within the intellectual who cuts himself off from the immediacy of life experience through his intellectual theories, as Apuleius did, there remains a kind of hunch or idea that certain things can only be made conscious through being suffered or lived . . ." A wealthy man, he himself may never have been forced to endure pain and suffering in his privileged life. As a philosopher and a scholar, he may have lacked the aggressive and resilient nature that a warrior or a laborer tends to develop in order to free himself from a strong maternal influence. She continues,

> Apuleius probably had an enormous mother complex which took the form . . . of being threatened by an overwhelming . . . archetypal feminine principle. If a man is too much impressed by the figure of his mother, whether by her fault or by his own disposition, she interferes with his contact with reality, with women, usually inhibiting or eating up his *chthonic* [earthy] sexual personality. He may, being oversensitive, not have a strong enough masculine brutality to escape the mother and fight his way to freedom. Instead he escapes into intellect where generally she cannot follow.[4]

In Apuleius' tale, the hero falls down an Alice in Wonderland–like rabbit hole into the realm of lived experience. The author's literary creation can be interpreted as a text describing the development of a psychological process within his own psyche, depicting qualities vitally needed to free himself from the influence of the mother. Rather than flying off into the intellect, which I tend to believe was both his and his character's typical response to unexpected circumstances, Lucius/Apuleius responded to something unknown to him that was rearing its head, leading him in a new direction, toward manhood.

What greater affront to a snobbish, highbrow, eternal youth such as Lucius, the "light bringer," than to be changed into a reviled beast of burden. To people of the classical world, the ass carried varied meanings. The quality often ascribed to the animal was wanton lust, not too remote from the horny, insatiable behavior exhibited by young Lucius. The word's symbolic roots lead us to a key theme in the tale, that of Saturn. The planet associated with the ass is, in fact, *Saturn*. We know Saturn by his other name, Cronus, the god who eats his young out of fear that they will one day rebel against him and steal his power. His son Zeus outwits him, takes the throne of the gods, and banishes Saturn. Yet in his final stage Saturn becomes the wise and beneficent ruler over the Golden Age of happy men, in which the earth yields its fertile bounty and people live in harmony.

The often humorous tone of Apuleius' novel finds poor ass-headed Lucius bearing the brunt of pranks and abuses. Moreover, it is in Apuleius' very writing style, resembling carnival folk humor, that one discovers the paradoxical pairing of humiliation with comedy, sacrifice with renewal, travesty with transformation. The later carnival forms in the Middle Ages afforded the common folk a sort of cultural rite of passage, through which each person, during the carnival time, could transcend their humble position and toss away all inhibitions and limitations. This embodiment of their foolishness was where transcendence could be found, and it is a place where the fool plays a central role. In these plays and festivals, folklore and fairy tales, both King and Fool were enjoined and mocked, celebrated and sacrificed. The festive, playful, carnival spirit evoked the earthy, the sensuous, and the grotesque humor that parodied the ritual sanctity of official church and state. Carnival translates from the Latin roughly as "farewell to flesh," as in the Fat Tuesday Mardi Gras festivities preceding Ash Wednesday. Elements of these motifs are found throughout *The Golden Ass*. Apuleius' ebullient writing style can be closely compared to that master story-teller of medieval folk humor, Rabelais.[5]

Just as the midwinter festivals herald a return of the light, in his story the gaze of Apuleius never strays far from the promise of the dawn bringing with it the rebirth of Lucius from suffering and near-death. The ass-eared fool reigned during the ancient Roman festivals at the midwinter Saturnalia, which were viewed, according to Bakhtin, as a "true and full, though temporary, return of Saturn's golden age upon earth."[6] The Saturnalia traditions continued into the Christian era, and European folklore told of the "Christmas Fool," adorned with an ass-eared cap, who was killed by the "Spirit of the New Year," the infant Zeus.

Apuleius may have intentionally used a similar theme in his novel, where Lucius must carry the mantle of the ass-headed Saturnalian Fool and endure the endless shame of his imperfect, lowly position. "Lucius the Ass" must become Saturn's unwitting scapegoat while undergoing torturous sacrifices for a higher purpose that is only later realized. Within the fool may lie the trace of a king.

Through the struggles of Lucius we learn of shame as a teacher. It is through the bearing and working through of our shame and humiliation that we come to renounce all illusions of perfection, superiority, and certainty that we hold toward the world. We lie exposed, authentic, wounded. We come to accept ourselves in whole, including our foolishness and our flaws. The acceptance of the Fool is a transcendent moment, for it humbles us as well as opens us to a greater story. At the core of his storytelling, Apuleius has laid bare the hidden meaning of Lucius' odyssey. The boy must live in the punishing realm of Saturn the Father so that he can free himself from an over-identification with the maternal, and become a man capable of honoring, not using, the feminine. He must endure treatment as a devalued beast of burden. He is whipped, beaten, left for dead, even forced into lewd acts. He learns humility and he learns to endure pain like a warrior. Saturn's final, benevolent reign over the Golden Age of Men foreshadows something crucial in our story. A man like Lucius who fights to free himself from the mother will find within him a transformed Saturn nature. No longer the envious destroyer of children, he can stand as a bridge to the energies of a deeper masculine nature.

The Golden Ass and the pearl within it, the story of "Amor and Psyche," elucidate the problems I have undertaken to explore. Within the poison is contained the cure. The boy who is engulfed by his mother will discover his own point on which to take a stand only when the Saturnian mantle of manhood is thrust upon him. Living as the lonely ass brings humility, submission, pain, and recognition of the suffering of others. When Lucius ingests the antidote of the rose garland during a procession in honor of the Goddess Isis, his suffering is finally at an end. Lucius regains human form, a changed man, ready to serve life, not steal from it greedily.

In taking within himself the rose antidote, Lucius assimilates the ageless symbol for the heart, devotion, and the truest of all loves. Foreshadowed in the restorative treatment is his initiation into the mysteries of Isis that were popular in that day. Those ancient and secret rites reenacted the sacred union that joined a man in service to the divine. As we shall see, the spiritual renewal of young Lucius brings with it a deep sense of meaning, service, and humanity. His metal has been tempered in the fires of life through suffering the most humiliating, shameful, and torturous experiences imaginable.

The boy who goes searching in the land of his mother for mystical wisdom is transformed into an ass. He is taken off of his high horse, his seeming intellectual superiority, and forced to learn as a beast of burden. The influence of Saturn is felt throughout much of the novel and holds great psychological significance for the work on narcissism. Saturn, in his terrible aspect, crushes mama's boys that deny him. He is the lead weight tied to the eternal boy's lightness of being. He forces limitation upon the youth's unbounded freedom. He forces reality onto the dreamer. He brings balance. Lucius' embedded narcissism is uprooted and he is sacrificed upon the altar of Saturn so that he may one day become a man who can rightly serve the other—in her transcendence and her nakedness.

At one important juncture of the story, the author recounts how Lucius the Ass has been stolen by a gang of thieves, who brutalize him. But in the bandits' den he befriends a beautiful young bride, Charite,[7] who has been kidnapped and held for ransom. He makes a vow to himself to aid in her escape from the foul murderers, no matter what the cost, but the pair must wait for an opportune time before they can attempt to flee. There, to pass the time around the campfire, an old charwoman recites the immortal tale of the Princess Psyche who must also undergo great trials to win back the love of her life, her *Amor*, the divine son of Venus.


### *The Tale of Eros and Psyche*

The tale that the old charwoman imparts to Lucius and Charite is an ageless one, featuring themes with which we are all too familiar: *a possessive and seductive mother, her godlike son who can't take no for an answer, and his lover, the original woman who loves too much.* At center stage is Venus, goddess of love and beauty, jealous of any mortal daring to upstage her or to steal her precious boy's affection. Her son is Eros (*Amor*), wayward god of love, a grown-up Cupid and the proverbial eternal youth. And finally we have the mortal Princess Psyche, whose first sin was being born with grace and beauty so great that people throughout the land began to worship her as if she were the newborn Venus, thus neglecting the temples of the goddess herself. Given Venus' propensity for jealous vengeance, this was not a good idea. But the greatest affront to Venus is the fact that Psyche offers Eros a real human relationship.

Psyche's sisters are married off to respectable, albeit geriatric rulers of nearby kingdoms, men who would rather go off to war than become intimate with their wives. But no man could feel himself worthy of Psyche, nor did any dare come within a furlong of this "new Venus." Idealized, she sits alone in her ivory tower, untouched by life: the perfect woman in every narcissist's fantasy.

Psyche's father clearly cannot help his daughter into life. He sees how his daughter arouses awe in his subjects and fears the gods will punish this rebuke of Venus. After consulting the oracle of Apollo and receiving a terrible decree, he sends his youngest daughter to her apparent death. She is to march at the head of a funeral procession, dressed in bridal robes. Then, at the summit of a mountain, she is to be sacrificed to her "bridegroom," described by the oracle as a monstrous and fiery-winged serpent. Like the virgin left chained upon the altar to feed the dragon, Psyche bravely accepts her fate and awaits her murder. Yet the fierce dragon is none other than the divine youth whose arrows of love can enflame men's hearts to unimaginable and destructive excess.

Enraged, Venus has ordered her son down to earth to avenge her and to destroy the upstart girl. But instead Eros becomes enflamed with desire for Psyche, the New Venus. This conflation of mother and lover reveals the incest fantasy that traps Eros in over-identification with the maternal. Having taken one look at his innocent, luscious prey, the God of Love could no sooner kill Psyche than swear an oath to eternal celibacy. He arranges to have his newest plaything secretly whisked away to an enchanted palace within a secret valley, far from the prying eyes of his mother. Nightly, *Amor* returns to Psyche's bedchamber for sexual bliss. In her imprisonment, Psyche is forced to yield to her unknown lover and is forbidden to ever gaze upon his face, for he departs before the morning light. She lies trapped within a gilded cage, simply an object of a man's desire.

The true intent of Eros' acts against both Venus and Psyche is hidden from both women, and may at this juncture in the story point to his hidden rage and hatred at his own entrapment within the feminine. He schemes to simultaneously deliver a lethal blow that will get both of them!

Initially, Psyche is the perpetual victim, passive, helpless, and clueless. In her first terrifying night, as Apuleius informs us, "her fear of the *unknown* surpassed by far the fear of any peril that ever she had conceived."[8] She must submit to this dark and powerful spirit. Yet, in time, she grows to love him, despite his anonymity. But when Eros allows Psyche's jealous sisters to visit her luxurious prison, they poison the innocent girl's mind in hopes of horning in on the obvious windfall that has befallen their sister. Only when they enflame her thoughts with fear that her anonymous husband is in fact a terrible monster with the head of a thousand serpent coils is the passive Psyche stirred to action, finally willing to risk all just to see her lover's face.[9] That night, she lifts an oil lamp from a hiding place beneath her bed and casts its light upon the face of her sleeping husband, intending to cut off the deadly serpent's head with a razor. Only then does she realize that she has taken up with a god. She is so startled that her hand starts to shake and a drop of the lamp's hot oil falls upon his shoulder, deeply burning him. When she pricks her finger on one of his love arrows, in the flickering light of a dawning consciousness, she *falls in love with Love.* Startled awake, Eros bolts from her arms and flies away, despite her mournful protests. His little love nest has been exposed and now he must escape.

He returns to his mother's palace, wounded and seeking sympathy, knowing he could never bear to stand up for himself against the ire of Venus once she comes to learn of his disobedience.

What follows in the very moments after love is awakened is a suffering and loss that is nearly unbearable. The flame that brings consciousness is so rarely painless. It is only when Psyche, in the dark, sheds light upon her unconscious condition, ultimately wounding Eros and driving him away, that she can begin the task of consciously loving him. Psyche's act of burning Eros with the lamp's oil signifies the lovers' sacrifice of the fiery passion that has seized them in a mutually blinding possession.[10] In renouncing the safety of the lover's Garden of Eden, Psyche must face the uncertainties of existence alone, for the first time in her life. To survive, the now-pregnant Psyche must surrender herself to the vengeful Venus and her abusive handmaidens. She must undertake four impossible tasks at the hands of her enraged mother-in-law, while Eros goes home, like a whipped pup, to his mother's house to nurse his wound. Now all Psyche's thoughts turn toward restoring her union with Eros.

In her first task, Psyche must sort a heap of seeds into distinct piles. The girl is helpless, but she receives assistance from a colony of ants that do the work throughout the long night.[11] In her second task, Psyche must ford a stream to bring back strands of golden fleece from Apollo's sun rams. In the height of the noonday sun, these great beasts are fierce and foul tempered, ever ready to slice her to pieces with their horns if she dare confront them directly. Just as she attempts to cross the stream, a reed softly sings to Psyche, imploring her to wait for the right time to proceed, to wait for the sun to begin to set before attempting to cross. Sure enough, as the daylight begins to dim the beasts lie down to sleep on the hillside. Psyche crosses the stream and picks strands of the golden fleece from the sticker bushes along the banks of the river.[12]

In her third task Psyche must fill a crystal vessel with waters that flow from falls high upon a jagged peak. These waters are the source of the dreaded River Styx. This, too, is beyond her capacities, so she is aided by Zeus' eagle, who flies to the source and fills the container.[13] In her fourth and final task Psyche descends to the underworld to retrieve a box of beauty ointment for Venus from the goddess of the Underworld, Persephone. Psyche is warned ahead of time to "resist pity" for various characters along the way that ask for her help, for to do so would entrap her for eternity in the land of shades.[14] She succeeds in acquiring the beauty ointment but decides to keep it for herself, believing the ointment will make her irresistible to Eros and compel her long-lost husband to return to her. Through her willful act she has disobeyed Venus' final command, and when she opens the box on reaching the surface, she falls into a deathlike sleep.[15] Eros, observing it all, will not sit idly by any longer. He breaks from his mother's chambers, flies down to the place where Psyche lies, and awakens her. It is love that awakens the sleeping soul.[16]

Through her developing strength and resilience, and her ultimate faith in love, Psyche fulfills all of Venus' tasks. Her courage inspires Eros to leave his mother's house to find and free his lover from her deathlike sleep. In that loving act, *Amor* finally acts like a man, freed from lunar orbit around mother's earth, no longer under her domination. The two lovers ascend to the halls of Olympus and into the welcoming arms of the gods. Psyche drinks the ambrosia of immortality and later gives birth to their daughter, *Voluptas*. Yet this flight away from the human condition gives the story a characteristically incomplete ending. It mirrors so many other great romances where young lovers must perish and leave this world because their idyllic love can exist only in the great beyond, never with feet planted firmly upon the ground. As we return to the text of *The Golden Ass* we find this theme repeated.

Back in the robbers' den, Lucius and Lady Charite are rescued at long last by her brave husband, *Tleptolemus*. The couple's joy, however, is short-lived. Like the tragic troubadour's tales of fatal love (*Liebestod*), the lovers' souls find eternal union only in the afterworld. One is murdered by an envious competitor, while the other, in grief, takes her own life, unable to bear an existence without her beloved. Meanwhile, Lucius is sold from one cruel or neglectful owner to the next. He is subjected to the worst indecencies that humanity has to offer. Our author has plunged his protagonist into the realm of the *shadow*.

A traveling band of eunuch priests become Lucius' new owners, hawking their Syrian Goddess Cybele to the crowds they entertain. These debauched priests stage frenzied dances replete with acts of sadomasochism and bloody self-mortification—all for show—meanwhile lining their robes with the silver they glean from the audience. These were half-men, androgynous, squealing "girls," as their master called them, far from the celibate priests you might expect. They lusted greedily over the poor men they could lure into their clutches. They identified so mightily with the goddess that every remnant of their masculine being had been devoured by her. The author affords us here an extreme picture of a man trapped in the mother complex.

Apuleius describes how Lucius is led from one auction to the next. In his final trial, a convicted murderess, "though condemned to be eaten by wild beasts," is ordered first to become his "bride" through an act of bestiality, all before a jeering public.[17] Such a disgraceful prospect finally jars Lucius to action: he races six miles to a secluded beach and falls asleep. Startled awake by the glorious full moon rising from the sea, he purifies himself seven times in the water and offers heartfelt prayers for help and mercy to the "Blessed Queen of Heaven" in all her innumerable forms and names. As he falls back to sleep, a transcendent vision of beauty arises from the sea—the Goddess *Isis*—universal mother, mistress of all the elements, the unifying manifestation of all known gods and goddesses.

In the dream Isis promises to deliver Lucius on the following day, during the annual Spring procession, when her priests lead the people down to the seaside to bless the ships for safe travel in the new season. She instructs Lucius to eat the rose garland that she will command her High Priest to carry. In return for his transformation from ass to man, she asks—no, expects—that he will devote himself to her service for the rest of his days. All this comes to pass. Sloughing off the ass's hide, Lucius undergoes initiation into the sacred mysteries of death and rebirth, emerging as a priest of Isis and Osiris. The boy Lucius has freed himself from enslavement in the realm of the mothers and become a man, one capable of service, sacrifice, and passionate devotion.

## *The Eros Template*

Eros is an unrepentant, narcissistic lover who retreats from all emotional attachments. He takes the first steps toward maturity and love only after suffering and enduring a life-changing wound that opens him. We find him brought to life by countless writers and artists in many guises and circumstances throughout the long, meandering history of the Western world. Eros, son of Venus, husband of Psyche, is the prototype of the many versions of the puer aeternus we will meet in this book. We recognize him through the actions of men who leave behind the scattered wreckage of lost relationships. This type of man harms many women in their search to find the diamond in the dung heap of love and relationship. He's the one who leaves a goodbye note, is caught with the best friend, or turns cold and distant when the "L" word is spoken. It is ironic that these men who give so little are loved so much. This is due, perhaps, to their aura of specialness, or to their accomplishments, attractiveness, sensitivity, charisma, charm, and creativity, or even to that pitiful little-boy-lost quality that can evoke a mothering response in the most independent of partners.[18]

Apuleius' "Tale of Amor and Psyche" is the classical story that best charts the course of these men's romantic, narcissistic, and even predatory love. It is embodied in the character of Eros as well as in that of Lucius, the hero of *The Golden Ass*. These stories follow Eros and Lucius through their wounding and suffering, and toward the possibility of mature love, humility, and devotion. Regarding this from the standpoint of the male (as opposed to that of women), one can extract from Eros a *template* that outlines the key qualities of one pattern in narcissism—that of "mother's perfect little god," who habitually seeks instant pleasure in paradise but never in mutual relationships.

Here are some of the common themes of narcissism in the *Eros Template* extracted from "The Tale of Amor and Psyche." They are generally found embedded in our notions of romance and love, and are met throughout Western history.

*Mother's special boy*. He is the divine son of his mother. He is so special, and he knows no bounds. He can't take no for an answer. His desires and impulses must be gratified instantly. He is incestuously bonded to his mother, but as long as he does her bidding she protects him from the slings and arrows of the cruel world that may try to knock him down a few pegs for being so full of himself.

*His beauty is only skin deep*. He is a physically beautiful man but he lacks the capacity for internal reflection. His life centers around surface things: fulfillment of physical desires, attainment of beautiful possessions, and expectations of perfection. The great control and power that he must exert over his outer environment and relationships is a form of compensation for an emotionally unstable and chaotic internal identity that he cannot hold in check.

*Predator*. His desires are fueled by an internal lack, and when he becomes satiated he searches ceaselessly for a new object of desire and pleasure. He is a predatory hunter. He seeks the adrenaline rush of sexual conquest and power over the helpless victim. Like Psyche awaiting her sacrifice atop the mountain, she is merely his thing to be used to meet his needs.

*He seeks fusion in relationships*. He maintains his control over the love object by keeping her in the dark about who he really is. She has no identity separate from his, and as long as she is fused with him she is not an object to be related to but is compelled instead to be an object of his desire alone. He unconsciously seeks to relive the fantasy of incest with his own mother in his own little Garden of Eden, by finding her substitute, the newer version of Venus—young Psyche.

*He is split between his mother and his lover*. His loyalty is split between the need for mothering and the desire for the mature love of a woman, a division that interferes with his maturation and prolongs his stay in eternal youth. Alternatively, he is tossed between his longing for the untouched virgin and his desire for pleasures that only the goddess of love may bestow.

*Idealization and devaluation of the object of love*. He is always in search of the ideal, perfect woman. Because she is only human, the woman merely plays a role in his perfect fantasies and he has no idea who she really is. The moment she begins deviating from his expectations his feelings turn cold or destructive. Her imperfections arouse all sorts of uncertainties and insecurities within him, and to avoid those unstable feelings he must devalue her. Using her to maintain his stability and his illusions of perfection, he can also blame her when she lets him down. He sets things up so that he never has to look within to his own weaknesses. He rids himself of his own bad feelings by dumping them into the devalued woman.

*The narcissistic wound leads to negation of the other.* Owing to an unstable identity, he is full of exaggerated sensitivity and therefore is easily slighted and wounded, which leads to negation and devaluation of his ideal love object. Because the internal feelings prove too unbearable to look at, he instead chooses to retaliate against any perceived betrayal that causes him pain. He will easily abandon and evacuate the woman from his mind if it will allow him to avoid suffering.

*Continual return to mother to avoid the difficulties of life.* He will seek the old familiar re-treat to his mother's rooms to heal the narcissistic wounds inflicted by what he sees as a cold, cruel world, a world that demands to meet him as a real person. He is split between the need for security, sympathy, and maternal comfort, and the instinctive hunger for sexual gratification.

*Feigned innocence serves to mask his own destructive, hateful impulses.* By splitting off his awareness he turns a blind eye to the terrible mother and her group of vengeful handmaidens who fall mercilessly upon Psyche when she surrenders herself to Venus. By involving himself so exclusively in bemoaning his own mistreatment, Eros feigns innocence. His guilt lies in his complicity. A man such as this can bat his eyelashes innocently while he compartmentalizes his hatred and aggression, though it will often seep out indirectly, passively.

*The mother-bound man destroys all links to human relationships.* Mother-Venus and her handmaidens threaten Psyche with death if she fails to fulfill any of the impossible tasks set before her. They hope to destroy any links to love, dependency, and vulnerability. As in the previous paragraph, Eros feigns innocence as the dirty work is done for him, thus in-sulating himself from real life and real relationships and the pain that might ensue. These destructive handmaidens exist within the mother-bound man as protecting and persecut-ing objects, encapsulating him in a shell and protecting him from the risk of an intimacy that might cause him pain. He stays safe within mother's orbit, unwilling to break free of her power. On a conscious level he is only cognizant of his role as the "offended party" and will not own responsibility for the violence he inflicts on others when defending himself against perceived threats to his self preservation.

*The wounding that pierces the narcissistic shell.* In the end, Eros has suffered through his wounding and his separation from his wife Psyche. The bearing of shame plays a vital role in deflating one's omnipotence (although this step is not as clearly elucidated with Eros as it is with Apuleius' main character, Lucius). Eros develops within himself the courage and resilience to defy his mother's wrath and to return to Psyche. The wound that Eros ultimately bears exposes the false self that he has perpetuated in order to maintain his illu-sion of control over life. He chooses the life-giver,[19] as Neville Symington calls it, with all its uncertainties.

*Repairing the capacity to love.* A psyche must develop a resilience and cohesiveness in order to bear the vicissitudes of life, and from this, love in its transcendence may emerge. In the story, Eros comes to see this in Psyche, as he realizes the depth of her sacrifice and devotion, all for the sake of love. Her courage has touched something within him that inspires him to break out of his prison and seek connection and love in a human way. He discovers the capacity for care and the meaning of sacrifice. He repairs his marriage, but only after the couple suffer through separation, pain, and loss. Through a process of great suffering in which the capacities for *transcendence* emerge, Psyche, recognized as a man's inner *psyche-soul-anima*, transcends the maternal complex in which she has been mired. Love frees the soul.

## Notes

1  Apuleius, *The Transformations of Lucius otherwise known as The Golden Ass,* translated by Robert Graves (NY: Noonday Press, 1951).

2  Marie-Louise von Franz, *The Golden Ass of Apuleius* (Boston: Shambhala, 1970), 56.

3  I owe a great debt to Marie-Louise von Franz, whose commentary on *The Golden Ass* lays the foundation for this body of work.

4  von Franz, *Golden Ass of Apuleius,* 21–22.

5  Apuleius, *The Golden Ass.* See Graves, "Introduction," x.

6  M. M. Bakhtin, *Rabelais and His World* (Bloomington, IN: Indiana University Press, 1984), 7–8.

7  Charite's name—charity—can be traced back to the Greek word for the "love of God," or *agape.*

8  Erich Neumann, *Amor and Psyche* (Princeton, NJ: Princeton University Press, 1956), 11.

9  At the deepest level within the psyche, symbolized by her emancipation from the darkness of the bedchamber, we may view Psyche as the image of a man's inner feeling, his feminine nature—the *anima*—coming out of the dark and into relation with him.

10  This is the only variety of love that mama's little prince could offer within his enchanted paradise—one of instant fusion, the rapture of momentary pleasures soon to fade and die, and freedom from all struggles. Psyche, with one abrupt stroke, has put an end to the illusions spun by the web of erotic love. Psyche, as *psyche*, must wound and be severed from her unconscious, immature, idyllic, romantic, and self-centered relation to love, so that she might love on a deeper level. When new possibilities emerge from the psyche, consciousness increases and love can be freed from its contamination with the maternal, just as Eros must separate from his mother. In the myth of Psyche and Eros we find the first lines of poetry or prose ever written that laud the struggles of the human psyche to free love and desire from the drives of mother nature, and to move toward a state of conscious loving, caring, and relating.

11  This is a lesson in differentiation of chaotic, instinctive energies.

12  She learns to trust her intuition to find the right time, and resists the destructive impulse to "ram ahead" without reflection.

13  This speaks to the inability of the ego, by itself, to contain the waters of life and death. In times of difficulty the energies of the Self may emerge and come to our aid when the ego shows the resilience to endure the struggle.

14  This can allude to regression in psychotherapy and analysis, where we must work at not getting stuck in the unconscious.

15  Here Psyche, as the emerging conscious psyche, is attempting to differentiate from the unconscious that is signified by the realm of the gods and goddesses.

16  In *The Myth of Analysis*, James Hillman recounts the lover's tale as an inner text, describing "processes that go on between eros and psyche." By awakening Psyche from her deathlike sleep, Eros has finally broken free of the mother. Love profoundly affects the psyche. *"Only Love" (Eros)–mature Love (freed from the binds to mother), "can awaken an unconscious Psyche"* (my emphasis). James Hillman, *The Myth of Analysis* (Evanston, IL: Northwestern University Press, 1972, 55, 57). Surely these tasks undergone by Psyche must teach us something about how the psyche develops so we may learn to love more deeply.

17  Apuleius, *The Golden Ass*, 260.

18  We may pause to reflect upon why some women may seek the eternal youth, the "soft male," in order to avoid the threat of the strong patriarchal influence from their own past.

19  Neville Symington, *On Narcissism: A New Theory* (London: Karnac Books, 1993), 80. The "lifegiver" is the choice opted for by the patient, rather than the default to the "narcissistic option." The lifegiver may be signified by an internal or external object, such as the good-enough breast, or good-enough therapist, that the patient seeks. It may be compared to one's opening to the Other, in Levinas's terms. It is the choice for life and relationship rather than the deathlike, perpetual sameness of narcissistic encapsulation.

# PART ONE

# NARCISSISM IN THE ROMANTIC
# THE MOTHER, HER SON, HIS LOVER

*She summoned her winged headstrong boy, that wicked boy . . . armed with arrows and torch aflame . . . wantonness and lust are his by birth. . . . 'I implore you by all the bonds of love that bind you to her that bore you . . . avenge your mother . . . and sternly punish this rebellious beauty. . . . Cause the maid to be consumed with passion for the vilest of men . . .' So spoke She, and with parted lips kissed her son long and fervently.*[1]

> —Venus here calls upon her son, Eros, whom she is sending off to destroy her rival, Psyche.

## *Introductory Remarks*

As the fable of "Amor and Psyche" unfolds we learn of humanity's waning devotion to the love goddess, Venus, mother of Eros. Her altars have been desecrated and abandoned as the exciting news of the arrival of the "New Venus" spreads across the land. The narrator of the tale proclaims, "No, this time the earth, not the sea, has been impregnated by a heavenly emanation and has borne a new Goddess of Love, all the more beautiful because she is still a virgin."[2] Psyche is the symbol of purity—chaste, innocent, a virginal ideal, and completely untouchable by human hands, whereas Venus' sexual conquests and seductions are legendary. She is, sadly, used goods, abject, a devalued whore, thrown upon the garbage heap by a faithless world, traded in for the sparkling and mysterious new bauble in the marketplace.

Apuleius describes how Venus laments her mistreatment at the hands of mortals who have forgotten who she really is: "the first parent of created things, the primal source of all the elements . . . the kindly mother of all the world."[3] For Apuleius and the Greco-Roman world, Venus is not merely the eternally young and beautiful vamp lying seductively upon her couch casting her spells as Goddess of Love. She reveals her true nature as the primal source of all creation and is therefore linked back to the Great Mother and the ancient fertility goddesses whose rites of initiation flourished in the great agricultural civilizations of Mesopotamia, Egypt, and Greece, long before the Christian era.

In this context, therefore, Eros, is Venus' eternal *son and lover*, the *puer aeternus*, bound by the bonds of love to serve her as fertility god and never to leave her orbit. The wanton lad has come to know only too well his mother's amorous and incestuous entreaties. Her seductive influence causes him to roam the world, inflaming human passions and lust to indiscriminant excesses with his arrows of love. In one sense Eros, her offspring, manifests the forces of Venus in the world through these arrows. His phallus is hers; he is bound to her, existing merely as a moon revolving closely around her planet.

Venus dispatches Eros on a mission to destroy the mortal Psyche, the "New Venus," who has unwittingly become the target of all Venus' displaced hatred. He is torn between loyalty to his mother and the young beauty's charms, and ultimately he succumbs to his desire to possess this pure and untouched ideal. While awaiting her sacrifice Psyche is spirited away off the mountaintop and brought to the secret palace of Eros.

We can only wonder how cognizant Eros must be of the resemblance Psyche bears to his own mother, or to the implications of the pull toward incest therein. In the days that follow, Eros offers Psyche the only kind of love that his mother's little prince could know—the foolish promise of a short-lived paradise where no struggle is permitted and no conscious relationship can ever really develop, for the lover will never reveal his face in the light of day. Enraptured by her passionate and mysterious husband, Psyche lives at his complete mercy. The two lovers live in a timeless oneness, a dreamlike fusion removed from ordinary life, as lovers often do.[4] The enchanted paradise in which Psyche is held captive dramatizes every immature romantic love encounter in which the other carries for us our idealized projection of our twin.[5] The paradise of love encapsulates the twins in a deadening and perpetual sameness as a defense against difference and the unknown, just as Psyche dreads the unknown during her first night in the enchanted palace, alone and terrified.[6]

●  ●  ●  ●  ●

To put what we have just heard into theoretical terms: When a man projects his own soul image upon another, narcissism distorts, even contaminates love, particularly romantic love. In fact, to maintain his projection he colonizes the other so that she will continue to meet his expectations. The mother is the first love of our lives, and naturally male feelings of love become mixed up with maternal influences, both positive and negative. Part of a man's feelings for his mother, then, are projected onto the objects of his love.

*Anima*—the soul of man, the living essence and spirit of life within—transcends all complexes, and can never be located in another person; it emerges instead through the discourse and endless process of engagement with life. When a man's ego becomes entrenched in the mother complex, however, he turns away in fear from the uncertainties of life, an action that prevents the deeper encounter of self with other. For a man to free his love from the kind of narcissism found in romantic yearnings he must struggle to free his *anima* from the erotically charged projections, infused with elements of the mother complex, that have permeated his early life. In so doing he exposes narcissism's illusions and his own disavowal of love.

The anima's disentanglement from her identification with the mother complex is clearly exemplified in the liberation of Eros and Psyche from the influence of Venus at the climax of the story. The triangle at the heart of the "Tale of Amor and Psyche," comprising mother, son, and lover, embodies three dimensions of the mother problem in a man enveloped and dominated by overwhelming maternal influences, both negative and all too positive. His imagination has been distorted in its perceptions of love and romance—in his ideas of how love is "supposed" to be and how he is to manipulate it to fit his romantic image. He learns to insulate himself from the shattering effects of the alterity of love upon his fixed beliefs. The illusions of love that are depicted in the tale of Psyche and Eros echo many of the same themes portrayed throughout the long history of tragic love and romance in the Western world.

The narcissistic defenses that are mounted against men's emerging capacities to love take a number of forms, which we will meet in the chapters that make up Part One of this book. These defenses are present in the earliest mental life of the infant, for instance, in its archaic fantasies of restoring a traumatically lost (imagined) maternal paradise. In a further example, the helpless infant defends against the dread of the mother's unconscious affects flooding him, his defense taking the form of repression of these unfathomable messages. Later, in the adolescent and adult male, defenses take the form of splits in the psyche between needs for mothering and the desire for seduction and pleasure, and between the craving for carnal passion and the longing for the purity of true love. Lastly, the dissolution of the self into romantic and passionate fusion states is another form of defense, a defensive retreat from life indicating a symbolic return to the mother.

British Object Relations theory understands these defensive phenomena as forms of what it calls "defensive or libidinal narcissism." In this form of narcissistic defense, Ronald Britton writes, one attempts to "preserve the capacity for love by making the love-object seem like the self"[7] (through twinning and fusion). Alternatively, one may aggressively annex the other's unique and separate identity as a means of restoring control to one's threatened sense of self.[8] The Tale of Psyche and Eros abounds with examples of this defense, such as the incestuous claims Venus places upon Eros in order to possess and control him. In turn, Eros internalizes his mother's fear of annihilation (her fear of being abandoned by humanity) by identifying with her aggressive need for control, as we see in his sexual conquest and possession of his young bride, Psyche.[9]

The boundaryless union within the paradise of Eros and Psyche acts, for a brief time, as Eros' form of retreat and protection from the difficulties of life and the uncertainties of change, until he inevitably loses Psyche. Likewise, the mother-bound man—and the twin he is often drawn to— repeatedly swings between dependency and rejection, often being caught up in roles that reenact his primitive fantasies of fusion with and then loss of the mother.

In Eros' split between his mother and his lover one can see the familiar dilemma of a man who finds himself suspended in the choice between wife and mistress. On the one hand, from one perspective he needs to maintain a stable and secure home-life that only a devoted wife, one who is more like a mother to him, can provide. On the other, he is drawn by the intoxicating allure of the mistress who will stroke and stimulate him. In his need to be aroused and satiated by the one, then soothed and nurtured by the other he has negated the distinctiveness of both women and has instead merely annexed them. This, too, is a form of defensive narcissism: he forces each woman to be as a mother to him, although they play out opposite roles.

Masochistic elements of defensive narcissism can be recognized in the tragic myth of the puer aeternus' fatal entrapment in the realm of mother. As his mother's son he is subject to her desires and bound to orbit her world. His phallus is hers to use. He is hers to consume in pleasures leading to ecstasy and annihilation, known in the French as *jouissance*—the ultimate submission.

In some cases, patterns of submission, fusion, and masochism may appear in the field between patient and therapist as well as in the interactions of intimate partners. A therapist's mind may be aggressively colonized by his narcissistic patient, for example, whose needs or demands feel overwhelming, depriving the therapist of his ability to think at moments. The therapist may also feel used and powerless for a time, much like the masochistic object in an intimate relationship.

What has been felt as a profound failure in maternal containment in infancy, producing narcissistic defenses in its train, can sometimes be worked through in the analytic relationship. This is crucial to the emergence of capacities for care and concern thwarted in the early life of the patient.[10] When the analyst's capacity to survive the patient's attacks without retaliation or abandonment is demonstrated to the patient, it can elicit regret or guilt in the patient for having hurt the one he has depended upon. Through the transference relationship the "analyst as mother" is experienced as containing and capable of metabolizing the aggression of the patient's infant part. This is often followed by the patient's capacity for care and concern for the analyst and the possible harm done to their relationship. The narcissistic state is transcended through this achievement of care for the other.

These themes are discussed in the four chapters of Part One. The first chapter, *The Great Round*, highlights the condition of the child's original oneness with mother, followed by the inevitable wounding and disruption of that state with the loss of the maternal body. This profound loss will prompt the individual's eternal longing to return to the state of imagined wholeness and completion. In certain cases, owing to his mother's dominating psychological influence and need—which her son feels compelled to meet—he will become over-identified with the psychology of the *puer aeternus*. In this state he is dissuaded from becoming a separate individual because separateness is viewed as a threat to his mother. This reaction explains his need to insulate himself from life when things become too difficult, and to inhibit the development of capacities for mature love.

Chapter Two, *The Death Coniunctio: Tales of Fatal Love*, describes the compulsion to dissolve in the fantasy of oneness, as in the lovers' fusion of ecstatic pleasure and suffering (which I identify as a form of Freud's *death drive*). This addictive pull to act out the romantic illusion of paradise also takes the form of a compensatory refusal to live in the world or to bear life's difficulties. In one's fantasies, the continual longing to find "the one" with whom to feel complete, followed by catastrophic collapse when the fantasy fails to be realized, is seen as a submission to the inner "death mother." These outcomes reflect a weak and immature ego's lack of internal boundaries and an immersion in the mother complex—whether in its positive or negative aspects.

Chapter Three explores the problem of *The Split Feminine: Mother, Lover, Virgin, Whore*,[11] as a split in a man's psyche between his ideals of pure love and his hunger to fulfill earthy, erotic desires, often referred to as the problem of the virgin and whore. Another typical enactment of this form of splitting will find a man swinging between his need for mothering provided by a stable (maternal) wife, and his desire to be seduced and enthralled in an affair: these are the internal poles of mother and lover. He deprives both women of their unique individualities, uses and colonizes them, and relegates both to different yet static forms of mothering him. The biblical story of Jacob and his two wives, the culture of the Courts of Love, the twelfth-century Cathedral at Chartres, and the cult of the Cathars all signify the cultural, religious, and historic split in the Feminine.

The fourth chapter—*Analyst, President, Surgeon: The Split Feminine in Contemporary Man*—continues to explore the theme of the mother/lover split in the male psyche. Here I examine the likely impact that maternal loss and ambivalence may have had upon the early lives of two renowned public figures—Carl Jung and Bill Clinton—as well as a patient who was once a noted plastic surgeon. Each man has been buoyed by stabilizing women in maternal, caregiving roles on the one hand, and infused with passion for women who carry their projections of anima or seductress on the other. The emotions evoked for these anima women bring inspiration, destabilization, or ruin to the lives of these men.

## *Notes*

1   Neumann, *Amor and Psyche* (Princeton, NJ: Princeton University Press, 1956), 5.

2   Apuleius, *The Transformations of Lucius otherwise known as The Golden Ass.* Translated by Robert Graves NY: Noonday Press, 1951), 96.

3   Neumann, *Amor and Psyche*, 4.

4   "Sexuality cannot in itself build depth of character and if sexuality is used as an empathic bridge to another person where deep ties are otherwise lacking, it can be destructive of the development of the love capacities. Romantic love is based on empathic feelings between individuals who see themselves reflected in each other. Such love thrives on withdrawal from the world of problems where faith and analytic thinking are required. The pleasures of romance justify its selfishness and often lead lovers to feel that the outer world is a hostile place. Behind romantic intensity lies a shallowness in the creative love capacities." Paul Rosenfels, *Love and Power* (New York: Libra Publishers, 1966), 92–93.

5   Twin refers in this context to the type of narcissistic couple who individually are insufficient without their "other half." One is the ideal projection of the other's internal image of perfection, and vice versa. They often look and act much alike, and this actually increases over time, because, due to their withdrawal from the world, they depend increasingly upon each other to regulate each other's behavior.

6   See Apuleius' quote in the Prologue.

7   Ronald Britton, "Narcissism and Narcissistic Disorders." Paper presented at Northwest Psychoanalytic Society, EBOR Conference, Seattle, September 30, 2005.

8   In the internal object relations Freud describes the hysteric patient needing to play a part of one of the parents in the "primal scene," where others are invited to look on, and where the patient does not feel excluded. So, in defensive narcissism there is a turning inward within the patient of the image of one of the primal couple that the baby identifies with. That good part is then projected into the analyst or an ideal outer love object. In this sense the libido is object seeking in defensive narcissism, contrary to Freud's earlier belief that narcissism was un-analyzable due to the inability, he believed, for the analyst to be an object of the patient's transference. Robert Oelsner, "Introduction to the work of Ron Britton." Pre-lecture paper presented at the Inter-Institute Guest Lecture Series, Seattle, Washington, March 19, 2008.

9   To a lesser extent aspects of "destructive narcissism," defined as the hatred and obliteration of all links to another, are to be found in these three scenarios, as well. However, Part Two explores cases of destructive narcissism more fully. Defensive and destructive forms of narcissism may at times appear to overlap or segue one into the other.

10   See Chapter Four.

11   This term is borrowed from Peter Mudd's paper, "Jung and the Split Feminine," in the Round Table Review, 6(1) (1998), 1.

## CHAPTER ONE

# THE GREAT ROUND

*For what the center brings*
*Must obviously be*
*That which remains to the end*
*And was there from eternity*[1]
—Goethe

Jung and others warn us that deleterious consequences befall a man who cannot re-nounce his over-identification with the internal mother within—a circumstance that will keep him narcissistically removed and unadapted to life. In this chapter I present a number of narratives from myth and legend, as well as vignettes from clinical practice, that depict this immortal drama of the union and separation of mother and son. In the medieval Grail Legend of *Parzival,* the hero's traumatic birth provides an example of the process through which an infant can internalize his mother's negative affects, which will then obstruct the child's growing consciousness and need for separation. Here I also pres-ent the case of a former patient whose death exemplifies his retreat from life and whose entrapment within the negative maternal complex led him to suicide in the hope of find-ing eternal freedom from pain.

The ancient myth of Attis and Cybele provides a related template, one that tells the poignant tale of a divine son, the *puer aeternus*, born to the Great Mother, who castrates her beloved boy for attempting to grow up and leave her. In the last section of the chap-ter I discuss the dream of a patient struggling for freedom from the mother complex. The dream's heroic patterns of initiation suggest unrealized possibilities for the transcendence of psychological incest and castration at the hands of mother. The missing father looms large throughout each of these narratives.

• • • • •

The narratives of creation mythology and the mystery rites of death and renewal, found at the beginnings of civilization in such places as ancient Egypt, Greece, and Mesopotamia, provide the earliest patterns of men's fantasies for a hoped-for return to the mother's *body paradise.* This fantasy is the source of the dissolution of boundaries and the urge toward incest between son and mother.

Before there was a splitting apart of all opposites into heaven and earth, so the myths tell us, life was contained within the World Parents, in an idyllic state of oneness without beginning or end, the Great Round of the mother of all things. Ancients pictured this as an egg or a calabash gourd, or as a serpent encircling itself and swallowing its own tail. It was called the *uroboros.* It is not too great a leap to imagine a resemblance between these mythic origins and the infant's primal existence within the womb and the first months of life. Despite the irretrievable loss of the maternal vessel during the birthing process, the baby and mother exist seemingly as one entity. The Jungian analyst Erich Neumann explains,

> So long as the infantile ego consciousness is weak and feels the strain of its own existence as heavy and oppressive, while drowsiness and sleep are felt as delicious pleasure, it has not yet discovered its own reality and differentness. So long as this continues, the *uroboros* reigns on as the great whirling wheel of life, where everything not yet individual is submerged in the union of opposites, passing away and willing to pass away.[2]

Imagining the infant internalizing the unconscious somatic experiences of its mother while in utero and upon birth, French psychoanalyst Julia Kristeva describes what she calls the *semiotic*—the infant's *representations* of primitive affects, existing *prior* to verbal symbols. Kristeva associates the semiotic with the affects of the mother's body, or *chora.* Chora—a Greek term found in Plato's creation story, *Timaeus*—is described as a maternal container that enables all phenomena to be, but that cannot be named or identified, as its existence precedes language.[3]

Kristeva envisions an original wounding, suffered before there are words, that cannot be defined through the symbolization of language. It may be described as a sense of fundamental lack and a despairing sorrow for the *loss of the maternal body,* and in psychoanalytic work it can be glimpsed through the upwelling of unconscious experience—body symptoms, dreams, and other bits of primary process. Paradoxically, it is in the abject loss and unending mourning arising from the child's separation from mother, with no realistic chance for his return to her, that he is spurred on to resuscitate her within his imagination. In time the imagination gives rise to the capacity for symbolic representation through language. The human subject reflects the dialectical discourse between the maternal affects of *chora* and what Lacan and Kristeva would see as the paternal representations of language and its laws. For Kristeva all creativity comes from this gap between the body affects, with their bits of primal fantasy, and the symbolic; loss and melancholy are the mothers of creativity.

Symbolic representation is therefore a step removed from the enigmatic experience that produces the maternal affects, and it will attempt to provide substitutes for the irreplaceable loss. Symbolic representation may even be used to deny the importance of the maternal that has been lost. It is for this reason that postmodernists like Lacan and Kristeva consider that the moment we use language and the symbolic to define our experience we have separated ourselves from the experience, in a kind of reproduction or imitation of that loss. In this sense language is seen as a masking of our split self and a disavowing of the unnameable wound—and hence a narcissistic alienation that appears intrinsic to our human development, even as it is matched by a strange yearning to return to what has been lost.

This description parallels Winnicott's seminal thinking on the separation of psyche from soma in the earliest days and weeks of a newborn's life. Winnicott perceived the original state of the infant as possessing an undivided psyche and soma. It is ultimately the failure and breakdown of the maternal environmental container that leads to the development of a mind, born in loss, that must compensate for the environment's collapse. Psyche and soma—mind and body—are split forevermore.[4]

In concert with Neumann's insights, drawn from the myths of creation, psychoanalyst Stephen Mitchell uses the metaphor of cosmology to speak of the beginnings and development of psychological life. The universe began in a state of *primal density*, a term Mitchell borrowed from psychoanalyst and philosopher Hans Loewald, wherein everything was heavy, dense, and collapsed in upon itself. Everything was everything. The Big Bang theory suggests that when the cosmos exploded out of this state matter was differentiated into discrete parts. Mitchell describes how Loewald's vision of the origin of mind, likewise, sees the earliest experiences of psychological life as evidence of the tension between the primal density from whence we came and our differentiating minds. Whereas the primal density signifies the lack of separation of mother and child, or the perception of the lack of differentiation of inside and outside, past and present, or fantasy and reality, the differentiating mind, through thought and language, can isolate us and create boundaries and a sense of individuality, and can help in adaptation. Perhaps this implies the eventuation of a great effort, a "big bang" through which those parts of the child emerge, facilitating growth and the adaptation whereby the child may break free of the magnetism that maintains him within the fusion of this primal state.[5]

Given that the infant's comfort and security is founded in part upon successful nursing and feeding, it is striking that the ancients would choose the symbol of the tail-*eating* serpent to dramatize this initial stage in the creation myth as a metaphor for the oral but undifferentiated state of early life. If the infant fails to internalize these basic nourishing processes due to the collapse of the "object mother,"[6] destructive feelings of despair, hopelessness, dissociation, deep frustration, envy, greed, aggression, and even as Neumann would say, "the sadistic desire to devour its mother"[7] can result. When the baby's needs for nourishment and containment within the nurturing bonds of its mother are frustrated or denied, we can only imagine the ensuing desperate internal struggle for survival. In phantasies of the baby aggressively tearing the breast to bits, or, conversely, its inconsolable collapse into despair and loss of all hope, we see images of baby and mother enacting the roles of both predator and prey.[8]

· · · · ·

In the beginning of the Arthurian legend of *Parzival*,[9] Queen Herzeloyde, nine months pregnant with Parzival, awakens writhing and wailing in pain from a terrible dream foretelling her beloved husband's heroic death in battle. The author, von Eschenbach, writes:

> She thought a falling star was sweeping her into the air where fiery thunderbolts struck upon her with violence. These flew at her all at one time, and then her braids crackled and sang with sparks. With a crash the thunder made its rush and burst in a gust of burning tears. As she came to consciousness, there a griffon wrenched her right hand away. Then all was changed. She imagined fantastic things—how she was nurse to a dragon that tore her womb, and how this dragon took suck at her breasts, and how he swiftly fled away and left her so that she never saw him again. Her heart was bursting out of her body, and yet her eyes could not help but see that thing of terror.[10]

This prescient dream afflicted the radiant queen just at the moment when her husband's squire arrived at the castle to tell the sad tale of his lord's death. It unleashed unending grief and sorrow for her dead lover and even alluded to her future abandonment by her son, when the time would come for him to leave her. In this moment of bad tidings, Herzeloyde fell into a listless, suicidal depression, not caring if she or her unborn son would live or die. She barely survived Parzival's birth.[11] At the last moment, she regained consciousness, prayed for the strength to live, and gave birth to the child who was the fruit of her and her husband's love.

Upon her recovery from the traumatic birth and the grave events preceding it, the queen took her baby boy in her arms, and she and all the ladies in waiting gazed intently at the little penis between his legs: "He could not be other than fondled and cherished, for he was possessed of the organ of a man," writes von Eschenbach.[12] Through her child, Parzival, Herzeloyde was both mother and wife to her dead husband, whom she bore within her and gave birth to from the seed of his life.

One can only imagine the traumatic beginnings and the ongoing instability suffered by a newborn male subjected to such a collapse and burdened at birth with his mother's depression, anxiety, and trauma of loss. It brings to mind Bion's idea that the absence of a containing mother is a psychological catastrophe.[13] One might understand the powerful tendency of the mother to pour all of her love into the child, to protect him and to control him, as a defense against the unbearable pain and fear of reenacting her abandonment. As her child grows up, any signs of his autonomy or need for separation poses a threat to his mother's stability. By inducing guilt in him for causing her the pain of reliving her loss, she impedes his growth.

In the story, Parzival was shielded by his protective mother from all the dangers and hardships of a warrior's life and raised in the woods as a simpleton. This prevented him from growing up and leaving the nest until fate intervened. Beneath the mother's veil of protectiveness was an aggression that annexed her son's unique identity and turned him into an object of her needs and desires, signified by the flurry of the queen's handmaidens, who excitedly fondled her baby boy's genitalia.

• • • • •

The boy who is overidentified with the role of *puer aeternus* lives in the charmed circle of the mother who keeps him all to herself. Lurking beneath her charming surface is the *devouring mother*—that primal density, as Loewald says, carried by the mother and personified in our unconscious tendency to sink back into inertia and passivity. Thus the birth of consciousness is prevented by our fear of the uncertainty that may bring danger. When the son introjects his mother's depression or her abject terror of abandonment, his narcissistic defenses are triggered through his identification with the *puer aeternus*.

In narcissism, the traumatic failure and loss of maternal containment at birth, as in Parzival's story, impedes the development of core structures in the infant's psyche that allow the infant to negotiate differences between self and other. In consequence, the ego, identified with the *puer aeternus*, becomes inflated by a highly primitive and unarticulated *mother complex*. The mother complex then acts more as a narcissistic defense against the danger of retraumatization that accompanies the uncertainty of a mutual relationship. In reaction to the child's early trauma, in other words, the unarticulated maternal complex loses its ability to mediate as a self structure between consciousness and unconsciousness, or self and other. Instead, it induces states of ego fusion with the mother and withdrawal into fixed emotional patterns that shut down possibilities for experiencing the multiple dimensions found in relations with people seen as whole persons. The complex's unarticulated core resembles Kristeva's unknowable affects of the maternal body, existing before word or memory, that are irreparably lost to the infant, but that the child tries to resurrect through imagination. These fantasies of return to the maternal paradise, however, are merely reproductions and imitations that alienate and insulate the individual from his core of experience and his relationships.

In the mythic drama of the puer as it appears in the tale of Parzival, we find allusions to incest. But the kind of primitive allusions to incest that unfold in this context should be considered symbolic, not concrete or sexual. In the words of Erich Neumann, incest here speaks imaginatively to:

> a form of entry into the mother, of union with her, . . . it is more a desire to be dissolved and absorbed; passively one lets oneself be taken, . . . melts away in the ocean of pleasure. . . . The Great Mother takes the little child back into herself, and always. . . . there stand the insignia of death, signifying final dissolution in union with the Mother . . . . Cave, earth, tomb, sarcophagus, and coffin . . .[14]

In concert with these yearnings for dissolution, the narcissistic mind is stirred by vibrant, infantile longings and grand mythic fantasies. What passes for glorious merging with the all-embracing mother, however, is in fact a *marriage of death*, a disintegration of the self, a victimization, and a crumbling of the integrity of the boundaries of the psyche, which are necessary for maturity and selfhood. The hoped-for stability of an individual identity does not come to pass, and one finds only withdrawal from actual life, and oblivion. In Kristeva's formulations, the longing for return to the mother's body is soon followed by terror and dread.

Jung's poetic words poignantly capture this state of longing, carried on into later life by the narcissistic mind as it seeks again and again to return for the hoped-for ambrosia of eternal life, despite the inevitable cost of the loss of one's very self:

> [The puer's] Eros is passive like a child's; he hopes to be caught, sucked in, enveloped, and devoured. He seeks, as it were, the protecting, nourishing, charmed circle of the mother, the condition of the infant released from every care. . . . No wonder the real world vanishes from sight![15]

While these are but passing moments of emotional possession, they can distort the perception of reality and fill a man's mind with longing for what might be. "What is" can be violently denied, for there are times in life when his imperfections, frustrations, and failures may throw him into unbearable despair and panic. If, however, he relinquishes the fantasy of mother coming to the rescue to care for all of his needs and desires, and throws his whole weight into the scales of manhood to fight his way out of her membrane, then he stands a chance of embracing real life and relationships. That road leads to maturation and emotional development. If on the other hand the smallest of offenses triggers narcissistic sensitivities that catapult him out of a relationship and send him reeling for cover, then he will reach back for grandiose fantasies while in retreat, because they serve to split him off from any pain. He desires only to sink back into his illusions of mother's soothing paradise. What he ultimately finds there is psychic death—a death of the soul.

•  •  •  •  •

I am reminded of a patient with whom I once worked, a man who searched in vain for an eternal paradise free from pain. He was driven by powerful emotional currents, ones that compel an individual to throw caution to the wind and sail headlong into the concealed rocks, driven hopelessly onward by the entrancing song of the deadly sirens. His underlying hope is to merge with the suckling mother in her embrace, where at last he might find safety, yet what she offers is instead sweet poison and death.

After several years of psychotherapy, my patient tragically withdrew from treatment against my recommendations. He had quit his job because he could no longer bear the pressure of going to work. He was single, and lived off his meager savings until the money was apparently all gone, and he had cut off most of his friends. Several years after he quit therapy I learned that he had committed suicide at 48 years of age. But he once told me a story that has stayed with me.

In the late sixties he had gone to a rock concert and had taken a large dose of LSD. His mind "just drifted away," as he put it, and he became dissociated from normal feelings and perceptions, far beyond any effect the drug might have had. Existing in his own little world, reality as we know it ceased for him. He couldn't talk. His friends led him around like a zombie. They were unable to break through to him and could not get him to open up and return to his senses, so they left him to be looked after by some friends on a hippy farm in the country. Several days later he wandered off into the woods and found a huge redwood tree in a clearing. He knew that the only way he could return from this dissociated psychotic state, or, in his words, the only way for his soul to return, was if he clung to that old tree. There he sat, as if in a vegetative infancy, his disintegrated mind dwelling in a primal state of fusion with the Great Mother Tree. He lost all track of time while hugging the redwood, feeling as if he was being absorbed into its great life force. Finally, a deep sobbing erupted from some primordial place within him, and after what seemed like hours he felt himself coming back from the dead and reconnecting to life.[16]

In retrospect, my patient had taken a wrong turn in the hallucinogenic labyrinth, owing to some emotional contents that proved too terrifying or fragmenting to bear. So he split off from his body, lapsing into a dissociated state. Greek mythology tells of the sojourns of initiates in the underworld, where an individual might suddenly encounter *Hecate*, the Greek Goddess of the Crossroads, who offered visions of ecstasy and enlightenment but also delirium, fragmentation, and madness. It was as though my patient had encountered the goddess of the crossroads, but she was not bearing the gift of enlightenment. She was bringing madness.

Sometimes, through madness and wrong turnings, one comes face to face with what shatters yet ultimately transforms and deepens one's being. With nature's indomitable life force coursing through his veins, my patient could at last break out of the internal dead space encapsulating and isolating his being. His flowing tears brought life out of death, propelling him out of the vegetable and into the animal world again, at least for a time. For, as I learned so many years later, this sensitive and creative soul did not possess the stamina to live in this often harsh and demanding world, and soon became Her victim, *the very food* for the Dark Mother.

The witch in the Tale of Hansel and Gretel is just such a mother of darkness. In escaping the hunger and death offered by an unloving stepmother, Hansel and Gretel became lost in the woods, but then found and entered a kindly grandmother's gingerbread house, believing that they had at last found abundance, safety, and an idyllic and nurturing caregiver. This was an illusion meant to entrap. What Hansel found instead was a devouring witch who wanted to fatten him up to eat. Only through cleverness and the will to live—kill or be killed—were the children able to turn the tables, burn the witch in her own oven, and break the spell.

In profound contrast, what was missing from my patient's conscious will was a courageous, aggressive resolution to fight for his freedom and his very life and to flee from the clutches of the devouring mother. Ultimately he lacked within himself the capacity or the resilience to contain his enormous mental pain. Perhaps at some point, feeling too betrayed, he abandoned all hope of recovering the good mother within, the one who came to his aid those many years ago in the woods, and simply turned away from life. Perhaps his only recourse was to devalue and reject the internal nurturer he once idealized. This devaluation finally took the form of a wish to die, a wish disguised within the longing for freedom from pain.

Only in a fantasy of death can one believe it is possible to be free from the suffering innate in human existence. This may be one way of understanding Freud's death instinct, which will be a focus of the next chapter. In my speculations I could imagine an inner assassin unleashed within my patient, hatefully turned against himself, dashing all hope. But in truth one can never really know.[17]

• • • • •

The previous case vignette describes an ancient and desperate longing to return to the hoped-for fullness and abundance of a secure beginning, and the terrible consequences to a man's integrity if he succumbs to the Dark Mother's call. In the myth of the Great Round, the son is born from the womb of the mother and the endless circle opens. He enters the world of opposites, a world he responds to ambivalently. He is her special creation, his phallus heralded and glorified by Her. In time he must return to Her again, for it is She who demands his sacrifice, and she will feast upon him in death, for the sustaining mother and the devourer are both one and the same flesh.

The ancient agricultural myths and the mystery rites of spring renewal celebrate the *hieros gamos*, the sacred marriage between the Earth Mother and her *son and lover*, the god of vegetation. He is joyously born to the Great Mother, personified as the first blades of grain or wheat or corn in spring, then glorified as Her consort during the summer growing season, and ultimately sacrificed with great lamentation at harvest time. He descends to the underworld to the womb of his mother, and during the winter darkness impregnates her with his divine seed. At the time of the spring equinox he is ceremonially reborn in the mystery rites that dramatize his rebirth from the underworld, as the Great Round begins again with the new planting season.

Quite an endless and tumultuous existence for that son of hers, whom the Roman poet Ovid named *puer aeternus*, the eternal youth. In the mythology these boys are almost always androgynous. They are beautiful, often magically born from the earth's vegetation and raised by the mother without much male input, as in the story of *Parzival's* traumatic birth and early life. Naturally the feminine influences dominate and arrest the development of their nascent masculine personality. They don't have the strength of will to break free from the gravitational pull of the earth mother. So they go on and on, from year to year, orbiting as a moon around the earth, never developing to maturity nor fighting for their individuality.

The depiction of the *puer aeternus*, with his unstable life, early death, and many rebirths can be used clinically to understand the mother-bound young man whose own life and narcissistic behaviors so closely mirror that of the *puer*. In truth, such a young man, adored and depended upon by his mother (and the women who are mothers and lovers to him), is forever being pulled back into the feminine sphere of influence. She has gobbled him up, and his own psyche has become identified with the complex of the *puer aeternus*. The eternal youth longs to avoid the difficulties of life, whereas the mature consciousness, like Nietzsche's "tragic man" building sandcastles on the shore that he knows will one day be washed away, accepts the vicissitudes of life and learns to transcend the cycles of the Great Mother.[18]

What the puer acts out in the world is a royal life, with little awareness of what lurks beneath, driving him. According to von Franz,

> If a man is a mother's boy and lives as though he were eternal, as if he did not need to adapt to reality and a real woman, if he lives in savior fantasies as the man who will one day save the world or be the greatest philosopher or poet, he is wrongly identified with the puer aeternus figure. He is identical with a god, and he has not yet detached his ego complex from it. It has not yet grown out of the archetypal background, and the puer is sheer destructiveness. Such boys, who are stuck in the mother complex, are absolutely unformed . . .[19]

A man unconsciously living out this myth will attempt and fail at love through a series of fits and starts, because life and real love make demands upon him, force him to work at them, and are never perfect. He can be easily daunted or hurt by confrontation or judgment, necessitating hasty retreat to a safe harbor. Sadly, he never matures enough to see relationships through to a more sustaining level. Why should he, when he feels in the back of his mind that his mother will be there with open arms when the world once again turns cold and hard. At times the nurturing bosom of mother takes the form of a maternal woman who always takes him back; at other times it manifests in his emotional retreats from life through addictions, intellectualism, womanizing, depression, or romantic sentimentality, to name just a few of the forms his retreat may take.

## *The Myth of Attis and Cybele*

The ancient Greek Tale of Attis and Cybele depicts this timeless and tragic dance between mother and son. Contained within the tale are the world parents, their androgynous and primal offspring, and the virgin mother goddess who is impregnated from the fruit of a tree and gives birth to a beautiful son. The goddess's unbounded love is matched only by her dread at the thought of losing him to another woman. She would prefer to see him castrated and dead rather than permit him to leave her. Here is the story, as I tell it.

> The great god Zeus fell asleep upon a rock that secretly contained the spirit of the Great Mother. The two divinities merged in passionate embrace, and his semen fell upon the rock. Ten months later, a babe like no other emerged from it. His name was *Agdistis*, and he was a savage, lustful and untamable creature. He contained both male and female sexes within him. No one could stop his wanton excesses and destruction, for he viewed himself above the laws of god and man.
>
> Finally, the crafty wine-god Dionysus tricked the thirsty beast into gulping down his brew, thinking it water, and Agdistis fell into a deep slumber. The god tied a long cord to a tree and bound it to the penis of Agdistis. Startled awake from his drugging the creature bolted up and was castrated on the spot. Torn from his body, his severed penis and flowing blood were swallowed by the earth and up sprang an almond tree on the very spot.
>
> *Nana*, who was called by many, *Cybele*, the great goddess of Asia Minor, came upon the flowering tree, plucked from it an almond which she set in her lap, and magically conceived a child. Her son was called *Attis*. He grew into a youth of exquisite beauty. His mother loved him passionately, in all the ways that a woman loves a man.
>
> [Here the tale takes many turns and there are many different versions. One story tells of the unfaithfulness of Attis.] When he tried to leave his mother for the love of a young nymph, Cybele drove him to castrate himself and die beneath a pine tree, so that he would belong to no one but her. His spirit entered the pine, and from his blood sprang violets. Cybele sat lamenting beneath the tree, mourning his death, and all

growth ceased upon the earth. Not until Zeus declared that the pine tree would never die, that it would stay evergreen, did life begin again.

In the ancient spring rites of renewal in honor of Cybele, her eunuch priests would cut down the sacred pine tree, representative of her fallen son, and carry it in solemn procession into the temple. There they adorned its branches with violet wreaths, the offering meant to stimulate new growth. To its stem they attached the effigy of Attis. In the earliest ceremonies that reenacted the sacrifice of Attis, the priests would actually mutilate themselves beside the tree, and bury their severed parts in the earth. They too sacrificed their manhood to pledge themselves faithfully to the service of the Great Mother. Amid much lamentation, the effigy of Attis was placed in a tomb and sealed. The next morning the tomb was opened, and when they found that the god was no longer there, great joy arose amongst them, for Attis was reborn! What followed were orgiastic fertility rites throughout the land, proclaiming the resurrection of spring and the promise of abundant growth.

The characters in this renewal myth personify a number of aspects of narcissistic states. Agdistis, the androgynous and ferocious offspring of the Gods of Heaven and Earth, embodies the preverbal, primal density that lies at the root of life's beginnings, poignantly evoked by the imagery of the myth. Within life are the undifferentiated opposites of masculine and feminine, beast and god. It is from the seed of Agdistis that the eternal youth springs—Attis, the son and lover to the Great Mother. Like Agdistis, the narcissistically bound man has no boundaries or limits. He lives at the complete mercy of that primal center, seen darkly through impulsive, nonreflective behavior and blindly driven emotional reactions. There are no psychic structures within to contain or to mediate the energies of life, no subject relating to object. He has always been told that he can never take no for an answer. Like a sociopath, he feels no laws pertain to him, and no human suffering softens his cold heart. He is a hungry hunter always on the prowl for weak prey.

Curiously, Agdistis, Narcissus, and Eros (as in Cupid's arrows) are all hunters. Like these mythic figures, some narcissistic men cannot contain all their needs and so they hunt down their prey, merging with them, feeding off their psychic energy, as a way to fill their sense of lack. What may drive certain narcissistic acts is a great hunger to eat and be eaten, to dissolve, to merge into this ecstatic feast, where everything is condensed into everything else. No distinction exists in this individual's mind, only an androgyny, an unboundaried oneness where everything is as it was at the beginning. At one moment he is the hunter and in the next, like young Attis, he is his Mother's prey.

At the crux of the Attis and Cybele myth lies the paradoxical mystery of the phallus. In all the ancient myths of creation the son's phallus is treated as an object endowed with magical fertilizing properties. As Earth, his Mother longs for her son's seed so that she may bring forth new life. He has grown up into adolescence and his penis has taken on more prominence in the mother-son drama. But once his usefulness has been exhausted, as with the reaping of the fall harvest, Attis is castrated by his mother. In turn, the sacrifice of the son's phallus leads to renewed growth upon the barren earth.

Like the emasculated young god, such a young man displays no overt struggle, nor does he demonstrate the capacity to endure pain through which he might differentiate or adapt. Cybele's attack upon Attis reveals the aggressive quality of a mother's envy. It saps her son's initiative. He never adequately separates and therefore lacks any real sense of self. Bound up in narcissistic fusion he has overidentified with his mother. As long as he never strays he remains eternally hers. As Symington has written, it is the "option repeatedly chosen,"[20] having been learned in the dawn of life by an infant besieged by unbearable terror when facing the volatile changes of a dangerous and unpredictable environment. Mother Cybele's loving embrace changes in a heartbeat to the cold grip of the Death Mother.

Parents' narcissistic love can colonize their child and convey to him the sense that any overt sign of his autonomy is a threat to them and must therefore be discouraged.[21] Attempts to meet his needs outside their special enclosure will be met with resistance and disapproval. But as Jung says, "he makes no more than a series of fits and starts, for his initiative as well as his staying power are crippled by the secret memory that the world and happiness may be had as a gift—from the mother."[22] The result is tantamount to the fattening up of Hansel in the fairy tale. These conditions encourage his crippled attitude toward life and his inability to develop an enduring and resilient self, capable of withstanding separation as well as the attempted castration at the hands of the mother when he tries to break away.

It is the birth of the trickster element that saves Hansel. Consciousness often begins not in innocence but with the trickster's disruption of constrained reality. The trickster's creative action may signal emerging qualities of agency in the self and a differentiation that shocks the child out of his passive state in relation to the mother.


## Clinical Vignette

The following clinical vignette illustrates the struggle and failure to leave the mother. It describes the misery and pain enveloping a young man who is clinging to the memory of a "kind and good-hearted woman" he had met scarcely two months earlier. The wreck of a lady now standing before him revealed herself to be a drunken dance-away lover who cut herself off sexually the minute she began to care for him. Her typical response was to sabotage the new relationship by going off behind his back for a night of (seemingly) meaningless sex.[23] To top it off, despite all the evidence, it took everything short of a crowbar to pry him away from this woman. His typical caretaker's savior fantasies hid a more sinister and alluring pattern, one that he felt helpless to resist. The prospect of a life without this woman felt like a rejection too terrible to bear. His loss of who he imagined her to be brought up great suffering in him, along with desperate but unsuccessful attempts to restore their union. In this young patient we find, beneath his devotion, a deeply persecuted soul.

What constitutes the powerful and sometimes deadly erotic pull that brings such ill-fated lovers together and will not let them loose, at least not until a soft-hearted lad (with a weakness for drugs) has come within a hair's breadth of corrupting himself by falling back into vices he had struggled so hard to overcome? Such a scene is typical in the life of a mother-bound man who is desperately seeking to fulfill a fantasy of romantic oneness with a woman he imagines as other than his mother. Instead of escaping the mother, however, he finds himself in the role of rescuer to an equally lost soul. Clearly there must have been some inner drama that he felt compelled to reenact, some promise of divine love, replete with many passionate swings of emotional suffering. The couple lived through so many of those late-night, gut-wrenching scenes that often climaxed with the tender surrender in which the two became one, but which in the end required his own near-sacrifice. On the conscious level, once the infatuation stage receded, he saw that his beloved was not what he imagined her to be. From the unconscious standpoint, however, she may have been just what the doctor ordered!

On the conscious level, such a man may consider it his duty to restore to health the beautiful and wounded woman who needs him, but unconsciously he is living in terror of severing a fusion between mother and child.[24] My patient had longed for a Sleeping Beauty with thorns around her heart whom he could rescue. Instead, he wound up as Beauty's frozen, helpless prey. This outcome was not unlike what befell Briar Rose (the Sleeping Beauty), whose doting parents, in attempting to surround the christening of their baby girl with only goodness and light, set the stage for a dangerous attack from the dark side. By denying her participation in the christening ceremony, the parents compelled the "thirteenth fairy" to place a vengeful curse upon the kingdom.[25]

One can observe here how the enigmatic core of the mother complex may be ceaselessly retranslated throughout a lifetime, without ever being resolved, while its unconscious power and dynamism remain invisible to consciousness. As in the case of my patient, instead of becoming conscious, the complex erupts in the intersubjective emotional field through the other person, in the form of dark, powerful, and destructive desires and hungers. Even as the man maintains his patina of goodness and innocence, he sees himself as victimized and helpless.

Akin to the magical paradise that held Psyche and Eros, an impenetrable briar forest surrounds Briar Rose. It can be seen as a metaphor for the "devouring Dragon-Whale," described by Neumann. This term refers to a state of captivity that characterizes the effects of the mother complex. "The danger of engulfment," he writes, "is often disguised by the lure of a [regressive] paradise which, like the gingerbread house in the tale of Hansel and Gretel, conceals a devouring monster."[26] The aggressive and destructive power of the complex is often projected, remaining in shadow form, unarticulated to consciousness.

My young patient was one of two brothers who, despite being in their early thirties, had not been able to drum up the energy needed to emancipate from home. He used marijuana multiple times a day, which seemed to reinforce his rather passive attitude. His mother loomed large. She was a saccharine-sweet caretaker, rescuer, and martyr supreme who would do anything for her children (including maintaining their dependency). The father was as wispy as a ghost and rarely left his room. He spoke only in monosyllabic sentences so as to avoid, as much as possible, his wife's emasculating criticism. Her rage wasn't entirely unjustified. Perhaps she longed for a "real man" and her critical tongue reflected her disdain for his weakness. Not surprisingly, the dance of rage and passivity in my patient's mother and father resembles his own disavowed aggression and power, acted out through his lover's dark and destructive desires.

A short time after the collapse of his short-lived romance, my patient reported a dream. In it he is trying to leave his house (where he still lived with his mother and father). As he walks along the driveway a giant snake is blocking his departure, and many tiny snakes are writhing around in the front yard. He awakens, fearful and daunted by the obstacle.[27]

In failing to overcome the giant snake, he is perhaps prevented psychologically from freeing himself of entrapment in the mother complex. Such a larger-than-life image suggests that a great reservoir of libidinal energy has been building up unconsciously, inaccessible as yet to the ego. He cannot attack it or overcome the snake in the fashion of a sun-hero, who, once he has sacrificed the Mother, creates the world from the libido gained by his release from her.[28] The great monster and its babies may very well represent the mother complex in its devouring aspects. In another sense, however, the serpent may signify the Holy Other—uncanny, awesome and frightening, that has blocked the path of the dreamer, and that is now challenging him to fight for his life.

The last time my patient had attempted to move out of the house, he fell into a manic, religiously themed psychosis requiring hospitalization, in part brought on by the abrupt loss of a love relationship, as one might guess. Could the image of the giant snake signify his terror of dissolution of self, through madness or death, evoked by another failed love affair? Or could the snake be the servant of the Self, seeking to confront the passive, mother-bound ego, attack its fixed attitudes and fears, and force him to fight for freedom from the belly of the whale so that he can become a man? Perhaps both alternatives are valid. My patient is confronted here by the terrible truth—*mother and lover are one and the same*, though they differ in their guises. Both the alluring lover who draws him to the brink, and his dear mother who will keep him safely tucked away from all harm at any cost, are representations of the *Death Mother* who means to obliterate him or to devour his vitality so that he may never leave Her.[29]

The unchallenged snake signifies the dreamer's sense of captivity in the magical incest role of the *puer aeternus*, whose ego lacks the vitality necessary to free him from the mother's realm. Unable to navigate through the regression that threatens to overcome him, he remains trapped in the alluring cycle of fusion with the death mother—in a deadly excite-ment of submission—with no hope of independence from or transcendence of the com-plex. Any mortal whose ego is unconsciously identified with the *puer aeternus* is doomed to eternally reenact the drama in *concrete* form. For only a god or hero (as signifiers of a *psy-chological* process) may overcome the incest prohibition and the engulfing mother complex and act forcefully to bring more cohesion and differentiated wholeness to the psyche.

According to Jung, mythic heroes, appearing in dreams and symbols in the analytic work are the psyche's "personifications of libido."[30] In certain circumstances, he tells us, their conquering of the dragon or serpent Mother represents a kind of "regression toward incest" so that they may be "regenerated or born again as a renewed whole."[31] The hero or sun-god myths of descent to the monster's lair to confront her and bring back the trea-sure hard to attain, are motifs that can appear in clinical material, where they may signify possibilities of emergence and transcendence. Through his regeneration, the hero restores to ego-consciousness split-off energies trapped in the complexes. His actions reflect the enhanced capacities of the ego gained through the ego's ongoing assimilation of shadow contents. Endowed with sufficient substance, the ego transcends its identification with the mother complex.[32] This development is equivalent to the ego's heroic conquest of the psyche's incest stage as it gains the capacity to withstand the pull back into the maternal body. Should the dreamer turn away from the call to arms, however, it may signify a timid acquiescence to the omnipotent power of the mother and a fearful avoidance of the nec-essary phallic, male aggression. When we deny our own shadow we invariably submit to those in the real world who carry the shadow of power that we project upon them.

My patient, for example, showed no discretion when it came to his appetite for mari-juana. He'd smoke anywhere, anytime. He succumbed to a form of the death instinct that lay under the *jouissance* of the drug high. (For more on *jouissance*, see the next chapter.) In his typical brushes with the law he would be pulled over for speeding or tail-light infrac-tions. The traffic officer would detect the odor of pot, or discover a smoked roach dangling from the ashtray, and my patient would promptly be cited or arrested on the spot. As much as he bemoaned his cruel luck and disdain for "The Man," it never ceased to amaze me how often his bad behavior met with instant retribution.[33] It was as if some part of his psyche repeatedly orchestrated these interventions by The Law, which forced him into treatment to face his addictions and his entrapment in the devouring mother. Like his father and brother, he lacked the substance and resilience needed to break free of the spell—a sense of what Lacan terms *the name of the Father*, the paternal authority of the Law. Instead, his male, phallic power took shadow form in projections, often onto authority figures whom he identified as persecutory and brutal, and who were most obliging in acting out his drama in the concrete world.

In summary, a man's lifelong identification with the *puer aeternus* figure and his repeated emotional retreats to the safety of his mother complex represent his attempt to stabilize threatening and primitive maternal affects that he has internalized. This primitive complex stunts his psychic development rather than acting as a mediator, suggesting that the archaic mother complex behaves as a narcissistic defense against his fear of psychic obliteration. This fear is often initiated by unsignified, unarticulated, and unbearable core experiences of the loss of the mother, and the traumatic failure of maternal containment at birth and in the first months of life.

Throughout life the grandiose fantasy of return to an embryonic paradise within the mother's body is repeatedly chosen to fend off the terrors of alterity within the psyche and in the world of mutual relationships. A retreat to the negative internal mother can be located beneath the idyllic fantasy of romantic bliss that colonizes individuality, whether of oneself or the other. In the other extreme, withdrawal to the Death Mother may be realized in the fantasies of a suicide that is expected to bring one freedom from life's unbearable pain.

For a man to find the way out of this endless, narcissistic cycle he must undergo a process of breaking his identification with the mother complex. This process is often characterized by the development of a resilient and reflective psychological standpoint and portrayed in the motif of the emerging Father. This motif is the subject of subsequent chapters, particularly Chapter Ten.

## *Notes*

1 Johann Wolfgang von Goethe, *West-Eastern Divan*, "II. Book of Hafis: The Unlimited" http.//www. readbookonline.net/title/3242, (accessed 6/2/09). Cited in Erich Neumann, *The Origins and History of Consciousness* (Princeton, NJ: Princeton University Press, 1970), 5.
2 Erich Neumann, *Origins and History of Consciousness* (Princeton, NJ: Princeton University Press, 1970), 16.
3 Plato, *Timaeus and Critias*, translated by Desmond Lee (New York: Penguin, 1977), 52.
4 Donald W. Winnicott, "Mind and Its Relation to the Psyche-Soma" (1949), in *Through Paediatrics to Psychoanalysis* (New York: Basic Books, 1975), 243–54.
5 Stephen A. Mitchell, *Relationality* (Hillsdale, NJ: Analytic Press, 2000), 3–4.
6 See Chapter Four.
7 Erich Neumann, *The Child* (Boston, MA: Shambhala Publications, 1973), 76.
8 See the work of Melanie Klein.
9 The name means "piercing through the middle."
10 Wolfram von Eschenbach, *Parzival*, translation and introduction by Helen M. Mustard and Charles E. Passage (New York: Vintage Books, 1961), 58–59.

11  In Jacob's story in the Book of Genesis, his mother felt great despair during her pregnancy. She suffered from suicidal thoughts, just as does Herzeloyde, when Jacob and his twin brother, Esau "jostled each other within her, and she said, 'If so, why should I live?' " Genesis 25:22.

12  von Eschenbach, *Parzival*, 63. This hearkens back to the fertility Goddess's glorification of her divine son and his phallus, whose seed impregnates the earth mother in the darkness of winter, and who is reborn as the first blades of grain or corn in Spring.

13  Personal communication with JoAnn Culbert-Koehn.

14  Neumann, *The Origins and History of Consciousness*, 16–17.

15  C. G. Jung, *The Collected Works of C. G. Jung* (Princeton, NJ: Princeton University Press, 1970), 9ii, 11. (Henceforth, all citations to Jung's *Collected Works* will be designated as *C.W.*, with volume and page number.)

16  Such an act is not without its historical precedent. European folklore as late as the seventeenth century is replete with stories about the worship of sacred groves and trees that had curative powers and could bestow fertility. The sick would often tie themselves by ropes to the massive tree trunks so they might transfer their illness to the tree. Paul Sebillot, *Le Folk-Lore de France* (Paris: Guilmoto, 1906), III, 367–442. Sebeillot's definition is cited in Henri F. Ellenberger, *The Discovery of the Unconscious* (New York: Basic Books, 1970), 188.

17  Richard Alexander, "Some Notes on the Origin of Despair and Its Relationship to Destructive Envy," *Journal of Melanie Klein and Object Relations* 15(3) (1997): 417–40.

18  Friedrich Nietzsche, "The Birth of Tragedy," in *The Birth of Tragedy and Genealogy of Morals*, translated by Francis Golffing (Garden City, NY: Doubleday/Anchor, 1956), cited in Steven A. Mitchell, "The Wings of Icarus: Illusion and the Problem of Narcissism" at http://www.wawhite.org/Journal/mitchell_art5.htm, 7.

19  Marie-Louise von Franz, *The Golden Ass of Apuleius* (Boston: Shambhala, 1970), 96.

20  Neville Symington, *Narcissism: A New Theory* (London: Karnac Books, 1993), 36.

21  Jean Knox, "The Fear of Love: The Denial of Self in Relationship," *Journal of Analytical Psychology* 52(5) (2007): 546.

22  *C.W.* 9ii, 12.

23  It may indeed have had meaning for her, perhaps in an unconscious sadomasochistic longing and desire for "Dionysian ecstasy" and destruction.

24  This man's terror is due to an unconscious imperative that was present in his original mother-child relationship to the effect that under no circumstances is the child to abandon the mother. Alice Miller describes the kind of mother who originally enforced such a rule, a parent whose deprivation and emotional insecurity compelled her to appropriate her children's dependency needs into a reversal of roles whereby they had to take care of her. Children of this kind of mother (or father) learn to attend to their parent's needs and gratification as a way to secure the caretaker's love and to avoid losing that security. Alice Miller, *Prisoners of Childhood*, (New York, NY: Basic Books, Inc., 1981), 7-8.

25  In this fairy tale, a deathlike sleep lasting one hundred years has overcome the kingdom of Briar Rose. The "thirteenth fairy" was the one causing all the fuss. Excluded from the christening banquet upon the princess' birth, she had cast a vengeful curse.

26  Neumann, *Amor and Psyche*, 74–75.

27  Curiously, this dream occurred on the eve of St. Patrick's Day. Being a nonpracticing Catholic for many years, he had not recalled that Patrick was famous for driving all the snakes out of Ireland. In bringing Christianity to the Celtic pagans, the saint was in fact driving out the old nature religion of the Mother Goddess.

28  In the Hindu myth of Indra, found in the hymns of the Rig Veda, the fertility god rides into combat against the great serpent, Vritra, who stands guard over the waters of life. Upon his elephant,
Ganesha, and wielding his thunderbolts, Indra kills the serpent, looses the waters that generate
life, and brings forth the rising sun. Cotterell and Storm, *Ultimate Encyclopedia of Mythology*, 374.

29  See the myth of Attis and Cybele.

30  *C.W.* 5, 255.

31  *C.W.* 5, 255

32  Jung speaks to the mythic significance of dream symbols such as snakes or dragons, as produced
by the psyche of a mother-bound man who has no father to stand at his side. "Dragon and snake
are symbolic representations of the fear of the consequences of breaking the taboo and regressing
to incest." (That is, the fear of the primitive pull back to the mother's body.) Such a symbol corresponds to the "negative mother-imago and thus expresses resistance to incest, or the fear of it."
*C.W.* 5, 255.

33  Neville Symington, "Phantasy Effects that which It Represents," *International Journal of Psycho-
Analysis* 66 (1985): 349–57.

## CHAPTER TWO

# THE DEATH CONIUNCTIO
# TALES OF FATAL LOVE

T he tales of great love that are woven into our shared cultural psyche present an idealized image of love as union. In each lover's surrender to the other, two separate beings symbolically die to become one. We find this theme of longing for oneness embedded in all classic romances, however fleeting or tragic, and this same yearning to be one is what is emulated in all lesser human love. The same theme is observable in the mystic's spiritual marriage to God.

We also see this theme in Jung's concept of the *coniunctio* as the inner marriage of opposites, which he identified as a transcendent, *psychological* process. Jung's analysis of medieval and ancient mystical texts points out countless images of the coniunctio throughout history. When attempts are made to concretize this metaphorical, divine union through projection onto a human object, however, it becomes a defense *against* human intimacy, relationship, and transcendence. Edward Edinger has coined the term the *death* or *lesser coniunctio*,[1] defining it as the psychological state of a "premature union of insufficiently separated [inner] opposites,"[2] which appears as an internal image that the subject feels compelled to project and externalize onto an object. Rather than an inner marriage signifying the inner cohesion of the self, or what Jung called a differentiated psyche, the death coniunctio exerts an unconscious pull upon a weak ego to submit to the enthralling image of the one with whom it longs to merge. Complexes that underlie a deadly coniunctio take possession of the ego due to its lack of foundation, threatening its loss of psychic integrity. This precipitates the danger of a dissolution or fragmentation of the immature ego due to the lack of cohesion and differentiation in the psyche.

This drama is drawn into the world of relationships. The identification with the death coniunctio is acted out concretely in instances of immature erotic enthrallment in the oneness with the other. To compensate for the ego's inner deficiencies, such relationships often feature an incestuous engulfment or an over-identification with the maternal, as the lover is under the illusion of becoming hopelessly spellbound by "the one." While the couple may lose themselves for a time in the highly charged emotions that the death co-niunctio produces—swinging between elation and the despair of loss—this state contrasts starkly with the desire for internal spiritual, or psychological, union described above.

We encounter the death coniunctio in the metaphor of the *hieros gamos*—the sacred marriage between the Earth Mother and her son and lover, found in the ancient myths and mysteries of the matriarchal civilizations. In these myths the son is often depicted as the god of vegetation, whom the Earth Mother gives birth to, consorts with, and sacrifices by her hand. The death coniunctio lies unmistakably at the heart of the son/lover's plight. In the vocabulary of Jungian psychology, in the hieros gamos the immature male ego is in the grips of the mother complex, which exercises a negative influence upon men's no-tions of romance and its tragedy. In this chapter I will explore the dynamics of this deadly love by drawing upon examples from myth, legend, and literature, as well as from clinical material.

• • • • •

Many will recall, from earliest childhood, stories of immortal love, such as the fairy tale of the slumbering princess Briar Rose (or Sleeping Beauty), imprisoned for a hundred years in a tower, with her castle surrounded by a forest of thorns.[3] At the appointed time, as Briar Rose is awakened from her century-long sleep by a kiss from her prince, the briar forest that encapsulated her castle is suddenly transformed into blossoming roses, and life is again awakened in the court of the once-barren king and queen.

In the pages of *Genesis* we read of young Jacob, his long sojourn in the wilderness finally over, gazing upon the beautiful vision of the unknown woman at the well who would one day be his wife and the love of his life.[4] A passage from the *Zohar*, the great Jewish mysti-cal text, reveals the meaning of the well as a place of *sacred union*. From Jacob's first sight of his beloved Rachael, the text reveals, "The secret of the well is that it only rises when it sees its union, that is, its spouse. . . . Jacob thought: I want to take a wife to join the *Shekhinah*,[5] the secret of the well."[6] In the biblical texts the union of one's soul with its beloved symbolizes love as a spiritual path to union with the God of Creation.[7] From the union of Rachael and Jacob, the trace of the *Shekhinah*, the indwelling *feminine* presence of the Divine, descended into the world. According to Rabbi Areh Kaplan, in the Kabbalistic interpretation of scripture the marriage of the Hebrew Patriarch and Matriarch, Jacob and Rachael, symbolizes the "ultimate union of heaven and earth, of God and creation,"[8] of the *Lord* God with *Shekhinah*, the Sabbath Bride.

This age-old recognition of the Love of God in the longing for union of lover with beloved reemerged in the medieval courtly cult of *Amor* (love.) It took form in the fabled

Arthurian romances, those high tales of love and death immortalized throughout Europe by the traveling minnesingers.[9] Sir Lancelot of the Lake, famed and tragic hero of Arthur's Round Table, was doomed to live his life possessed by a forbidden love for his Queen and best friend's wife, Guinevere. Born of mortal blood, Lancelot was said to be bewitched by the faerie magic of the fabled Lady of the Lake, who fostered him. Here we glimpse the power exerted upon a man from his earliest years by elements of the feminine.

Yet Lancelot and Guinevere, those "spellbound reckless lovers,"[10] as Heinrich Zimmer writes, could somehow be forgiven, redeemed, immortalized, and even emulated by the world and each generation that followed, owing to their deep suffering and helpless enchantment by the forces of magic. Of their forbidden love Zimmer says, "Each was related to the other, not as a human being, but as to a discovery of a lost, required, separated portion of the soul. They were not two, but one: each a projection of the unconscious of the other . . . their normal human biographies . . . annihilated in this demonic spell . . ."[11]

We find these same themes underlying certain religious mystical traditions.[12] They differ only slightly in their intensity from the sensual and romantic love stories cited above. The devotional poetry of Saint John of the Cross and of the Sufi poet Rumi, as well as the ecstatic visions of Saint Teresa of Avila, poignantly reveal the human soul's deep suffering and passionate longing for union with the experience of God, as Beloved.[13] The words of Saint John of the Cross allude to his longing for oneness with the Divine, signified by a "total transformation in the Beloved in which each surrenders the entire possession of the self to the other."[14]

No more sublime an image exists of the profound reunion of Lover and Beloved than the seventeenth-century masterpiece, *The Ecstasy of St. Teresa*, by the sculptor Bernini. The work depicts a scene described in the Saint's autobiography and *The Interior Castle*, a compilation of her mystical writings. Bernini's sensuous and erotic work depicts the saint as she swoons in ecstasy, both pleasure and pain written in her face as God's angel withdraws the arrow that has pierced her heart. Here is Eros, in the thinly veiled guise of an angel penetrating the heart, as an image of sacred union between Spirit and Earth.[15]

We turn now to the work of psychological union. The *union of lovers*, depicted in Eros' act of rescuing Psyche from her deathlike sleep and Briar Rose's awakening by a kiss from her Prince, has been symbolized for ages in art, myth, fairy tales, and religious and secular literature and drama. As an inner image appearing in dreams and the like, it signifies the emergence and renewal of life and fruitfulness through the power of True Love, and presents us with far-reaching psychological implications: the hope, Hillman writes, of "awakening" the "sleeping *soul* through love."[16] We can only hope for such an awakening, for the psyche only hints at the emergence of unrealized, transcendent possibilities. Actualizing these possibilities in the future must depend upon our ability to free ourselves of the complexes of the past, which keep us fixed and divided from ourselves.

From Jung's researches into ancient and medieval symbols of the coniunctio we find a timeless metaphor for the psychological work that produces emergent and vital symbolism from the unconscious, which transcends the sense of separation and limitations of the ego, and moves toward a more cohesive psychic wholeness. Jung recognized that the *self*—the regulating center of the psyche that transcends conscious functions of the ego—could be represented in the images of the coniunctio—the process of psychological union of opposites within a person. He labored tirelessly to provide ancient and medieval images portraying the human struggle to recover lost portions of the soul. The marriage of opposites within the psyche is represented in such timeless, mythopoetic images as King and Queen, spirit and soul, heaven and earth, *Luna* and *Sol*. The product of their union, gained from the struggle between conscious and unconscious, emerges as something new that signifies a transcendence and broadening of the ego's boundaries. Clinicians too recognize the fruits of a long and difficult analytic process in our patients' greater capacity for inner connection, psychic cohesion, and deepening human relations—what Jung might consider the process of *approaching* wholeness. But obstacles abound for such achievements, in part due to our cultural fear and dread of what we cannot control or understand.

The dark phases of *Luna*, as the moon, arouse just such dread. *Luna* symbolizes the cycles of nature, *eros*, mutability, the irrational, the unconscious, and all things stemming from the mysteries of the *dark feminine*. Since the early days of Christendom these things have been vilified, feared, and marginalized by a cultural consciousness that instead privileged her "essential spouse," *Sol*, representative of the Sun's light of consciousness, stability, rationality, and the masculine spirit. It is in *Sol and Luna*'s union or in their conflict and antinomy, Jung maintained, that the self in all its ambiguity emerges in psychological transcendence, and in love.

Such a luminary as Saint Augustine, for example, implored his faithful to cleave to the immutability of *Sol* and the Church, as a shield for those weak souls susceptible to the enthralling seductions of the *dark feminine*. In his late-fourth-century AD writings, we find a startling departure from Saint Teresa's image of the heart pierced by Love's arrow. If you compare Augustine's commentary on Psalm 10.3 with the original Hebrew text, he adds a bit of poetic license to the Latin Vulgate: "They have made ready their arrows in the quiver, to shoot *in the darkness of the moon* at the upright of heart."[17] He believed that wounding was a result of man's wickedness, and to his weakness in the face of the pleasures of the senses, which he ascribed to the dangerous moon and her waning and waxing influences. He urges the "wise man" to cling to the stable and spiritual sun, and shun the entreaties of *Luna*.

From this injunction we may catch a glimpse of the split found in the psyche of European culture, and perhaps appreciate the struggle we face today in finding union with the opposites within.

Whatever we hate or repress of the psyche, and whatever remains unlived, survives quite richly in the unconscious imagination. It takes the form of blind emotional possession or projection onto those segments of the population that we marginalize or think little of. The witch hunts in seventeenth-century Salem or during the McCarthy era of the 1950s suffice as cultural instances. But like the dark side of the moon, these elements remain far from the light of consciousness. For those souls, however, who Augustine might perceive to be weak and unable to resist the seductions of *Luna* and her maternal influences, an opposite kind of danger lurks. Instead of being the predator, they become the prey. We are of course speaking of the problem of the *puer aeternus* and his incestuous union with the mother. While immersed in sensual pleasures that she bestows upon him, he becomes her captive and meets his ultimate demise in the mother-realm, as described in the language of pagan, matriarchal, pre-Christian mythology as the *hieros gamos*.

What we might call a pull toward incest—when the *puer* man retreats from life and moves toward all things mothering and infantile—may be, as Jung has shown, a longing for the "latent state that precedes regeneration."[18] The puer can't, or won't, do the work against nature, the *opus contra naturam*—the struggle to overcome the unconscious patterns of the complexes. It is not real incest that is sought, Jung writes, but an "urge to get back to childhood,"[19] an incestuous union that he hopes might give rise to the energies of psychological rebirth. As Jung says, "Yet the longing for this lost world continues and, when difficult adaptations are demanded, is forever tempting one to make evasions and retreats, to regress to the infantile past, which then starts throwing up the incestuous symbolism."[20] This is what Freud might consider secondary narcissism.

Such a pull could explain to some degree the compulsive nature of the narcissistic current in the *puer* man, who returns again and again to the well in hopes of renewal. Sadly, as Jung informs us, these actions lack the energy of the instinctive self to back them up, and are "an artificial product . . . in the long run . . . incapable of life."[21] The incestuous desire, in Jung's thought, is not for the purposes of cohabitation, but rather the fantasy of finding some way of returning to the mother's body in order to be reborn from her, as portrayed in all Sun myths.[22] What appears as a regression of the ego back to the mother/unconscious in service to the self, giving rise to the rebirth of heroic energies needed for life, instead degrades in puer psychology into a perpetual collapse in on oneself. This occurs because the man identified with the *puer mythos* lacks the vitality of life. According to Jung, "The lovely apparition of the *puer aeternus* is, alas, a form of illusion. In reality he is a parasite on the mother, a creature of her imagination, who only lives when rooted in the maternal body."[23] Here the mother is a personification of the collective unconscious, whereas the *puer* epitomizes a nascent consciousness that can only succumb to unconsciousness.

Eros' role as *puer aeternus* in Apuleius' tale alludes to the incest motif in the sense of his longing to be rooted in the maternal body, subordinating the youth to his mother, Venus. By extension, the same longing for fusion is true for Eros and Psyche, the young woman who was, after all, considered to be the "new Venus," born of mortal flesh, not divine. This enthrallment to the object of desire represents an identification with the death coniunctio. As Edinger indicates, this is "what happens when an immature aspect of the ego embraces the unconscious: it undergoes death or dissolution. For the immature ego, it is very dangerous to have any dealings with the unconscious."[24] This warning points to the usual basis for the incest taboo. A man in an erotic obsession will continually search out "the one" who will complete him, but what he finds beneath the image of such a deadly coniunctio is the *death mother* and her incestuous embrace. In some cases he will repeatedly project this image upon a particular type of woman or girl who fits the picture of his perfect twin, yet their pleasurable fusion invariably degenerates into a destructive dependency and a dissolution of self. His psyche is fixated at too immature a level and lacks the strength to break free from the intoxicating, erotic longing to return to the fantasy of the mother's body.[25]

This dynamic is described in the more obscure version of the Narcissus myth, as told by the second century Greek traveler, Pausanias, in which Narcissus has fallen in love with his twin sister.[26] It is when she dies that out of longing for her he goes to a spring, knowing that it is only his own reflection that he sees as he gazes into the waters. To gain some relief from his grief, or perhaps to obviate it completely, he then imagines that he sees her reflection looking back up at him. Her image is merely an extension of his own mind, but in his subjective gaze he believes that she will be his fulfillment, his completion.[27] In narcissistic twinning of this kind, like Eros or Narcissus, we seek our own image of the ideal through unconscious projections upon relationship partners. Like Psyche in the dark bedchamber, enthralled with her unknown lover, we lose ourselves in the brief reverie of union with our own soul image each time we fall in love. Enthrallment, in its barest definition, alludes to captivity, being spellbound, and even enslavement. There is no real hope for vis-à-vis relationship, for every lover lives in the dark.

The medieval Courts of Love retold countless tales of fatal love—the "Romances of Death"—wherein doomed, star-crossed lovers would long and suffer for their idealized love object, their passionate devotion never requited or consummated. Sacrifice and selfless renunciation of impossible or forbidden love was sacralized as the purist form of love, one that could only find expression, as Denis de Rougemont writes, in the "passion and longing for death which passion disguises."[28] Often these sacrificial lovers would die from grief over the loss of their beloved, comforted only by their faith that their souls would be united forever in heaven. The symbolism of souls joining in death is apparent in the two rosebushes, one planted over the grave of Tristan and the other over Isolde, that grow in time to entwine as one. In Wagner's opera, as Tristan lies on the verge of a self-willed death, he cries, "Yearning now calls. For death's repose."[29] Tragedies like these encompassed end-less and ecstatic cycles of longing, suffering, renunciation, fusion, and self dissolution—described in the French as jouissance.

The underlying motive of Freud's theory of the death drive is the compulsion to repeat. That is, the compulsion to recapitulate loss, nothingness, and annihilation (as when baby's mother goes away, for instance), then gives way to the satisfaction of return, abundance, and restoration of life (upon mother's return). The subjective idea of death lies at the core of the symptoms we feel compelled to repeat, no matter how painful they may be, such as traumatic loss, self-destructiveness, sadomasochism, and other psychopathology. Para-doxically the motive behind the impulse toward annihilation, in Freud's view is the hope of returning to an earlier undifferentiated state of inorganic life. From life comes death, which itself is, according to Freud, the dialectic "origin and aim of life."[30] Thus we see the repetition of trauma that will bring dissolution, so that within it, paradoxically, we may begin again anew.

Lacan, on the other hand, would suggest that we are compelled to go back to the past out of fear, because we must deny the depths and the void of the unknown. What we think of as the past is an attempt to explain the unexplainable, and the intoxicating pull of the death drive is therefore a refusal to live. The fatal lovers of the courtly tales embraced the addictive experience of *jouissance*—the ecstasy in pleasure and pain. By their sacrifices they repeatedly sought dissolution back to an original inanimate state, maintaining the idyllic belief that they would be connected forever in death. Repetition compulsion underlies this ideal, reflecting the hunger to "know death," to explain away the incomprehensible and the unknowable, owing to an inability to accept death's inscrutable mysteries, and to bear life's uncertainties.

In the hopeless fusion of yearning for the twin emotions of passion and suffering, aris-ing in this kind of Dionysian death and dissolution, there can be no substantive, bound-aried sense of being; no stance *in the name of the Father*—that paternal, Lawful authority. When the divine son dissolves into his mother's embrace, he loses all sexual definition, and essentially becomes a hermaphrodite.[31] In this grandiose state he stands above shame, above the Law like a god. However, to submit to the *Symbolic Order* of things is to undergo a castration and to suffer the finiteness of our being. The "paternal" world of language and representation is ruled by what Lacan calls the Law of the Father, and Jung logos, creating a new style of human discourse that sets the boy apart from the cycle of incestuous dis-solution of his ego into the churning seas of maternal affects. (See Chapter One.)[32] We are no longer gods. As if awakened from a dream, we are cast up on the shore—cold, alone, and humbled.

The tales of Sir Lancelot and his queen, which I mentioned earlier, touch upon many of these themes. Chretien de Troyes, the poet of Marie of Champagne's court, was the author of this cycle of Arthurian romances in the twelfth century. A learned man, his legends wove together the Celtic sacred mysteries of the north with the troubadour's songs from the courts of love in southern France.[33] He was certainly not unaware of the mythic Greek and Roman themes that arise in his tales. According to Chretien, it was rumored that Queen Guinevere cast a spell of enchantment upon her pitiable paramour, compelling him to love no one but her, even though the moments they shared were so rare and fleeting. Lancelot could find no happiness in the arms of any other woman.

Romance, as pursued in the historical Courts of Love, and described by analyst John R. Haule, demands that

> the knight dedicate[s] all his efforts to the service of a lady he may have no hope ever of marrying. He is inspired by an erotic spirituality to do great deeds. . . . Such a spiritual love exists outside of convention and free from the procreative instinct. . . . Because they cannot be married, their love is forced into an essentially spiritual form, or else it is illicit.[34]

Otto Rahn's romantic tome describes the troubadour's poem as an "homage to his lady. . . . On his knees, the troubadour would swear eternal fidelity. . . . As a token of her love, she would give her paladin-poet a golden *ring*, and as he stood up, a kiss on his forehead. This was always the first kiss and many times, the only one."[35]

In the famous story of "The Knight of the Cart," Lancelot underwent many trials while pursuing Guinevere, who Heinrich Zimmer describes as "the life and soul of King Arthur's court."[36] She had been abducted by a dark knight who was in fact the Lord of the Land of Death. Zimmer sees Lancelot as a mythical savior, and the soul he is rescuing from Hades, Guinevere the Queen, as "the feminine life-giving principle, the highest symbol of chivalrous love . . . life force in its visible human incarnation."[37]

In his quest to retrieve his Queen, Lancelot overcame great trials. He endured near-mortal wounding, imprisonment, and temptations of the body. These were like the stages of initiation common to the ancient hero-myth cycles, where one outer garment of the ego after another is shed. In "The Knight of the Cart," to test the great knight's love, his challenge was to bear the shame of dismounting his charger and stepping into the pillory cart for all the world to see. But he hesitated for just an instant before climbing aboard, and that was his undoing. We know from many of the courtly romances that shame and sacrifice are wise teachers that temper the arrogance and omnipotence of narcissism.[38] The knight's reckless, arrogant, and unreflective nature, indicative of the immaturity of youth, is brought into question by trials that cause the shattering of his egotism and the awakening of his shame and humility. Such is the case with Lancelot. Thus, in place of her gratitude and a tearful reunion after a long absence, Guinevere snubbed her hero, despite his heroism and sacrifice. Dumbfounded and mad with pain, Lancelot attempted to kill himself. Only after witnessing his desperate act did Guinevere relent and proceed to explain herself. With the omnipotence of a goddess, she knew of his hesitation and would not tolerate his slightest ambivalence, demanding of her servant utter devotion, obedience, and willingness to submit himself to the greatest shame and dishonor, all in the name of love. He then begged her forgiveness for his affront, and when she assented he remained, in Zimmer's words, "bound indissolubly, blindly, and forever, to the goddess of sheer life force."[39]

One would be hard pressed to avoid the comparison of the young hero to the *puer aeternus*, glorified and then sacrificed by the earth goddess he loved and served, who was both his mother and his lover, and whose planet he was destined to orbit. In Chretien's Queen and the knight who served her, we see allusions to those matriarchal myths and rites of the *hieros gamos* that honor both the goddess who must be obeyed and her son/consort/sacrificial victim.

The story of Lancelot's suffering, madness, longing for oneness, and redemption through love bears transcendent elements as well as hints of the death coniunctio. Kristeva posits that the experience of love's separation and utter loss, an experience that reflects a fundamental lack that is ours from the beginning of life, indissolubly gives life to the passion for oneness. She cites three narratives—religious-mystical, creative, and psychoanalytic—that express this imaginal longing to be one in transcendent ways.[40] Love and the desire for union—born of loss, transcendent through suffering—as depicted in the romances like those of Lancelot and Guinevere, offer undeniable examples of mystical transcendence through love. Narratives like these may plumb the depths of melancholy, suffering, and abjection to recognize it, give a name to it, and generate cathartic rebirth.[41]

In what Kristeva describes as a "*mania*, born of paranoia,"[42] she locates a fourth narrative that is not transcendent but defensive; it is one that for me resembles a form of narcissistic fusion with its allusions to the death coniunctio. The imagination arising from this melancholy becomes an end in itself, so that the subject's feelings of inner lack and longing become adhered to his colonized object of desire. This results in a hoped-for but illusory vision of wholeness and union that may stave off the terrors of uncertainty and utter nothingness.

The dire consequences of this process may be glimpsed in the plight of Lancelot, who descends into madness and suicidal depression as punishment for his failure either to please Queen Guinevere's impossible demands or to calm her violent jealousy. The melancholic longing, self-suffering, and even suicidal imaginings that I recognize in the troubadours' tales of fatal love become, as Kristeva writes, "a reuniting with sorrow and, beyond it, with that impossible love, never attained, always elsewhere, such as the promise of the void, of death."[43]

The star-crossed lovers—those tragic, often masochistic characters spellbound by love's allure, struggle to find earthly happiness and pleasure that is so rare, impossible to maintain, and that is ultimately denied. They continually enact patterns reminiscent of the death drive, with its promise of freedom from earth's endless suffering through a future reunion in paradise. Here we see how an aspect of narcissistic defense is personified in the tales of fatal lovers, one that brings a state of transient fusion and dissolution of the subject with its object of desire. The need to preserve the subject's control over a threatening environment lies beneath the urgency to merge and together, "rise above" ordinary space and time. As the Queen's power of enchantment over her knight shows, she has assumed possession of her lover and he is made to seem like a part of her. But for Lancelot, his unique and separate being is lost in the death coniunctio.

One can recognize here the wish for death as a means of ridding oneself of the painfulness of life, with its alterity and uncertainties that may threaten one's sense of identity. But the fantasied union in the afterlife with an identical, ideal object is a disavowal of life that casts a pall of deadening sameness around the dyad, like that of Narcissus spellbound by his fixed reflection in the pond. Only in the fantasy of death's encapsulation may a narcissistic identity be preserved against the threat of collapse at the hands of the internal or external alterity of the Other.

In their songs and tales the troubadours could imagine the purity of union with their beloved only when it was cleansed by the death of the flesh; their desire was ignited by lack and the longing they felt in their suffering and separation from the beloved. Therefore erotic pleasures were often (though not always) sublimated through the troubadors' sublime poetry, and elevated in their imaginations through longing for love's ideal. The heretical religion of the *Cathars* arose simultaneously with the practices of courtly love in the south of France in the twelfth century, and the two are therefore considered by many to be interrelated. The Cathars believed themselves to be like fallen angels in Satan's corruptible earth. (See Chapter Three for a more detailed discussion.)

This apparent dualism privileges the hoped-for world of spiritual love in the great beyond over the immediacy of the human encounter that is fraught with complexity and limitations. It may be put into a contemporary psychological context when we recall Kristeva's original premise: Evoked from the infant's wounding and irretrievable loss of the maternal body/paradise is an impossible longing to imaginatively restore what has been lost. This longing is projected into religious experience, creative work, love, and through what I would consider the compulsive repetitions found in the death instinct. These compulsive repetitions, I believe, act as narcissistic defenses against unbearable pain, and are a means of coping with the trauma of the original loss, as well as subsequent traumas that retranslate the original wound. Fearing its repetition in the threatening encounters with the other, the individual returns within his imagination to the fantasy of death—the preanimate world of perfect oneness in the state of the death coniunctio. Psychologically, however, it is a return to the death mother that the son seeks where he will remain safe and infantilized, perpetually enacting the painful but well-trodden patterns of the mother complex.

The writings of Heinz Kohut suggest that the idealization of the love object, illustrated throughout the medieval tales of love, originates from primitive configurations of narcissism that he views as normal and essential to our development. As infants and small children we need to idealize our parents and take in the parental images as a mirror of our self. This mirroring process enables the baby to hold onto the ideal image, or what Kohut calls the self-object, until it is possible to develop enough of its own ego strength.[44]

According to Kohut, for the infant to form a nuclear self it needs the parents to mirror back a sense of omniscience and power. Owing to the sense of connection between parent and infant, the baby identifies with the omnipotence of its idealized parents. If one compares this early narcissistic state to the union of lovers in the troubadours' ballads, both are marked by fusion between a self and an object that are loved as one. One can understand how the beloved becomes the center of her lover's world, and why the lover's very existence is predicated upon being part of the beloved.

While the "eternal promise of reunion with the primary maternal object,"[45] Gediman writes, represents the primitive fantasy underlying these unions, realizing such an ideal is a sheer impossibility when the ecstatic lover overvalues his beloved. She is, after all, just a human being. Given this dilemma, it is clear why so many of these tales embody themes of fatality and tragic loss: the narcissistic state cannot be realized except through death and the imagined perfection of Heaven.

One might consider "being in love" as a transitory and idyllic spell under which one sees only a subjective trace of himself while gazing into the narcissistic mirror of his lover's eyes. However, "loving" is an active verb, implying a mature and substantive capacity to love actively, not for what one hopes the lover will be, but for who she really is.[46]

The act of loving transcends narcissism, because it implies a relationship between two, not a oneness. Jung informs us, in speaking of the psychological state of the *coniunctio* and the union of opposites, that "one is not a number; the first number is two, and with it multiplicity and reality begin."[47] The number *one*, which the merging with the death coniunctio implies, alludes to an unrealized state of potentiality; only by the division of one into two can the world become real. The blind sense of indissoluble fusion into oneness, Jung implies, is more accurately seen as a refusal or inability to bear the tensions of the intimate, human, vis-à-vis relationship with the other. Beneath that more provisional attitude lies the hope of a potential life that has not yet begun. Yet the pull toward oneness is chosen repeatedly by those who fear the uncertainty of the actualized, embodied, good-enough life that is going on in the present. The momentary encounters and flashes of oneness with the fantasied other are at the same time violent defenses against seeing the other as a whole person who one holds ambivalently, inasmuch as she contains both good and bad qualities.

●　●　●　●　●

Eventually the sun set upon the age of courtly love, itself a resurgence of the mystery traditions of antiquity. Yet as the Swiss philosopher Denis de Rougemont concludes in his classic book, *Love in the Western World*:

> The history of passionate love in all great literature from the thirteenth century down to our own day is the history of the descent of the courtly myth into 'profane' life, the account of the more and more desperate attempts of Eros to take the place of mystical transcendence by means of emotional intensity.[48]

What was celebrated in the poetry of the troubadours and in the practices of courtly love was a mystical theology that bordered upon heresy, because it honored the transformative powers of Eros—unquenchable, yet filled with suffering and sacrifice. When that era passed into history, what remained were its outer forms that largely degraded sacred love to the concreteness of the profane. Yet five hundred years later another attempt was made to resurrect some of the vestiges of these ideals in the new philosophy of *Romanticism*.

## Romanticism

Among their many rich innovations to art and philosophy, the Romantics believed in the existence of an invisible world of spirit within nature, a world that could never be rationally understood or known. It is for this reason in part that Romantic ideals have decried the *Enlightenment's* unrelenting quest for knowledge through the use of reason, scientific thinking, and rationality.

Among the ideas brought forth in Romantic art, prose, poetry, and philosophy was a renewed interest in the notion of finding *ideal* love and beauty, even if it could only be longed for or dreamt of. Both the philosophies of the early Greeks as well as that of the eighteenth century philosopher, Immanuel Kant, had significant impact upon the Romantics' conception of the ideal. According to Plato, those things that can be perceived by the senses are merely imperfect copies of what he spoke of as "eternal ideas," and that Kant would later call "forms." These are not individually held, but are universally built into the psychic makeup of us all. Jung often cited Kant's great influence upon his philosophical ideas. He was fond of saying that "epistemologically" he took his "stand in Kant," offering as evidence his theory of the archetypes, which closely resemble the "forms."[49]

Yet when we put forth any idea that presumes to explain the original, essential truth of the mystery and plurality of life and nature, a mystery that in truth is unknowable, we unwittingly create a dualistic hierarchy. Something basic, flawed, but vitally human may get cut off and devalued in the process. Such is the case when an allegedly higher good is claimed to be found only through seeking aesthetic beauty and love's ideal. This devalu-

ation of the other reveals a profound split of psyche and soma, a kind of narcissism, embedded in personal and cultural attitudes. (One may even propose to trace the existence
of this division of mind and body to infant development, notably through Winnicott's
seminal thinking about the original unity and splitting of the psyche-soma, resulting from
the loss of a stable maternal environment, as discussed in Chapter One.) As a consequence,
within this devaluation—and despite Romanticism's rich contributions to art, music, and
literature and its important challenge to the march of the Enlightenment—there lies a split
that reveals the shadow of romantic love and its ideals of beauty, as well as the shadow of
Romanticism itself.

In speaking of the Romantic poet John Keats (1795–1821), art historian Sonia Cavicchioli states, "The sensibility of the English poet . . . reveals the nostalgia of one who. . .
. considers the beauty of classical art to be the manifestation of an ideal civilization, one
that was infinitely happier than the present one."[50] Keats the Romantic intuited that in the
longings for ideal love there stirred the "'essential beauty' of the soul of all things . . . revealed through love."[51] In the full flood of new love, shortly after reading Apuleius' novel,
Keats composed his "Ode to Psyche."[52] His is the first attempt to view beautiful Psyche not
as some relic from the archaic age of myth, but as the inner soul of man, *awakened* by the
creative fires of Love—*Eros*.[53]

Through Keat's fertile imagination, James Hillman describes how he could "enter into
the identities of other beings. . . . His worship of the feminine placed him in danger of
identification with Eros."[54] We might be led to think of Keats as an exquisitely sensitive
young man, over-identified with and possessed by his anima in all her vicissitudes, and
deeply split off from his chthonic male power.[55]

## *Creativity and the Artist*

Helen Gediman's ideas about narcissism in relation to Romanticism, creativity, and the
artist enlarge upon Kohut's theories, and may shed a more positive light upon Keat's
over-identification with the objects of his art. Gediman cites the early psychoanalyst Lou
Andreas-Salomé and her writings about the narcissism of twinning, whereby creativity is
recognized as a process for transforming the narcissistic state. "Twin narcissism," Gediman
writes, "is a term for fusion of self and object that is evocative of an early ego state common
to infants, lovers, and some creative artists."[56] The artist, composer, or poet's identification
with the object of his inspiration may be experienced as a powerful identification with all
of life, where self and object collapse into each other.[57] Kohut concludes, "The creative individual. . . is less psychologically separated from his surroundings than the non-creative
one. The I–you barrier is not clearly defined."[58]

There are acts of creation that Kant speaks of as *sublime*—creations that transcend category, so beautiful that they evoke pain, forgiveness, even terror of the infinite's proximity. In Kristeva's idea of *chora*, one's melancholy without the other is the basis for all creativity. From this perspective art may function as the transcendent, so that the artist is in touch both with maternal wounds suffered before thought or word, and with the capacity to translate his affects into symbolic understanding.[59]

On the other hand, Andreas-Salomé could see qualities of the Liebestod, the romantic fantasy of love-death, underlying the subject's identification with his object of ecstatic love or inspiration. When excessive or overvalued, it can annihilate both self and object.[60] Both Keats and the clinical vignettes that follow provide, I believe, ample evidence of this.

Three short years before his untimely death at age 25 from tuberculosis, Keats met and fell hopelessly and tragically in love with a neighbor, Fanny Brawne. His overwrought letters to her speak of love's longing for something that no one person could possibly give to him. As both self-reliance and health ebbed from his body, he often cast himself in the guise of her helpless victim. It seems odd that such a delicate and intelligent soul as his could fall into over-idealization of Fanny, a perhaps not so worthy object of love who was described as rather ordinary and unassuming. Yet in the midst of this enthrallment his poor body lay wracked with suffering as he saw his life slowly fading away. His passionate longing for this unattainable love while at the very door of death lent a ferocious meaning to his life until the tortuous end, and seems to echo certain aspects of the Liebestod.[61]

Underlying the swings between idyllic fantasy, torment, and anguish in Keat's last years, one may sense the presence of the original split between psyche and soma. The denied shadow aspect of nature might well reveal its ominous and destructive face when a diminished existence cannot endure or embody a substantive life, a response that speaks to the psyche's compensatory tendencies. As Jung notes, "Whenever an instinctive force . . . is driven into the background through a one-sided . . . [conscious] attitude [or, I contend, a debilitating illness of the kind Keats experienced] . . . it leads to a dissociation of personality."[62] That is, when Keats's body began to betray him, and he was no longer able to express his physical passions, an instinctive force in Keats became split off and fell into the shadow. Fantasies that expressed the agony of separation and longing for love's idyllic paradise came to be dominant and overvalued in his mind, perhaps as forms of compensation for his diminished physicality. The paradise he longed for became, in the end, death's repose—the shadow of the body.

Keats's poetic longing for the spiritual purity of unconsummated love and the fantasy of ecstatic dissolution in the oneness of eternity that he projected upon this literal, meager, human relationship, ended in the early death of this grand soul. Though frail in body and debilitated by illness, his beautiful mind soared in seeming defiance of the physical end. Yet the psychic contagion of the death coniunctio had become concretized in an impossible longing to return to a maternal paradise free of life's pain.[63]

## *Clinical Vignettes*

The death coniunctio can be located in the compulsion to lose oneself repeatedly in the romantic fever of a new love's enthrallment. In these moments conscious intention seems powerless and futile in the face of the force generated by the unconscious dynamic. Such an unconscious and compulsive loss of self may in some cases be a form of defense or even denial of a primal terror existing at one's core. This brings to mind the baby's loss of its earliest maternal containment, or its entrapment by an all-engulfing mother, as her thing to be used. The following two clinical vignettes depict both these aspects.

As if pointed toward a homing beacon, one may be repeatedly drawn to the same heart-wrenching failures in love. A 50-year-old man sought me out for therapy when his wife of twenty years and the mother of his four children suddenly asked for a divorce. His career was in shambles. He was devastated and blindsided by it all. He came into therapy hoping to gain some clarity and understanding of how this could have happened.

In his college days he was a "hopeless romantic"—a folksinger, poet, and songwriter. His songs were confessional, filled with themes of love, loss, and longing for the one true love of his life that always seemed to elude him. His spirits lifted whenever he spoke of his music, so I encouraged him to tell me about that period of his life. In one session he recited the lyrics to a song that captured the essence of his romantic odyssey, entitled, "Nothin' Left of Me." One after another he recalled each hoped-for love affair, how he poured himself into them—and how they all ended in ruin. They took everything he had until there was "nothing left." As he recited the words it occurred to me that this pattern had the quality of a repetition compulsion. That is, his idyllic fantasies and projections had a compulsive nature to them, and they were repeatedly followed by suffering and melancholy.

In my mind I also considered the archetypal nature of his creative suffering, as we have observed it in the love songs of the earliest bards. The Greek Orpheus, from whose sweet voice and lyre resounded the most beautiful music in all the world, lost his beloved Eurydice on their wedding day. From his loss sprang the first tragic songs of love and death. Europe's first operas featured the dramas of the Liebestod, which reflected the resurgence of the Orphic religion at a time in the fifteenth century when the church was beginning to lose its grip upon the people.

The Orphic mysteries were based upon Orpheus' journey down to the kingdom of Hades to retrieve his wife and the events that followed. Within the Underworld, Orpheus sang and played his lyre for King Hades and Queen Persephone, and moved the royal couple to compassion. They relinquished their hold upon Eurydice, with but one condition, and she was free to return to the land of the living with her husband. Mere steps from freedom, and in the light of the upper world, Orpheus glanced back, just to be certain that she was following him. That singular moment broke the one condition for her freedom—that under no circumstances would he be permitted to look back to see if Eurydice was there behind him. Did his act reveal his mistrust, or a lack of faith, or could it signify the protectiveness and need that Orpheus felt for her? The answer is not given, but after that instant she was lost to him in the land of shades until the end of his days. Mad with grief Orpheus roamed the land until one day he was seized by a band of maenads—priestesses of Dionysus—who, in a mad frenzy, ripped him to pieces like a sacrificial animal. His head was thrown into the river, where it magically called out for Eurydice and eventually floated to the shore, where it became an oracle. His voice transcended death.

The encounter with the mystery of the other is eternally disruptive to our desire for things to remain stable and the same. Does this tale teach us that in the matters of love and faith we can never look back? In other words, must love be lost when we attempt to control or possess it? And if so, perhaps what underlies our desperate need to know is the impulse to annihilate the uncertainties of life and to love with guarantees, thereby thwarting any possibility of being abandoned, as in the trauma of a baby who loses his mother. Are the perpetual projections of our wholeness onto others ultimately no more than an attempt to possess their irreducible uniqueness in order to maintain sameness and to insulate us from future trauma?

My patient's story mirrors much of this discussion. He described feelings of his own finiteness, of never feeling he was enough. He needed to merge with the magical other, whom he hoped could restore what was lost in a childhood where he was subjected to a cold, unaffectionate mother. Instead, he would either feel dead after sexualizing a relationship once he had gained possession of the woman, or he would become swallowed up by his addiction for her, only to be discarded in turn. He spoke of his brooding state following the broken relationships as one of "mooning the loss," like a lonesome coyote crying at the moon. The repetitive nature of his melancholy belied a loss that was perhaps never sufficiently mourned. Melancholy takes the place of mourning when ambivalent and unresolved issues surround the loved object who is lost, dead, or deadened. In this case, all my patient's lovers had assumed the role of his mother. In the course of our work together he began to recognize, in the drive for magical specialness and the ensuing failures, that he had been reenacting the drama of his maternal longing and loss throughout his lifetime. With the dawning awareness of the origin of his grief and anger in the absence of maternal love, which he recognized all too well within his marriage, he began to move forward into the next phase of his life, with sadness yet wisdom.[64]

The dream of a 55-year-old artist poignantly reflects his earliest fear of—and fight against—becoming ensnared throughout his life by women who would fill the role of being a mother to him. He had recently left a long marriage with children, his instinctive demands having been curtailed by a maternal wife who desired companionship and love, not of the flesh and blood, erotic variety, but of agape—a shared Christian love and charity. In fact, he had left her in his mind years before, and had pursued a string of scattered affairs in order to meet the needs he felt were denied him. His story reflects the problem of the split feminine, a theme that will be the focus of the next chapter. At the time of this dream, a new relationship awaited him, one with a younger woman who aroused and quenched all the fire and thirst he carried for pleasures that he had repressed during his many years of marriage. Yet despite the powerful connection between them, the prospects of another commitment down the road left him tentative and feeling weak at the knees. He dreamed:

> I am climbing a hill to get away from something or someone. I go through a narrow passage where two large, round rock faces come together in a chasm. I'm sliding down easily, like it's ice, and I've already committed myself to slide over the edge where now I can't get back up. The chasm has narrowed and I've become stuck, wedged, trapped there. Way below me I see people playing on the beach. This is the worst thing that's ever happened to me. I'm stuck here alone, part way, with no hope of getting free, my life being taken away.

Despite the obvious associations to his current predicament, that of being stuck between his judgmental family, the soon-to-be ex-wife, and his new lover, I believe that this potent dream has captured the primal terror at his core—the ancient feeling of being trapped. This is the theme of his life, beginning with his grandmother, an endearing, steadfast anchor in his first years of life, who provided stability and regimen in his daily life while his mother and father were away for long periods of time. He was a sensitive boy—the baby of the family—and he relied upon her greatly. Yet he also admitted how intrusive she was. He spoke of a complete lack of boundaries, which meant he was forced to submit to her thorough inspections in every area of his personal hygiene and toilet habits. Trapped in the ambivalence in which his need for separateness from her invasiveness could also be construed as an aggressive rejection of this much-needed maternal object, he learned to avoid her over-closeness by becoming secretive and avoidant. Over time my patient found ways to use his charm and wit to avoid any conflict or situation he couldn't control, yet in his denial he was unable to see how he manipulated people as if they were objects to be kept in place. This control had become the indirect form that his split-off and much-needed aggression had taken.

Beneath my patient's placating and passive persona was a deep terror of intimacy, which he experienced as entrapment, the loss of self, and an ancient fear that people would ultimately dig into him—cannibalize him, and take everything of value away that he created. The needed maternal embrace that his wife provided became, in time, suffocating and dead, resembling the enfolding love of his grandmother that ultimately threatened to engulf and entrap him. His marital deadness necessitated his escape into the arms of lovers promising dissolution in the pleasures of erotic bliss. The scene in the dream of gaiety on the beach, inaccessible from his place of entrapment, conveys this desired ideal that remains always just beyond his reach.

But if one looks more closely, my patient's compulsive pattern resembles aspects of the death coniunctio. Hoping that his flight from the death mother might bring him the freedom of happy love, he instead falls headlong into her clutches a second time. His longing to merge with her is predicated on the fantasy of a paradise where all of his needs will be fulfilled. However, this is inevitably followed in his mind by the primal terror that if he does surrender to her he will ultimately be entrapped and obliterated. So he lies stuck, suspended in time, above life and above those who pursue him, with no means of evading death. The dream appears to confront his illusions of escape with this deeper truth. By considering the dream image from a different perspective, the chasm in the rocks that wedges him in makes escape from his circumstances impossible, and forces him instead to stay and face the terror of his vulnerability and dependency. This may speak to the possibility of intimacy's deeper surrender, and the shattering of my patient's fixed orientation that maintains his fear of entrapment, which he anticipates in every relationship.

• • • • •

In summary, all these stories highlight aspects of the death coniunctio and portray, at some level, the human longing to transcend death through ecstatic suffering and love.[65] In the death coniunctio, the insufficient or immature ego is drawn to dissolution in the fusion with the (m)other, with no hope of transcending the pattern. In the tales of the *hieros gamos*, the son is trapped again and again in the death drive that underlies the repetition compulsion that keeps him safe within the orbit of his Mother. Though turbulent, masochistic, and chaotic, this return to death and then to life again is addictive, as it maintains the illusion of certainty and the tyranny of perpetual sameness that is a common feature of narcissism. The death coniunctio often lies beneath the illusions of falling in love, and can foreclose upon a man's capacity to love in an active way—where the other is treasured for her differences and her individuality, and her lover in turn for his capacity to reveal to the other what is authentic within himself.

## Notes

1  Edward Edinger, *The Mysterium Lectures* (Toronto: Inner City Books, 1995), 85.
2  Edinger, *Mysterium Lectures*, 85.
3  Aspects of this fairy tale, like that of "Beauty and the Beast," descend from Apuleius' tale of "Cupid and Psyche."
4  Recalling the Biblical story, Jacob had left his mother and father, Rebecca and Isaac, and twin brother Esau, as a thief in the night, having conspired with his mother to steal the older twin's birthright and blessing from his enfeebled old father, Isaac. Fearing Esau's murderous rage, Jacob fled to the homeland of his mother's brother, Laban, a renowned Syrian sorcerer and pagan priest. His two daughters, Leah and the beautiful Rachael, whom Jacob glimpsed at the well, were Jacob's first cousins.

5   *Shekhinah* is the feminine emanation of the Divine Creator.

6   Rav P. S. Berg,. *The Essential Zohar* (New York: Bell Tower, 2002), 170.

7   See *Song of Songs.*

8   Areh Kaplan, *Innerspace* (Jerusalem: Moznaim Publishing, 1990), p. 109.

9   Minnesingers, or minstrels, were bards who honored *Minne*, the ancient goddess of nature. In German, the name refers to courtly love of a higher, ideal nature, possibly even a transcendent nature of eros, in contrast to *liebe*, or erotic love.

10   Heinrich Zimmer, *The King and the Corpse* (Princeton, NJ: Princeton University Press, 1948), 161.

11   Zimmer, *King and the Corpse*, 160.

12   The spiritual theme of an inner oneness produced from the union of the two is expressed in the Gospel of Thomas, where Jesus explains how one will enter the Kingdom of Heaven. "When you make the two into one, and when you make the inner like the outer and the outer like the inner, and the upper like the lower, and when you make male and female into a single one, so that the male will not be male nor the female be female . . . . then you will enter [the Kingdom.]" *The Nag Hammadi Scriptures: The Revised and Updated Translation of Sacred Gnostic Texts,* Edited and translated by Marvin Meyer, "The Gospel of Thomas" #22 (NY: HarperCollins, 2007), 142-143.

13   Spanish mystics like Teresa and John were deeply influenced by the Biblical "Canticles," or *Song of Songs.*

14   St. John of the Cross, "Spiritual Canticle," in *The Complete Works of Saint John of the Cross, Doctor of the Church*, translated and edited by E. Allison Peers from the critical edition of P. Silverio de Santa Teresa (Westminster, MD: Newman Press, 1964), vol. 2, 223.

15   The revelation, made immortal by the sculptor's inspired hands and heart, is faithful to her experience, as recalled by the Saint in her own words:

> Beside me, on the left hand, appeared an angel in bodily form, such as I am not in the habit of seeing except very rarely.... He was not tall but short, and very beautiful; and his face was so aflame that he appeared to be one of the highest rank of angels, who seem to be all on fire. They must be of the kind called cherubim, but they do not tell me their names.... In his hands I saw a great golden spear, and at the iron tip there appeared to be a point of fire. This he plunged into my heart several times so that it penetrated to my entrails. When he pulled it out, I felt that he took them with it, and left me utterly consumed by the great love of God. The pain was so severe that it made me utter several moans. The sweetness caused by this intense pain is so extreme that one cannot possibly wish it to cease, nor is one's soul then content with anything but God. This is not a physical, but a spiritual pain, though the body has some share in it – even a considerable share. So gentle is this wooing which takes place between God and the soul that if anyone thinks I am lying, I pray God, in His goodness to grant him some experience of it. Teresa of Avila, *The Life of Saint Teresa of Avila by Herself* (London: Penguin Books, 1957), 210.

16   James Hillman, *The Myth of Analysis* Evanston, IL: Northwestern University Press, 1972), 54.

17   *C.W.* 14, 26, my emphasis.

18   *C.W.* 5, 234.

19   *C.W.* 5, 235.

20   *C.W.* 5, 235–36.

21   *C.W.* 5, 236.

22   *C.W.* 5, 223–24.

23  *C.W.* 5, 259.

24  Edinger, *Mysterium Lectures*, 38

25  Again, some men who need to act this out are not only doing so at the behest of their own infan-tile longings to return to a fantasy of a once perfect symbiosis with the mother, as both Freudian and Jungian analysts originally believed. They may be enacting the kind of attachment their origi-nal mother demanded precisely because she could not feel anything unless her child enlivened her as her only source of aliveness. This raises the question of a certain deadness within the original relationship that had to be relieved by manic defenses. When uncovered analytically, the dead-ness in their relationship may turn out to have been due to a form of identification with a *different* internal mother object, one that French psychoanalyst Andre Green calls the Dead Mother. This idea contrasts with Edinger's mother of the death *coniunctio* whose enthralling, desirous, and in-cestuous image draws the child to its death and dissolution. The Dead Mother Complex that Green formulates is one in which the man has been deeply impacted by his original mother's depression, which may in turn have been caused by feelings of loss and bereavement over a loved one that in-clude feelings of intense betrayal. It is the child's job, therefore, to try to revive the mother through passionate loyalty. The mother's function as a source of life and vitality, internalized by the child, has suddenly turned dead and distant due to her profound loss, and the child must redeem her. The impact of such an internal dead mother object will have great effect on the child's future capacities for non-incesutous loving relationships. Andre Green, *Life Narcissism Death Narcissism*, translated by Andrew Weller (London: Free Association Books, 2001), 178-9.

26  Pausinias, *Description of Greece*, 9.31.8. At http://www.theoi.com/Text/Pausinias9B.html (accessed 1/15/11). Translated by W.H.S. Jones.

27  We may understand the motif of Narcissus' unrenounced loss of his sister and the obviation of his pain through the melancholy fantasy of reunion with her as a variant of the dead mother complex that Green describes. When there is a failure of the young ego to separate from the dead mother, that ego, in a narcissistic way, "relentlessly endeavors to retain the primary object and to *relive its loss repetitively*." (My italics.) The early ego is fused with the [lost] mother object and feels empty as a consequence of its depletion. Depression, deriving from this early narcissistic wound-ing, intensifies the feeling of emptiness. Hence, we see Narcissus' inevitable wasting away. Green, *Life Narcissism Death Narcissism*, 195.

28  Denis de Rougemont, *Love in the Western World* (Princeton, NJ: Princeton University Press, 1983), 51. [London: Faber and Faber, 1940.]

29  de Rougemont, *Love in the Western World*, 50.

30  For Sigmund Freud's "Remembering, Repeating, and Working Through," 1915/1958, 39, see Jon Mills, "Reflections on the Death Drive," *Psychoanalytic Psychology*, 23(2) (2006): 373–82; Freud's quote is at page 378.

31  Note the conjunction of the names Hermes and Aphrodite (Venus).

32  Lacan's Name of the Father proceeds out of the Symbolic order, which is Lacan's version of the Other. This new order emerges in articulation with the Imaginary that had previously dominated the child's thinking—this Imaginary level of thinking being similar to primary narcissism and the child's maternal fusion with the Same, the seed-ground of all narcissism.

33  It should be noted that the troubadours' poetry of love was equally influenced by Sufism, where the lover surrenders not to an outer woman, but to his spiritual beloved—God. Psychologically, this could be considered the anima, or religiously it may transcend the bounds of psyche.

34  John R. Haule, *Divine Madness: Archetypes of Romantic Love* (Carmel: Fisher King Press, 2010), 3.

35  Otto Rahn, *Crusade Against the Grail* (Rochester, Vermont: Inner Traditions, 2006), 4.

36  Zimmer, *King and the Corpse*, 162.

37   Zimmer, *King and the Corpse*, 170.

38   Ladson Hinton, "Shame as a Teacher: 'Lowly Wisdom' at the Millennium." In *Proceedings of the 14th International Congress for Analytical Psychology*, edited by M. Mattoon, 15–16. Einsiedeln: Daimon Verlag, 1998. 15–16. See also the story of *Parzival* in Chapter Ten of this volume, "The Emergence of the Father."

39   de Rougemont, *Love in the Western World*, 179.

40   In this work, refer to the religious-mystical examples of the Spanish mystics; for creative works, Bernini's *Ecstasy of St. Teresa* and the "Song of Songs" provide illustrations.

41   Richard Kearney, *Poetics of Imagining: Modern to Post-Modern* (Edinburgh: Edinburgh University Press, 1998), 199.

42   Kearney, *Poetics of Imagining*, 199.

43   Julia Kristeva, "On Melancholy Imagination," in *Postmodernism and Continental Philosophy*, edited by Hugh Silverman and and Donn Welton (Albany NY: State University of New York Press, 1989), 15, cited in Kearney, *Poetics of Imagining*, 197.

44   "Winnicott, Kohut, Neumann, and others observed that the mirroring of the infant by the mother must be seen to constitute the basis on which the adult's feelings of identity and self-worth will rest." Mario Jacoby, *Individuation and Narcissism: The Psychology of Self in Jung and Kohut* (London: Routledge, 1985), 200.

45   Helen Gediman, *Fantasies of Love and Death in Life and Art* (New York: New York University Press, 1995), 23.

46   Gediman, *Fantasies of Love and Death*, 16.

47   *C.W.* 14, 462.

48   de Rougemont, *Love in the Western World*, 170.

49   Jung distorted Kant by saying that archetypes were basically noumenal, and not phenomenal as well as noumenal.

50   Sonia Cavicchioli, *The Tale of Cupid and Psyche: An Illustrated History*, (New York: George Braziller, 2002), 224.

51   For Aileen Ward, *John Keats: The Making of a Poet* (New York: Viking, 1963), 160, see Hillman, *Myth of Analysis*, n52, 54.

52   In a long letter to his brother and his brother's wife, which included an early version of his Ode, Keats embarks upon a discourse into the nature of "how souls are made." Below, a few lines of his poem give us but a glimpse of this psychological idea:

> Surely I dreamt to day; or did I see
>
> The winged Psyche, with awaked eyes? . . .
>
> Yes I will be thy Priest and build a fane
>
> In some untrodden region of my Mind . . .

From Robert Giddings, editor, *John Keats, Selected Letters* (Oxford, UK: Oxford University Press, 2002), 236–37.

53   Hillman, *The Myth of Analysis*, 54–55.

54   Hillman, *The Myth of Analysis*, 54–55.

55   Critics and literary figures of his day portrayed his writings as effeminate and lacking in a masculine energy. In speaking of his relationships to women, his attractions often toppled over into identification in his sympathetic nature. Conversely, he seemed to fear being entrapped by the

feminine and sapped of his male power. See John Mee, "Introduction," xxx, xxxi, in Giddings, *John Keats, Selected Letters*.

56  Gediman, *Fantasies of Love and Death*, 20.

57  Lou Andreas-Salome, "The Dual Orientation of Narcissism," *Psychoanalytic Quarterly* 31 (1922), p. 5, as cited in Gediman, *Fantasies of Love and Death*, 24.

58  Hans Kohut, "Forms and Transformations of Narcissism," *Journal of the American Psychoanalytic Association* 14 (1966), p. 259, as cited in Gediman, *Fantasies of Love and Death*, 24.

59  Kearney, *Poetics of Imagining*, 198.

60  Andreas-Salome, "Dual Orientation of Narcissism," 12–13, as cited in Gediman, *Fantasies of Love and Death in Life and Art*, 23.

61  Giddings, *John Keats, Selected Letters*, 368. In a letter dated November 1, 1820, less than four months before his death, Keats writes, "The persuasion that I shall see her no more will kill me. . . . I should have had her when I was in health. . . . I can bear to die – I cannot bear to leave her. . . . O that I could be buried near where she lives. . . . If I had any chance of recovery, this passion would kill me. . . . I have coals of fire in my breast. It surprised me that the human heart is capable of containing and bearing so much misery. Was I born for this end? God bless her . . ."

62  *C.W.* 16, 229.

63  In Keats's four-thousand-line poem "Endymion," we may detect a certain autobiographical foreshadowing of the young poet's tragic life. (The writing of his first long poem hounded him throughout its many fits and starts, until its disappointing completion—in his own estimation as well as that of the merciless critics'.) The Greek legend tells of the Moon Goddess whose love for the mortal shepherd is so great that she cannot bear to lose him, so she places him in everlasting sleep so that he might remain eternally young. The psychological meaning that might be derived from the myth hints at the typical early death of a man over-identified with the archetype of eternal youth, who exists in a deathlike sleep of fantasy and dreams imposed upon him by a powerful maternal influence, which removes him from a life of substance and reality. Keats revisions the tale from the perspective of Endymion's love for the Goddess, as a way of expressing that Romantic longing to find in reality an ideal love that has previously existed only in one's imagination. He goes off in search of the Goddess and inadvertently falls for a mortal woman, who turns out to be the Goddess in disguise. Keats's poetic sojourn links back to the motif of a "self-destroying transcendence in which he might achieve a blissful personal unity with all creation." In the last lines of the poem the shepherd dissolves into the spiritual oneness with all of nature. See "Keats, John," in *Encyclopedia Britannica* (Chicago: University of Chicago Press, 1991), vol. 6, 780.

64  Again, we can reconstruct the process in such a patient's infancy. The child's compulsion to be lost in play, imagination, creativity, and later intellectual pursuits could be recognized as attempts to overcome his mother's traumatic loss, and the loss of meaning that has left her "dead." This is one of the paths to puer aeternus identification. As von Franz tells us, a man identified with the archetype of the puer aeternus may seek to fly above life to get away from the dead mother using strategies like fantasy, intellectualism, aesthetic expression, or brief romantic liaisons, as a way to sustain the illusion of aliveness. Such a man is in fact living with a hole in him created by the original mother's coldness and withdrawal. While his woman-idealizing fantasies, creative pursuits, and romantic involvements offer needed sublimations of impulses that have not been gratified in reality, the sublimations, however godlike, cannot stabilize his compromised psyche because he is still too vulnerable to any wounds that may be aroused by his attempts at a love life. His psychic pain will inevitably resurrect the dead mother in him. This time, it is *his* coldness and withdrawal that he subjects his partner to. This is the puer aeternus neurosis. Green offers the key to understanding the malignancy of this pattern in the following formula: While the dead mother

is in ascendance in the psyche, it blocks the possibilities for love. Green, *Life Narcissism Death Narcissism*, 180-1.

65  For further references, see films such as *Wuthering Heights* (also the novel); *The English Patient*, *Somewhere in Time*; and *American Beauty*, to name a few.

## CHAPTER THREE

# THE SPLIT FEMININE
# MOTHER, LOVER, VIRGIN, WHORE

**M**any men are compelled to enact throughout their lives, as Peter Mudd notes, "a deeply split mother imago, or so-called feminine element . . . "[1] In marriage, they may rely upon their wives primarily to provide them with maternal care, in order to manage and stabilize their emotional well-being. This may lead to great boredom and deadness in these relationships owing to men's need to maintain control and certainty, though often there are swings in the other direction. There, they are attracted to women whom they fantasize will bring them back to life. They endow these women with their own missing qualities, who then most often take on the form of the *femme inspiratrice*—the lover who acts as inspiration and initiator into the creative, sexual, or spiritual dimensions of body and soul.[2]

In the vignettes that follow you will recognize new aspects of the themes introduced in earlier chapters. From boyhood, the mother–son fusion is marked by engulfment and/or abandonment, and this is often combined with the boy's poor relationship to his father who is either missing, too harsh, or helpless. A man attempts to win his freedom from the wife/mother by losing himself in the illusion of a magical other, but this soon collapses into a mother problem of another variety—that of the death or lesser coniunctio.

To shed some light on the possible theoretical factors underlying this strangely normalized and common male behavior, I will bring out the abandoning, destabilizing, or devouring roles that the maternal figure or figures have played in the boy's earliest period of life. It is these traumatic influences that may trigger his terror of psychic annihilation, prompting his defensive need to find safe harbor through splitting off. When unquestioned or unbroken, this internal pattern is acted out again and again on the stage of relational life.

An equally prevalent drama revolving around the split feminine can often be seen first in the fantasies of male adolescents, who project an idyllic image of perfection and true love onto one whom they hold above them. Some men carry this attitude throughout their lives. Their lady is often too pure to be touched, and the lovesick male is willing to wait an eternity for her, silently suffering all the while. These aesthetic sentiments are reminiscent of certain aspects of the troubadours' code in the age of courtly love, where it was believed by many, including the nineteenth century French historian, Claude Fauriel, that "[w]hatever turns into a reality is no longer love."[3] Both historically and today, lovers' virtuous purity, unrequited longing, and sacrifice are glorified over physical necessity. For certain men in our historical moment in time, the inner ideal that is pined for but never realized may signify a concealed longing to retreat to the *clean room of the mind*, above and beyond what are regarded as the taint of life and the limitations of flawed human relationships. Their failure to find perfection is used to justify their disavowal of life and devaluation of the other.

Conversely, these contemporary men may at the same time feel compelled by another voice within them to seek instant gratification for their lustful desires, and this time in the real world. They are drawn to a different type of woman that their mind imbues with vampish and purely sexual qualities. Internally, the primal longing for a return to the original fusion may be the driving force behind their drive for sexual consummation, although it is mixed with the terror of becoming lost in the symbiosis. They yearn to experience the enigmatic life of the other but are so terrified of it that they turn it into something that is the same as what they already know—that is, dead. Therefore the search always continues.

These opposing types of relationships are regularly enacted in the world, and we can also recognize them within the psyche as images of the virgin and the whore. Desire is split between these polarities, separating the heart, aesthetic sensibilities, and spiritual ideals, from the sexual, physiological drives for pleasure. At the same time such men colonize the women they use, constraining the woman to enact a one-dimensional role that fulfills only the man's own needs and fantasies.

Virgin and whore, mother and lover, or some combination of each, are archaic, binary, often opposing images of the split feminine, manifesting in all historical times, and may therefore express certain aspects of an emerging spiritual dimension of the psyche. The following section will provide examples to clarify this idea. The impact of these images upon our attitudes, beliefs, and behaviors surrounding matters of the heart is undeniable, and our failure to take their cultural and historical significance into account seems shortsighted.

This chapter's initial section provides ancient and medieval examples of the split feminine in broadly religious and romantic contexts. Resonances of these historical illustrations will then be shown in the context of modern human dramas.

We begin with the story from Genesis of Jacob and his two wives, one from whom descends the kingly line of the Hebrews, and the other who is Jacob's beloved. We follow with the history of the Gothic Cathedral of Chartres, honoring Mary, Queen of Heaven, which was built over the ancient remains of a grotto to the pagan Virgin of the Underworld. We then discuss the Cathars—the "pure ones"—the heretical sect which at the very least inspired the poetry of the court of love, and who venerated the highest form of the feminine spirit in heaven while negating the desires of the earthly world as evil and corrupt. A courtly tale of Lancelot, from this era, depicts the knight caught between his longing for Guinevere and the loyal and devoted "Lady of Shallot."

I will then discuss the related dilemma in modern men, approaching it through what some men experience as an unavoidable dichotomy in love and marriage—that is, the belief that one can have passionate love or marriage but not both in the same partner. For this reason some men behave as if they must be enacted by different women who play out different roles for them. This is not an unavoidable dichotomy for these men as much as a splitting process in their psyches. In other words it is a defensive reaction by which a man attempts to maintain psychic equilibrium, despite his internal feelings of dread, loss, and uncertainty, through projection of this internal split onto the objects he attempts to control in the world.

## *The Story of Jacob and His Wives*

By adhering to the moral severity dictated by the Laws of their One God, the ancient Hebrews removed themselves from the influence of the Great Mother. Psychologically, their disavowal of and separation from the ancient rites of the goddess represents the beginning of individual consciousness and the awakening of the capacity for a reflecting mind. This act of separation prevents our habitual surrender to the endless sensual desires and the unconscious patterns of our nature. But, when a spiritual attitude marginalizes feelings of love and passion, a heavy price is paid. As Joseph Henderson comments, this division "proceeded . . . from a different religious need in which the instincts of the mother [goddess] and her repetitive compulsion of sacrifice could be sublimated to achieve a more permanent attitude of devotion to the Holy Spirit." At the same time, he continues, "it led to great inner tension, forcing a repression of those natural longings of Jewish patriarchal figures to bring the feminine principle of love into their religious life to soften the harsh law of obedience to the will of the Lord God . . ."[4]

The Biblical story of Jacob and his two wives represents an attempt—an unsuccessful one, I believe—to rectify this split in the Hebrew psyche. From the womb of Leah issues forth the kingly line of David, whereas Jacob's beloved Rachael and her child, Joseph the Dreamer, carry disguised yet unmistakable qualities that link their lineage with the earlier worship of the forsaken and reviled *Astarte*. Astarte is the goddess known in biblical scripture as the "whore of Babylon," originally the Phoenician and Canaanite lunar goddess of fertility and love.[5] Her devotees celebrated her incestuous union with the dying and resur-recting god of vegetation who is both her son and consort.

As we are told in Genesis, when Jacob emerges from the wilderness, his long journey from his father's house complete, he gazes upon his cousin, Rachael, coming with her flock to the watering place. She is beautiful and loving, and he weeps at seeing his kin, for looking into her eyes is like seeing his own mother. Rachael is the daughter of his mother's brother—Laban—an Aramean sorcerer of some repute, who serves the goddess Astarte.[6]

Jacob's only desire is that he and Rachael might be wed.[7] However, he must contend with his deceptive uncle, who negotiates a deal that calls for Jacob to work seven years for him in return for his daughter's hand in marriage. Many years later, on the night of the wedding, Laban deceives him. The bridal veil conceals the older sister, Leah, who Jacob mistakenly takes to bed. But his father-in-law allows Jacob to wed Rachael as well, so long as he promises to toil another seven years for Laban. For Jacob to possess his beloved, he allows himself to be manipulated by Laban into taking two wives. Jacob is brought down from his righteousness by his own desire. Of course not only did Jacob bed both wives but their handmaidens, as well, all for the sake of God's commandment that the Hebrews be fruitful and multiply! (Torah Law written long after this period, however, forbids the tak-ing of more than one wife.)

Twenty years later, Leah and her handmaidens have produced sons that will, in turn, father the twelve tribes of Israel, and the kingly line of David, Solomon, and the future messiah. As his wife and mother to his progeny, Leah draws Jacob into social conformity and adaptation to the responsibilities of carrying on the patriarchal line. Rachael, on the other hand, Jacob's beloved and favored wife, is jealous of her sister's fertile womb, herself having given birth only to one son, Joseph.

Nowhere in Jewish commentary do we find the notion of Rachael's link to the ancient mother goddess; however, portions of scripture suggest this. For example, on the morning that Jacob flees with all of his family, wealth, and livestock from the lands of his envi-ous father-in-law, Rachael goes into her father's tents and steals his idols. Her father is a great sorcerer and uses these statues for divination purposes. Torah scholars suggest that Rachael took the idols so that Laban couldn't divine their whereabouts. I believe another interpretation is warranted. Is it possible that this theft indicated her own attachment to these same gods, revealing an unconscious attachment to her father and his beliefs, thus prompting his desperate pursuit? Laban overtakes their caravan and admonishes Jacob for the theft, of which Jacob is unaware of. Not knowing that the thief is Rachael, Jacob invokes the name of God, casting a death curse upon the guilty party and dares Laban to search his camp to find the idols. Rachael has concealed them well inside her saddlebags, and is excused from climbing off of her camel, claiming that it is her time of the month. (Men have traditionally stayed far away from women during their moon cycle, claiming that the menstrual blood is unclean. Perhaps what lies beneath this age-old repulsion is the irrational dread of the feminine mysteries and a primal terror of the mother's power of birth and death.)[8]

As Jacob's caravan approaches the outer boundaries of the Holy Land, Rachael, who is carrying their second son, Benjamin, goes into labor and dies while giving birth. She is said to be only thirty-six years old. Some commentators claim that Torah Law must be obeyed within the bounds of the Holy Land, and that Rachael's death is related to the fact that she was Jacob's second, and therefore illegitimate, wife.

An aspect of Rachael's name derives from the word *ewe*, which traditionally signifies a precious possession as well as a lamb, considered a sacred animal of sacrifice in pre-Christian, pagan rites. In speaking of Rachael, Torah commentator Rabbi Elie Munk writes, "She seems destined to have a life like a flame which blazes up and burns intensely before going out. Her brief existence will be rich, even violent. Her love for Jacob will be her whole life . . ."[9] With the sacrifice of Jacob's love, severe patriarchal law is symbolically restored.[10]

Jacob's lament is profound. These words, from Thomas Mann's *Joseph and His Brothers*, describe the deep split within Jacob, whose unyielding adherence to God's Law led inadvertently to his beloved's demise. "This was Jacob's mistake. He had two passions in life: God and Rachel. Here they came in conflict; and yielding to the spiritual he brought down disaster upon the earthly one."[11]

Now Jacob transfers all his love for Rachael to their son, Joseph. He fashions a coat of many colors for Joseph to wear, a coat said to be made from Rachael's wedding garment. It is an affront to the sensibilities of the patriarchal sons of Leah, being essentially equivalent to a boy wearing a dress in a college football locker room in the 1950s. His father's show of blatant favoritism enrages his half-brothers, who cruelly plot to kill Joseph. Instead, they throw him down a well and then sell him into slavery in Egypt. They return to their father with Joseph's coat, ripped and bloody, claiming that poor Joseph was attacked and eaten by wild beasts. Their act resembles the ancient rites of death, dismemberment, and rebirth.

Once again, Jacob's grief is boundless. His hoped-for heir is lost forever, or so he believes.[12] Joseph is Jacob's only link to Rachael—the embodiment of his soul and his deepest love. She is the signifier for the feminine traditions hidden deep within the story. Unbeknownst to Jacob, however, Joseph is not dead, but rather goes on to become an interpreter of the pharaoh's dreams, foretelling years of great abundance followed by terrible drought and famine. Because of this he is appointed the sole regent over all of Egypt, with authority second only to the pharaoh. Any hope of repairing the split in the feminine lies in this next generation, with Joseph.[13]

Having received the news of Joseph's death, Jacob wearily retreats to his tents, content to commune with the Holy Spirit—the *Ruah Ha Kodesh*—as Leah's sons rise to prominence. With each profound loss, first his beloved Rachael, then his son Joseph, Jacob withdraws more and more from the world of men. In Egypt, during the seven years of famine that

Joseph foretells, the waters do not flow and the rains do not fall to water and feed the live-stock and crops. However, the true famine suffered by the family of Jacob is a grief for the lost feeling that feeds the human heart through relatedness and love. Jacob's heart is left parched, just like the sands of the wilderness, yet in the world beyond this one, where he communes with invisible things of awe, he lives as one with his beloved, his *Shekhinah*.

### *The Split Feminine in the Medieval Era*

Folk legend tells the story of Saint Patrick, who expelled a demon serpent from the soil of Ireland in the fifth century. In lopping off the head of the great pagan serpent he is said to have put an end to the powers of the Celtic nature goddess and her fairy folk. Yet that was far from the end of it. Her ancient religion continued to flourish secretly, in underground grottos, in midnight full-moon rituals, and in the legends and myths from the pagan past. Celtic oral traditions told tales of a good king named Arthur and his Knights of the Round Table. Arthur's father, aptly, was named Uther Pendragon, *The Head of the Dragon*, hinting at his ancient connection to the old ways. Celtic legends also merged with the burgeoning mythos of the new religion, Christianity, with the most enduring of these tales revolving around the search for the mythical cup of renewal, the Grail, with its roots planted in both Celtic and Christian mysteries.

In 1066, the Norman lord known as William the Conqueror defeated King Harold at the Battle of Hastings and won the crown of England. King William was descended from Norsemen, marauding Viking pirates who preyed on northern England and seized the northern portion of France, now known as Normandy, from the descendants of Charlemagne and Roman Christendom. In time, the Norsemen too succumbed to conversion to the new religion. The flaming sword of Truth brandished by the Normans' patron, Saint Michael, blazed a bloody path to glory and conquest.

Yet at the very height of these European warriors' power and might, something miraculous had begun to occur—a profound resurgence of creative spirit, honoring and inspired by the emergence of a divine feminine image of the Queen of Heaven—Mary. This was evidenced in the works of art, literature and architecture, and in the ideals of chivalry and courtly love. It had been more than a millennium since human hands and hearts had expressed such profound sensitivity and beauty in their works and ideas. Simply behold the Gothic Cathedral of Chartres, built to immortalize in stone *Notre Dame*—Our Lady, Virgin Queen of Heaven. Chartres, renowned for its tales of miracles and healing down through the ages, also houses a statue of the Black Virgin and Child in an alcove within its crypt, one of scores of shrines throughout Europe that venerate the Black Queen of Heaven. How could such beauty, refinement, and religious devotion have blossomed throughout

Europe during the twelfth and thirteenth centuries, a time of constant war, brutality, and bloodshed?

At the center of this renaissance was Eleanor, the French Duchess of Acquitaine, a towering spirit of the twelfth century. Eleanor had two daughters, Alix and Marie, by her first husband, Louis VII, King of France. In 1164, the two sisters married two brothers, with Alix wedding the Count of Chartres, and Marie the Count of Champagne. These three women were at the heart and soul of this flowering of cultural and spiritual rebirth. The beautiful prose of Henry Adams captures the essence of their influence upon European consciousness:

> [W]hile the Virgin was miraculously using the power of spiritual love to elevate and purify the people, Eleanor and her daughters were using the power of earthly love to discipline and refine the courts. . . . The ideals of Eleanor and her daughter Marie of Champagne were a form of religion. . . . [Each] knew what a brute the emancipated man could be. . . . [T]hey used every terror they could invent, as well as every tenderness they could invoke, to tame the beasts around them. . . . [T]hey made a school which they called their Court of Love, with a code of law to which they gave the name of "courteous love."[14]

The practice of chivalry and courtly love provided a form that would curb the brute instincts of the medieval knights. The old values of might makes right gave way to defense of the weak.

In the view of many historians, the cult of courtly love arose from—or in concert with— the Cathar heresy, as it was known of by the Church of Rome, in the southern lands of Provence and Languedoc in France. There is considerable debate as to how this religious movement took root there. When Rome was at its height it acquired lands in the geographical location of what is now modern France. Upon Rome's collapse the Byzantine Empire formed from its eastern lands. According to Denis de Rougemont, Persian *Manichaeism*, a dualistic form of gnosticism, spread through the Byzantine Empire and took root in southern France and northern Italy as Catharism. From there it came together with another Persian movement that migrated from Turkey, the Arab courts, and mystical Sufi sects of Iraq, until it reached Moorish-occupied Andalusia in the south of Spain. It arrived in Spanish Catalonia and southern France, which directly borders it, according to de Rougemont, as "one of the most extraordinary spiritual confluences in history,"[15] in which Islamic love poetry was transformed into troubadour verse. Other scholars of Catharism, have pointed to archeological finds that link the ancient seagoing Phoenicians to settlements on the southern shores of Provence, where the religion originated.[16] As the first seafaring traders, the Phoenicians would have been well acquainted with the teachings of *Mani*—the founding sage of this Persian form of gnosticism.

Among the Cathars, it was thought that true love could never be experienced between a man and a woman in this earthly, carnal existence, for this plane was thought to be evil and corrupted. Only the soul, our angelic essence, trapped down in the earth and matter, was divine. Following this belief the Cathars forbade the pleasures of sexual intercourse to their elite devotees, believing that the act imprisoned the soul within the body. They viewed marriage as an organized vice. Casual sex was tolerated among the larger body of their followers, because it was felt to relieve instinctual pressures with no fear that the soul might be entrapped. The dualism apparent in these beliefs rejects the human and privileges spiritual love.

For the Cathars, only through the Queen of Heaven, the spiritual bridge connecting man with God, could one enter the Kingdom of Light in the Heavens. Only by overcoming the temptations of the flesh, the seductions of Venus, and renouncing this world could the Cathars be pure and attain salvation in the next life. In Catharism Jesus was relegated to the status of a mere angel. The appeal of this purist religion, which glorified and idealized the feminine spirit in the form of the Queen of Heaven, became quite threatening to the Patriarchy of the Church, which banned it as heresy. Later, the Cathars' center of influence in the south of France and Catalonian Spain was crushed by church-sponsored crusades, forcing the old beliefs underground.

Upon Eleanor's wedding to Louis the troubadours of her court in Acquitaine accompanied the new queen from the southern lands to the north. Eleanor divorced Louis, and then married her second husband, Henry II, descendent of William the Conquerer, two years before his ascension to the throne of England in 1154. It is generally accepted that the poets of her court of love transmitted their doctrine of *amor* to the storytellers of the Arthurian romances in England. A common thread connected the two. As de Rougemont tells us, the Cathars "drew certain features of its mythology from its Celt . . . background." The ancient Celtic religion of the Druids "taught a dualistic view of the universe and made Woman into a symbol of the divine."[17]

As Robert Johnson writes, while the ideal of courtly love initiated "a revolution in our attitudes towards the feminine values of love, relationship, refined feeling, devotion, spiritual experience, and the pursuit of beauty, it also left a strange *split* in our feelings."[18] The internal split that Johnson alludes to pits the pure and sacred ideal of the feminine, embodied in Cathar orthodoxy against the woman who embodies the elemental earth, the irrational, and the sexual. Nothing speaks more poignantly to this symbolic problem than that extraordinary work of art that is the grand Gothic cathedral at Chartres.

Eleanor's daughter, Alix, came to Chartres as its countess around 1165, close to twenty years after the slender spires of the first cathedral had been built. By fifteen years before her arrival, the undertaking of the beautiful stained-glass work had already commenced. In 1194 a fire destroyed much of Chartres. After the blaze, pilgrims used the great crypt to conduct services—the same crypt where the shrine to the Black Virgin stood. Reconstruction of the Cathedral of Notre Dame at Chartres began in 1195, so that by 1206 the choir services could resume. The daughter of Alix, Queen Blanche, figured greatly in all these undertakings, completed over thirty years. Today the cathedral stands as a testament to the extraordinary creative spirit permeating that era.

Alix and Blanche, Eleanor's daughter and granddaughter, were royalty—regarded by their subjects as the earthly representatives of the Virgin Mary, Queen of Heaven. They dictated the tastes at their court, and the artists whose inspired hands carved the exquisite stone images and fashioned the stained glass windows sought to do what pleased them, as if in doing so they were pleasing the Virgin Herself.

Historically, the village of Chartres was named for the *Carnutes*, a Celtic tribe. These were pagan Druids, who created a thriving center atop what was once a neolithic site until it, too, was destroyed by the Normans in the ninth century. In that same period and place, certain references point to the worship of the Black Virgin. The mysterious origins of the cult of the Black Madonna throughout Europe have been traced back to the Egyptian goddess Isis, and her son Horus. The briefest of comments upon this rich topic will have to suffice here as to the cult's historical development and controversial implications.[19]

An ancient grotto to the Great Mother, referred to as the Virgin of the Underworld, is said to exist beneath the foundation of the original twelfth-century church at Chartres. In the Druidic period, according to Ean Begg, it was known as the "cult of a holy well 'of the strong,' and of 'The Virgin who will Give Birth,' our Subterranean Lady."[20] Like so many places sacred to the Old Ones, the ancient temples were buried and built over, and their power usurped by the Church. "Our Lady" of Chartres must certainly bear the dual mantle of both Queen of Heaven as well as Goddess within the Earth, however veiled our eyes may be to the latter, or how split off she may seem in this dualistic hierarchy that privileges light over dark. Her Gothic cathedral, whose towers reach to the sky to capture the most light, was built to honor the Heavenly Virgin Mother and Her Child, while the meaning and origin of her fertile, elemental nature has been purposely buried over time, due perhaps, to the potential threat it may hold for the Church and its traditions. The truth has not been easily accessible and this fascinating line of inquiry has only been brought to our attention in relatively modern times.

Ironically, if any flaws at all were evident in the pure and perfect lines of the Gothic edifice, they lay in its attempts to reach into the heights of heaven with such slender spires. Thin columns necessitated use of wood in the vaulted ceiling, making its walls and other supports unsound and more vulnerable to fire and collapse. Says Adams, "the Gothic architects . . . needed light and always more light, until they sacrificed safety and common sense in trying to get it."[21] Isn't this almost always the case? When we reach too high and too far toward the pure and perfect spiritual light, the dark opposite, denied and marginalized, will bring about our collapse and deflation, until we are brought down into solid earth and humble matter. It is notable that the *bases* of the towers and the *crypt* alone were all that remained of the burnt-out edifice of Chartres after the fire of 1194.[22]

It was Marie of Champagne's court poet, Chretien, who fashioned the first written version of the old Celtic tale that came to be known as the *Count of the Grail*, or *Parzival*, as Wolfram von Eschenbach's later version was called. Wolfram claimed to have received the story from a Provencal troubadour named Kyot, and elements of the Cathars' heretical religion are present in both texts.

The Grail knights, as Wolfram tells us, were called *Templeise*. von Franz and Emma Jung links them with the Cathars, and also comment that, "The possibility that the Templars were spiritually influenced by certain movements of Islam, especially esoteric, Gnostic ones, cannot be dismissed out of hand.[23]

The Templar Knights were charged with guarding the road to Jerusalem, and they were housed on the grounds of what was once the Temple built by King Solomon in that ancient city, from which their name is derived.[24] They were, most likely, in search of ancient relics and treasures buried beneath its foundations—most notably, the Arc of the Covenant, once housed within the Holy of Holies.[25]

King Solomon's African Queen of Sheba, is likely to have served as the inspiration for the Black Shulamite, the beloved who appears in the Song of Songs, which Solomon is credited with writing. She captured the imagination of the medieval mind, as evidenced by the odd reference to "Solomon's wife" in Chretien's *Count of the Grail*, and the twelfth-century carvings of the Queen of Sheba at Chartres. Here we see the link with the Black Virgin and Chartres. In later traditions, such as alchemy, Sheba would be inseparable from the image of Sophia, the early Gnostic embodiment of divine feminine wisdom.[26] The Canticles, as the Song of Songs was called, also served as the religious inspiration for the Spanish mystics' ecstatic meditations upon their union with the Beloved.

It was Marie, Chretien's sovereign, who first inspired the literature of courtly love and religious mystery. Chretien claimed that she had given him the idea for the story of *Lancelot* and that several of his Lady's characters were modeled after her life and person. The courtly tale of "The Lady of Shallot" laments the tragic end that befalls Elaine, the sacrificial victim of Lancelot, a man terribly divided in his feelings for the two women that love him. This story, paraphrased below from Bulfinch's version, clearly shows the narcissistic aspect of splitting, and prepares us for a more personal and contemporary view of the problem of a man's splintered mother imago.

> Sir Lancelot is wounded in battle and is nursed back to health by Elaine of Astolat. She is hopelessly in love with him but as soon as he recovers he cannot wait to depart from her for he longs to gaze once more upon Guinevere's lovely face. Elaine cannot bear to live her life apart from him. Her life failing, she steps onto a boat and floats down the river toward Camelot. Sometime later, Lancelot, spying a richly ornamented boat that comes aground, goes to investigate it. There he finds the beautiful "lilly maid of Astolat"—lying in death's repose. Within her purse is a letter addressed to King Arthur. In reading

its contents aloud to all the Knights of the Round Table, he speaks her words: "Lancelot of the Lake, the most accomplished of knights and most beautiful of men, but at the same time the most cruel and inflexible, had by his rigor produced the death of the wretched maiden whose love was no less invincible than his cruelty."[27]

In this tale of the Liebestod, one can see contemporary themes from depth psychology that speak to the shadow of romantic enthrallment. Lancelot represents the evasive lover who fears any mutually felt tenderness, care, or concern. Beneath his evasion may lie the dread of being possessed and entrapped in the death mother whose needs he fears will empty him. He bolts for the exit, in search of the fantasy of paradise in the timeless oneness of the lovers' fusion—a twin narcissism. This is ultimately a masochistic fantasy, for in fact Lancelot longs for what he can never have in Guinevere. But in his feelings of lack he remains suspended above life as a defense against the threat of human love that could shatter his narcissism. After the battle at the beginning of the tale, as he lies critically wounded and completely vulnerable and dependent upon Elaine, it is she who stays with him and nurses him back to life. Herein lies his cruelty, for when it counts, he cannot tolerate her dependency upon him.

The mantle of Elaine, the pure "lilly maid," is an allusion to the cult of Mary and the promise of idyllic love in Heaven. Here, Guinevere, Elaine's rival for Lancelot's desires, embodies Venus or Eve, the sensuous object of his unrequited and transient longing. The courtly man's divided psyche can never be healed, for neither love can ever be realized. Elaine's last great act of sacrifice exposes him for the coward that he is by publicly shaming him. Bearing shame is a typical device used in Arthurian romantic tradition to evoke humility. As we shall see, in clinical work, the shameful truth is often the only thing that can shatter the fixed narcissistic orientation.

## *The Contemporary Problem*

The maternal split in the contemporary male psyche may show itself outwardly in the man's fragmented view of women as idealized, then devalued, objects. In his mind, he swings like a pendulum from one pole to the other, never settled, never fulfilled. His divided desire to possess the virgin or the whore echos a much broader religious idea. In this psychic split, he clings to idealization and purity only to fall prey to primitive, emotional, and sexual "weaknesses." The split he experiences is like that of a baby who is unable to bear ambivalent feelings toward his mother and who sees her as two separate people, one good and one bad.

In the state of romantic enthrallment, a man dealing with this split may get completely carried away, longing to merge and melt all boundaries away in endless bliss with "the one." And those who drink of this intoxicating ambrosia cannot conceive of approaching such an all-encompassing event sensibly, rationally, or cautiously, regardless of how transitory the actual experience may be.

However, once the ideal object of his love and desire is lived with and sexualized, and his passions are sated, a psychic deadening and devaluation often follows. She is no longer that pure and perfect being. On the contrary, she is a real, flawed human being. At this point, the narcissist will repeatedly turn a blind eye to the challenge of the real human encounter, content to merely skim the surface, trolling for the easy catch.

This deadening loss of feeling is followed by a tendency to want to fill the lack, to project anew, and to once again search for the state of fusion with a fresh image of She who embodies his ideal. Here it's important to remember that eros—desire—is based in lack, and is always trying to fill the gap of uncertainty. The Greek word *eros* suggests, as Anne Carson writes, a wanting, a lack, "a desire for that which is missing." However, "that which is known, attained, possessed . . ." is no longer an object of desire.[28] The lover wants someone he does not have; once his prey is caught, he soon grows tired of possessing her.

The observation of infants and their object relations helps us to understand the basis of this split. Clinicians posit that in order to feed safely and thrive, babies must be able to separate aspects of the good mother from the bad. In this primitive mental state, the all-good and nurturing mother is capable of containing all her baby's needs. Therefore she could not possibly be the same bad object who can be experienced as threatening, abandoning, and traumatizing to her baby, due to an inability, at times, to bear its anxiety, demands, or neediness. It is suggested that the suckling infant could never feel secure enough to maintain a good feed if it believed that the same mother was capable of instilling in him such anguish and terror that is attributed to the bad-object mother. Hence each new moment of reverie between mother and infant is all that exists, as the unbearable and traumatic history is obliterated.

Splitting at this primitive level is thus life-sustaining and normal. Healthy development and adaptation occur when the maturing baby can begin to tolerate the mother's going away because he trusts she will return. In his acceptance of her ambivalent, imperfect nature, she is permitted to be simply "good enough." To a degree, splitting remains part of normal development, a tool of nonverbal communication as well as a defense against a sometimes threatening world. It is when the retreat back to the infantile "Garden of Eden" is habitually chosen, in lieu of the difficult adaptations to life's challenges, that we may discover narcissistic and dissociative disorders interrupting growth and maturation.

The experience of splitting can be likened to the way the brilliance of the midday sun hides the moon, stars, and planets from sight. Men who still hold to infantile defenses live in the sun of a similar blind illusion—or a feigned innocence—that these heavenly bodies, these real alternatives, do not exist at all because they cannot be seen or accepted. Such a man may fight to the bloody end to defend his one-sided position, because his profound dissociation serves the very necessary function of defending a brittle self against the threat of uncertainty and instability.

## *The Dichotomy in Love and Marriage*

> [L]ove cannot extend its rights over two married persons. For indeed lovers grant one another all things mutually and freely. . . . whereas husband and wife are held by their duty to submit their wills to each other. . . .[29]

This judgment handed down in 1174 by Marie of Champagne's court of love declared that marriage and love were incompatible. Granted, Marie's court of love arose in reaction to feudal laws wherein marriage was a legal way for nobles to appropriate the wealth of their ladies' estates. Yet despite the impact of the Enlightenment many men still face the same dilemma when attempting to imagine the lover and wife inhabiting the same woman. No less sage a voice than C. G. Jung's seems to convey the same sentiment, when Jung acknowledges passion's incompatibility with domesticity and marriage in a letter written in 1958:

> Marriage . . . increases the need of licentiousness, not only because matrimony gets stale, but also because of a certain need . . . associated with the hetaira-nature of the sex object. . . . There are women who are not meant to bear physical children, but they are those who give rebirth to a man in a spiritual sense.[30]

Jung rationalizes the dichotomy by suggesting that when one is a wife and mother, it is hard to be a "hetaira," a term going back to ancient Greece and Rome referring to courtesans as companions. Bachofen chose to use this term when writing about what he imagined as the earliest stage of prehistory, a time when humanity lived in polygamous tribes, so that women did not know who fathered their children.

Although Jung's analysis may hold merit, it does not speak to the modern man's culpability in the inevitable suffering that ensues from this passionate triangle. It avoids the discussion of how and why a man could maintain both his wife and his lover in such fixed roles in their opposite camps, and why he is unable to hold or imagine the feminine in his mind as a cohesive multidimensionality. I believe that these enactments of separation are illustrative of the split in a man's feminine unconscious, and that their deconstruction may reveal them to be forms of narcissistic defense. Such separations are initiated by perceived threats to a man's control and stability, threats that are reminiscent of deficits carried forward following early maternal trauma, loss, and the fear of annihilation.

A husband who depends on the safety and stability of the maternal embrace of wife and family may also search out clandestine sexual encounters that promise ecstatic, short-lived pleasures in the arms of the mistress or the "other woman." In other scenarios as Toni Wolff maintains, the *femme inspiratrice*—the "inspirational woman,"[31] whose life seems diametrically opposed to that of the dutiful wife/mother, waits secretly in the wings, standing ready to awaken the unconscious creative juices within the man. Her rites of initiation lead a man into uncertain territory, and not without occasional catastrophic consequences.

The man in a steady relationship may seek an escape, hoping to enliven his otherwise stable and sterile life through an infusion of what he imagines to be the mysterious and exciting unknown. It may lie somewhere off in the future, as yet unlived, just a fantasy. Ironically, it is often his own urgent need for control and stability within his marriage that ultimately deadens the marriage in the first place and keeps his partner at a distance. Perhaps what he truly dreads is this deeper unknown, discovered only through the human encounter—the real relationship—rife with turbulence and emotional conflict. In any event, he often jumps ship, always seeking freedom in the new, the young, or the exciting. Sadly, untold pain awaits the innocents who get dragged into the mess when the truth is finally revealed, for this evasion is in fact a terribly hostile act, one he does not recognize as such. The wives and children always bear the brunt of it.

Often in the final, desperate act of the drama, the man who suffers from this deeply split internal mother image will swing back again toward the soothing arms of the one who is a mother to him. He may adopt this convenient solution to the conflict for no other reason than to receive his wife's stabilizing containment as his spouse and the mother of his children. He will inevitably discard the other, or perhaps string her along to hedge his bets. What is certain is that she will be cast adrift if there is any question as to the maintenance of his security, for that is always primary. This whole process is not an initiatory one; the conflict that ensues from his actions does not bring about a transcendence of the inner split. On the contrary, in Jungian terms, this end result would be an example of the regressive restoration of his persona.

In the next chapter contemporary vignettes lend substance and support to these ideas developed here.

## Notes

1 Peter Mudd, "Jung and the Split Feminine," *Round Table Review* 6(1) (1998): 1.

2  Toni Wolff, "Structural Forms of the Feminine Psyche," translated by Gela Jacobson. *Psychological Perspectives* 31 (1995): 82.

3  Claude Fauriel, *Histoire de la poésie provençale* (Paris: J. Labitte, 1846), vol. I, p. 512, as cited in Denis de Rougemont, *Love in the Western World*, translated by Montgomery Belgion (Princeton, NJ: Princeton University Press, 1983), 34.

4  Joseph Henderson and Maude Oakes, *The Wisdom of the Serpent* (Toronto, ON: The Macmillan Company, 1963), 22–23.

5  Astarte was known by many names and her worship was disseminated throughout the peoples of the Middle East, including the Arameans. Some researchers believe that she was not a moon goddess. The crescent-shaped headdress she was often depicted as wearing, they contend, was not a symbol of the moon, but rather that of the cow.

6  Aramea was located roughly in the area that we now know as Syria.

7  Here we see the tribal practice of cross-cousin marriage, where the sister's brother's daughter may be joined with the sister's son. This is an attempt to move one step away from the taboo of incest between brother/sister and mother/son, and similar connections, while still honoring the power of the kinship libido.

8  Rachael's name has interesting etymological roots. Its last syllable, as Racha-*el* alludes to the plural and *feminine* name of God, found in *el*-ohim and *el*-ohenu—"our God," and in the many aspects of God, signified by the legions of archangels, such as Rapha-*el*, Gabri-*el*, and Micha-*el*. This name for God can most likely be traced back to a mountain god identified with the supreme deity of the Canaanite pantheon of deities: *El.* Arthur Cotterell and Rachel Storm, *The Ultimate Encyclopedia of Mythology* (London: Hermes House, 1999), 329. Curiously enough, the Arabic letters *al*, from which *Al*-lah is derived, can also be linked to the ancient idea of the cycles of the *moon* and its many phases. Here again lies the hidden power that *Luna* exerts over the flow of waters and the fertility cycles of life.

9  Rabbi Elie Munk, *The Call of the Torah* (Brooklyn, NY: Menorah Publications), 1994, 403–404.

10  See the story in Genesis of Jacob's sons, who murdered all the men of a neighboring tribe while they were recovering from circumcision. One had fallen in love with their sister, Dinah, and defiled her. Jacob would permit their union only if his people submitted to the rites of circumcision—the symbol of the Hebrew's covenant with God. As the men lay suffering, all were slain by the vengeful brothers.

11  Thomas Mann, *Joseph and His Brothers* (London: Vintage Random House, 1999), 252.

12  Henderson and Oakes, *The Wisdom of the Serpent*, 22.

13  His "death and rebirth," from imprisonment to rulership of Egypt, represents a regression back to the feminine traditions.

14  Henry Adams, *Mont-Saint-Michel and Chartres* (New York: The Heritage Press, 1933), 195–196.

15  Denis de Rougemont, *Passion and Society*, translated by Montgomery Belgion (London: Faber and Faber, 1956), 102.

16  Otto Rahn, *Crusade against the Cathars* (Rochester, VT: Inner Traditions, 2006), 54.

17  de Rougemont, *Love in the Western World*, 124.

18  Robert Johnson, *We: Understanding the Psychology of Romantic Love* (San Francisco: HarperSanFrancisco, 1983), 71.

19  This reference pertains to the Merovingian heresy of France, which allegedly depicts Mary Magdalene as the Holy Grail that bore the son and royal line of Jesus. The Order of the Prieure Notre-Dam de Sion, reportedly in continuous existence since the twelfth century, was said to have been established in order to restore the bloodline of the Merovingians to the throne. In some ancient centers of influence, the Magdalene was worshipped alongside Isis, Cybele, and Artemis, as their cults intertwined. No less a figure than King Louis XI was a devotee of the Black Virgin cult, and believed Mary Magdalene to be of royal French lineage. Ean Begg, "Evidence for Continuity for the Black Virgin Tradition," in *The Cult of the Black Virgin* (London: Penguin Books, 1985), 14–16.

20  Begg, *Cult of the Black Virgin*, 21.

21   Adams, *Mont-Saint-Michel and Chartres*, 89.

22   I imagine that the Crusaders of that era, infused with the glorious and righteous mission of lib-
     erating Jerusalem from the heathens, suffered a similar ignoble deflation at the time Jerusalem was
     wrested from them in 1187 by Saladin and his Moors, who drove the Crusaders out after a hundred
     years of European occupation.

23   Emma Jung and Marie-Louise von Franz, *The Grail Legend* (Princeton, NJ: Princeton University
     Press, 1960), 16. Begg's sources suggest that many of the statuettes of the Black Virgin found their
     way aboard the Knight's Templar caravans back from the Holy Land, leading to speculation that
     the Templars' secret traditions honored the Queen of Heaven. This may suggest that they shared
     common ground with both the Manichean traditions of the east and west, as well as the Prieure de
     Sion, the organization that purportedly founded their order.

24   E. Jung and von Franz, *The Grail Legend*, 152.

25   According to the Old Testament, the Arc contained the Ten Commandments that Moses brought
     down from Sinai, and the priestly clan carried it throughout their time of Exodus from Egypt, un-
     til Solomon built the Temple in Jerusalem to house it. The Holy Spirit—*Ruach Ha Kodesh*—would
     descend upon the Arc in a fiery cloud to deliver the Word of God. Only the purest of the priestly
     line could be present in the Holy of Holies to witness the miracle.

26   Ethiopian legend tells of Solomon's marriage to the Queen of Sheba, and how their son was en-
     trusted by Solomon with the sacred Arc.

27   Thomas Bulfinch, "The Story of Lancelot: The Lady of Shalott," in *Bulfinch's Mythology*: *The Age
     of Fable, The Age of Chivalry, Legends of Charlemagne*, foreword by Alberto Manguel (New York:
     Modern Library, 2004), 367.

28   Anne Carson, *Eros the Bittersweet* (Normal, IL: Dalkey Archive Press, 1998), 65, as cited in Karol
     Marshall, "Eros the Sweetbitter," paper presented at the Forum of the Northwest Alliance for Psy-
     choanalytic Study, Seattle, Washington, May 8,1999, 2.

29   de Rougemont, *Love in the Western World*, 34.

30   C. G. Jung Letter to Carol Jeffry, June 18, 1958, in Ronald Hayman, *A Life of Jung* (New York,
     Norton, 1999), 70.

31   Toni Wolff, "Structural Forms of the Feminine Psyche," 82.

## CHAPTER FOUR

# ANALYST, PRESIDENT, SURGEON
## THE SPLIT FEMININE IN CONTEMPORARY MAN

I
n this chapter I will attempt to show, through psycho-biographical vignettes and a clinical example, that the split feminine in men is not an isolated occurrence, but affects men in all walks of life. I view it as a form of defensive narcissism that isolates men from emotional impact that is threatening to their need to maintain safety and sameness. Although these are relatively brief descriptions, they will be helpful in illuminating the common threads that are found in the early lives of two well-known contemporary men, C. G. Jung and former President Bill Clinton. Following these explorations, a case history from my clinical work elucidates the traumatic early-life conditions that lay beneath a gifted surgeon's descent into sexual addiction, alcoholism, and the ruin of his family and career that contributed to his premature death.

• • • • •

The two biographical sketches with which I begin illuminate a theme introduced in the previous chapter, namely the impact of maternal instability, which in these cases was present from the time of each man's birth. Based on the biographical facts at hand I speculate on how this instability could give rise to a split in the maternal imago, and consequently to "polygamous components," as Jung describes them, in the adult personalities of the two men.[1] To restore emotional balance in their lives, Jung and Clinton compelled their wives and lovers to fulfill precise roles for them, reflective of each man's fluctuating need for safety or freedom, and nurturance or passion.

## C. G. Jung

Jung's psychological anamnesis, beginning prior to his birth, is well chronicled in his own autobiography as well as by several major biographers. The rich material drawn from these sources and presented in the following section affords us a detailed exploration, albeit a speculative one.

At the beginning of his career the renowned psychiatrist Carl Gustav Jung, who at the time was twenty-eight years of age, commenced psychoanalytic treatment of Sabina Spielrein, an eighteen-year-old psychotic patient. Scarcely a year before that, Jung was married to 21-year-old Emma Rauschenbach.[2] Spielrein was the granddaughter of a Jewish rabbi. She was dark and beautiful, and possessed of a mysterious depth of emotion and spirit missing in Jung's relationship with Emma, whom he viewed as stable and grounded. Emma was an essential and safe harbor for him and the mother of his children, yet she lacked the capacity to inspire his fiery depths, to *initiate* him. Perhaps, too, it was Jung himself who lacked some basic courage to bear the emotional intimacy demanded of marriage.

From the powerful psychological and emotional bonds established between patient and doctor came the seeds for the repair and healing of Spielrein's damaged psyche and a deepened capacity for relatedness on her part. But the turbulent currents of their unconscious analytic relationship threatened—and perhaps succeeded—in carrying the two away.[3] This unconscious process later came to be known as the "transference-countertransference." Jung could not distinguish his emotions, nor aspects of himself, from a psychological state of partial identity with Sabina—the magical oneness of subject and object that the anthropologist Lévy-Brühl has described as a "participation mystique."

Jung and Spielrein's absolute-influence over each other catapulted both of them headlong into an intoxicating and delirious kind of fusion.[4] She had a mystical, clairvoyant way about her that aroused powerful feelings in Jung. "We could sit for hours in silent ecstasy," she wrote. "My love for him transcended our affinity until he could bear it no longer and wanted 'poetry.'"[5] Clear incestuous elements heightened their titillation. In her analytic treatment with Jung, Sabina had revealed childhood memories of aroused, incestuous, sexual feelings with her father. In her fantasies and dreams Jung became interchangeable with her father and brother, and the hoped-for "father" of their forbidden and mythical child, Siegfried.[6]

Incestuous elements can emerge in any relationship that is based upon a hierarchical authoritarian structure, including that of a doctor and patient. The doctor must be mindful and vigilant in the maintenance of the necessarily delicate boundaries, and in the awareness of his own unresolved issues, so as to avoid doing inadvertent harm through enactment. Lacking the benefit of this clinical awareness, Jung acted out his erotic countertransference through their shared *coniunctio*, which helped to resolve Sabina's psychosis. Yet ultimately, in the second act of their drama, he caused great harm to her by pulling back from the emotional intensity of the relationship. By then, their fantasy of idyllic fusion had taken on roller-coaster, nightmarish qualities owing to dangerous inner contents that were rising to the surface in Jung, contents that stemmed from his earliest life and had never been resolved. A review of Jung's first years, drawn from various sources, will speak to this process. The evidence supports Peter Mudd's assertions that Jung suffered from a "troubling split in the mother imago"[7] giving rise to "polygamous dimensions" in his psyche[8] that began with his painful relations with his mother.

C. G. Jung was born on the shores of Lake Constance in rural Switzerland in 1875, scarcely two years after the death of an older brother who survived for only a few days. This was a terrible loss for his mother, who had lost several other earlier pregnancies, and it may have contributed to his parents' later marital difficulties and separation. Jung could not recall much physical care from his mother aside from the normal care and feeding. Perhaps she felt too overanxious, so soon after the death of the earlier boy, to allow her new baby to feel held, contained, or relaxed in her arms.[9]

At age three young Carl developed eczema, due in part to emotional stress, although at about this same time his mother was hospitalized in a mental ward in Basel for a depression related most directly to her marriage. Carl was cared for both by a maiden aunt and a young, dark-skinned family maid. He was deeply troubled by his mother's departure and he never forgave her for going away.[10] He clearly recalled the young maid who cared for him while his mother was away, and the comforting feelings she instilled within him. He remembered nestling his head on her shoulder, and how different this was from his experience with his mother, in whose arms he never felt completely relaxed. So strange and mysterious was this maid, yet familiar and connected to him in a way that he could not describe. He spoke of her in terms usually reserved for a mother. He felt he had known her always. She came to represent, as he writes in *Memories, Dreams, Reflections*, the "whole essence of womanhood," what he would later come to describe as the *anima*.[11] Through this precious relationship Jung may have felt the first glimmers of a distinct yet unknown Other that he experienced separately from his mother—around whom a great ambivalence grew.[12]

At a deeper level, the parents' troubled marriage, the unstable emotional environment for young Carl, and his mother's depression were all typical expressions of an inadequate mourning process for the firstborn who lived for only a few days. In many cases of this kind a great deal of pressure is often placed upon the next child, in the form of impossible parental expectations, to compensate for the lost child. He would always be compared with that "little angel in heaven." Mudd describes a tendency in the parents toward overprotectiveness that can give rise in the child to a kind of a "confused narcissistic equilibrium." In other words, Jung might have grown up with a sense of specialness and calling as the child that lived, the one that must be preserved at all costs. His specialness could reflect one side of a fractured psyche, the other being the battering experiences of total abandonment and loss by his mother which he endured at three.[13] This "profound environmental instability," Mudd adds, would leave Jung "vulnerable to intense fears of abandonment, annihilation, and death."[14]

Jung's unstable early life, clearly affected by his mother's abandonment due to depression and possibly psychosis, coupled with a retreat into his own rich fantasy life,[15] was mitigated slightly by the nurturing experience of his maid and his aunt. This ambivalent attitude toward the primary women in his life proved to be the original source of the split feminine within Jung. Peter Mudd has suggested that these polarized and contradictory inner feminine images kept him in a perpetual state of imbalance that threatened his internal stability. Says Mudd, "On one hand woman was experienced as an abandoning, dangerous, unreliable creature, on the other a reassuring, redemptive figure full of eternal strangeness and wonder."[16]

Such were the powerful internal dynamics driving Jung's doomed relationship with Spielrein. Perhaps unable to tolerate the tension of their fusion, he attempted to break things off several times, but was met with the hell's fury of a scorned woman on each occasion.[17] Dependency had always had dire consequences for him, and if the stories of their love affair were true, he had become too deeply involved. Perhaps he sensed that such identification with or dependency upon the object of his desire might trigger within him the primal terrors of abandonment or annihilation.

The roles that Emma and Sabina were compelled to play in relation to Jung enacted his internal split. They can be seen as forms of his narcissistic defenses. Jung's need to withdraw and return to the conventional and safe confines of hearth and home, where he could regain his sense of authority and control, protected him from the risks entailed in forming bonds of trust and achieving deeper emotional surrender. At the same time, the concretizing of grandiose, incestuous fantasies of fusion with the enchanted other might insulate him against even deeper fears of a dependency that could bring fragmentation and abandonment. According to Hegel, "To be loved by another we give over our self to the other and we actually enslave the other."[18] Jung enslaved Sabina through her passionate longing and romantic notions of love for him. Out of a desperate need to maintain psychic equilibrium Jung sought power over the object of his desires in this form of twin narcissism, attempting to use her to fulfill his need for that missing part of himself. (This twin narcissism, as we recall, derives from the early state of fusion of the infant with its mother.) But the relationship fell apart, as Peter Mudd writes, "When Jung failed to control Spielrein, to compel her to play the precise intrapsychic part which he needed, the spell broke."[19] Jung consolidated himself back home with Emma, while at the same time entering into another powerful relationship with a younger, former patient—Toni Wolff, who was to become his mistress. Their relationship lasted thirty years.

Two significant events in Jung's later life suggest that he may have developed to a point where he could look at the situation reflectively, armed with the wisdom gleaned from painful experience and, perhaps, a deep remorse. In 1944 the *shattering other* was visited upon him in the form of a devastating heart attack that brought him to the brink of death. After his recovery, in 1946 he wrote *The Psychology of the Transference*, in which he spoke of the erotic transference between a patient and doctor. At its heart, he recognized the transference as an inner experience of union with one's own very soul that may be evoked in the therapeutic relationship, but that is misunderstood when it is concretized and acted out. He dedicated the essay to Emma, perhaps as an *apologia*, perhaps as a confession. Jung's wounding is our wounding—that is, the wounding of all men who have found themselves swimming in those same turbulent seas, struggling to navigate through the treacherous straits between *Scylla* and *Charybdis*. This favorite analogy of Jung's is a reference to the devouring sea monster and the dangerous whirlpool, respectively, who guarded the most perilous straits in the Classical world.

### *Bill Clinton*

While former President Bill Clinton's history shares common themes with Jung's, the source material about Clinton does not provide the psychological nuances that are the focus of Jung's memories and reflections. The ideas set forth here have been drawn mainly from historical data, and are therefore more tentative and speculative than those in the preceding section.

Bill Blythe, William Jefferson Clinton's father, died three months before his son came into the world. It had been love at first sight for Clinton's mother, Virginia, when Blythe walked into the hospital where she was working. They courted for only two months and were married. Blythe promptly shipped out overseas to serve in the war effort. He returned for a week at the end of 1945, and Bill was conceived. After Blythe returned for good the couple was together for only three months when he was killed in a car accident in 1946. Born by Caesarian section three months later and one month premature, Bill was a fatherless son of a widowed mother. One can only imagine the impact of this background upon a new baby, born to a mother in the midst of such grief and loss, with the insecurity of facing the prospects of raising her son alone, without his father. It is reasonable to ask whether Virginia's difficult emotional state could also have placed undue stress on the pregnancy itself, and have been a contributing factor in the premature birth of her son.[20]

Bill's mother went to live with her parents. "Mammaw"—Bill's grandmother, Edith—ruled the roost, while his grandfather, though kindly, was very passive.[21] Bill was immersed in the mothers' world, with the two women competing for his love and attention. His grandmother ran a structured, disciplined household. She ordered his life, regulated his sleep to the minute, and pushed food into his mouth. She was said to have a bad temper.[22] Her daughter Virginia adored her daddy but feared her mother.

When Bill was one year old his mother left home to attend school for two years, leaving him for months at a time in the able and sure hands of his Mammaw. Virginia hated to leave him but she was also anxious to get away from her mother's influence. When Bill was 4 his mother married Roger Clinton, who, according to biographer David Maraniss, was "a freewheeling sharpie from Hot Springs . . . who ran a car dealership in town" and dealt bootleg whiskey on the side. "He loved to drink and gamble and have a good time." He was also a womanizer.[23] Roger Clinton was an alcoholic, abusive man, who took young Bill and his mother away from his grandparents and the only place he ever knew as home.

It was an erratic life for the young family. The sources indicate that Bill lacked positive male mentors in adolescence. He did not have the kind of strong father energy needed to guide and initiate him into the world. In high school Bill played in the band with the girls. He never competed in sports, nor did he serve in the military later on in his life. But he was bright and capable and the public service and scholastic awards piled up.

The evidence speaks to tragic and abrupt losses in Bill's earliest life—the widowing of his mother just before his birth, her intermittent departures from his life from the time he was a year old, and the loss at 4 years of age of his grandmother and the highly structured routines she provided for him when the family moved away with the new husband. Early losses are often the source of states of despair in a man. The absence in a boy's life of mitigating masculine influences to lean on for strength can accentuate the need, later in life, to seek out more controlling relationships to help manage unbearable states of dread.

In the two mothers who love him we can see the basis in Bill's first years of life for his internalization of the split in the maternal imago, and the mother-bound tendencies that accompany it. One is loving and permissive—more like a big sister than the mother, but she can't always be counted on to be there. She leaves him for months at a time when he is only a year old. The other is more like the "phallic mother," who runs a tight ship and maintains a stable, loving consistency. While he is safe in his Mammaw Edith's capable but somewhat compulsive and domineering care, at the same time one can imagine fantasies of passive-resistance, rebellion, and retaliation arising toward that same caregiver. He could exert similar resistance toward others who would take her place later in his life—in their "devouring mother" aspects. The instability in Bill's childhood and youth was exacerbated by growing up with an alcoholic stepfather who disrupted what security he had. This instability might underlie the stark dichotomy reflected in the contrast between his need for the woman who would control his every move and his simultaneous resistance to being controlled by her.

The spouse of an alcoholic often stays with him, maintaining a codependent relationship out of fear of being abandoned, but at the cost of her children's well-being. If the mother has been emotionally besieged by such an existence, her children can experience her diminished presence as a form of maternal deprivation, even if it is unintentional and not malicious. Often children compensate for the intermittent care at home by excelling in school and extracurricular activities that keep them away from home as much as possible. Since it is unclear whether the Clinton home conformed to any of these typical family patterns, any conclusions drawn from this line of inquiry are highly speculative, yet worthy of consideration.

With this background in mind, we can conjecture about the possible forces motivating Clinton's behavior, leading up to the well-publicized soap opera that fixated the nation for the last years of his presidency. Hillary may have possessed the same containing and structured qualities as his grandmother. Perhaps he relied on his more "phallic wife" to provide order, security, and the drive that spurred him on to do great things. Gossip within the psychiatric communities of Washington and Little Rock, for whatever it is worth, posited that Clinton was greatly dependent upon Hillary and was driven to sexual acting out whenever she left town, or after emotional meltdowns between the couple. As the stories went, he simply could not bear the terrible feelings of abandonment that accompanied her anger or her emotional and physical withdrawal from him.

In this context, his sexual conquests can be seen as serving his narcissistic defenses. Perhaps he targeted younger subordinates or star-struck women who looked up to him, in an attempt to magically restore his own sense of power, or as a means of coping with unbearable feelings of loss. After the conclusion of their notorious affair, Monica Lewinski was said to regard Bill Clinton as the most selfish man she knew. This characteristic would reflect his use of the desired object not so much for sexual gratification, but as a thing to be colonized and as a means of stabilizing himself emotionally. Like Jung, Clinton too was confronted, altered, and perhaps humbled forever by a life-threatening heart attack and surgery that took him years to fully recover from. Perhaps in the year of intensive psychotherapy following his surgery he came to glimpse a trace of the hidden architect behind his shameful fall from power and his close brush with death—that shattering and enigmatic *Other*. Its impact alone is capable of deflating an inflated persona that constantly yearns for assurance from the adoring crowd, so that something new, more substantial, and true can emerge from the shards of his life. I'm not sure if we will ever know.

## Clinical Vignette

At the pinnacle of a brilliant career in plastic surgery, a 45-year-old man makes a destructive choice that marks the beginning of a slow descent into alcoholism, sexual addiction, and premature death fifteen years later. He becomes enthralled with a callgirl who awakens sexual drives within him of a sadomasochistic nature. Like a man possessed, he doesn't hide the behavior well at all, and his wife of twenty years divorces him. His daughter, whom he had little to do with in her early years, continues to return the favor. He and the woman have a tumultuous, on-and-off relationship that eventually disintegrates. But this is only after she toys with his affections, and exploits him for vast amounts of money and jewelry. Her abandonment drives him mad. Pathetic, and desperate at times, he begins to abuse alcohol and pain medications, originally prescribed for chronic headaches, and eventually he loses his practice.

This man's tragedy is reminiscent of the German film classic, *The Blue Angel*,[24] in which Marlene Dietrich plays a sexy cabaret singer who seduces a prim and proper professor away from his ivory tower at a boys' school. His captivation is so complete that he gives up everything to be with her, even submitting to the donning of face paint and a costume to play the role of a clown in her show. His abject humiliation and self-disgust lead in the end to his suicide.

My patient, whom I saw for only a brief period of time, was an only child from a middle-class Jewish family from Chicago, with a distant and stern father and an overbearing, invasive, and overprotective mother. As a child, his mother pushed him to study all the time. His future as a surgeon had been mapped out for him since he was 8 years old. While other children played in the schoolyard or at the park, his mother insisted that he stay in and study. She worried neurotically about his health. With the slightest sniffle, his anxious mother would send him to bed, or poke and prod him with enemas and a never-ending assortment of over-the-counter remedies. He grew to hate her and her complete absorption in every facet of his life. Yet he passively acquiesced to her every demand, perhaps out of a sense of helplessness in fending for himself.

His father never stepped in to protect him, nor did he teach him how to be in the world. Perhaps his disengagement from his wife and son grew out of his own need to escape from his wife's emotional neediness, which she then deposited into her son. He allowed his son to be sacrificed. After his father's death, my patient learned that he had had a lifelong mistress. His distance and betrayal may have had a profound emotional effect on his wife, who in turn may have attempted to meet her unrequited needs through her only child.

My patient's memories of his earliest life were inaccessible to him. One unforgettable event from his childhood, however, stood out like a template for the primitive mental state that took hold of him throughout his life, compelling his oscillation between the extremes of the mother imago. When he was a boy of 7, he stayed home from school with the flu one day and watched a black-and-white film from the forties on TV; it was called *The Curse of the Cat People*.[25] It was the most terrifying film he'd ever seen. He was spellbound, caught like a deer in the headlights.

According to my patient's recollection, in the thrilling climax of the film a young girl is trapped in an old house with a woman who feels murderous jealousy of her that she conceals beneath a feigned concern. She calls the girl downstairs to do harm to her. In this supernatural tale, for that is what it is, the souls of two twin sisters, one good and one evil, are locked in a struggle over control of the woman's body that they are both trying to inhabit. One intends to strangle the girl, the other to protect and care for her. As first one and then the other calls to her, the trusting child slowly makes her way down the stairs, doubt and uncertainty gradually taking hold of her. My patient was unsure who or what would be awaiting the child at the bottom of the staircase: a loving embrace or the cold grip of death around her throat. In the end, the good soul banishes the evil one forever, but the terror he felt for this innocent girl, as she is seemingly led to slaughter, stayed with my patient forever.

This painful dramatic reenactment brought into startling relief the primal split within him. His desperate need for a mother who could love, affirm, and protect him contrasted starkly with his fascination with the emotionally penetrating woman who ate away at his native sovereignty, a woman he was powerless to stop. Of note here, is that my patient's retelling of the film differs significantly from the actual plotline, so that the synopsis above represents his reconstruction of the original he experienced at age seven, seen through his own internal lens.[26]

My patient's panicked reaction to the story reflects, I believe, his terror of the hidden, devouring, and vampyric aspects of the mother complex beneath his own mother's worry, hypervigilance, and penetratingly intrusive caretaking. Her overbearing presence infantalized him. He couldn't take a step without coming under her scrutiny and enduring a barrage of machine-gun-fire questioning. As he got older, his hatred of her incessant pestering took on a passive-aggressive and avoidant form. He learned to stay away as much as he could. Later on, in his marriage, he assumed a similar passive and infantile role.

With his mother in firm control of the rudder of the ship of his life, and his father a distant and crotchety nonentity, my patient was accepted into medical school, never questioning the course he had taken.

The long covered-over crack in the veneer opened in 1965, just after examinations midway through medical school. The crises that ensued threatened to shatter his mother's best-laid plans for her son—plans which were, in fact, her own unrealized wishes that she had appropriated her son to live out for her.

It was a time when the message of the young poet and folksinger, Bob Dylan, had seized hold of an entire generation of youth, and his visions affected my patient deeply in disquieting ways. Dylan's words spoke to the restless, questioning, and searching young man, fomenting seeds of rebellion in his imagination. Over that school break, he took a guided acid trip, breaking through the illusory bonds that entrapped him in a dutiful life that he had not chosen for himself. For those brief moments of clarity, he glimpsed the possibilities of freedom from the constraints of his ego's narrow orientation.

The days that followed the LSD experience were tortured ones for him. He was prepared to quit medical school, yet in the end turned away from that drastic course. Perhaps, in hindsight, this was the beginning of the end. We both pondered what course his life might have taken had he stepped away from medical school, or his specialty field of elective plastic surgery, that kept him mired in a larger-than-life world, serving a clientele composed of the rich and famous. He spoke with wistful melancholy about those days in 1965, as if he would never get over the death of a dear friend.

Despite an esteemed reputation and a brilliant career, at home my patient behaved like a lazy child who couldn't do anything for himself. His wife became the captain of their social calendar and the regulator of hearth and home. He acted helpless and avoidant around their baby. Over time, as he settled into a life of luxury and pleasure, boredom and deadness began to seep into his marriage and life. It seems that he had maneuvered his wife into becoming a milder version of his mother. I would conjecture that his acting-out, which destroyed his marriage, was in some ways an expression of the hatred and aggression he felt toward his internalized entrapping mother, whom he projected onto his wife.

This man's turn to the seamy side of life, filled with intoxicating and insatiable hunger for sexual and drug-induced *jouissance*, would ultimately lead to the loss of his medical practice and a dangerous form of deflation—a second shattering of his brittle ego. This wounding, however, was not transcendent. Instead, it led to a slow erosion of his mental capacities. The process seemed more closely to resemble the repetition compulsion inherent in the death drive, a dissolution of self in the death coniunctio, a fantasied return to the oceanic existence before birth. The brief moments of fusion he found with his partners in his years of womanizing could never be sustained, for they robbed him of any individual agency, and he slowly got lost in an alcoholic oblivion. In hindsight, one could theorize that his alcoholism became a form of the original maternal captivity that, ironically, he had spent so many years attempting to extricate himself from.

Perhaps this type of man is secretly driven by an unrenounced bond with the death mother that he cannot free himself from. The unending fantasies that he projects onto women are formed from the maternal images within his psyche. These fantasies may take on such opposing guises as, for example, the enchanting innocent or the femme fatal, that both enthrall and lure him away from the real, sustaining, difficult, human relationship. It is this dual complex that poisons his mind, killing off any feeling for the real woman once the fantasy has been lived out, driving him onward toward the next short-lived affair. Confirmed womanizers can resemble swarming locusts who get their fill and then move on, leaving only devastation in their path. At the same time such a man may be filled with enormous fear and hatred for all things feminine. This is evidenced by the sadistic power he exerts over women—because, at the deepest inner level of his being, he feels completely devoured by the Mother. This may have been just the case with my patient. His advancing alcoholism turned this once renowned physician into an object of pity—a tragic man.

• • • • •

As we see in the lives portrayed here, the split in a man's maternal imago is formed from narcissistic defenses originating in infancy, defenses created for protection from experiences of maternal deprivation or engulfment. The men at the mercy of such a split learn only to swing between idealization and devaluation of the other, separated from or suspended above the human dimension that may wound and initiate them.

The men whose stories we have just heard all seem to have been severely handicapped in their early lives by the absence of the kind of father who would be capable of providing boundaries and protection against a storm of overpowering maternal affects. These sons must ultimately find the father within themselves—the missing element that a man draws upon for the courage to plunge into the unknown depths of life and to bear the suffering, losses, and vicissitudes of real human relationships. It is by bearing the shattering experiences he encounters there that a man can transcend narcissism. If meaning can be made from these experiences, it is all worth it. And if not, and a man continues to repeat the same old worn-out patterns, then his suffering has been a meaningless waste.

It is important to value greatness in a man, but the kind of greatness that is not based in the number of accomplishments he has achieved, or the amount of fame, wealth, and power he has amassed. Rather, we must look to his values, for who he has come to be as a man, and for how he has learned from the experiences that have wounded him. A man who has had to learn the meaning of integrity and humility the hard way places his family's well-being above his own self interests and grand designs. Such a man has learned how *to* love, and is often loved by many. Though he may never have the experience of worldly power and renown, he may achieve riches far more enduring—a level of human relatedness where responsibility to the other is primary and holds its own rewards. Standing bravely in the gaps of uncertainty and choosing curiosity in place of foreclosure is a humble place to begin.

• • • • •

In the West, our romantic myth, from antiquity up to the present time, has conflated the illusion of erotic love with mystical transcendence—"a oneness with the Divine." This *mistake* can be understood through a closer scrutiny of our earliest psychological processes, which reveal the trauma of the infant's primal loss of the enigmatic paradise of the mother. The infant's loss occurs too early in life to be reflected on or put into words. Its grief is therefore so unbearable that it must be disavowed. Each subsequent loss resembling the earliest one is met with the same repudiation. The individual will attempt to restore these lost maternal affects in his mind by reproducing them in fantasy, creating expectations that in later life may take the form of endless retranslations of romantic encounters. These may appear in several ways.

One approach aims to make the object of desire into something familiar so that its sameness provides a way to maintain control over an uncertain, threatening environment. However, this snuffs out any possibilities for mutual love. Another way involves seeking to merge with an ideal object in the illusion of oneness that reenacts the original, maternal fantasy. But because what underlies this desired merger is an insufficient ego, this attempt inevitably collapses, initiating the repetition of traumatic loss and the fragmentation of the man's ego. In a third possibility, a man may choose a long-term maternal relationship to mitigate his internal insecurities related to fear of loss or abandonment. Yet the constant regulation eventually deadens the intimacy of the relationship, and the man then seeks passion or inspiration from a new, secret object of desire. But the momentary state of fusion soon collapses, either from his fear of loss of control, or for other reasons cited earlier. In all of these ways the man projects the maternal split in his psyche onto the women in his life, who are compelled to act it out.

These attempts to restore the infant's irretrievably lost maternal paradise, through fantasies of the "two becoming one" are, in fact, defenses employed *against* grieving for traumatic losses. They are all, in fact, evasions of the intimacy, vulnerability, and pain of separation that are required of mutual, *dual* relationships that come without guarantees. And evasions are narcissism's earliest defenses.


## *Notes*

1 Jung coined this phrase in a letter to Sigmund Freud describing this aspect of himself. See C. G. Jung, *Letters*, translated by R.F.C. Hull, selected and edited by Gerhard Adler in collaboration with Aniela Jaffe, vol. 1: 1906–1950 (Princeton, NJ: Princeton University Press, 1973. Bollingen Series 95.1). Cited in Peter Mudd, "Jung and the Split Feminine," *Round Table Review* 6(1) (1998): 5.

2 Upon their marriage Jung took ownership, according to Swiss Law, of her considerable wealth. There is some reason to believe that the match was engineered by the mothers of Carl and Emma.

3 In 1904 the violating and destructive effects upon the patient, attributed to the physician's loss of moorings and subsequent crossing of boundaries—especially sexual ones—had not yet been clearly described and guarded against.

4 *C.W.* 6, 456.

5 According to Sabina's diaries, this was, apparently, Jung's euphemism for making love, and though it has been assumed by some biographers that this took place, there has been no incontrovertible evidence, other than the diaries, that they had consummated their relationship sexually. However, Emma's jealousy of their relationship, fueled by Zurich's scandalizing gossip, was very real. Draft of a letter from Sabina Spielrein to Freud June 9, 1909 in Aldo Carotenuto, *A Secret Symmetry: Sabina Spielrein between Jung and Freud* (New York:Pantheon Books, 1984), 96-7.

6 Siegfried, the hero from Wagner's Ring cycle, was the child of an incestuous pairing of brother and sister. Sabina, a deeply romantic soul, loved and idealized the opera.

7 Mudd, "Split Feminine," 4.

8  Mudd, "Split Feminine," 5. At about this same time a brilliant young analyst named Otto Gross was sent to Jung by Freud (and Gross's father) to assist in his recuperation from drug addiction. Instead, it was Jung who became enthralled with Gross's radical ideas, which effectively deconstructed the country-boy Jung and his old-fashioned notions of fidelity. Gross was a hedonist who staunchly opposed patriarchal authority; he believed in polygamy, and claimed that he slept with his patients. These new ideas must have certainly had an impact on Jung in his treatment of Sabina. See Ronald Hayman, *A Life of Jung* (London: Bloomsbury Publishing, 1999), 100–102. In December of 1909 Jung wrote to Freud that "the prerequisite for a good marriage . . . is the license to be unfaithful"; see C. G. Jung *Letters*, vol. 1: 1906–1950, as cited in Deirdre Bair, *Jung: A Biography* (Boston: Little, Brown, 2003), 181.

9  Hayman, *A Life of Jung*, 10.

10  In his own words he "always felt mistrustful when the word 'Love' was spoken. The feeling I associated with woman for a long time was of innate unreliability." C. G. Jung, *Memories, Dreams, Reflections* (New York: Vintage Books, 1965), 8. Conversely, "Father" meant to him reliability yet powerlessness. He did not elaborate, but one wonders if this sense of his father's powerlessness was in part a reaction to his own relationship with his wife.

11  Jung, *Memories, Dreams, Reflections*, 8, 9.

12  When his mother returned from the hospital she still fell into spells of depression along with happy moments. He began to regard her as two people. Though his mother was outwardly submissive, occasionally a terrifying "second personality" would burst through showing great power. He retreated more and more into the woods to play alone, enacting his own vivid fantasy life. *Memories, Dreams, Reflections*, 9.

13  Once he was walking across a bridge suspended over the Rhine Falls and he slipped through the railing, only to be snatched from death by the same maid, who caught hold of him in the nick of time. He wondered in his later reflections whether, beneath his "accident proneness" as a child there lurked an "unconscious suicidal urge or . . . a fatal resistance to life in this world." Jung, *Memories, Dreams, Reflections*, 9. This prompts the question as to whether this terrible fracture in the mother–son relationship was simply too much for a young child to bear.

14  Mudd, "Split Feminine," 5. The British psychoanalyst and pediatrician D. W. Winnicott, in reviewing Jung's autobiography, *Memories, Dreams, Reflections*, concluded that "psychotic illness must have set in by the age of four, and that Carl's personality was split as he defended himself. . . . His secretiveness was part of his defense system. . . " He also spoke of Jung's indomitable will to recover, owing to an understanding of his own psychosis. Although the number of Winnicott's dissenters in the Jungian camp was large, Michael Fordham, an eminent Jungian analyst, concurred for the most part with Winnicott's belated diagnosis. Hayman, *A Life of Jung*, 13. What the offended Jungians may not have fully understood about Winnicott's psychoanalytical theory, of course, was that these "islands of madness" he was describing were essentially a part of everyone's psychological makeup, albeit more or less pronounced depending on each case.

15  His later childhood years further paint a portrait of a dissociated boy, living a double life filled with secret rituals of fire-tending, magic stones, and a carved manikin to ward off evil that he kept hidden in the attic. In adolescence he swung between the persona of an inferior, disheveled schoolboy and a powerful, omnipotent personality with accompanying feelings of superiority. The latter aspect, a common narcissistic defense, allowed him to justify his isolation, which concealed how threatened he must have felt in relating to others.

16  Mudd, "Split Feminine," 5–6.

17  After her successful treatment at the hospital, Jung continued to see her, his rationale being that he was concerned she might relapse. He helped her to get into medical school and she assisted at

the hospital with his word association experiments, and in other capacities. They continued to see each other in informal treatment sessions, without pay.

18   Quote attributed to Hegel, from a candidate training seminar lecture by Peggy Crastnopol to the North Pacific Institute for Analytical Psychology, December 2002.

19   Mudd, "Split Feminine," 8.

20   Virginia claimed to have taken a fall, causing the early labor.

21   According to biographer David Maraniss, Bill's grandmother Edith was one of Hope's

> dazzling characters. . . . She was an imposing figure, short, wide and intense, with penetrating eyes. . . . She loved to wear her nurse's uniform. She was devoted to her patients. She was an ambitious and temperamental lady, apparently dissatisfied with her lot in life, being married to a good-natured fellow who everybody loved, but who couldn't put two nickels together to save his life.

David Maraniss, *First in His Class* (New York: Touchstone/Simon and Shuster, 1995), 22.

22   Again per Maraniss, *First in His Class*, 22:

> Edith had a mercurial nature, a rollicking sense of humor coupled with a mean streak most often directed at her daughter or husband. She had taken out the whip to punish Virginia for childhood indiscretions, and even when the daughter became a mother of her own and had outgrown the switch, she could not escape Edith's criticisms and orders. Nor could Edith's husband. . . . Her temper grew fiercer over the years. She was a yeller and a thrower . . ."

23   Maraniss, *First in His Class*, 31.

24   *The Blue Angel* (1930).

25   *The Curse of the Cat People*. 1944. Screenplay by DeWitt Bodeen. Directed by Gunther von Fritsch and Robert Wise.

26   In the actual plotline of the film, most importantly, the "good spirit" is not the dead sister of the evil woman, but is, rather, the girl's "invisible friend." In fact, she turns out to be the girl's father's first wife who had died earlier, and who reappears as her guardian spirit. Her image is superimposed upon the face of the sinister woman in the film's climactic final scene, prompting her to go to the woman and embrace her, which disarms her, just as the rescue party arrives. So in this case, the child's trust overcomes her fear, an experience far different from my patient's.

PART TWO

# THE PREDATOR BENEATH THE LOVER

*On some high mountain's craggy summit place*
*The virgin, decked for deadly nuptial rites,*
*Nor hope a son-in-law of mortal birth*
*But a dire mischief, viperous and fierce, . . .*[1]

—Ancient oracle of Apollo foretelling the sacrifice
of Psyche to her unknown husband.

### Introductory Remarks

Psyche walks at the head of her bridal procession to the top of the craggy peak, as Apuleius writes, "with the air of a woman going to her grave, not her bridal bed . . ."[2] Abandoned and offered up by her own father to appease Venus's destructive envy, she is left exposed and alone, obliged to submit to whatever fate awaits her at the hands of the fierce serpent of the oracle—Eros.

In the opening passages of his tale, Apuleius reveals what is at the root of Venus' hatred for Psyche: she has become the admired object of a fickle humanity that has coldly abandoned Venus without the slightest provocation, driven by an infatuation for a mere mortal.[3] As Graves quotes Apuleius, "nobody took the trouble to visit Venus's shrines. . . . her festivals were neglected, her rites discontinued . . . her altars were unswept and cluttered with the foul remains of months-old burned sacrifices, her temples were allowed to fall into ruins."[4] In fact, by the second century AD, when Apuleius first put quill to parchment, Venus had indeed begun to be cast aside by the nascent but burgeoning cult of Christ the Son, born of a Virgin Mother, who was sent by his Heavenly Father to redeem the earth.

Psyche does not meet her death on the craggy summit, for she is far too intoxicating a morsel for Eros to pass up. She has been thrown right into his arms, and he succumbs to

*99*

his greedy fascination for this fairest human flower, appropriating her for himself while betraying his mother in the bargain. Psyche's first night alone in the darkened bedchamber where Eros comes and ravishes his virgin bride is nothing less than an act of rape. Yet over time Psyche, too, bathes in the intoxication of erotic pleasure that conceals the painful fact that she is living in the dark—a literal captive of love. It is Eros who holds all the power, for, after all, *he* is a god. The powerful fantasies of submission, of being taken or seduced—these are intertwined with our notions of being swept away by true love.

The lovers' idyllic paradise comes to a violent end, brought about by the poisonous slander Psyche's shadowy sisters press on her. The sisters are motivated by their own destructive envy of what they believe to be Psyche's good fortune. They plot to ruin their naïve sister's nuptial bliss by persuading Psyche to betray her anonymous husband through exposing his identity. In this grand turn of events the predator now becomes the prey! And when the lamplight reveals to the unwitting Psyche that Eros is not the monster she had believed him to be, thus saving him the ignoble fate of having his head hacked off, he is rudely awakened by a drop of hot oil from her lamp, which scalds him. As Apuleius writes, "Cupid sprang up in pain, and taking in the whole disgraceful scene, spread his wings and flew off without a word." He doesn't desert Psyche straightaway, but alights on top of a tree, *looking down upon her* reproachfully, disdainfully. He says, "[Y]our punishment will be that I'll fly away from you."[5] Eros retaliates against her through narcissistic withdrawal which he justifies by the wound she has inflicted upon him, despite the fact that the oil failed to penetrate beneath the surface of his skin—*to get into him*. While no one is able to pierce through Eros' narcissism at this juncture in the tale, this scalding is just the first step in the process of his wounding, deepening, and bearing of loss.

As is characteristic in narcissistic dynamics, once the fantasy girl is known and deflowered, or when the figure of ideal perfection becomes sexualized, the woman comes to seem ordinary. Eros can cavalierly dispose of her on the slightest whim when his narcissistic mood changes. He becomes indifferent, recalcitrant, cold, or deadening, all of which are forms of defense against threatening emotional depths.


Part Two, "The Predator Beneath the Lover," discusses these destructive facets of narcissism in their role as the darker, predatory aspects beneath romance, erotic love, kinship libido, and their related fantasy formations, here based on the Psyche and Eros text presented earlier. Each of the chapters in Part Two investigates examples of *destructive* narcissism, which can be recognized in the violent need to annihilate otherness—to destroy links that create meaning. The severing of links occurs when one requires that both mind and body be insulated against the intolerable threat of the breach in changelessness that is posed by the alterity of the other who can never be known or controlled. Consequently, feelings of timelessness, being outside of time, or being frozen in time are common in destructive, narcissistic states. For in these, one wards off the perception of descending into time, and exposing one's vulnerability to traumatic change, loss, and death.

Such acts of primitive destructiveness are found in Venus's hatred and envy of Psyche, in Eros' disavowal and betrayal of Venus in favor of Psyche, and in Eros' abrupt rejection, devaluation, and abandonment of Psyche once she has wounded him with the oil.

The destructive narcissism that is the focus of Part Two differs in important ways from the defensive narcissism explored in Part One. The instances of defensive narcissism we saw in Part One included masochism, fusion, and the internal, negative identification with the puer aeternus. Each of these qualities underscores the stabilizing or stagnating, coloniz-ing or victimizing aspects of bonding. Defensive narcissism, however, still implies relation, albeit of a non-mutual variety, whereas destructive narcissism and its compelling drive to sever all links to alterity—to all difference—stands in dynamic polarity to these dynamics. Therefore defensive narcissism appears in some cases to overlap and devolve into destruc-tive narcissism, as in, for example, the narcissist's irreparable devaluation of his once ideal object.

In Part Two we find examples of destructive narcissism in acts of sadism, annihilation of the other, psychic encapsulation, and the personality's identification with negative senex attitudes. In destructive narcissism, the aggressive destruction of links places the subject in a position of sadistic dominance.[6]

British Object Relations theory provides a model through which to understand the primitive origins of destructive narcissism. From this theoretical perspective, the baby imagines itself to be excluded from identification with the parental couple in the primal scene, and this sense of exclusion evokes its primary destructiveness in the form of envy. Abject hatred of the subject's own excluded, unbearable parts is then projected into the outer bad object. This apparent badness is then used to justify the sadomasochistic destruc-tion of all links to that object and those parts of oneself like it. In destructive narcissism, (primary destructiveness) the death instinct can be recognized in this destruction of the bad object as other, as well as by the retreat into defensive encapsulation in order to main-tain the state of unchanging sameness.

But in defensive narcissism (primary narcissism) the death instinct is located in the "death of self" as the result of merging with the good object that is seen as identical and the same. The fantasy of death as a certainty then becomes a hedge against the violent Other and alterity. In these two narcissistic currents, love is not transcendent but engulf-ing, regressive, or disavowed, leading either to a loss of distinctiveness and integrity of self, or to the destruction of all links. The couple collapses into fusion and sometimes dissolu-tion. The person in the position of being the hapless prey of an enthrallment may suffer treacherous betrayal or even die of grief.[7]

Narcissism, as we will see in these next chapters, forecloses one's ability to recognize both the uniqueness and the ineffable trace of the Other in the face of one's companion. A man gripped by narcissism operates according to unrecognized assumptions—that all objects are intended for the ego's use, and that there is nothing in this world that cannot be possessed.[8] Narcissistic defenses attempt to insulate the ego-complex from every impact by the Other that might otherwise disrupt and threaten the ego's sovereignty.

## A Summary of Part Two

Chapter Five, *Hatred for the "Taint of the Human"* explores the motives behind the destructive hatred and rejection of the once-idealized and now devalued other. The chapter also describes the deeper processes that may underlie sociopathic and genocidal impulses, both in the psyche of the individual and culturally. The story of "Narcissus and Echo" and Oscar Wilde's novel *The Picture of Dorian Gray* give poignant portrayals of the disowning of our human imperfections and vulnerabilities. These dreaded elements are deposited into the abjected or discarded, hated other, while the ego clings to compensatory aesthetic ideals of purity, perfection, and beauty. A clinical vignette in which a patient recalls an experience in his adolescence highlights this theme.

Chapter Six, *Demon Lover and the Abuse of Imagination*, explores a hidden propensity in certain men to use sadism and cruelty as a means of control over their colonized partner, as exemplified by the doppelganger story of *Dr. Jekyll and Mr. Hyde*. This inclination is frequently cloaked in a persona of "goodness" that is too charming or overly compliant, and that covers aggressive, murderous impulses stifled in early life. A clinical example describes how such a man leaves no visible marks upon his victim; only a slow erosion of spirit reveals his tyranny over his partner's soul. The compensatory, obsessional fantasy life that revolves around sexual exploitation and sadomasochism is also described. The workings of this fantasy are illuminated through a sub-plot within the Parzival tale that describes a dark wizard, who, though his mind is bent, is possessed of enormous magical powers. His crastration has led to oedipal humiliation and hatred that drives him to entrap and possess, but never touch the four hundred maidens he imprisons in his enchanted castle. Like a phantom, he sets things in motion but remains unseen throughout the story.

Chapter Seven, *A Deadly Narcissism: Saturn's Crippled Eros*, considers a range of persons and characters familiar throughout both Western history and literature—from figures of cold and calculating intellect to villains mad with power—who personify a pervasive psychic and cultural deadening of men's capacities for relatedness. The privileging of intellect in the former acts to split them off from their more human, bodily lives, while in the latter self-righteousness and abuse of authority mask a merciless disavowal of the human other. They go by names such as Torquemada, Dr. Frankenstein, and Captain Ahab. These figures offer a glimpse into the negative *senex*—the old man—that dominates certain personalities through a form of deadly narcissism. Such men hatefully split themselves from the heart of *Anima Mundi* and their child spirit within. Dissenting writers who have challenged the impact of the Enlightenment, with its arrogant claims that all of nature's mysteries can be known and appropriated, have critiqued the pathologies and the cultural attitudes these figures embody. Prominent among these are an omnipotent disregard for human limits and a hatred and terror of alterity, uncertainty, the ineffable, and the impure.

The final chapter in Part Two, *Clemency on the Way to the Gallows: Transcending Trauma and Dissociation*, presents the memories and dreams of a patient in the concluding year of a ten-year analysis, as he was beginning to transcend experiences of violent and traumatic victimization in childhood. These acts of destructive narcissism were perpetrated by a monstrous father who evacuated his own murderous fantasies and self-hatred into his innocent son. As my patient's long-repressed emotional life emerged and was given voice in his dreams and in the analytic process, a greater dimensionality became apparent in his life and relationships, along with a lessoning of his post-traumatic memories.

## Notes

1  Apuleius, *The Transformations of Lucius otherwise known as The Golden Ass*. Translated by Robert Graves  (NY: Noonday Press, 1951) 100.

2  Apuleius, *The Golden Ass*, 101.

3  The birth of Psyche and her conflict with Venus represented a "critical event in human history," a failed attempt to resurrect the feminine spirit in a new form, *in a more human, related form*, at a time when the patriarchy was on the rise. Erich Neumann, *Amor and Psyche* (Princeton, NJ: Princeton University Press, 1956), 59. The Roman Empire and the Christian sect are clear examples of its recent surge, while Hellenistic Greek culture and the nomadic desert Hebrews fostered its earlier manifestations. The Great Goddess's vital connection to the hearts and minds of humanity at large was indeed dying, save for the few exceptions cited in Part One. She was more remote, with her life-giving powers receding into the archaic past. In time she was buried in men's minds, her parts dismembered, her nature split in two.

4  Apuleius, *The Golden Ass*, 97.

5  Apuleius, *The Golden Ass*, 118–119.

6  In the analytic couple, for example, the therapist may feel annihilated by the hatred present in the room that the patient can neither contain nor metabolize. The therapist must survive these onslaughts, thus showing that he is a viable object that won't wither away, but is alive in a way that the patient can make good use of, as Winnicott stresses.

7  Robert Oelsner, "Introduction to the Work of Ron Britton," pre-lecture paper presented at the Inter-Institute Guest Lecture Series, Seattle, Washington, March 19, 2008.

8  Hasan Rafeeq, *Aporia: Divining the Divine: The Role of God in Levinasian Ethics*. At http://humanities. byu.edu/philosophy/aporia/volume/vol.112/hasanto.html, 2 (accessed 3/23/05).

## CHAPTER FIVE

# HATRED FOR THE "TAINT OF THE HUMAN"

Ovid's tale of *Narcissus and Echo* is a lucid depiction of destructive narcissism, and in this chapter I will discuss some of its many aspects, both through its links to the story of Psyche and Eros, and through the lens of contemporary psychoanalysis. As its elements emerge, Ovid's story reveals the destruction of all links to the other and the retreat into an unreflective, eternal sameness, a death coniunctio, that precludes and prevents feelings of conscience and shame.

In the tale of Psyche and Eros, the influence of Platonic thought is revealed in the way Apuleius privileges the ideals of aesthetic beauty over life and nature. Plato's view that only those things that are beautiful are good reveals a kind of splitting and hubris that is inadequate to life because it is one-sided. In a brief clinical vignette on this theme we will see how a patient as a young adolescent boy continued to seek out experiences that allowed him to repeat the theme of idealizing and devaluing his object of desire, a process driven by these same hidden, narcissistic currents.

The dream of remaining eternally young and beautiful through hatefully splitting off one's disavowed vulnerabilities is poignantly depicted in the gothic horror novel, *The Picture of Dorian Gray*, first published in 1890. Here Oscar Wilde masterfully portrays the phenomenon of the *double*, in which the split-off moral conscience rails at its other half, the growing inhumanity in the main character.

Beneath such dramas lies the terror of the intimate gaze of the Other. When this terror is violently disavowed, what follows is a turn of events in which the *tainted other* becomes a thing—an abject, hated object.

• • • • •

In the striking moment when Psyche brings the lighted lamp into the bedchamber and awareness to her love-blinded eyes, she also burns her lover. Eros has now been seen as himself, and in retaliation he punishes his young bride by coldly flying away from her as the girl clings to him in desperation. The indignant Eros, Apuleius remarks, feels "foully betrayed" and admonishes Psyche from a "lofty place" before departing for good (or so it seems).[1]

Here it may be useful to point out the elements of narcissistic wounding in this brief portion of the text, in which the lover casts her objective gaze upon the beloved and sees him as he really is. Finding the other's gaze too shameful and penetrating to bear, the narcissist reacts by destroying all links to the other as he assumes a "lofty," devaluing stance toward the offender. By gazing upon Eros, Psyche has become the hated object that has entrapped him through her need for him.

In the context of the analytic relationship, one might identify Eros' reaction as one piece in a pattern of narcissistic defenses whereby the patient's own unbearably needy aspects are projected into the other and thus disavowed. This other's objective eye recognizes what the patient's subjectivity cannot and brings him face to face with his unmet dependency needs.[2] When the patient cannot accept this truth, and his shame and humiliation are simply too much to bear, these painful feelings must be hatefully split off and deposited into the dependent and devalued other. In the analytical situation, all of a sudden the therapist can't do anything right. He is seen in an inferior light, which serves the patient as a justification for his distrust and his emotional withdrawal through which he hopes to restore his omnipotence.

The story of *Narcissus and Echo* provides what may be the original source for the phenomenon of hating the taint of the other who carries what one disowns in oneself, in order to maintain the self's illusions of purity and perfection. We learn that at his birth it was predicted that Narcissus would live a long life, provided he *not know himself*. As he grew up, Ovid informs us, his "pride so cold" prevented the "many youths . . . and maidens" who "sought his love" from ever touching his heart.[3] Encountering Echo, he fled from her embrace saying, "Hands off! Embrace me not! May I die before I give you power o'er me!" Echo, who could only echo back his words, responded helplessly, "I give you power o'er me!"[4] Echo simply wandered away to live a lonely existence; but in time Narcissus too, was cursed by unrequited love. Out hunting one day he came upon a pristine and untouched spring and bent down to drink. There in the water his eyes met the gaze of his own reflection. He felt hopelessly drawn to the image, never realizing that the other he admired and burned with desire for was his very self. *He did not know himself!* Unable to tear himself away from the gaze looking up at him, or to touch the exquisite face mirrored in the water, Narcissus "wasted with love," Ovid writes, and slowly withered, disintegrated, and turned to ash, as if consumed by a "hidden fire."[5] All that was left of him was a narcissus flower with its white petals.

Narcissus repudiates Echo as the tainted other, and following this act he can only find refuge and a final resting place beside the clear spring that has never been touched by human hands. The spring clearly conveys the illusion of purity held by one who has never been initiated, who has never experienced limitations to his omnipotence. Nothing or no one foreign has adulterated the pristine purity of its beautiful, mirrored surface. Gunter Seidler expands upon this theme.

> [O]ne has to have encountered resistance, some other imposing a limit, before one can emerge from the process of untrammeled self effusion, unrestricted timelessness. Ethnologists would no doubt be able to point to initiation rites that confront a young person with repeated experiences of "limits" prior to formal admission to the group of adults. Obviously Narcissus has no such experiences to fall back on. Self-consciousness or self-recognition, which I contend are indissolubly bound up with experiences of alterity, are beyond his ken: "no youth, no maiden touched his heart."[6]

Narcissus is lost in his identification with the pure, untouched beauty of this tranquil refuge. But it is not a place of benevolence. We must never forget that the greatest atrocities in the history of humankind have been done in the name of purity and the hatred of difference. Nazi Germany's "final solution" for the Jews, and the Khmer Rouge's "killing fields" in Cambodia, are two noted examples.[7] To recall the words of Levinas, the failure to heed the call of the ineffable Other—whose trace is found in the face of the other in all her vulnerability, alterity, and imperfection—marks the origin of human violence.

Seidler envisions Narcissus' encounter with his reflection in the pond as exemplifying the ego's failure, in narcissism, to relate to the internal foreign other, a connection that could have forged internal object relations within Narcissus, and the "eventuation of a self." As he writes, "This reflection of the other in him would have enabled him—the sum of ego and other as self—to *relate* to another person. He would have developed the ability to differentiate . . ."[8] In other words, Narcissus might have found a way to relate to internal states existing beneath the surface. Instead, he comes to know himself only in a one-dimensional way, in that he sees only his ego and its literal external reflection in the pool. Because the ego's stance prevents the integration of the internal other and, therefore, the eventuation of the self, the external other is denied any capacity for personal autonomy, will, or intention, as well. Nor is there any hope for another to have any effect upon Narcissus. No one is there—or no one other than he himself. He annexes the other's personhood, but in the bargain he forestalls his own chance to acquire consciousness and self knowledge. After all, an "echo" is not an embodied response, only a hollow and imitative one.

Because he does not come to know himself in a differentiated, reflective way, essentially stopping at the surface, Narcissus slowly dissolves into the eternal cycles of flowering nature, a fate much like that of Endymion in Keats's poem of that name. To preserve the image, Narcissus must stand apart from the life-spring's gushing flow, and the flow of time. As

Seidler says, "The exclusion of alterity is bound up with the standstill of time. [Narcissus] does not age, he does not die a human death, he remains oddly timeless."[9]

The longing for eternal beauty, purity, and perfection exists in our fantasies and *eschatology*—the worldwide religious ideas surrounding the soul after death. The eternal maiden, Snow White, lies in a deathlike sleep, preserved within a glass coffin, awaiting the kiss that will awaken her. At the heart of this scene is the profound archetype of the hope for eternal life. Similarly, in the "Tale of Amor and Psyche," Psyche's fourth task takes her down to the Underworld to procure Persephone's box of *beauty ointment* for Venus. Instead the desperate young woman seeks to steal the ointment and keep it for herself, so that Eros will find her irresistible. She falls into a deathlike sleep until Eros comes to rescue her. He then brings her, once and for all, up to the home of the gods and away from this earthly world of mortals.

This theme has a number of parallels with the indulgent aspects of our modern culture. Grandiose narcissistic fantasies of staying eternally young and living forever are maintained through control over our bodies, as with adherence to rigid health and fitness regimes, the use of plastic surgery, and in exploiting the benefits of medical breakthroughs. This very control can reflect a kind of narcissism whose aim is to maintain an unchanging sameness in life, as with Narcissus at the pool. Beneath the surface lie the dread of change, uncertainty, pain, and decay. This is what it may mean for the mortal Psyche to fall into the unchanging sameness of deathlike sleep after she dared to open the box containing the eternal beauty of the gods.

In the following commentary, Marie-Louise von Franz exposes Apuleius' aesthetic and Platonist biases. She suggests that he probably inserted the quest for eternal beauty into the older, pre-Roman version of the Psyche story.[10] She describes the origin of these biases in this way: "A man's anima whispers to him: what is beautiful is also good, in the Platonic sense of the word (*kalon k'agathon*, 'the good and the beautiful go together')."[11] The dualism of idealization and devaluation becomes apparent, she believes, when beauty, purity, and perfection are held up as the highest values, because,

> [This] leads to a kind of aestheticism which is an inadequacy toward life, because life in every respect is a pair of opposites. It is beautiful but also ugly. . . . Chasing only beauty and aestheticism, even in their highest form, is a kind of hubris, an inflation, an unreal attitude. . . . Eternal beauty does not exist in nature; it is always varied by gruesomeness and horror.[12]

Marie-Louise von Franz is advocating for pluralism in the encounter with otherness—for making a space for what is left out when we make an assertion about what the truth is.

When Echo is devalued and spurned by Narcissus, she embodies the deep shame that he disavows in himself. Narcissus carries no awareness of himself or others. According to Seidler, "Con-science is bound up with the capacity to relate . . . the capacity for compassion . . . and with a fundamental capacity for shame."[13] Narcissus can see things only from his subjective perspective. He lacks objectivity and self-reflection, qualities that shame regulates. One feels shame when one is seen only as an object. When one is made aware of being extremely self-absorbed, the normal human response is shame. Narcissus is devoid of this response. With life maintained at the surface, Narcissus has no capacity for vis-à-vis relations outside, or for internal reflection inside, so that any chance that he might suffer feelings of conscience or shame is obliterated.

Echo is unable to express anything of her own; what she says must be identical to the expressed needs of the other. She adheres but does not relate. As Seidler puts it, "She loses herself to the other."[14] For every sadistic Narcissus there is, somewhere, a masochistically bound Echo, a pairing that hints at the bipolar complexes that indissolubly link two such partners. He, who will fight to the death to avoid submitting to someone having power over him, is complemented by one who can only imitate—not initiate—by echoing, "I give you power o'er me."[15]

In his paper on masochism, Emmanuel Ghent makes a useful distinction between submission and surrender. Ghent quotes Michael Eigen as saying that "One may surrender 'in the presence of another,' not 'to another' as in the case of submission."[16] When free of domination and control in submission, the "ultimate direction" of surrender, Ghent claims, "is the discovery of one's identity, one's sense of self, one's sense of wholeness, even one's sense of unity with other living beings." In submission, in contrast, "one feels one's self as a puppet in the power of another, [and] one's sense of identity atrophies."[17] Surrender implies the capacity for face to face relationship, wherein subject and object see one another while each allows him or herself to be seen by the other in a multidimensional way. Submission on the other hand, is a form of fusion in the death coniunctio, where the dominant subject annexes the individuality of the submissive object, and dimensionality collapses.

## Clinical Vignette

A patient's recollection of first love in early adolescence may illustrate more clearly the cycle of purity and devaluation discussed above, in which the object of desire is first possessed and then discarded, and the cold loss of feeling is then followed by the desperate longing for the now lost object. My patient described a disturbing period that began in his first weeks of junior high school. He was invited to a party where he met a girl who had come with another boy. A desperately romantic lad, he felt struck by lightning when he laid eyes upon her. She was his ideal picture of purity and beauty, and the two were instantly lost in love's enthrallment. Over the next few weeks he shyly courted her. They went to a movie and in the darkened theater she gave him encouraging hints that he could kiss her. He finally drummed up the courage as the credits were rolling and timidly gave her a peck. The next day at school he impulsively broke up with her. She was deeply hurt. Over the course of the next year he made a complete about-face and mooned for their lost love. She made the fatal mistake of falling for him again and the two kissed passionately one afternoon. The next week, at the junior high Halloween party, he coldly dumped her again. He was dressed as Dracula. She wore no costume. Once she was gone, he spent the ensuing year miserably pining away for her. She was so affected by his ruthless withdrawal that in the next year she gained a somewhat slutty reputation by leading several boys on with sexual favors. She toyed with their affections and then without warning proceeded to break things off, just as he had done with her.

My patient described in retrospect, as best he could, what he felt during this period. "I felt nothing for her once I had her. It was only when she was unavailable that I longed for her." We explored the feelings that were so deeply split in him at the age of 13. His unacceptable sexual feelings could never be reconciled with his ideals of pure love, so he simply split off all feelings for her whenever she wanted him. In this way he would not sully or dirty the image of the fair flower he believed her to be in his mind.

From another perspective, we might think about his coldness and loss of feeling as a consequence of a fear of closeness and intimacy. When she is brought into actual human relationship he is compelled to destroy the links between them. This is a kind of repetition compulsion undertaken to maintain stability and safety against her aliveness and unpredictability, which threaten to penetrate him. Only in the romantic fantasy of longing and losing her can he maintain the perpetual sameness. When the ideal object incarnates as the real girl in the physical world she is imperfect, and when he has possessed her, he loses any feeling of connection and must cut her off. The life-giving energies are felt only in the hunt; once the prey is caught, there is only psychic and emotional deadness in its wake. Only in the state of lack, when he has driven her away, can he restore the ideal image and long for what he has lost.

The romantic undertones of tragic love are evident in this story, as well as the privileging of the fantasy of love's ideal over the flawed, human experience. Even the Dracula costume my patient wore at Halloween suggests that in his dread of the tainted human he sucked away the girl's life's blood and turned her into a vampire as well. This is a painful illustration of the way fear and hatred of our own vulnerabilities can be ruthlessly split off and deposited into the most tender of victims.

## Oscar Wilde and *The Picture of Dorian Gray*

As Western civilization approached the end of the nineteenth century, the march of progress was accompanied by attitudes of pessimism and a belief in the slow but certain decline and degeneration of society. Nietzsche's view that human civilization, with its civility and moral veneer, was at war with its primitive nature added to a widespread sense of nihilism regarding the future of humanity.

However, the Neo-Romantic movement of the same time—though only a shadowy imitation of the original philosophy espoused a hundred years before—viewed the growth and advancement of European society as presenting a decadent spectacle to be reveled in.[18] The Neo-Romantics regarded culture as being in a state of decay, based upon the model of the Roman empire in its long decline. Through the eyes of its artists and poets, nature was stylized. Decadence had taken on, as historian Henri Ellenberger writes, a "rich and alluring corruptness."[19] With the individual worshipped and isolated from community, it was not surprising that narcissism became a characteristic feature.

Ellenberger continues, "Never, in the history of literature, did poets celebrate Narcissus and narcissistic heroes to such an extent. It has been shown that the Narcissus figure was a general symbol and incarnation of the spirit of that time."[20]

As the mood of degeneration and pessimism advanced with its perversions and decadence, Victorian propriety, correctness, and modesty fell into decline, usurped by the cult of eroticism.[21] Such notable artists as Toulouse-Lautrec and Gustav Klimt depicted their subjects—often prostitutes—tenderly and fondly. Just as the seductive symbol of the vampire has come to obsess our nightmares and grip our senses, so the late-nineteenth-century image of the femme fatale, the female vampire or "fatal woman," promised certain destruction to any man lured by her siren song.

Out of the zeitgeist of this time emerged Oscar Wilde, whose literary testament, so poignantly embodying this age, proved to be instrumental in his own destruction as an artist. Scarcely five years after the first printing of *The Picture of Dorian Gray*, Wilde's controversial novel was used as evidence that ultimately led to his imprisonment for sodomy. The witch hunt was fueled by a brutally prejudiced, homophobic, hostile English press. After serving two years' hard labor, the young dandy, in poor health, wandered throughout Europe for two years and died at 46 years of age, penniless.

Couched within the gothic horror genre, *The Picture of Dorian Gray* is a psychological novel about an eternal youth whose beauty was like that of a Narcissus or Adonis. In Wilde's narrative, Dorian's portrait had been painted by a gifted artist, an older man who had lost himself in idolatrous worship of his subject. The painter languished in homoerotic infatuation for the pure, idyllic image that he could possess only on his canvas.[22]

On the fateful day when Dorian first glimpsed his beautiful reflection in the painting, like Narcissus gazing into the pool, he offered up his very soul to the invisible powers if they would only freeze time in that moment, so that he might never grow older.[23] Little did he know what mysterious forces were set in motion at the sound of his words. In that fateful second he had become like those frozen princesses of myth and fairy tale, idealized and captured in the unchanging timelessness of eternal beauty's deathlike sleep. Here too one can identify the aesthetic dualism that privileges the Platonic ideal of the good and the beautiful, as seen in Dorian's attempts to freeze life as a way of controlling the terror of his own decay, ultimate death, and unknowable alterity—events that might open him to the experience of the Other. It is this control, characteristic of destructive narcissism, that one often observes in defenses against deprivation and lack in early life.

As a young man, Dorian Gray longed for what was denied him at a tender age. We learn that his father was a penniless nobody who ran away with his young mother. He was killed in a duel shortly after their marriage, the apparent victim of the wrath of Dorian's grandfather, a noble lord who could not bear to see his daughter marry beneath her. His beautiful young mother died when he was still a baby. This would have caused profound maternal deprivation. How could his dreams not be filled with images of his mother as some mythical, beautiful ideal? She was tragically lost to him, Wilde writes, "A beautiful woman risking everything for a mad passion. . . . The mother snatched away by death, the boy left to a solitude and the tyranny of an old and loveless man" (his grandfather).[24]

Spurred on by an aristocratic mentor, Sir Henry, who rivaled Goethe's Mephistopheles himself, Dorian Gray searched for the experience of pure feeling and sensual pleasures, invalidating any tender yearnings of the human heart for love.[25] His lack of a strong and supportive male presence would make him highly susceptible to his mentor's seductive philosophical rantings.[26]

Attending a Shakespearean play in a theater one day he became enthralled with a beautiful young actress, Sibyl.[27] With each immortal role she played he became more intensely smitten. He professed his undying love for her and spoke of marriage. He loved only the heroines she portrayed, of course, and the moment she spoke of leaving the stage so that she could assume the traditional role of wife and mother, Dorian's heart turned cold. She had failed to live up to his idealized projections, and he cruelly broke off the affair.

Upon returning to his flat he made a strange discovery. Gazing at his prized portrait Wilde describes how Dorian's face on the canvas had changed, as if "there was a touch of cruelty in the mouth" that seemed to intensify as he gazed upon it.[28] Unbeknownst to him, his devaluation and rejection of Sibyl led to the tender-hearted girl's tragic suicide. Sir Henry broke the news to him and quickly made sure to protect the boy from scandal while persuading Dorian to dismiss any guilt.[29] After his initial horror at the news, Dorian exhibited some pangs of conscience, but these soon gave way to a kind of detachment and even an attempt to romanticize her death. "Why is it I cannot feel this tragedy as much as I want to? I don't think I'm heartless. . . . I must admit that this thing that has happened does not affect me as it should. It seems to me to be simply like a wonderful ending to a wonderful play. It has all the terrible beauty of a Greek tragedy, a tragedy in which I took a great part, *but which I have not been wounded.*"[30]

In the film, *Eternal Sunshine of a Spotless Mind* (2004), we find a similar theme in which the pain of failed love affairs could be wiped "spotlessly" from the mind through neural technology (see Chapter Eleven). Beneath both the Oscar Wilde novel and the film lies the fantasy of ridding oneself of all the impurities associated with the bearing of shame, guilt, hatred, pain, and suffering. Only the perpetuation of goodness and light remain while all the unbearable aspects of emotional life are split off into other compartments of the mind, insulated by amnesia barriers to keep the bad sealed away.

As I view his story, Dorian Gray longs to restore the spirit of his dead mother in the hoped-for affair with Sibyl. This is a fantasy of fusion with the idyllic other that might obviate the unimaginable grief surrounding the infant's profound traumatic loss. When Sibyl fails to live up to his image of a goddess of love and beauty, he feels betrayed and hatefully rejects and disavows the young actress for her human flaws and ordinariness.

Psychoanalyst Neville Symington suggests that

> in the narcissistic illusion there is no other; there is only me. . . . there is a desperate clinging onto this delusion, only it is generally hidden because the person projects himself into some figure who is believed to be everything. . . . One of the ways in which I sustain the delusion that there is no other is to control this other.[31]

The narcissist establishes this control by projecting the idealized self into the other, thereby annexing the individuality of the other so that he may maintain control of his environment.[32] There can be no other out there to *relate* to for Dorian Gray, for Sibyl is only there as an appendage to be used to serve his own needs. Once her allure is dispersed the fantasy of ideal love turns to hate and disdain, for the environment becomes unstable.

Within the narcissistic state one is constantly attempting to live at the surface of things, to avoid being confronted by the uncertainty and fear of one's inner depths or the emotional depths of another.[33] This can be seen as a desperate effort to stabilize oneself against the threat of attack from unknown sources, and to control internal and external objects and events in the environment that might fragment the self. The fear of psychic fragmentation remains the narcissist's greatest psychological terror.[34]

When the illusion that one can maintain absolute control over life collapses, the internal narcissistic defenses attempt to protect the traumatized ego from the threat of annihilation. It does so by dissociating the ego's ideal from the hated parts and depositing them into separate compartments of the mind. Destructive and aggressive activity is directed against the hated parts, which are felt to be too unbearable to be seen or known.[35] Through the projection process in relationships, like that of Dorian upon Sibyl, his hatred for the abject child within himself is split off, as a form of what Bion has described as an attack on linking, and is deposited within the tainted other, Sibyl, who will now carry it. Hence Dorian's detachment from any real feelings of horror, grief, guilt, or care for the girl's senseless death. A cold cruelty takes their place, reminiscent of the demeanor of the tyrannical old grandfather who raised him. While Dorian Gray is Wilde's fictional creation, in him the author provides us with a keen portrayal of the movement from defensive narcissism to destructive narcissism.

In time Dorian came to experience every sensual pleasure without regard to limits or care for others, and in a strange synchrony the painting began to alter greatly, bearing, as Wilde explains, "the burden of his passions and his sins, . . . seared with the lines of suffering and thought."[36] And while his own face remained forever perfect and youthful, the portrait was to become a "monstrous and loathsome thing" he hid away in a locked and darkened room in his childhood home. This was the price paid, according to Wilde, for "[e]ternal youth, infinite passion, pleasures subtle and secret, wild joys and wilder sins," all things that he would come to achieve without fear of consequence.[37] He could somehow dissociate himself from any last semblance of conscience or shame and remain perfectly unblemished—unwounded—for although he could not, the painting bore all the traces of his excesses and crimes, even murder.[38] His greatest fear was that his dark secret would be exposed; he would do anything—even kill—to prevent its disclosure.[39]

One evening the portrait artist, Basil, came to Dorian's house to demand the truth from the man he once so idolized as to the public accusations of his scandalous debauchery. Dorian was filled with contempt and resolved in that instant to reveal the truth of the painting's dreaded secret to its creator. Basil was horrified at the sight. In Wilde's chilling prose he describes how the portrait had come to reflect the black state of his soul: "Through some strange quickening of inner life the leprosies of sin were slowly eating the thing away. The rotting of a corpse in a watery grave was not so fearful."[40]

Panic seized Dorian as he observed the full weight of his revelations dawning upon the artist. This was the objective and sometimes terrible eye of truth, the alterity that deflates narcissism's self-absorption for the sake of self-recognition. That is, seeing parts of oneself through another's eyes. The sudden exposure proved far too devastating for Dorian to bear.[41] The fear of exposure turned quickly to a flash of hatred and loathing, for it was the creator of this monstrous mirror, he reasoned, who was to blame for this evil. With this thought stirring in him, "like a hunted animal" he reached for a knife and plunged it many times into the artist's neck, until he lay lifeless on the carpet. Dorian was able to conceal the crime perfectly, just as he could bloodlessly separate himself from any human revulsion or shame for his heinous crime.

Desperate to maintain his pathological secret, Dorian Gray became a tormented man who longed to wash away the blood on his hands and regain his "rose-white boyhood."[42] For a fleeting moment he imagined confession, punishment, and atonement as the only means of cleansing his sins.[43] Yet the painting was a record of it all, and in the end its burden was something he could no longer bear. In that moment he knew that it must be destroyed. In his final act, seizing the same knife he had used to kill the painter, he set about to mutilate the grotesque reflection—the only evidence of his black heart. In killing the soul-life that had inhabited the painting he sought freedom from the past so that he might finally be at peace. The servants heard a crash and a terrible cry upstairs, and when they came to investigate they found a beautiful portrait of their youthful master hanging from the wall, and below it, with a knife in his heart, a loathsome and withered dead man. His true identity was confirmed only upon examination of the rings upon his fingers.

Oscar Wilde's use of the portrait as the uncanny psychological double serves as a metaphor for the way in which shameful and hated parts that are too unbearable to be seen or felt become split off and deposited in one's tortured core of being. These splits act like compartments of the mind that hold emotions the narcissistic ego-complex cannot face up to, for to do so would mean its fragmentation or annihilation. They contain the hated and loved parts, separated by an amnesia barrier that allows the narcissist to maintain his feigned innocence and his rationalizations, while his conscious personality, blank and devoid of conscience, is subjected to unremitting deadliness.

In three of the major, traumatic, affect-laden events in Dorian Gray's life, he fails to tolerate the emotional ambivalence that is so crucial for the achievement of whole object relations, that is, relationships with people seen as multi-dimensional, whole persons. Instead, he splits off feelings that could have led to the capacity for care and concern. From the experience of his horror and his brief pangs of remorse for Sibyl's death he skips quickly over any guilty feelings he might have and into romantic intellectualization and detached justification. In both his homicidal and suicidal attacks, first upon the artist, and then upon the hideous mirror of his own soul, he is gripped with the fear of exposure. This fear quickly changes to hatred and a desperate need to annihilate the threatening other. Without the normal capacity to tolerate his guilt and the ambivalence that accompanies it, he cannot show concern and responsibility toward another.

Winnicott points to conditions in infancy that lead a "loss of the capacity for concern." He envisions two images of the mother in the baby's mind: The environment-mother, who "receives all . . . affection and sensuous co-existence," and the object-mother, who is the target of the baby's excited, affect-laden phantasies, instinctive needs, and hateful impulses. When the object-mother fails to survive the baby's aggressive, hungry attacks, or the environment-mother fails to provide the guilty infant an opportunity for reparation for its destructiveness, care and concern cannot be achieved. They are replaced by "crude anxieties and by crude defenses, such as splitting, or disintegration,"[44] as found in cases of maternal deprivation and loss. I see all of these signs in the life and death of Dorian Gray.

● ● ● ● ●

In summary, we can observe how each of these dramatic, hate-filled enactments of dis-avowal of the taint in the human portray aspects of destructive narcissism. This is the violent impulse to destroy all links to threatening internal states of mind, as well as to the human other whose proximity imperils one's stability and control. The bad that is inside of us cannot be tolerated and must be evacuated and deposited into the victimized object who must bear it for us. The lifelong damage done to those who have found no other way to resolve their deprivation is often irreparable, save for the few bright souls who find a way to transcend their circumstances. Without the capacity for feelings of guilt and shame, which require reflection, relatedness, and the processing of our grief, we cannot repair our wrongdoings, nor can we offer, experience, or receive care and concern for, or from, the other.

## Notes

1 Erich Neumann, *Amor and Psyche* (Princeton, NJ: Princeton University Press, 1956), 27–28.
2  The "objective eye" may come from the partner who confronts the narcissistic behavior, or in the analyst's transference interpretations.
3  For Ovid, "The Legend of Narcissus and Echo," see Ovidius Metamorphoses, translated into the German by Hermann von Breitenbach (Zurich: Artemis-Verl., 1958), Book III, 11.354–355; see also Gunter H. Seidler, *In Others' Eyes: An Analysis of Shame*, translation by Andrew Jenkins (Madison, CT: International Universities Press, 2000), 78.
4  Ovid, "The Legend of Narcissus and Echo," in *Metamorphoses*, Book III, 11.392–94; see also Seidler, *In Others' Eyes*, 78.
5  Ovid, "The Legend of Narcissus and Echo," in *Metamorphoses*, Book III, 11.509–10; see also Seidler, *In Others' Eyes*, 79.
6  Seidler, *In Others' Eyes*, 80. For last quote see Ovid, *Metamorphoses*, Book III 1. 355; see also Seidler, *In Others' Eyes*, 78.
7  We can see the powerful parallels between the sociological and psychological currents. In Seidler's view, in order for the other to be perceived by the subject in a vis-à-vis manner, the subject must "display a number of features that accord with the subject's own, and a number which are . . . nonidentifiable, alien, inaccessible" (Seidler, *In Others' Eyes*, 89). To Narcissus, as well as to the perpetrator regime, these ambiguities and differences are intolerable and must be rooted out of the garden in order to maintain certain control over their victim groups through splitting.
8  Seidler, *In Others' Eyes*, 82 (my italics).
9  Seidler, *In Others' Eyes*, 82.
10  Marie-Louise von Franz, *The Golden Ass of Apuleius* (Boston: Shambhala, 1970), 134.
11  von Franz, *The Golden Ass*, 130.
12  von Franz, *The Golden Ass*, 132.
13  Seidler, *In Others' Eyes*, 86.
14  Seidler, *In Others' Eyes*, 83.
15  Ovid, "The Legend of Narcissus and Echo," in *Metamorphoses*, Book III, 11.392–94; see also Seidler, *In Others' Eyes*, p. 78.

16  For the Michael Eigen quote, see Emmanuel Ghent, "Masochism, Submission, Surrender," *Contemporary Psychoanalysis* 26(1) (1990): 215–16.

17  See Eigen in Ghent, "Masochism, Submission, Surrender," 220–21.

18  Far from the idealism of the earlier Romantic period, which reflected a deeply intimate bond with nature, Neo-Romanticism reflected the industrialization of society and its artificiality.

19  Henri F. Ellenberger, *The Discovery of the Unconscious* (New York: Basic Books, 1970), 280.

20  Ellenberger, *Discovery of the Unconscious*, 279.

21  The words we use today to describe sexual perversions—sadism, masochism, fetishism—came into the mainstream through the literature and art of the late nineteenth century.

22  "Taking the term *narcissism* from an English writer on the psychology of sex, Havelock Ellis, Freud had introduced it in 1910, explaining that homosexuals, choosing themselves as their love object, look for a young man they can love as their mother loved them." Ronald Hayman, *A Life of Jung* (London: Bloomsbury Publishing, 1999), 163. Freud had originally conceived of narcissism as a condition where the ego is thought to be like a reservoir that sends libido out to objects but absorbs it when it flows back. "The narcissist withdraws emotional energy from external reality, turning it back on himself to become his only love object." Hayman, *Life of Jung*, 164. To what extent a tale such as Wilde's may have informed Freud's ideas on narcissism is not known.

23  "If it were only the other way! If it were I who was to be always young, and the picture that was to grow old! For that… I would give everything… I would give my soul for that." Oscar Wilde, *The Picture of Dorian Gray* (New York: Dover Publications, 1993), 19.

24  Wilde, *Dorian Gray*, 26.

25  Goethe's *Faust*, with its themes of bargaining for eternal life in exchange for one's soul, and the consequent wanton disregard for human limitations or moral boundaries, clearly informed Wilde's rendering of his main character and his mentor.

26  Wilde, *Dorian Gray*, 16–17. Sir Henry sees Dorian as a pure, blank slate upon which he can inscribe his Neo-Romantic ideals: "Someday, when you are old and wrinkled and ugly, when thought has seared your forehead with its lines, and passion branded your lips with its hideous fires, you will feel it, you will feel terrible. Now wherever you go, you charm the world…. You have a wonderfully beautiful face, Mr. Gray… And beauty is a form of Genius – is higher, indeed, than Genius…. It has its divine right of sovereignty. It makes princes of those who have it…. To me, Beauty is the wonder of wonders. It is only shallow people who do not judge by appearances…. Yes, Mr. Gray, the gods have been good to you. But what the gods give they quickly take away. You have only a few years in which to live really, perfectly, and fully. When your youth goes, your beauty will go with it… Time is jealous of you… Don't squander the gold of your days, listening to the tedious, trying to improve the hopeless failure, or giving away your life to the ignorant, the common, and the vulgar. These are the sickly aims, the false ideals, of our age. Live!… Be always searching for new sensations…. A new Hedonism – that is what our century wants. You might be its visible symbol…. But we never get back our youth… Our limbs fail, our senses rot. We degenerate into hideous puppets, haunted by the memory of the passions of which we were too much afraid, and the exquisite temptations that we had not the courage to yield to. Youth! Youth! There is absolutely nothing in the world but youth."

27  *Sibyl* is also the name for the mythical earth goddess who is both mother and lover to her son, *Attis*.

28  Wilde, *Dorian Gray*, 66.

29  "If you had married this girl you would have been wretched…. One can always be kind to people about whom one cares nothing. But she would have soon found out that you were absolutely indifferent to her…. I say nothing about the social mistake, which would have been abject, which,

of course, I would not have allowed, but I assure you that in any case the whole thing would have been an absolute failure." Wilde, *Dorian Gray*, 73.

30   Wilde, *Dorian Gray*, 73 (my italics).

31   Symington, *Narcissism: A New Theory* (London: Karnac Books, 1993), 86.

32   Jeffrey Sattinover, "Puer Aeturrnus: The Narcissistic Relation to the Self." *Quadrant* 13(2) (1980): 75–108.

33   Symington, *Narcissism: A New Theory*, 54.

34   Ladson Hinton, "Narcissism, the Unknown, and the Passion for Being." Paper presented to the Jungian Psychotherapy Association, Seattle, Washington, September 22, 2001, on Hans Kohut's theories.

35   Donald Kalsched, "Daimonic Elements in Early Trauma." *Journal of Analytical Psychology* 48(2) (2003): 148.

36   Wilde, *Dorian Gray*, 66.

37   Wilde, *Dorian Gray*, 77.

38   The projected "dual personality" had captured the imagination of the times, finding its way into the literature and art of the last half of the nineteenth century. In the phenomena of the "doppelganger," the *double* could be signified as a mirror or twin (Narcissus), a portrait (Dorian Gray), the "alter-ego" or *shadow* (Jekyll and Hyde), and so on. Concurrently, the rise in popularity of psychological research into dissociation and "spiritist" phenomena, multiple personalities, and somnambulism opened the door to an understanding of the many levels and states of mind existing autonomously, or "split off" from, waking consciousness.

39   The "pathological secret" can be observed in Hawthorne's *The Scarlet Letter*, where the spurned husband of Hester Prynne secretly knows the identity of her "co-adulterer" and sadistically drives the young parson into unbearable fits of despair and guilt, and, ultimately, to suicide.

40   Wilde, *Dorian Gray*, 115.

41   Seidler, *In Others' Eyes*, 80.

42   Wilde, *Dorian Gray*, 162.

43   Ellenberger, *Discovery of the Unconscious*, 44–45. Protestant reformers did away with the Catholic requirements of confession and instituted instead the practice of the "Cure of Souls," arising in the seventeenth and eighteenth centuries. This practice involved the minister's obtaining of a confession of some terrible secret, which would facilitate their cure. This practice of uncovering the pathological secret became known to the general public and was incorporated into many psychological novels such as *The Scarlet Letter* and *The Picture of Dorian Gray*.

44   D.W. Winnicott, "The Development of the Capacity for Concern," (1963), In *The Maturational Processes and the Facilitating Environment* (Madison, CT: International Universities Press, 1965), 78.

## CHAPTER SIX

# DEMON LOVER AND
# THE ABUSE OF IMAGINATION

The term *demon lover* conjures up fantastic, underworldly images, and is, therefore, a product of *psyche*.[1] Robert Louis Stevenson's story of "Dr. Jekyll and Mr. Hyde" investigates such a doubled situation, which has come about following the splitting-off of hatred and violence that is denied consciously. In defensive narcissism aggressive attacks work to destroy the other's separateness and individuality; at the same time they compensate for one's threatened sense of safety and control. This sadistic *predator beneath the lover* leaves no visible marks upon his victim, only a slow and relentless erosion of spirit as the predator exerts a tyranny over the soul. Such an imaginal shadow double often runs counter to a man's timid, placating, or charming persona, which may appear to emanate goodness in the world. In actuality he maintains a feigned innocence as paralysis gradually incapacitates and imprisons his partner.

A Jekyll and Hyde type character can learn to become exactly what the lover fantasizes, and then, once she (or he) is entrapped, or "in love," the shadow side emerges. For example, one patient I worked with had learned to become a placating, pleasing little boy over the course of a long marriage. Yet without warning he would strike like a silent viper, revealing hidden sadistic propensities. As our analytic work progressed, he revealed aggressive, murderous impulses in his early life, which we recognized as attempts by the child's ego to split off hated vulnerabilities and to deposit them into another.

Such men can be identified by narcissistic defenses that mark preoedipal mother–child bonding that has gone wrong. The steps of this process are beautifully depicted in contemporary analyses of the *Dracula* mythos, from which the projected fantasies of "vampyric mothers" and "monstrous babies" are derived.[2]

In severely split personalities, predatory and perverse sexual pathology can take on a life of its own in powerful fantasy life. In one form, thin-skinned ego states are encapsulated through fantasies of erotic submission that allow the disavowal of relationships; the result is an autistic, insular life at the surface. Such fantasies stem from the traumatic wounds inflicted by a parent, or shared by both the mother and the son in the early infant–mother relationship. This dynamic is exemplified in a portion of the Grail Legend describing the castrated sorcerer Clinschor, who has captured countless women languishing within the seemingly impenetrable walls of his Castle of Wonders. No one has ever gazed upon him but it is known that he never touches the women he possesses. The acts of this sorcerer reveal abuses of imagination—compensatory, often split-off, addictive fantasies revolving around sexual violation. In the consulting room patients describe how they obliterate un-bearable feelings of humiliation and shame, through defensive reenactments that take the form of fantasies of power over weaker and more vulnerable objects. Cleverly hidden and compelling, such violent defenses are often never confronted by an ego complex that is frequently rigid and brittle. All-consuming mental constructions of this kind thus stand in and compensate for the anticipated dangers inherent in a lived life, rife with uncertainty.

Demon lovers abound in classical stories. Psyche is sacrificed to a viperous and fierce bridegroom who whisks her away to a magical palace. She is entrapped by her demon lover, and made a captive of Eros, who comes in the night and takes her as his bride. Many stories reminiscent of Psyche's captivity contain inferences of sexual violence. The maid-en Persephone in Greek mythology was abducted from her mother, raped by Hades, and forced to reign over the Underworld kingdom as his queen for half the year. In the Unicorn Tapestries, produced in France about 1490–1505, we witness the fierce unicorn lured to the garden by love and laying its trusting head in the lap of the virgin, who betrays him as the hunters and their dogs move in for the kill. In *Beauty and the Beast*, Beauty is forced to choose the dangerous Beast over her loving father, and to live as his captive within his bewitched castle.

Stevenson's story of "The Strange Case of Doctor Jekyll and Mr. Hyde," of 1886, is a more recent rendition of the demon lover motif, albeit a twisted version of Psyche's cap-tivity in Eros' palace. The classic 1941 film[3] stars Spencer Tracy who plays both the good doctor and his shadowy, doppelganger twin; Ingrid Bergman plays the coquettish and vivacious dancehall girl who becomes enthralled by him. The kind but all too human Dr. Jekyll has found, he believes, the formula for separating the good from the evil in the hu-man soul. Despite his honorable intentions, his action unleashes a sadistic murderer onto the streets of late-nineteenth-century London.[4]

When his beautiful fiancée is forced to depart for the European continent, Jekyll is un-able to bear her loss. He succumbs to his desire for the lovely and titillating barmaid who once threw herself unabashedly at the handsome young doctor. However, he needs the ruthless guile of Hyde to accomplish the seduction and betrayal. Here is the split feminine at work within the man. He is unable or unwilling to endure the long months of waiting for his virginal bride-to-be, a woman from a "good and decent" family. He succumbs to the burning need for instant gratification with the seductive peasant girl who enflames his lust. As Hyde begins to assert himself, submerging the personality of Dr. Jekyll for longer periods of time, we see him stalk his prey, watching and observing from afar. When Hyde sets his black eyes upon her, she appears overcome by a frozen terror. He lusts for her total submission. He toys with her at will until the girl is broken—a beaten and tortured captive. As the weeks pass, she loses her spark, her smile, her earthy sensuality. In their place rise abject terror, constant dread, total submission; she becomes a soul destroyed. When the serum wears off and Dr. Jekyll returns to normal, he comes to visit her, assuring her that Hyde will trouble her no more. As if he were a knight in shining armor he promises her that she is safe, at long last, and she believes him. Allowing a tiny ray of hope to return, she busily prepares her escape. But suddenly all hope is dashed as Hyde steps through the doorway, dragging her back into his clutches. Because she has dared to defy him, he becomes enraged. Wrapping his powerful hands around her throat, he coldly snuffs out her last breath.

After his crimes are revealed, Hyde cloaks his identity in the host, Jekyll, and repeatedly pleads his innocence to the authorities. "I've done nothing I tell you, I'm Dr. Henry Jekyll." Eternally innocent until the fatal shot to his heart, his defiance only screens a deeply hidden or split-off destructive sadism.

Jekyll's denial is vigorously upheld. He righteously fights to the death to maintain his feigned innocence. He will lie even to himself. Self-denial of this kind makes up a significant portion of the narcissistic defenses. Amnesia barriers are erected to prevent the aggressive and hateful attacks from being traced back to his own black heart. Lacunae, like islands of blank space, empty of thought, cover terrible deeds. He must maintain his innocence or he will be exposed to what he believes will be merciless retribution. This could relate to damaged early objects that become parts of a persecutory superego.

Mr. Hyde embodies a sexuality that is cold, brutal, and unrelated. Destructive narcissism underlies his murderous impulse, for it aims at complete annihilation of otherness and any separate identity of the object. "Hyde" resides not in some subterranean source within, but is rather the "hide" of the animal—its protective skin—worn to obliterate any semblance of tenderness and feeling, both from within or from without.

Wives and lovers, the casualties of such psychological terror, may suffer violation for many years while enduring the torment of such relationships. They may become entrapped by the charming and endearing Dr. Jekyll part, who is good to them during the daylight hours. Whenever any sexual intimacy is sustained, however, the Hyde part in the man's psyche may lash out when his partner is the most vulnerable, coldly killing off the eros between them. However, in these situations usually nothing so obvious as Hyde's brutality is unleashed on his victim. Keep in mind an additional meaning of the name Hyde: such a man will *hide* his sadism, even from himself. The telltale signs of his handiwork are found in the deterioration over the years of his partner's core sense of value in her native sensual-ity and spontaneity.[5] The following example will help to clarify these ideas.

## Case Vignette

The course of a male patient's analysis revealed a childhood subject to the affects of an ex-tremely depressed and unfulfilled mother. He was swamped by her black, brooding moods, and at times alternately devoured or sucked dry by her overmothering and neediness—cast adrift by cold withdrawals, gobbled up to fill her emptiness, then demolished by her poisonous attacks.

In the extreme cases where a mother's "love" for her child can be devouring and patho-logical, she may be experienced as vampyric—as one who drains her son of his life force and his autonomy. As Barbara Almond writes, "The mother whose psychic equilibrium depends on control of her children and gratification through them is a psychological vam-pire. The mutual enthrallment of vampire and victim parallels a mother-infant attachment that is distorted by the negative side of maternal ambivalence."[6] In other extreme states of mind, a mother's containing function may be compromised by depression, fatigue, or emotional distress. She may tend to project her own hatred into her baby, and envision his needs as ruthless, parasitic, too much—a monstrous baby, one whom she must disavow as her only way of surviving.

In my patient's case, he learned while very young to anticipate his mother's mood swings and to offset their impact through placating behavior. He became her special little man and the light of her life as a means of protecting himself from her projected hatred, neediness, and withdrawal. The fulfilling of his own needs was subject to her moods. No sense of agency and separation, so critical at two to three years of age, could develop in the young child, due to the blurring of her needs with his own. This very helplessness itself may be the unremembered origin of the disavowed hatred, aggression, and violence that may inhabit a man throughout his life. They can erupt at times when his vulnerability is the most threatened, culminating in attacks on all links and destruction of any remnants of intimacy and love.

Violent fantasies of this kind, with their basis in the helplessness and vulnerability of infancy, bring to mind the "most Gothic of Gothic novels"—*Dracula*,[7] and the traumatic early life of its author, Bram Stoker. The rich psychological insights of Barbara R. Almond's work, "Monstrous Infants and Vampyric Mothers in Bram Stoker's *Dracula*," inform my commentary. Her paper focuses not only on the typical sexual interpretation of the vam-pire, but also exposes the underlying preoedipal, primitive developmental dynamics.

For the first eight years of his life, Bram Stoker was a bedridden invalid, completely helpless and dependent upon his mother. While Count Dracula evokes terror as a monster whose ruthless needs leave his victims spellbound and helpless, Stoker the child invalid may have, in Almond's words,

> struggled with conflicts over passivity, dependence and surrender, a surrender that took on sexual meanings [in later development]. Pleasure in passive yearnings, as well as terror, could have permeated his feelings toward a mother who both ministered to him and saved him, while she frightened him with stories about others who succumbed to contagion, weakness and death (in the cholera epidemic she had witnessed during her own childhood).[8]

Stoker's fantasy of a powerful, superhuman predator, on one level, can be seen as a compensation for his own infantile feelings of utter helplessness and passivity. The Count feeds through possession and invasive penetration, which suggests elements of a destructive narcissism that denies "dependency and need by substituting omnipotent fantasy and ruthless exploitative behaviors."[9] In this light he may function as a symbol for the archetypal defenses that arise to protect the helpless child against uncertainty and the possibility of sudden maternal loss, by way of his unrelenting pursuit and power over his objects of prey.

My patient recalled a critical early memory from his fourth year, which may connect some of these ideas. In the recollection

> He was a child, walking with his father along a trail beside a fishing pond. A mother duck was parading her ducklings in formation along the bank. The boy rushed up and in his excitement scooped up the last straggler in his hands. He was seized with a violent impulse and started to squeeze the life out of the innocent creature. When his father screamed his name, he felt as if stabbed with a knife. Coming to his senses, he threw the duckling down on the ground. The shaken duck waddled into the pond to rejoin its mother.

Where could this violence have come from, we wondered?

In an active imagination, we learned that the boy hated the vulnerability of the baby duck. He associated this to his sense of feeling smothered by his mother, and of his own needs being smothered. He was filled with horror and excitement at the power that he felt over life and death, as he held the tiny creature in his hands. This violent need to "squeeze the life out of the baby," in clear view of his ordinarily absent father, was a cry for help to be rescued. Instead, his father screamed, punished him, and never attempted to find out more about his murderous impulse. It was as if the boy were enacting his mother's suffocating need and rage while projecting his own dependent vulnerability into the baby duck. What he needed, in the unconscious enactment of the play, was for the father to come forward and to protect him from being strangled and engulfed by his needy mother. He needed the boundaries provided through the *Father principle*, and that give a sense of safety, so that the father and his son could explore his underlying violent reaction. Instead his father unleashed his own punishing reactivity, and shamed his son.[10]

A man who is possessed by the Hyde or Dracula figures within is as disengaged from the healthy masculine parts of himself as he is from his inner soul image—the *anima*. In considering the duck scene, what if my patient had not been shunned by his father, but had instead been scooped up and held close and talked to? What if his father had gotten to the bottom of his son's terrifying impulses, or found a way to talk to him about normal aggressive feelings? Might he not have displayed a presence of being in his boy's life? In so doing he might have provided his son with an indispensable boundary, enabling the boy to deal with his entrapment in the devouring mother, an entrapment containing perhaps the pull toward a deathlike *jouissance*.

Marie-Louise von Franz elaborates on the masculine problem. When a man has not integrated his masculine qualities (a common feature in certain men who perpetuate the pathology of the *puer aeternus* type), he can become quite destructive, egotistical, brutal, and unfeeling toward women. "When a man falls for one-sided cold sexuality, he wounds the woman within as well as the woman without."[11] This occurs, she contends, because he is identified with and insulated in a kind of fusion with his negative mother complex and remains out of touch with his own feelings. His *anima* has been wounded and lies suffering.

The contemporary problems my patient was experiencing were in fact a continuation of his problems with his mother. His own wife was forced to deal with difficult medical issues, depression, and chronic pain, which often became the focus of attention in the household. These he unconsciously associated with his mother's black moods, a connection that was brought to awareness in the treatment. He had learned once again to be the good boy, to placate and to attend to all her needs, rather than risk the feared threat of annihilation if he spoke up and engaged in conflict. Instead, his wife became the victim of his cold withdrawal or seething, destructive narcissism that took the form of aggressive sneak-attacks that shamed her for not meeting his needs. In confronting his behavior, she would be met with hours of fierce denial of any guilt for the wrongdoing. ("I've done nothing, I tell you. I'm Dr. Henry Jekyll!")

In time, when he could speak without needing to anticipate and control the outcome, it became possible to separate out his identification of his wife with his mother. There were signs that the conflicts were normalizing between the couple. He found that the direct approach, which included his honest admissions, apologies, and felt regrets for his occasional bad behavior, could be met, and that the difficulties could be put to rest quickly. To his relief and surprise he ventured into a vis-à-vis relationship without the world falling apart.

## The Abuse of Imagination

Internal, compulsive, and sometimes perverse, erotic fantasies of *psychic violation* are another outgrowth of narcissistic dynamics. Deep, ancient wells of humiliation and vulnerability are split off into sealed compartments of the mind, which are regulated by repressive and sadistic defenses that prevent feelings of inferiority from subsuming the ego. The weak and wounded inner objects are conjured up and projected into seduction fantasies and rituals of triumph and submission as a means of restoring the mind's control.

When does human sexuality and erotic fantasy degrade into perversity that denigrates one's capacity for compassionate surrender, that betrays another's innocence through seduction and forced submission, or that objectifies, fetishizes, or erases the flesh and blood, soulful being of the other? The concern of this section focuses more on a man's predatory and perverse *imagination*—and not on his sexual practices—as an indicator of his extreme isolation and narcissistic defenses. However, a brief discussion is necessary to describe how perverse relations may originate and developmentally progress.

In the case of perverse erotic fantasy and practice, the childhood subject often becomes the object of parental abuse and/or seduction, and is cast into a victimized or entitled role. These kinds of parents aim to deceive, corrupt, and titillate their children. They enter into what Ruth Stein calls "perverse pacts,"[12] where they disguise hateful, suspicious, and destructive affects as (feigned) love and excitement, which flood the child's undeveloped mind. These distortions confuse its understanding of love which it carries forward into adult sexual practice. Perversity may be a form of defense against the subject's psychotic and annihilating anxieties. Sexual ritual may serve as narcissistic protection against the shattering psychic reality and revelations of shame and dread that must be split off through revenge and triumph.

Returning to the hidden abuses of the imagination, here we may find a man who appears to the world to be beyond reproach, the very pinnacle of moral propriety, who may in fact be concealing a secret part of himself and a dangerous split within his psyche. Or perhaps the man who is a Caspar Milquetoast to the people who know him may be feeding voracious pornographic addictions within his imagination. Such a man may hunt for thin young prostitutes with whom to act out perverse, predatory incest fantasies, or may entertain sadomasochistic sexual fantasies marked by themes of domination, submission, and fusion. If he does act out in the world, he never seeks out a real person with whom to have a multidimensional relationship, but only an object of desire he could use to fulfill his fantasies. It is the addiction to the titillation and the adrenaline rush of instant gratification, the virtual fantasy, and the secrecy that he is drawn to, not the real person. These are all forms of enchantment that concretize omnipotent, incestuous fantasies, and that are sought in order to restore the fragmented self through triumph over the submissive object.

When someone abruptly leaves or rejects a hoped-for new relationship it can drive a fragile, thin-skinned man to restore himself by cruising the strip in search of the anonymous prostitute, strip bar, or seamy lap dance—the sure thing. He may surf the Net obsessively to find pornographic Web sites for masturbatory release. He will animate the world with enveloping and devouring projections. His internal sonar will home in on those violated souls out there on the crowded boulevard who match his frequency, when their eyes capture one another in the fixed stare of momentary fusion. Who is predator and who is prey in those instances of capitulation to the hunger to eat and to be eaten?

The short-lived encounters of psychic violation, physical or not, collapse the mental boundaries into an undifferentiated amalgam. I consider these fused states to be another form of the death coniunctio,[13] where submission and absorption into the fantasy of the other segue seamlessly into triumph and colonization. The illusion of oneness may mask the infantile rage that seeks ruthless possession of the denied and long-ago lost breast. Enactments of this kind ultimately serve to insulate and protect against the threat of wounding and penetration by the relational world, as well as by the world of internal objects. They all dramatize forms of emotional management, and once they run their course they may quickly extinguish an individual's life force, like the deflation of a manic state that pulls the psyche down into underlying deadness and depression.

The primal source in each of these "polymorphously erotic practice[s]"[14] produces exciting, electrically charged affects and images. These contents may originate from the flooding and destabilizing of the infant's preoedipal psyche by the mother's overwhelming affects or deprivation. They may be translated into present form in the fantasies of merging, devouring, dissolving, and shapeshifting of one's gender identification and sexual roles with the other. They appear to be expressions of the enigma that keeps drawing us back to our maternal origins, perhaps in the hopes of bringing stability, healing, and understanding to what is perhaps life's earliest mystery.

• • • • •

The *burn wound* of Eros, inflicted in the darkness of the bedchamber, caused injury to the surface of Eros' skin, the outer surface organ that held him together and kept him contained. The man who repeatedly falls back on the narcissistic option maintains a symbolic life at the surface as a defense against an inner instability of identity that mirrors unstable relationships in the earliest years of life. He has learned since early childhood to aggressively insulate himself from this kind of penetrating and fragmenting attack. It is for this reason that the skin is, symbolically, his most vulnerable place.[15] As Symington indicates, "[t]he source of action in the healthy person is from within. The source of action in the narcissistic person is at the surface. The surface has to generate action through getting figures within and without to stroke and stimulate this surface."[16]

Clinical research in the field of infant object relations aids our understanding of the earliest causal factors that initiate the narcissistic patterns that maintain a life at the surface. Thomas Ogden considers the "autistic-contiguous position" as the earliest form of infant comprehension of sensation. He describes the first dawning of life as a state in which the infant experiences varying degrees of otherness against its skin, such as a soft, yielding breast or the hard edge of a crib. One feeling against the body might evoke a sense of calm, warmth, and nurturance, while the other may evoke sensations of the skin as a protective armor and crust that keeps out cold, pointed, and uncomfortable objects.[17]

"[A]utism is narcissism," Symington argues, albeit "an extreme form" of it, citing Frances Tustin's studies of autism. He informs us that "psychic autism" results from the premature violation and severing of the mother–infant bond, after which the infant, in desperation, turns away from the cold world and creates a protective fortress or "second skin" around this "black hole of despair" within.[18] The child is like a burn victim who perceives his primary skin as exquisitely fragile, and recoils from even the slightest touch. This second skin serves as a defense that encases the mushy body-self against anxieties, such as the "terror of falling or leaking into endless, shapeless space."[19]

An infant who lives through such unbearable loss by employing autistic defenses must live life at the surface, and does so through imitation. The infant is shaped by outer objects that alter the surface, and imitates them, whereas normal children have a more "fully developed sense of an inner space."[20] Recall the plight of Echo who could never penetrate the defenses of Narcissus, and whose only means of expressing her unrequited love was to *imitate* his voice. One thinks of such imitations as a sort of adhesive tape, as in the case of enthralled young lovers who enter into a state of twinship to one another. In an alternative version of the Narcissus tale, it is his dead twin sister that he longs to see in his mirrored reflection on the surface of the pond. He pines for her unto death, incapable of turning his gaze from the illusory reflection of the twin that he cannot mourn, willing his reflection to be that of hers out of fierce denial. But true mourning involves internal reflection and relationship to alterity.

Again, images of the undead come to mind—vampires who haunt the living and who never change or die, and which may signify the "denial of unbearable object loss."[21] Dracula is an unconscious creation of Bram Stoker's mind, the internal product of an invalid child's helplessness and passivity. The fantasy of lethal, unbounded powers provides a counterweight to the child's sense of utter weakness and victimization.

Francis Ford Coppola's mesmerizing film, *Bram Stoker's Dracula* (1992),[22] begins with the premise that Dracula's ruthless victimization throughout the centuries stems from his unbearable, unmourned grief. Coppola's prologue depicts the "liebestod motif"—fatal love—reminiscent of the "Legend of Tristan and Iseult." It is 1462 and Constantinople has fallen.

Prince Dracula goes to defend his homeland in the Caucasus against the Turks. His beloved bride fatally mistakes the meaning of the color bearers—the banners carried by his army as it returns from their Holy Crusade. She believes that the colors indicate that his army has been defeated and that their prince has been slain in battle. Bereft of all will to live without him, she plunges from the tower to her death. Because she has committed suicide the bishop proclaims her soul forever damned, whereupon, in his madness, Dracula curses God and the Church. Murderous hatred for all living things fills his black heart. Once-angelic fountains issuing forth the pure waters of life transform into grotesque demons spewing out rivers of blood. "Vlad the Impaler" is born, signifying the unmourned and violent denial of his unbearable grief and loss.

Both Dracula and Narcissus cannot mourn their loved ones—bride or twin sister. Two forms of narcissistic defenses may be erected to deny the losses. One is enacted through violent retaliation, while the other is marked by passive, melancholic longing and the avoidance of life.

Despair and unmourned loss may languish unseen beneath the autistic defenses in the narcissistic person because they are simply too overwhelming to bear. For example, one patient, just prior to recovery of early sexual abuse memories, dreamt that his skin was like an insect's hard exoskeleton. Rather than face the pointed barbs and hard edges of outer life, or the "appalling loss that has not been mourned"[23] that exists deep inside the black hole he dare not enter, the narcissistic person assumes instead the passive, easy position. Turning back to the infantile experience of the unboundaried "marshmallow mother"[24] he disavows any hint of male aggression.

He may maintain his life at the surface in the outer world by seeking fusion with a twin who will stroke and stimulate his literal skin. In this erotic enactment very primitive forms of communication can be expressed. Through his control over the partner he receives certain kinds of stimulation and touch, enabling him to literally feel his skin; without that he may fear falling prey to massive anxiety about oozing into unbounded, endless space. However, for him no real person is out there, only an object he has vampirized, a tool to be used, an extension of himself enabling him to remain fixed at the surface.

He may also enact solitary autoerotic sexual fantasies with an internal object in the inner world to preserve that passive position. These powerful images of the infantile autistic era are evoked in any sexual play, as all the action and aliveness must stay at the surface so that he can maintain control over the violating world and the unlived pain within. His inner depths at that point are unknowable and lie in complete chaos. He bathes in soothing, tranquilizing motions, reminiscent of what I imagine to be like a return to the oceanic life in the womb.

What appears to be lacking in cases of this kind is the struggle to incarnate normal forms of power and aggression in the world. I view these states as abuses of imagination that substitute for real life by enacting a fearful avoidance of the lived life, which is viewed as if it might bring down the castrating, crushing hand of the father. The following legend poignantly describes the effects of these deadly dynamics upon the integrity of both the subject and his targeted objects.

### The Grail Legend of Sir Gawan and the Sorcerer, Clinschor

The metaphors of medieval legend may continue to inform our understanding of the origins of this traumatic split and withdrawal into the hidden and impenetrable lair of this predator of the imagination. In Wolfram von Eschenbach's retelling of the Grail legend of *Parzival*, we find the story of Sir Gawan and a sorcerer of enormous power, Clinschor. Sir Gawan, as the *sun-hero*, must undergo terrible ordeals in order to break the dark magician's "mighty enchantment" that has entrapped within his Castle of Wonders four queens and four hundred maidens, each one more beautiful and alluring than the next.[25]

Within the unbreachable fortress walls the eunuch Clinschor is coldly incapable of loving any of these beauties, so he vengefully hoards them like a collector of butterfly specimens, cutting them off from the life-giving essence of the world of men. If he can't have them then nobody can. He lives in a kind of psychic deadness and depression, powerless to externalize his sexuality. Symbolically, he has caused the earth to grow barren.

Clinschor is a Saturnian figure. Saturn's relation to sexuality and sexual disorders is dual: The Roman god is patron to eunuchs and celibates, but the animals sacred to him are the lusty goat and ass. However, and most importantly, Clinschor's lechery and lust have inwardly twisted themselves into the realm of *imagination*, seemingly as "dirty thoughts" or far more pathological obsessions, because he has been violently castrated, rendering him an impotent eunuch.[26]

We might consider his acts upon the captives in the Castle of Wonders to signify psychologically the internalization of an envious hatred and a retaliation against life for an unbearable early trauma. The ruthless smothering of vitality and vulnerability—feelings perceived to be out of reach—is set off by the experience of a sense of abject humiliation and powerlessness. As a parallel to being locked away in such an impenetrable castle, we might consider that all the stages I have described occur at an unconscious level within the person hopelessly possessed by these complexes. Clues about the sorcerer's history may add credence to my line of thinking.

Clinschor was once a famous duke until he fell into disgrace for being caught by the king in the arms of his queen. In retaliation for his betrayal he is castrated and turned into a eunuch, "nevermore to give pleasure to any woman. But that has meant suffering for many people."[27] Driven by his shame and humiliation he traveled to the birthplace of all magic, somewhere near Persia. There he learned the black arts through which to heap bitter vengeance upon all who came under his spell and had mocked and scorned him. "For the shame done to his body he never again bore good will toward anyone, man or woman, and when he can rob them of any joy, especially those who are honored and respected, that does his heart good."[28]

Psychologically, the source of such destructive envy is a hatred toward the "first woman" as unending adoration turns suddenly to devastating betrayal. We can observe in this medieval tale a reenactment of the primal scene immortalized in the myth of Oedipus. In Freud's reinvention of the Greek tragedy, he envisions the idyllic fusion of baby boy and mother as shattered by the castrating power of the father, who threatens the baby for daring to stake a claim on a mother who is already taken. The boy's omnipotent fantasies must be deflated in order for him to accept his human limitations, to grieve the loss of the suckling mother, and to adapt to life. He is the third, left outside the paradise of two. In our tale by Wolfram, the brutal king as father castrates his son, Duke Clinschor, for desiring his queen mother. He has trespassed on forbidden territory, gone beyond all boundaries, and has been violently punished for it. In return he has vowed forevermore to heap revenge upon all those feminine creatures who have come in the wake of the queen.

Lacan revisions the oedipal role of father in his version of the primal scene. Normally during the oedipal stage of development the father's entrance into the mother and child's dyadic relations signifies the opening of the child's closed system to the world of the third. Here the father is a needed, redeeming figure for the young boy, whose *no* teaches the lad boundaries and individuality, and provides a much-needed separation from the mother's engulfing world. However, if the father's *no!* is too sadistic or castrating, as in the earlier story of the child and the duckling, then the boy is rendered powerless to embody and live out his phallic potency. He can instead become, in extreme cases, like Clinschor, mired in fantasies of triumph and retaliation over weak and submissive sexual objects in order to compensate for his own inferiority.

When the father himself is bound by narcissism he will try to crush his son's grandiosity and enthusiasm at every turn out of an envy and hatred of it, in much the same way as his own father might have done to him. Compulsive seduction fantasies return the individual to the wounded area in his own psyche as a means of restoring himself. However, he identifies with the role of the abuser, as a response to the violation of his wounded child part. Typically, in abuse cases, the child will grow up and either see himself as an abused victim, or will identify with the abuser and harm his own children as a means of avoiding his own pain.[29] The intensity of feeling is found in the abusive action that glues him back together and obliterates the intolerable experience of vulnerability, humiliation, and grief.

The dark lord of the Castle of Wonders who holds dominion over the earthly sphere is defeated by King Arthur's nephew, Gawan, the true and valiant knight whose power derives only from the spiritual light of the sun. Throughout the Grail legends, Sir Gawan leads us on many perilous adventures into lands under spells of enchantment. These resemble stages of descent into underworld realms ruled by the Lord of Death himself. Gawan is a true sun hero, for his great powers wax from midnight to noon, and wane from afternoon until midnight.

> In this latest adventure Gawan is ferried across the water to the shores of an enchanted island. He is beseeched by the ferryman to refrain from any inquiries about Clinschor's Castle of Wonders, seen off in the distance, for, he warns, "there is misery beyond all misery."[30] Gawan is warned to prepare himself to meet death if he proceeds into the mystery hidden there.

> No honorable knight seeking to win the freedom of these maidens has ever returned alive from this place. He who survives the trials presented here becomes lord of the realm, frees the maidens from their "spell of bondage," and becomes "lord consort to the Queen," an allusion to pagan rites of fertility.[31] Upon approach, Gawan learns that the outer gate is tended by a trader with a booth overflowing with unimaginable treasures. He leaves his horse there and proceeds within the gates. He stands within walls that could sustain a thirty-year siege, if need be. Towers rise high over the ramparts. The great hall with its vaulted arches and bright decorations is completely empty, save for rows and rows of vacant beds. A door, which he enters, leads to a chamber where the first of many trials awaits him. There he finds the "Wonder Bed," created by his unseen host, Clinschor the Magician.

> Forewarned not to surrender his armor, chain mail, sword, and shield before he lies down to slumber, the knight attempts to leap upon the ruby-wheeled bed, which has begun to whirl around the jasper stone floor like a wild, untamed bronco. As he holds fast to it, the bed proceeds to crash him into the walls, seeking to unseat him, but Gawan holds on. When that trial passes, a rain of five hundred stones, propelled by magic slings, smashes upon the shield that protects him. This trial is followed by five hundred arrows shot from crossbows, all aimed at the figure lying upon the bed. And as if that were not enough, a great lion is unleashed upon the knight, which he fights with until death greets the great beast, bathing both hero and animal in a sea of blood from both their wounds. Half dead, he is tended back to life by the grateful maidens and Queen of the Castle of Wonders, who have been freed from their confinement through Gawan's acts of courage.

We know the lion to be a common symbol for the Gnostic's *Demiurge*, the dark power in matter that gives rise to all evil in the world. At one level Gawan as light-bringer has finally brought awareness to an entrenched unconscious complex. What was hidden in the dark has been revealed so that life and growth might resume again, as signified by the fertility and release of libido embodied in the ladies in waiting.

At another level, in the battle between hero and villain for control over the maidens caged within the Castle of Wonders, we see the archetypal struggle between the purity of heaven and earthbound evil. There are sources that clearly link elements of the Arthurian Legends to the Gnostic traditions that underlie Cathar philosophy. If these sources can be relied upon, then the enmity between the two alludes strongly to Gnosticism's dualistic split. The champion of God's spiritual world has overcome the sorcerer who rules Satan's evil, material one.[32]

This apparent, underlying Gnostic dualism, provides the perfect metaphor for the psychic split in a man whose pretentious mantle of goodness disguises—even from himself—an imagination perverted by the traumatic wounding to his native phallic identity. From a psychological perspective, the idyllic Gawan is like the ego's persona, *too* good and pure, and a far cry from the all-too-human figure of Lancelot—that brilliant yet pathetic bundle of passions and sorrows.[33]

Gawan, despite his gallantry and "huge sword," doesn't appear to be too excited about his new role as chief consort of the castle, despite having the pick of any number of beauties. One has the sense that he'd much rather go off to the next adventure and leave the lovemaking to someone else. Owing to Gawan's origin as a true solar hero, his character may originate in earlier mythic sources than does Lancelot's. For that reason the symbol of Gawan may be subsumed to more general, mythic principles, whereas Lancelot is more personal and multidimensional. They can be thought of as similar figures existing on different planes, in the same way that one might differentiate myth from fairy tale.

Meanwhile, Clinschor remains hidden, surveying his realm from a secret room. Never will he confront any situation directly. He is a typical paranoid—distrustful, well-defended, forever on guard, watching. Even in defeat he is never directly confronted or driven out. Seldom do we catch sight of the persecutor within ourselves, either. We can only feel the effects of his handiwork in states of fear, foul moods, anxiety, withdrawal, depression, or in our outbursts of rage, cruelty, and perversion.

To give one example, a narcissistic lover may impulsively lash out in uncharacteristically hurtful ways while languishing in a foul mood, or his words or behavior may indirectly cut his lover deeply. Astonishingly, he will plead absolute innocence of the act, in the most genteel voice he possesses. His protestations suggest how incapable he is of inflicting such pain. Indeed, he needs us to believe what a pure and good soul he is. It is as if some unseen alien entity has swooped in from his dark lair and done the dirty work, then vanished, leaving the doe-eyed one batting his eyelashes. He will fight to the death, proclaiming his innocence all the while. This is the true nature of one who is hopelessly split-off from his darker impulses. We must never forget the words of the oracle, that long life would be granted to Narcissus so long as *he not know himself.* Like Clinschor, as long as he remains unrevealed he maintains his power over those he has entrapped.

For this reason I identify the *demon lover* as a split-off internal object who is conjured up as a compensatory reflex in order to obliterate rising feelings of humiliation and helplessness that stem from attacks upon one's vulnerability in early life. As I have shown, later in life a false persona of goodness, passivity, and compliance may be erected, one that lies in complete opposition to the internal object, in order to maintain a feigned innocence and personal safety in the world. This false self will prevent detection of the secret perpetrator and the wounded feminine (or child-part) that has been entrapped. Here an individual may fear the threat of retaliation from any male authority for any outward show of aggression, even though this process typically remains an internal inquisition, an analogy Clinschor and his Castle so beautifully capture.

If we feign innocence of this secret perpetrator, its presence will remain a mystery, at least until the day we face the facts of the marginalized lives we have lived and the damage we have done. It is no easy task to exhume those well-guarded compartments of the mind containing our shameful and humiliating wounds.

A patient's simple act of announcing what he has been afraid to expose can often begin to break the spell of silence brought on by unwanted abuse memories or post-traumatic stress reactions. In enforcing their young victims' silence, perpetrators can remain anonymous and keep their power over the victim through terror. For the victim, the abuser is introjected, lurking within as a conjured-up internal object, forbidding the truth to be told or his own identity to be revealed, for that would expose the violations too. Breaking his taboos of silence, the patient can start the road to recovering his lost and abjected parts. Through the work of analysis a strong, containing relationship appears to be the prerequisite for such a vital change. When the original, idealized transference takes a turn and the analyst must now bear the projection of the bad father or mother, the first steps are being taken toward exposing the sadistic object hidden within.

## Clinical Vignette

A repetitive pattern emerged in one of my patients whose oversensitivity made the penetrating emotional conflicts with his wife intolerable to bear. He would lash out at her in retaliation, causing painful separations that sometimes lasted for days at a time. Often during these periods of severance he would submit to passive sexual fantasies of being stroked and stimulated by an unknown seductress, which would lead to masturbation and orgasm. This behavior would annihilate all feelings of vulnerability associated with his painful conflicts with his wife, and substitute for them feelings of pleasure in association with submission without tenderness.

In this pattern we see the patient's thin skin being narcissistically wounded by what he perceives as his wife's emotional attacks, necessitating the formation of a second skin through his violent retaliation and retreat into fantasy to restore himself. By splitting off from his internal feelings and external relationship he seeks the soothing, anesthetizing fantasy of submission in narcissistic fusion.

I wondered about where his compulsive behavior may have originated, and this evoked in him the memory of his initial sexual fantasies as a boy of 12. They revolved around his passive submission to a beautiful but cold seductress who was his captor, and who would arouse him by probing or stroking or rubbing against him. He never assumed a dominant role in any of these enactments.

An individual's first sexual fantasy can often be seen as the template for and key to understanding the early wounds of childhood that underlie lifelong patterns of self-protection that prevent intimacy and growth. Underlying the scenario is the imprint of the mother's original seduction, her fascination with—and possession of—her baby boy's penis. Such a preoccupation could be attributed to the mother's profound depression and her own traumatic early life, in turn evoking her own need to restore herself and be enlivened through the forbidden *jouissance* between mother and her golden boy.[34]

The infant's vulnerability and helplessness, when submitted to his mother's ambivalent feelings such as aggression, deprivation, or neediness, may arouse tremendous anxiety and rage in response to his unmet needs. These feelings can then mutate into a "revengeful and perverse sexuality . . ." where seductive desires may appear to be of an oedipal, genital kind, but are enacted in a more primitive orality, as we see portrayed in the *Dracula* myth.[35] Alternatively, the infant may be enveloped in a titillating yet terrifying fantasy of the mother who "can give and withhold, and therefore gratify or persecute through control and deprivation,"[36] characteristic of the perverse pact spoken of previously.

In my patient's adolescent fantasy of his forbidden act of submission, his captor gave him permission to be aroused by her probing and stroking. He excitedly engaged in an illicit act, forbidden yet godlike, that mirrored the alluded-to incestuous scene. The original preoedipal seduction was then endlessly retranslated throughout his life, substituting for his engagement in real life.

Over our time together he has slowly come to realize how his wife's emotional responses could set off his retaliation and regressions to adolescent, child, and infant states of mind. He has begun to learn to sit with these emotional reactions and, by doing so, to separate the present from the past, his adult ego from his puerile moods, and his wife from the mother complex. Through this reflective process he is developing a primary skin, sufficiently resilient enough to tolerate the vicissitudes of emotional life and the demands required of him as a husband and a father.

• • • • •

This chapter has brought to light an elusive inner object, a split-off, shadowy double. His existence may come into being due to early traumatic factors that thwart or deform the emerging phase of phallic aggression. These disavowed, wounded inner parts of the psyche may be projected into relationships, as well as identified in the archetypal images of the *wounded feminine* within a man. Objects of desire are colonized, their individuality subsumed in the fusion, so that certainty might be restored to a paranoid ego complex. This is a common feature found in defensive narcissism. In its extremes, the urge for power and ultimate triumph over the submissive and dependent object may lead to perverse erotic ritual and violent annihilation of the other. Here we see the undeniable traces of destructive narcissism that underlie the violent splitting off of unbearable feelings of humiliation and self hatred. The ego is thus insulated against any incursions by the Other that may shatter its sameness and control.

## *Notes*

1   Although we are considering the images of the demon lover as *shadow* contents within the psyche of a *male*, an evocative object relations treatment of the demon lover in *women's* psychology may be found in Susan Kavaler-Adler, *The Creative Mystique: From Red Shoes Frenzy to Love and Creativity* (New York, NY: Routledge, 1996). Eerie characters that portray examples of the seductive demon lover are usually thought to be aspects of a feminine psychology, that is, images of a woman's "negative" *animus*. They are found in Celtic *Silkie* stories; *The Harlequin Lover*; Captain Bluebeard; Dracula; *The Phantom of the Opera*, and similar tales of this kind.

2   Barbara R. Almond, "Monstrous Infants and Vampyric Mothers in Bram Stoker's *Dracula*." *International Journal of Psychoanalysis* 88 (2007): 219–35.

3   *Dr. Jekyll and Mr. Hyde*. 1941. Screenplay by John Lee Mahin, Percy Heath and Samuel Hoffenstein, based upon Robert Louis Stevenson, *The Strange Case of Dr. Jekyll and Mr. Hyde* (London, UK: Longmans, Green & Co., 1886), Directed by Victor Fleming.

4   In Stevenson's story we see a biting indictment of science and progress and the arrogant disregard for the limits of nature. This parallels Nietzsche's notion of modern man being caught between his false morality and buried, violent animal instincts.

5   In Lawrence Olivier's classic portrayal of Heathcliff in the film version of Emily Bronte's *Wuthering Heights*, in Heathcliff's wife you will see the same hollowed-out face, the mark of many years of enduring his hatred of her, for no better reason than that she was not his long since dead, beloved Cathy.

6   Almond, "Monstrous Infants and Vampyric Mothers," 223.

7   Almond, "Monstrous Infants and Vampyric Mothers," 233.

8   Almond, "Monstrous Infants and Vampyric Mothers," 221.

9   Almond, "Monstrous Infants and Vampyric Mothers," 233.

10   A child will often be caught between a depressed, withdrawn, and needy mother and an inaccessible or useless father who cannot save him. Here too see Green's *Life Narcissism Death Narcissism*, Translated by Andrew Weller (London: Free Association Books, 2001), 178.

11   Marie-Louise von Franz, *The Golden Ass of Apuleius* (Boston: Shambhala, 1970), 76.

12   Ruth Stein, "Why perversion? 'False love' and the perverse pact," *International Journal of Psychoanalysis* 86 (2005): 775.

13   See Chapter Two.

14   Stein, "Why perversion? 'False love' and the perverse pact," 775.

15   Randolf Severson, "Puer's Wounded Wing: Reflections on the Psychology of Skin Disease," in *Puer Papers*, edited by James Hillman (Irving, TX: Spring Publications, 1979), 137.

16   Neville Symington, *Narcissism: A New Theory* (London: Karnac Books, 1993), 54.

17   Thomas H. Ogden, "Analyzing the Matrix of Transference," in L. Bryce Boyer and Peter Giovac-
     chini, eds., *Master Clinicians on Treating the Regressed Patient* (Northvale, NJ: Jason Aronson, 1990),
     49.

18   Symington, *Narcissism: A New Theory*, 106, 105, 81.

19   Ogden, "Matrix of Transference," 43.

20   Ogden, "Matrix of Transference," 44.

21   R. M Gottlieb, "The Legend of the European Vampire: Object Loss and Corporeal Preservation."
     *Psychoanalytic Study of the Child* (49) (1994): 465–80, as cited in Almond, "Monstrous Infants and
     Vampyric Mothers," 223.

22   Bram Stoker's *Dracula*. 1992. Screenplay by James V. Hart, based upon Bram Stoker, *Dracula* (New
     York, NY: Signet Classic, 1897, 1965), Directed by Francis Ford Coppola.

23   Symington, *Narcissism: A New Theory*, 105.

24   Symington, *Narcissism: A New Theory*, 106.

25   Wolfram von Eschenbach, *Parzival* (New York: Vintage Books, 1961), 297.

27   von Eschenbach, *Parzival*, 345.

28   von Eschenbach, *Parzival*, 346.

29   Symington, *Narcissism: A New Theory*, 74–75.

30   von Eschenbach, *Parzival*, 296.

31   Heinrich Robert Zimmer, *The King and the Corpse*, edited by Joseph Campbell (Princeton, NJ:
     Princeton University Press, 1948), 82.

32   For further thoughts on this subject see Chapter Three. Emma Jung and Marie-Louise von Franz,
     *The Grail Legend* (Princeton, NJ: Princeton University Press, 1960), 131–32.

33   See Chapter Two.

34   Due to his internalization of the mother's depression and withdrawal, the patient's reenactment
     of the scene will inevitably lead to its opposite—deadness and coldness—once the excitement of
     fusion has been sated. According to Andre Green, "The [internal mother] object is [psychically]
     dead . . . hence it draws the ego towards a deathly, deserted universe. The mother's blank mourn-
     ing induces blank mourning in the infant, burying a part of his ego in the maternal necropolis. To
     nourish the dead mother amounts, then, to maintaining the earliest love for the primordial [moth-
     er] object under the seal of secrecy, enshrouded by the primary repression of an ill-accomplished
     separation of the two partners of primitive fusion." Green, *Life Narcissism Death Narcissism*, 195.

35   Almond, "Monstrous Infants and Vampyric Mothers," 222.

36   Almond, "Monstrous Infants and Vampyric Mothers," 223.

CHAPTER SEVEN

# A DEADLY NARCISSISM
# SATURN'S CRIPPLED EROS

Western literature and history show us countless images of men whose ruthlessness is concealed beneath pious visages. The truth of their lives is depicted by the imagination of artists seeking to expose these villains hiding, often with impunity, beneath their robes of power and sanctity. In the pages that follow, I present portraits from a gallery of well-known cultural images of this kind, iconic figures encased within their deadly narcissism. Here I am thinking of narcissism in a more general sense to mean the violence and hatred for the enigma of life that arise in response to a traumatic injury to the self, as well as the envy of those who have access to something of which the subject himself is deprived. Historical figures like Nero, Hitler, and the Grand Inquisitor Torquemada come to mind. In personalities like these, defensiveness and a terror of life generally underlie a psychic deadness and sterility that hardens them against differences, whether in people or in ideas. A deep malice, justified by their defensive conviction of moral superiority, arises in conjunction with this separation from psychic aliveness.

I begin the chapter by investigating the extent to which this fear of life provokes fragmentation in the psyche, inducing in certain men "negative senex attitudes" that envelop them in depressive, deadened, and rigid states of mind. The thinking of certain theologians and philosophers also reflects the negation of the body, illustrated, for instance, in the anti-material, anti-body prejudices in the philosophy of Plato and in Judeo-Christian theology, such as that of Augustine. The horrors of the Spanish Inquisition take this dualism to the extreme as we see in the hatred of difference lying beneath its moral righteousness and certainty.

A moralistic and fundamental *truth* that fits all, sustained and upheld by an authoritarian judgment, serves to insulate the individual from the uncertainty that lies beyond the capacity *to know*. In Milton's *Paradise Lost* and Goethe's *Faust* it is Satan who whets men's desires for forbidden knowledge and drives them to excesses. These literary works expose the dark side of modernity and the Enlightenment, with its indomitable drive for knowledge and reason, which is at issue in the novels of Shelley, Hawthorne, and Melville, as well. Each of these authors implores mankind to seek not the inflated heights of heaven but a "lowly wisdom." As we will see, Andrew Samuels's writings on "original morality" and the "moral imagination" call upon one to face the enigmatic shadow and one's own capacities for evil.

In the modern era, society and individuals sometimes violently marginalize the other who is regarded as impure, vulnerable, or different, and in doing so make choices that create conditions conducive to acts of genocide, destructive narcissism, and sociopathic violence. The chapter concludes with a brief case vignette of an elderly German woman, raised during the war as a Hitler Youth, who had to find a way to confront the unimaginable truth that destroyed her youthful ideals and her delusions of innocence.

## Negative Senex

Each of the historical and literary figures discussed in this chapter embodies certain negative aspects of the archetypal *senex*, which, in the Latin, means "old man." Words such as *senator* and *senile* also derive from that Latin term. Negative senex attitudes can take the form of intolerance for anything that threatens the fixity of one's habits or belief systems. As James Hillman comments, "Melancholy, anxiety, sadism, paranoia, anality, and obsessive memory ruminations reflect this archetype."[1] The negative and dangerous father Saturn—devourer of children—turns dry, poisonous, and deadened when he is split off from the eros of his child. The two—*senex* and *puer*—appear in the psyche as opposites on a continuum. We discussed the puer's impact in earlier chapters and now we see the other side of the split in the senex. According to Hillman,

> this crucial psychological problem arises from a fundamental split between senex and puer within the same archetype. Negative senex attitudes and behavior result from the split archetype, while positive senex attitudes and behavior reflect its unity; so that the term, "positive senex" or "wise old man" refers merely to a transformed continuation of the puer.[2]

Hillman is describing here the internal parts of a psyche that is fragmented instead of cohesive and coalesced. The negative senex temperament can be cold or distant, arousing loneliness and depression in one who recoils from a robust engagement in life. A psyche engulfed by the complexes feels fractured and calcified. The consciousness of the senex is that of an outcast who feels set apart, yet who holds fast to the cold, hard, and immutable reality of things. Hillman continues. "[This] coldness is cruel, without the warmth of heart and heat of rage, but slow revenge, torture, exacting tribute, bondage."[3] In his negative aspect Saturn rules the realm of death, standing at his appointed station with scythe in hand ready to sever life from limb, renouncing the materiality of human desire. He puts an end to hope and the infinite possibilities of what might be. "[Such an] end gives the pessimistic and cynical reflection as counterpart to puer beginnings."[4]

• • • • •

For two thousand years Greek philosophers, Judeo-Christian theologians, and mystics in the West have meditated on the enigmatic *pneuma*—spirit—and its often privileged relationship to matter and the body. The words matter and materiality derive from the Latin root, *mater*—or mother. Ever since Eve's defiant act that severed humankind from Paradise, she has been linked to the seductions of the serpent, to sexuality, sin, and evil. Issues of priestly celibacy, maintenance of the sanctified holy place, revulsion for the impure fluids of the body (and particularly menstrual blood), all point to a rejection of the "whore Eve," the mother of all mothers.[5]

The Virgin Mary, who redeems Eve, was commonly described by medieval European theologians as being without a child-bearing womb. In the writings of these men, Eve's vital feminine being was excised from her. Their limited minds could not envision the Mother of God as a natural woman. This has profound implications. The spark of divine creation, innate to the human body and its senses and emotions, has been lost from sight and covered in a dry husk. This bloodless, idealized, and intellectualized vision of Mary was partly a by-product of the medieval religious mind, cloistered away and aspiring to ascetic heights and spiritual detachment through the severing of its links to the world of phenomena and sensual desire. These ascetic attitudes were also in part a reaction to earlier historical antecedents—such as the excesses of Roman authority and, later, the barbarism following the fall of the Roman Empire.

### The Death of Socrates

In his fictionalized depiction of Socrates' last days, the *Phaedo*, Plato portrays the critical moment in which his teacher severs himself from his wife's deeply felt emotions as if they were of no consequence. On the day that Socrates awaits his execution in prison, his wife *Xanthippe* and their son sit with him in his cell. As his students file into the room to say goodbye, Plato tells us, "she cried out in lamentation and said as women do, 'Oh Socrates! Here is the last time your friends will speak to you and you to them!' Socrates glanced at *Criton* and said quietly, 'please let someone take her home, Criton.'" The text continues, "then some of Criton's people led her away crying and beating her breast . . ."[6]

Socrates goes on speaking without so much as hesitating or mentioning his wife's painful outburst. Considering that he will never see her or his son again it is striking that he simply cuts her off. Where is his compassion for her grief or his capacity to bear her pain? After all, it is she who will be left alone to raise a son and bear his loss. In Plato's depiction, Socrates seems to coldly dismiss Xanthippe's "female emotionality," unable or unwilling to honor her profound suffering. He and his students appear content to simply detach themselves from the upheaval.

Apuleius, long a student of the Neo-Platonic school of philosophy, begins his tale of *The Golden Ass* with an erotic vignette about a man named *Socrates*, whom he portrays as a love-sick sex slave who comes under the spell of a witch. Apuleius' story seems to make a mockery of his great teacher. The story epitomizes the dangers that a woman's emotionality and sexuality hold for a man who succumbs to them.

> A fellow traveler named *Aristomenes* relates a story to Lucius about a chance meeting with his old friend at the baths, a man curiously named Socrates. He is shocked to see his old friend in a filthy, disheveled state, a wreck of a man, in tattered cloak, appearing to be a street beggar. It seems that the old man had disappeared and was thought to be dead. His grief-stricken family had since fallen into ruin as a result of his disappearance.
>
> Cleaning the old boy off at the nearby inn, the traveler manages to eke the sad story from his lips. He had been robbed by bandits and had barely reached an inn run by an attractive older woman named *Meroe*. Feigning pity for him, she fed him without charge and offered him a bed at the inn—hers! Under her pressure he gave in to her ardent desires. He described a sort of sickness that slowly came over him that made him weaker and weaker of will as time wore on. *Socrates had become a sex slave* to a witch possessed of fantastic powers.
>
> Like the sorceress *Circe* who beguiled *Ulysses*, Meroe could transform men into animals who dared to defy or betray her, or attempt to leave. She could invoke the dark powers of the spirit realm to cast her deadly spells. By sharing his dire tale, Socrates has dared to expose the enormity of her evil powers, and because of this, neither he nor his friend will ultimately escape the wrath of the scorned witch. Through the "astral plane" she visits identical dreams upon both men, wherein she and her sister *Panthia* burst into their room, slit Socrates' throat, take his blood for ritual purposes, and pull out his heart. They leave poor Aristomenes trembling beneath the bed like a tortoise, threatening to tear him to pieces while severing his private parts to hang from a tree like some castrated priest of the Great Mother goddess, Cybele. Both men awake apparently in one piece, shake off the dreams and hastily hit the road.
>
> When they stop for a meal along the way, Socrates goes sickly pale, and while bending over for a sip of water beside a crystal brook, his throat wound reopens. A sponge falls out that the witch had used to sop up the blood from the gash, and a trickle of blood oozes from the cut, whereupon he drops dead by the witchcraft! These apparent nightmares were, in fact, deadly real. Aristomenes, a broken man, forsakes his homeland and everyone in his life—his wife, children and all his holdings, and exiles himself to another province, never to return again.[7]

It is unlikely that Apuleius would have used the name of Socrates if he had not intended to make a point, satirical or otherwise. Socratic philosophy values disciplined thought and detachment from the baser human eros. It privileges the aesthetic ideals of pure and perfect beauty existing beyond our world. The philosopher seeks the attainment of *apatheia*, a state of mind detached from emotional disturbances and passionate life. But perhaps apatheia may lead to a repression of what is lifegiving, as well. In presenting such a base and repulsive image of the great Socrates, pulled violently and irresistibly down into the passions of the body, Apuleius may be pointing up the imbalance in a life devoted only to the ideal. He puts this glaring split in bold relief, in the autobiographical figure of his hero Lucius, who, as we have seen, comes to learn this lesson all too well while living as a lowly beast of burden.[8]

## *Saint Augustine*

Augustine was well-versed in neoplatonic philosophy as well. The tenets of neoplatonism underlie many of his early theological writings. One of Apuleius' harshest critics, Augustine was a fellow countryman born near Apuleius' own birthplace of Madaura in North Africa. Both were schooled at the university in Carthage. Both studied oratory in Rome. Each experienced a great religious conversion, Apuleius to the *Isis-Osiris* mysteries and Augustine to Christianity.[9]

Augustine describes his life before his Christian conversion as one filled with pagan lust.[10] Book Two of his autobiographical *Confessions* begins with these disclosures: "I will now call to mind my past foulness and the carnal corruption of my soul. . . . In that sixteenth year of my flesh, when the madness of unlicensed lust took rule over me and I resigned myself wholly to it . . . I walked the streets of Babylon and wallowed in the mire thereof as if in a bed of spices and precious ointments."[11]

The sainted chief architect of Church law underwent his startling conversion to Christianity in the late fourth century. Whereas his father was not even Christian, his mother was influential in his conversion. Augustine's theological reflections on his transformation deeply influenced the spiritual course of Catholicism and its conception of redemption from sin and mortality. With broad brushstrokes, Augustinian theology promised each Christian soul eternal life, provided the faithful confess their sins and renounce all desires of the flesh. Those desires and temptations were viewed as a corruption of the will and Satan's handiwork.

Feminist theologian Rosemary Radford Reuther points out the Platonist influences that underpin basic Augustinian ideology:

> Despite Augustine's affirmation that all that is, is from God and thereby good, there remains in his thought the Platonic version of the anti-body, anti-mate-

rial hierarchy. God as Supreme Being is immaterial, and one is in communion with God by turning "upward" to the immaterial, against those bodily "lower things," which have lesser being and goodness . . .[12]

Reuther's comment suggests also that Augustine retained certain aspects of his prior Manichaean dualism.

Imploring the faithful to "turn upward," Augustine authored edicts requiring celibacy among priests as well as abstinence for householders, save for the purposes of childbearing. These injunctions to the flock could be viewed as a compensation for Augustine's own tremendous inner conflict and guilt at the time of his conversion, a conflict stemming from the clash between his wayward life of selfish excesses in youth and his experience of God's transforming grace that freed his will to do good.

Augustine came to this crossroads only through the teachings of experience, only after having lived a robust, albeit unfulfilled life. Yet his compelling teachings implore his brethren to skip over the earthy life that he lived. They are reminiscent of the advice of a protective father who tries to save his sons from the mistakes of his own ill-begotten youth, only to stir rebellion in the headstrong son and meek subservience in the passive one.

Even late into his reborn religious life, however, Augustine struggled with the dark bodily desires that his superior moral consciousness identified with his dissociated and devalued former self. Historian Henri F. Ellenberger comments on a sort of multiple personality within Augustine: "Considering the change that had taken place since his conversion, Augustine remarked that his old pagan personality, of which nothing seemed to remain in his waking state, still must exist since it was revived at night and in his dreams."[13] In his *Confessions* Augustine reports that he said to God, "Am I not myself, O Lord, my God. And yet, there is so much difference betwixt myself and myself within the moment wherein I pass from waking to sleeping or return from sleeping to waking."[14] He is describing the representation of repressed shadow contents of his unconscious. Through the moral dictates of a superior will, Augustine could banish this double personality to the shadows of the night, but, like a bad spirit, it would arise again to possess him in his dreams.

## *The Shadow of Morality*

The endeavor to attain a pure and chaste life through sheer force of mind and the repression of impure thoughts and physical desires often leads to merciless self-torment. In such cases, the failure to keep these "impurities" at bay triggers judgmental attacks upon oneself. As a consequence, these abjected parts are projected onto others, enabling the subject to restore himself behind a mask of self-righteous moral superiority. Yet the underbelly of that stance is always sadism.[15]

Admittedly we can never fully determine the unconscious motivations behind an individual's acts of cruelty and malevolence, and both "good" men and "bad" men exist in every culture. Given this qualification, the Spanish Inquisition with its atrocities, the Nazis with their eugenics programs and Final Solution for European Jewry, the Ku Klux Klan and its racially motivated lynchings, and the Khmer Rouge and its killing fields in Cambodia, will serve us as examples of social groups or elements of society acting as perpetrators, and seeking to weed out difference in the name of *purity*.

## *Torquemada and the Spanish Inquisition*

In 1478, the Jewish and Moorish influence upon all walks of Spanish culture and economy was at its height. As the Moors and their higher culture were being driven from Spain's shores, the final defeat occurring at Granada in 1492, the ruling powers sought out new "devils" to wage their crusade against, and soon found an old enemy "within"—the Jews and *conversos*, (Jews who had converted to Christianity). For decades of the fifteenth century Spain witnessed periodic bloodbaths of Jews and conversos who became the scapegoats for frenzied mobs that blamed them for unsubstantiated crimes against the "true faith." During this time a fanatical popular movement arose, becoming an especially fervent preoccupation of the nobility, a movement that obsessed Spain well into the sixteenth century. It was called the cult of *sangre limpia*, "pure blood"—and it glorified pure, white, Christian blood.

The brittle, righteous fanaticism of these groups may have been symptomatic of a profound social anxiety and mistrust resulting from the interface of strange and different cultures. The Catholic nobility, growing ever more jealous of the Jews' growing wealth and power, set up a secret court so powerful that it was not even accountable to the Pope in Rome. Its formal charge was to weed out all heretics—those not of the true faith, and to eradicate what it considered to be the Jews' evil influence in Spain. The Spanish Inquisition was officially established in 1482. A year later the infamous Tomas de Torquemada (b. 1420, d. 1498), a Dominican Catholic priest, became the first Grand Inquisitor. Torquemada stepped onto the stage at a critical time when the Church believed that it was being threatened and weakened from within by "infidels," the "impure," and the "unholy." While posing as devout Christians by day as a means to maintain their basic freedoms, lands, wealth, and positions, by night these *Marranos* (Jews who feigned conversion) secretly kept the religious traditions of their forefathers and mothers.

By Torquemada's decree some two thousand accused heretics, Jews, and nonbelievers, were burned at the stake, beheaded, died in prison, or were tortured to secure confessions of guilt, allegedly to purify and save their souls. Then in 1492 he persuaded the King of Spain to expel all Jews who refused to be baptized.

Ironically, Torquemada himself may have had something to hide. His own grandmother was herself a *converso*, a "New Christian," originally of *Jewish* descent![16] What internal forces would compel Torquemada's vehement beliefs, sanctioning the annihilation and expulsion of any semblance of his own heritage? First or second generation converts, wishing to prove their conviction and loyalty, tend to be the most zealous. The need to evangelize and convince others of the rightness of their beliefs can be seen as an attempt to justify and solidify their own faith. This may shed light on the impact of Torquemada's grandmother's conversion on him, and his own disavowal of his Jewish origins. I do not believe, however, that it is a sufficient answer to the deeper question of what would motivate such malevolence toward fellow human beings, much less his own family line. Perhaps we will never really know, for despite his name being synonymous with that period of history very little is actually known about Torquemada's life or the workings of his mind.

John Edward Longhurst attempts to answer the question of the origin of Torquemada's malevolence. From his perspective the Grand Inquisitor was a creation of his time. Longhurst admonishes those historians who condemn Torquemada as a "unique vessel of Satan," while failing to understand him as a product of an entire age "caught up in a wave of persecution and murder," an age "which creates a man's attitudes and shapes his destiny. But," he cautions, "we do not therefore have to condone the result."[17]

Torquemada was certainly of strong temperament and unshakeable convictions, a man who had completely devoted himself to executing the programs of the popular will, including a program that happened to fall in line with his own passionate beliefs—eradicating Judaism in Spain. As a man of his time, he struggled with the social unrest and anxiety stirred up by the collision of cultures that threatened his fixed beliefs and way of life. I imagine that he saw himself as a humble servant and righteous champion of his beloved Church and queen. He had been Queen Isabella's confessor since she was a child and was her closest ally and personal advisor. Anthony Bruno paints a more cunning and opportunistic side to the erstwhile humble friar. Apparently, Torquemada even encouraged Isabella to marry King Ferdinand of Aragon in order, as Anthony Bruno writes, "to consolidate their kingdoms and form a power base that he could draw upon for his own purposes."[18] Reportedly, it was Torquemada who originally nudged the royal couple to petition the Pope to sanction the Spanish Inquisition, a request the Pope granted.

Contradictions abound regarding Torquemada. He has been described as an unflinching ascetic, known to wear horsehair shirts beneath his robes to humble himself, yet the great fortune that he accumulated during his career through the Inquisition's confiscation of Jewish and converso lands was large enough to commission the construction of the grand monastery of Saint Thomas of Aquinas in Avila.

Torquemada's reach extended beyond his religious mission of expunging the sins of heretics. He urged Ferdinand and Isabella to seek the expulsion of all Jews who did not submit to true conversion. When two wealthy Jews offered to pay the monarchs thirty thousand ducats to allow the Jews to stay in Spain, Ferdinand wavered. Torquemada was incensed and went to the court of the king carrying a crucifix. Historical accounts report him to have said, "Judas Iscariot sold Christ for thirty pieces of silver. Your Highness is about to sell him for thirty thousand ducats. Here he is. Take him and sell him."[19] He slammed the crucifix down and stormed out. This scene indicates to me the enormous license the older monk allowed himself with the younger king and his queen. Ferdinand did indeed sign the expulsion order in 1492, beginning the exile of all Spanish Jews from their homeland. Torquemada's grand vision had come to pass.

At the zenith of his power and influence Torquemada traveled with an armed guard of two hundred and fifty, to protect him from threats against his life. It is said that in his later years he became paranoid and suspicious, in constant fear of being poisoned or assassinated. Some stories claim that he placed what he believed to be a unicorn's horn beside his dinner plate to ward off any poisons that might be slipped into his food. He had resorted to superstition! Like others who have abused their positions of power, says Bruno, "Torquemada was apparently blind to the inconsistencies of his own life."[20]

None of these narratives give us much more than a glimpse into his person. Were his acts the result of sadism and hatred, all for the sake of the soul's purification through confession, or was he simply an agent of a malevolent, paranoid time? Was his secret purpose to cast the Jewish people in such a reviled, inferior light as a way of splitting off his own inferiority and alterity, or were his unilateral actions a result of what he believed to be religious revelations that eclipsed all else? We will never know for certain, but perhaps both are true.

Without any definitive evidence, my *fantasies* lead me to imagine Torquemada as the type of man who felt he could magically destroy all links to his past by exiling the abjected other, ridding his world of any trace of association to them that might threaten his power and his violent maintenance of control. Despite the priestly robes he wore to camouflage the truth of his ancestors and the truth of what he had become, it was still the grandson of a Jew that he saw gazing back at him every morning from the mirror.

The scapegoat groups whose existence threatened Torquemada's fundamentalist beliefs and vision of religious purity were met with swift and absolute judgment. Torquemada seemed possessed by extreme internal contradictions, as evidenced by the contrast between his apparently humble asceticism, and his impassioned, righteous dogmatism. Yet he also displayed a Machiavellian cunning, a cold pragmatism, and a penchant for torture.[21] What he regarded as his righteous calling seemed to be mirrored by the zeitgeist of an incensed populace, and the two factors combined may have provided an outlet for the psychic energies of a hidden and dangerous split in his personality. The world has witnessed far too many periods in history such as this, where the false guise of righteous sanctity has been used to justify terrible acts of wickedness and brutality. But perhaps the world has never known of a man better suited—*born for the role* you might say—to fulfill the gruesome task which Church and state called him to perform.

In looking beyond the personal figure to the *archetypal* one, the Grand Inquisitor is a representation of a deadly narcissism that grips a man and compels him to rise above what he regards as his trivial human existence among the tainted mongrel mess that is humanity. Men who lack much capacity for human relatedness must often compensate by pedantic adherence to rigid moralistic dogma and a compulsive attention to duty, order, and regulation. This is sometimes not so black-and-white, for some men can be savages in certain respects, as in their dealings with the world, yet very related in others, as with their families. This contradiction is a true mystery.

At what point does a self-righteous, moralistic stance become something sociopathic and monstrous—a shameless pretense covering the hatred of vulnerability, a lack of care or concern for the suffering of others, the violent annihilation of difference that arrests growth and change? It is ironic that fundamentalism of this type, which adheres to absolutist, foundational ideas, does so more from a *lack* of a true moral barometer.

• • • • •

More commonly, an individual who clings to a straitlaced persona of goodness follows the moral dictates of society obediently and with good intentions. Nevertheless, he can in fact fail ethically and morally if his responses to the human cry are not compelled by his own internal sense of responsibility but instead, by a need to keep in step with the social expectations that require him to be good and to act accordingly. In this case he risks nothing, for his performance can border on sanctimony of a kind that resembles the actions of a "company man." While far different from the sociopathic inclinations described in the previous paragraph, this man's actions may be no less hypocritical. There are, however, occasions in such a man's life where he is confronted by someone or something that tempts him away from the deadness in his life that is the inevitable result of the need for perpetual safety and pretense. From the traditional religious perspective, the evil within has erupted on the scene. Sometimes the temptress (as is often the case) dangles the hope of aliveness in front of him, and sometimes it brings about his ruin. Literature is filled with characters who stepped off into the unknown because the devil made them do it.

In Western literature *Satan* has been the primary symbol of a man's impulse to turn away from his moral stance and the path of righteousness. Satan is the Tempter in the Garden and the one who tests God's favorite, Job. The mystical tradition of kabbalah associates Satan with the Archangel *Sammael* who inhabits the place of judgment and severity on the Tree of Life.[22] The kabbalists do not, however, identify Sammael with absolute evil. In their grand scheme of things he fulfills a necessary role by leading errant souls so far from grace that they must ultimately choose of their own free will (once they have seen the full impact of their actions), whether or not to return to a righteous life. Their system implies the existence of an all-knowing God with foreknowledge. This suggests that, in his omnipotence, God expects human beings to fail, to "sin," to be seduced by temptation, in the hope that they may learn from their suffering.

The biblical Satan whets humankind's insatiable hunger, pushing the pair in the Garden always onward toward unbounded heights and grandness. As William Blake contends, had the serpent not tempted Eve with the apple from the Tree of Knowledge of Good and Evil, we might still be as infants in the Garden, where everything is handed to us without a struggle. Only through disobedience and expulsion were Adam and Eve forced to develop a reflective consciousness and a free will.[23] *Lucifer*, the Light Bringer, brings about consciousness; the endless quest for unlimited power and knowledge, however, carries a dangerous shadow with it.

In John Milton's *Paradise Lost*, the Puritan poet re-visions the Genesis story of Adam and Eve, in which Adam disobeys God's one simple prohibition—Don't eat of the Tree of Knowledge. Milton's great work was composed in 1667, subsequent to the Restoration of the English Monarchy after the failed Puritan revolution and its grand disobedience of the King's absolute authority. The political themes of disobedience and rebellion for the sake of religious freedom, for which Milton suffered greatly, are loosely disguised beneath descriptions of Adam's and Satan's acts against God. This was a time when the people rose up against the despotism of the Baroque Age, where monarchs such as Louis XIV ruled under the proclamation, *L'Etat c'est moi*—"I am the State."

Milton's epic depicts Satan, the fallen angel thrust from Heaven and imprisoned in Hell for his failed revolt against God. Satan escapes and seeks revenge upon the newcomers in Eden, whom he deeply envies. Foreseeing Satan's incursion into Paradise, God sends his trusted servant, the Archangel Raphael, to remind Adam of his free will in choosing good or evil. He warns him of the consequences of transgression. Raphael is permitted to reveal the stories of Creation to Adam, who hungers for every scrap of "knowledge within bounds."[24] He presses Raphael for all that and more, but when he seeks privileged information about the celestial movements of stars, he has transgressed into the reaches of forbidden knowledge, and Raphael admonishes him for his arrogance. It is in these famous passages that Milton makes a plea for humility within human bounds.

> Heaven is for thee too high
> To know what passes there; *be lowly wise*
> Think only what concerns thee and thy being
> Dream not of other worlds, what creatures there
> Live, in what state, condition, or degree;
> Contented that thus far hath been revealed
> Not of Earth only but of highest Heaven.[25]

In one's lowly wisdom, the simple and humble joys of life may come to be known—a child's glee, one's gratitude for a second chance, the opening of the heart—and it is in these precious moments that life's deeper meaning may be discovered. Can we be *something* but not *everything*? The French expression *portée* comes to mind, that is, the limitations of one's reach. One needs to understand, with humble acceptance, one's own limits and capacities. In other words, we are just simple beings after all, flawed and human. From the writings of Montaigne in the mid-sixteenth century, come these words of restraint: "To make a fistful bigger than our fist, an armful bigger than our arm, to hope to step further than the length of our legs—these actions are impossible and monstrous. The same goes for man's attempt to rise above himself and humanity."[26]

In Milton's version of Puritanism the redeeming power of sacrifice and shame may bring a man back from oblivion and onto the road of responsibility, humility, forgiveness, and the awakening of integrity. As Jungian analyst John Beebe writes, "Learning to accept shame was the psychological point of the Puritan emphasis on original sin, and it is the moral achievement of Milton's Adam in *Paradise Lost*."[27] After their Fall from Grace, a penitent Adam laments to Eve,

> What better can we do, than to the place
> Repairing where he judged us, prostrate fall
> Before him reverent, and there confess
> Humbly our faults, and pardon beg, with tears
> Watering the ground, and with our sighs the air
> Frequenting, sent from hearts contrite, in sign
> Of sorrow unfeigned, and humiliation meek.[28]

Today in the glare of consumer-driven advertising with its greedy, pulse-pounding, sky's-the-limit message, promising always bigger, faster, hotter, these unpopular modest values may be difficult to find. In our haste to anesthetize our pain, to embrace the quick, easy answers, or to rid ourselves of our mortality and limitations, we stutter-step through life, perpetually moving, forever becoming, and rarely reflecting on the split in our human condition. Milton's humble message offers a counterbalance in an age flooded with paths to excess and indulgence and a resurgence of fundamentalist doctrine claiming to provide absolute truth.

For Jung, an individual self matures only with the recognition of a man's own capacity for evil,[29] after Satan the Tester has darkened the doorstep. Through the resilience of the self the shadow can be faced without the individual becoming possessed by it, or self-righteously denying it, or projecting it onto those whom one cruelly condemns. Out of the wrestling match that *Sammael* thrusts upon him, a man may come to the painful understanding that the burden of choice and responsibility is his—to be party to conscious acts aimed at the infinite good or toward totalizing violence. In my estimation this is the heart of what Jungians call *shadow work*, and it compels one to face his wrongdoings and the ensuing shame that comes from them. The bitter truth of this confrontation can break a man open. In the fortunate cases a humble standpoint arises; in ill-fated circumstances, however, what emerge are destructive impulses towards self and others.

These painful revelations may act to open one of life's seeming paradoxes: The blood of one's wounds is also the blood of all life—an overflowing source of all life and all human suffering. And in those rare, humbling, and painful moments a glimmering recognition can emerge: he is not alone. He has never been alone. For revealed in these moments of clarity, in gazing upon the other in his or her vulnerability and nakedness, lies a trace of a presence of the Infinite that shatters the illusion that we are autonomous beings, separate from humanity.


### The Serpent's Sting of Knowledge

In the late sixteenth century the figure of Doctor Faustus emerged from folk legend and onto the pages of great literature and drama, as envisioned by such a luminary as Christopher Marlowe. The fable tells of a man who sells his soul to the devil in exchange for superhuman powers and knowledge, signing the deal in blood. *Faust* was later taken up by the Romantic poet and dramatist Johann Wolfgang von Goethe in his classic play of 1808 and its sequel, written in 1833. Goethe's work has as its backdrop a cosmic wager between the Lord and the Devil over the question of Faust's damnation or salvation, suggesting to Roger Shattuck that "Goethe grafted Faust onto the Job story."[30] My intent here is not to delve into the deeply symbolic and universal themes found in the Prologue and Second Part of Goethe's *Faust* but rather to present the very personal tragedy that befalls Gretchen, the maiden who gives her love and surrenders her innocence to Faust, and succumbs to what I define as Faust's destructive narcissism. I will, however, also discuss how Goethe's tragedy reveals a shadowy underbelly of the Age of Enlightenment as it emerged out of the Baroque period.[31] Despite its great achievements in science, scholarship, and the championing of men's rights to use their own reason, the Enlightenment's inherent belief that knowledge can reveal all of life's secrets reveals the propensity for an inflated and gross disrespect for any human limits. In this era science had already undertaken a relentless and unbounded search for knowledge, and its staunch proponents had arrogantly come to believe that *all* knowledge was within the grasp of reason and the rational mind.[32] The learned Doctor Faust, who seeks to know all the secrets of the universe while immersing himself in sensual oceans of experience, personifies Goethe's vision of nineteenth-century European man, driven by the colliding forces of his age—the Enlightenment's zeal to know clashing with the ideals of Romanticism that arise in protest against it.[33]

As Goethe's drama opens, having reached the limits of scholarship in medicine, law, philosophy, and theology, which keep him suspended above life and seem to have gotten him nowhere, Faust complains, "There's nothing we can ever know."[34] The obliging devil *Mephistopheles* offers him an alternative: In exchange for his earthly soul he is granted any experience that he might desire. Faust accepts and plunges into a world of sensual experience and the occult. As Roger Shattuck comments, "he seeks and fleetingly finds pure pleasure, the rush of experience for experience's sake."[35] When Gretchen, the girl he has seduced, questions his faith, Faust speaks instead of "feelings," like a newly converted religious zealot:

> Just let it fill your heart, and when
> You feel highest bliss, why, then
> You call it what you will:
> Joy! Heart! Love! God!
> I have no name for it;
> Feeling is all,
> A name's mere sound, a haze that veils
> The radiance of heaven from view.[36]

Faust's delirious immersion in the pure feeling of the Romantic is transient. The real tragedy that he—or rather the Mephistophelian part of Faust that subsumes his ego—sets in motion begins with the poisoning of Gretchen's mother, followed by Faust's killing of her brother in a duel. With his last breath, Gretchen's brother curses his tainted sister. Now with child, having sinned in the eyes of God, Gretchen is obsessed by massive guilt, personified as evil spirits who press in upon her. Faust himself is spirited away to a Witch's Sabbath in the Hartz Mountains. Under their enchantment, a full year passes, and the distraught Gretchen, mad with guilt and despairing at Faust's abandonment, murders her newborn. For her crime she is sentenced to be beheaded. At the eleventh hour, Faust makes a futile attempt to rescue her from prison, but what he finds in her cell is a woman driven insane—a mere shell of the innocent maid he once loved. She refuses his help, preferring death for her crime and hoping for redemption.

In the opening to Part Two of *Faust*, Mephistopheles, with the help of nature spirits, provide a sleep of oblivion for Faust to help him forget the horrors past and the part he has played in them. He awakens refreshed, and in typical Faustian fashion attempts to stare directly into the sun—that is, "to experience truth in absolute terms."[37] Symbolically, Faust's yearlong enchantment and sleep of oblivion signify the feigned innocence, denial, unconsciousness, and dissociation through which a character subsumed in narcissism protects himself from his shame and his responsibility for the irreparable harm and suffering he has caused. In the predatory mind of a narcissist, the world is his to use, life's marrow is to be sucked bone-dry, then discarded. Faust bets Mephistopheles that "no feeling . . .

*no human attachment* will ever lure him into loyalty." That stony-hearted principle allows Faust to try anything a few times; as Shattuck writes, "Nothing is at stake beyond his own opulent survival."[38] His subsequent twenty-four years of "godlike flight"[39] come at the price of real human relatedness.

• • • • •

"Halfway between *Faust I* (1808) and *Faust II* (1833)," Shattuck writes, "there appeared in London an anonymous novel called *Frankenstein; or The Modern Prometheus* (1818)." The author was Mary Shelley who, at the tender age of nineteen, had amassed a wide body of knowledge of classical and modern mythology, from Prometheus to Milton's *Paradise Lost.* As Shattuck continues, "Most importantly, she takes aim at the Faustian motif of 'the serpent sting' of knowledge . . ."[40]

In 1816 young Mary Shelley came to live communally among the Romantic poets and idealists on Lord Byron's estate. Shattuck continues, "Surrounded by illegitimate births and infant deaths, they subsisted on high ideals . . . [and were committed to remaking the world] through liberation and revolution." The male group members refused to allow other concerns to stand in the way of the glory they hoped to achieve through their creative genius. Even at seventeen, Mary "perceived so vividly the vanity and selfishness of this existence. . . ."[41] I'd imagine that those "other concerns" that fell by the wayside might relate to deeper emotional connections, commitment, constancy, family bonds, and parental responsibilities. All needs personal and mundane simply paled beside the glorious fires of their Romantic ideals. As is characteristic of all narcissistic pursuits, however, idealization inevitably deteriorates into its opposite—cruel devaluation.[42]

Shelley's fable tells of a science gone terribly awry in its quest to conquer nature through the achievement of eternal life. A direct protest against Faustian excesses, her novella reveals our longing to be eternal as an endless disrespect of our human fragility and boundaries. It anticipates the exploitations that science has perpetrated in the name of progress. The denial of our limitations and of death can be understood through Shelley's story as an arrogant, greedy rejection of a humble life, a refusal to carry only what we can bear with our own two arms.

When the great miracle of science succeeds in reanimating the dead corpse, Shelley rails at the horror and catastrophe of the act. The good doctor has created a monstrous demon! Upon retiring to bed, Dr. Frankenstein dreams of embracing his beloved, who turns into the corpse of his mother, teeming with maggots. Shattuck offers a pointed interpretation of the dream: "Frankenstein, hoping to achieve a scientific miracle deserving admiration, discovers that he has violated Mother Nature herself."[43] In her prescience Shelley recognizes the mad quest for ultimate knowledge in the Age of Enlightenment as having wrought a terrible monster that has wounded nature, perhaps irreparably.

The Greek word *pleonexia* refers to the insatiable greed for excesses and the unattainable. It is the urge to reach out even for the moon and to refuse all limits. It must surely be the fire that spurs Goethe's Faust to limitless heights. In bold challenge to these excesses, Mary Shelley's observations resonate with the clear voice of John Milton a century and a half earlier, who, through his angelic guide Raphael, advocates a "lowly wisdom."[44]

Ironically, despite having crossed an ocean to escape persecution for their own, differing beliefs, the original Puritan colonists of New England were keenly distrustful and intolerant of differences, individuality, and the emotional life. Convinced of the depravity of "fallen" man, they adhered to a rigid moral severity in meting out justice. In contrast to the "moral achievement" of Milton's Adam in accepting shame, the New England Puritans placed greater emphasis upon guilt and the ostracism of individuals who disobeyed the laws of the community. Such guilt produces enormous distrust in one's own individual volition and creativity, while reinforcing the individual's reliance on group acceptance and compliance.[45] To be right with the world again one must conform and defer to the judgment handed down from the Patriarchal authority.

Nathaniel Hawthorne, author of *The Scarlet Letter* (1848), was a native of Puritan New England. One of his ancestors was a zealous Puritan judge who served at the infamous witch trials in Salem in 1692. The witch hunts had been a pervasive practice in the Baroque period. They were adopted by the governing authorities of the Puritan colonies to rid the Christian community of all it deemed impure, pagan, and satanic. Midwives and folk and herbal healers—mostly women—took the brunt of the assault upon the practices of the ancient ways. Hawthorne's family had lost wealth and prestige over the years, and he tended to view this as a sign of God's retribution for the shameful role they had played earlier in serving up such cruel justice with no hint of compassion. The redemptive power of love to prevail over a righteous and harsh authoritarianism becomes a central theme in his masterpiece.

In *The Scarlet Letter*, forbidden passions ignite between the saintly young minister of a New England village and a married newcomer who arrives in town without her husband. She becomes pregnant. As she is called before the tribunal of patriarchs who sit in judgment on her presumed adultery, she refuses to divulge the identity of her lover. She is branded with the scarlet letter *A* for adultery, and must wear the letter embroidered on her dress as a form of public humiliation. Given the backdrop of the witch hunts of the time, it is clear that these rigid and somber advocates of a severe puritan code are to be seen as having severed all links with nature, passion, and love. The heroine, Hester, is of the deep conviction that her actions were done in the name of love. In the face of intransigent abuses of power she remains strong and true to herself.

Then a third character emerges, her long-lost husband, who is filled with a steely, murderous rage for what he sees as her betrayal. Indignant that his lawful wife, his possession, would dare transgress against her master, he becomes obsessed with his desire for vengeance on the secret lover. When he deduces the minister's identity, he proceeds to torment the guilt-ridden man. Unable to bear his guilt any longer, the minister publicly confesses his act and dies in the arms of the woman he loves. The wicked man has essentially tortured his victim to death by exploiting his pathological secret and unbearable guilt. Inevitably Hester's husband is destroyed by the mania that has possessed him. She and her child depart for Europe with hope and optimism.

•••••

The crazed and driven quality we see in Hester's husband bears more than a passing resemblance to Herman Melville's Captain Ahab, in his obsession with the White Whale. During the time Melville was writing his novel the two writers were neighbors, and the younger of the two dedicated his now classic *Moby-Dick* (1851) to Hawthorne. Captain Ahab's blind lust for vengeance drives him onward, ceaselessly searching the high seas, forsaking all concern for the welfare of ship and crew, and all love for his own family, in his quest to destroy the great white whale that has taken his leg.

In his masterful prose, Melville describes Ahab's last moment of lucidity and humanity, just before the sound of the ship's alarm that finally announces the sighting of the white beast. As Ahab leans over the side of his ship, gazing into the deep blue, "that burnt-out crater of his brain," so long estranged from any touch of nurturing Mother Nature, finds a moment of compassion and grace:

> The stepmother world, so long cruel—forbidding—now threw affectionate arms around his stubborn neck, and did seem to joyously sob over him, as if over one, that however willful and erring, she could yet find it in her heart to save and to bless. From beneath his slouched hat Ahab dropped a tear into the sea; nor did all the Pacific contain such wealth as that one wee drop.[46]

In this moment at least, Ahab is encountered by the "deep blue"—that enigmatic Other—which overwhelms the wretched man with compassion and revelation. In the next passage Ahab discloses the sad and bitter truth of his own demise, his brutal yet honest confession flaying him open to his sins and wrongdoings. Bowing his "stubborn neck," Ahab acknowledges responsibility for his tragic actions. Such an act of transparency to oneself may dismantle entrenched beliefs and create the potential for redemption and forgiveness. Ahab peers into his "dry" and weary soul and asks of God only that his heart be opened at long last. He speaks to a shaken Starbuck, the first officer:

> [F]orty years on the pitiless sea! . . . forty years to make war on the horrors of the deep! . . When I think of this life I have led; the desolation of solitude it has been; . . . and how for forty years I have fed upon dry salted fare—fit emblem of the dry nourishment of my soul! . . . . whole oceans away, from that young girl-wife I wedded past fifty, and sailed for Cape Horn the next day, wife? wife?—

rather a widow . . . . Aye, I widowed that poor girl when I married her, Starbuck; and then, the madness, the frenzy, the boiling blood and the smoking brow, with which . . . Ahab has furiously, foamingly chased his prey—more a demon than a man . . . what a forty years fool—fool—old fool, has old Ahab been! . . . . I feel deadly faint . . . as though I were Adam, staggering beneath the piled centuries since Paradise: God! God! God! *Crack my heart*—stave my brain . . .[47]

Ahab's confession, uttered in this rare moment, stands for the possibility of bridging the chasm between the ego bound by narcissism and love's human connection—the responsibility for the other that transcends the sameness of egoism. Melville is reminding us that we may scour the seven seas, endlessly seeking to satiate the hunger for things we lack in our ordinary lives. But when all is said and done it is the human heart and the love we share that fills us, that brings forth the waters of life, and that transcends the emptiness and isolation of our being. He warns us not to look upward to the heavens, like Milton's Adam, whom Ahab refers to, but to search the soul in the eyes of our fellow men—the human face that bears a trace of the Other—to find what binds and heals.

[S]tand close to me, Starbuck; let me look into a *human* eye; it is better than to gaze into the sea or sky; better than to gaze upon God. By the green land; by the bright hearthstone! this is the magic glass, man; I see my wife and my child in thine eyes . . .[48]

In Ahab's brief moment of vision we ache for him, for those precious human connections, once severed, that now miraculously appear and grow like the "green land" before his very eyes. Sadly, the pain of the loss of his wife and child appears to be too great for him to bear. Just when the wounded man has shown himself to us, as the two speak longingly of returning to home and family, forsaking the hunt, Ahab's "glance [is] averted" to that "nameless, inscrutable, unearthly thing." Once again, the "hidden Lord and master, and cruel, remorseless emperor,"[49] seizes hold of him, crazing his mind. Is Melville not bringing into stark relief here the murderous quality of compulsion that destroys all links to life and vulnerability, the panic that lashes out against attachments and the dangerous uncertainties of life? In his depiction of Ahab's obsession with the whale Melville describes the deadly narcissism that swoops in and carries a man far away from the cries of human pain or suffering. Soon the final alarm is sounded, the spell is broken, and Ahab is sent scurrying to man the harpoon and meet his death. All life is again subsumed in blind hatred for Moby-Dick. Only in his final moment of awareness before the alarm sounds do we see fear ease its grip on him and a glimmer of humanity return.

In the end, entangled in ropes left by the impotent harpoons that perforate the indomitable beast's hide, Ahab, like a crucified Christ, glances up one last time as Moby-Dick dives down to the depths, carrying him to his death. The boundless hatred that Ahab holds for the white whale belies a profound terror for the primal depths of life and death—the dreaded, unknown Other—embodied in Moby-Dick. Ahab hates the whale because it represents the enigma of life, that enormous and unknown thing that can neither be killed off nor rationally understood. His only alternative is its extermination, and in choosing this it is he who becomes its prey. Perhaps Ahab's death signifies the inevitable and necessary sacrifice of those destructive, cultural attitudes that Melville's captain personifies.

Melville's *magnum opus*, viscerally real, yet symbolic, even prophetic, portrays the modern *ship of state* as an ill-fated whaling vessel, charged with decimating the oceans of their primal and majestic sea creatures. Born of the cultural narcissism arising from the Enlightenment, the belief in the superiority of logic and a science that could reveal all mysteries brought with it illusions of perfection, purity, and finite order, which, it was hoped, could stem the black tide of unimaginable terrors. Despite the enormous economic growth and material progress ushered in during the Age of Enlightenment, the enigmas of life were regarded as intolerable and unacceptable. Based upon these closed systems of knowing, industrial nations established policies designed to conquer and harness nature's forces, colonize and develop territories, and convert or exterminate indigenous races, their lands and resources stolen in the bargain.

Following the publication of his *On the Origin of the Species* in 1859, and especially after the turn of the twentieth century, Darwin's theory of evolution was appropriated to justify these abuses. His ideas were distorted by sociologists and political scientists who were bent on using them to further a kind of "Social Darwinism." This was, according to Ellenberger, "a philosophy that gave a seemingly scientific rationalization to the spirit of ruthless competition . . . ."[50] Social Darwinism has long been blamed by some historians for fueling the First World War.[51] The military argued that war and the maintenance of large armies were a biological necessity for survival. Criminologists sought to root out the unfit elements from society through capital punishment. Survival of the fittest was the law of the land, and all sorts of evils were perpetrated by the powerful in our so-called civilized, modern, Western society.[52] To achieve greater efficiency, perfection, and superiority over competing elements of society and among nations, scientific and technological advances were utilized with deadly results. Widespread application of these advances ranged from eugenics programs that sterilized and euthanized the mentally ill, to machines of world war, to wholesale, premeditated programs of genocide, and then to the development of the atomic bomb.[53] Some have argued that dropping the bomb made it possible for the war to end sooner, saving countless lives. However, many others contend that the postmodern critique of modernity was born from the madness of this terrible split in which millions would die, but the *trains would run on time!*[54]

Society tends to hate and fear what it does not understand or know, and to distrust what it regards as fringe elements—those that challenge or pose a threat to the status quo, or members of society who are weaker and more vulnerable. But the true challenge to the limits of knowledge lies in being able to bear uncertainty, ambivalence, and the tension necessary to prevent a premature foreclosure on truth.

## *Germany and Hitler*

Germany had been terribly betrayed after its defeat in World War I. The embargo that choked off all food supply lines extended long after the war ended. Money was worthless. People were eating shoe leather. The German people were broken and devastated. Amid all this a charismatic leader, invoking the words of Darwin,[55] vowed to raise the fallen spirit of Germany, and the German people followed blindly. The rage and shame of a tortured and suffering populace, bound by the Treaty of Versailles—the "Treaty of Shame"—was mirrored in their leader, Adolph Hitler. Despite the fact that the murders committed in the name of the Third Reich were legalized, required, and applauded, the excesses of Nazism and the Holocaust remain largely enigmatic. How can one possibly fathom the magnitude of evil underlying these acts? The deeply disturbed character of the leader of Nazi Germany provides us with an apt metaphor for the psychopathy of those times.

In his book, *Wounded Monster: Hitler's Path from Trauma to Malevolence*, Theodore Dorpat[56] suggests that Adolf Hitler's madness originated in the violence and trauma he experienced at the hands of his sadistic father, whose whippings and beatings nearly killed him. His mother, on the other hand, was depressed and guilty, in part, for marrying a man who was her uncle, and tended to be over solicitous and over-concerned with her son's cleanliness and health. At the same time she tended to neglect her young son, and failed to either protect him from his father's brutality or discipline him for his own violent rages. Dorpat believes that by the age of eleven a borderline personality had formed in the severely abused child, one marked by sadomasochism, a keen distrust for the world, and avoidance of shame.

The monstrousness of the man who emerged to lead Germany in the 1930s, Dorpat contends, was the product of post-traumatic stress disorder—"shell shock" as it was called then— the result of surviving four years in the German trenches during World War I, a seemingly impossible feat.[57] In 1915 Hitler suffered from numbness, headaches, and insomnia, and in 1918 he had a breakdown and was hospitalized for thirty days, during which he was mute and could not see. Dorpat contends that following this breakdown Hitler's character changed dramatically. Though his malevolence took root in childhood, his numbness and lack of empathy, guilt, or concern for human suffering were manifestations of his combat trauma.[58]

By 1925 Hitler had become a murderer. Dorpat claims that, as a result of the splitting-off of his inferiority, shame, powerlessness, and self-hatred, Hitler experienced a vitality, elation, and sense of power and omnipotence in the violence he idealized.[59] An obsessive personality overlay these dynamics, requiring order, perfection, and purity in order to maintain absolute control over his environment. The split-off bad feelings were evacuated onto scapegoats that Hitler could blame for every ill suffered by Germany after the First World War.

The persona that Hitler presented to the masses was that of an ascetic crusader for his motherland, although this idyllic portrait could hardly be further from the truth. His own mother was an object of idealization. Her death in 1907 had left him grief-stricken and broken. Idealization of women went hand in hand with their devaluation and denigration, a split typical of borderline and narcissistic personalities. Hitler's sadomasochism and sexual perversion are well documented. He proclaimed that the only woman he ever truly loved was his half-niece, Geli, Angelika Maria Raubel. When Geli's father died, her mother came to live with Hitler as his housekeeper, bringing along her seventeen-year-old daughter, and her sister. Hitler fell instantly in love with the young woman and over time grew increasingly controlling and possessive of her. In his utter incapacity to love, this may have been his attempt at replacing his dead mother as a love object.

A now declassified wartime document entitled, "A Psychological Analysis of Adolph Hitler," written by psychoanalyst Walter Langer and his colleagues, was commissioned in 1943 by the Office of Strategic Services of the U.S. government. It was based on firsthand testimony, and one of its principle informants was a former Nazi party leader, Otto Strasser, who fell into disfavor with Hitler and escaped Germany during the war. Geli had told him that her uncle would lie on his back and that he liked her to crouch naked over his face, which excited him, whereupon he demanded that she urinate on him. This form of sexual perversion is called urophilia; the vernacular term is "golden showers." This disgusted and repulsed her. Stories have also surfaced about Hitler's exacting and precise drawings of Geli's genitals as seen from below.[60]

In 1931 Geli shot herself with his pistol after a quarrel. Her suicide devastated Hitler. He became suicidal himself, and proceeded to create what amounted to a shrine to her in his house. He put up busts and portraits of her in every room, and forbade her name to be spoken aloud. Some historians suggest that it was after this episode that he became a vegetarian. As one writer puts it, after Raubel's death, Hitler's diet was "free of flesh."[61] It is worth considering that his apparent flight into purity and idealization followed his depravity and displays of contempt and hatred for women. Ultimately, it was the Motherland, Germany, that he held up as his ideal mother.

The next anecdote sheds light on the development of the masochistic component of Hitler's sexuality. The film star Rene Mueller confided to her director, Zeissler, that she had been invited to the Chancellery. She was certain that Hitler wanted to make love to her. They both undressed, but Hitler suddenly fell to the floor and began heaping insults on himself and groveling while he begged the actress to kick him and whip him. When she finally assented he became excited and masturbated to orgasm. They then dressed and sipped wine and chatted as if nothing had happened, and she departed. Soon afterward, Mueller visited London, where she had an affair with a Jewish man. Upon returning home she became a target of the S.S. In her distress she fell into morphine addiction. While recuperating in a sanitarium, she saw from her window a car full of S.S. men pull up to the curb. Fearing that they would torture or kill her, she leaped from the window and was killed by the fall.[62] Her death was apparently not an isolated incident. Of the seven women who were intimate with Hitler, six committed suicide or attempted it. Mueller's and Raubel's stories may be indicative of the murderous self-hatred that he felt compelled to project into the women who would become his denigrated sexual objects.

One last but telling incident, as told by Hitler's photographer, Heinrich Hoffman, occurred at a New Years Eve party where an attractive and excited admirer got Hitler under the mistletoe and impulsively kissed him. The look on his face was one of horror and astonishment, as if he were a helpless child. He fought back anger and embarrassment. The room full of people went quiet and cold. Hitler composed himself, politely thanked his hosts, and took his leave. Dorpat interprets this as a profoundly shame-avoidant reaction. Hitler's maintenance of supreme control in all situations, indicative of a narcissistically damaged personality, was his only means of avoiding humiliation and shame. His suicide at the end of the war can be seen as his final attempt to avoid the shame and humiliation of failure, weakness, and defeat.[63] In this choice we see a form of narcissism in which suicide, the ultimate form of the death instinct, is chosen as a means of insulation against the impingements of life.

Unaware of Hitler's pathology, the masses clamoring for change viewed him as charismatic and inspiring. He evoked heroic images of Nietzsche's "superman," and he brought about the resurgence of Germany's suppressed "will to power."[64] He attempted to wipe the slate clean through the systematic genocide of European Jewry—a wholesale obliteration of Hitler's own white whale. It would seem to be an attempt, as von Franz would say, to hop over the "hole in the staircase,"[65] in order to bury the country's wounded feelings in the unconscious. Historians have argued that the unbearable enormity of the German people's collective shame compelled the nation to seek scapegoats onto which to displace their pain and inferiority.[66] The evacuation of intolerable states of mind is surely a primary basis for all child abuse, racial violence, fanatical terrorism, and war, and it is perhaps the origin of sociopathic behavior as well. What is basic to humanity is lost if one's capacity to bear pain or feel shame for the harm that one's done to others is crippled. A people that cannot grieve its losses suffers dangerous consequences.[67]

The unbearable humiliation that pervaded Germany's broken people many years after their defeat in the first world war, brought about the split in the German psyche that I described in the previous paragraph. The excessive need for external control, regulation, and disciplined order, Jungian analyst Adolf Guggenbuhl-Craig believes, compensates for the unbearable terror and paranoia associated with the psyche's upwelling of feeling states that are often violent, chaotic, or painful. Any capacity for internal or external relationships is obliterated by these defenses. For example, when the Nazi party came to power it was considered one's national duty to report any behavior, even of one's neighbors and family, that varied from the strict moralistic values and authoritarian laws that governed the Third Reich. This exemplifies the way that societies and individuals who demand strict adherence to moral codes of behavior do so not only to maintain order but also as a way to compensate for their lack of *eros*. Eros is seen here as the indwelling capacity to relate compassionately toward others and to care about how one's actions affect another. When one possesses this inner awareness and care, it lessens the need to impose strict moral governance. A sense of being-for-the-other, in Levinas's language, replaces a severe form of moralistic judgment that is imposed by an outer structure.

Guggenbuhl-Craig warns that when nation-states or individuals lack the capacity for eros, they can verge on the genocidal or the sociopathic.[68] Vulnerability is driven underground and replaced by the compulsion to achieve perfection, order, and purity. Jungian analyst Ladson Hinton has decried the dangers of this search for purity and discussed its consequences.

> Genocide, with its nihilistic obsession with purity, is the ultimate illusion of the Clean Slate. These represent a hatred of life in its messy particularity. It is the terrible shadow of Modernity and is a living thing in the contemporary psyche. The desire for purity and perfection exists in all of us. In individual psyches one sees many images of sterile camps and prisons, and an emotional sense of a deathlike void. This is coupled with the narcissist's terror of the "taint of the human." We still partly live in this psychohistorical space. When the idea of the "Clean Slate" or "The Pure" arises, it is wise to wield the scalpel of the skeptic.[69]

• • • • •

Many years ago I worked with a patient who grew up in Germany during the National Socialist Party's rise to power and World War II. My patient recalled joining the Hitler Youth and taking part in glorious Aryan spring renewal rites in pristine pastoral settings. Listening to her stories I imagined Hitler's propaganda machine evoking mythic images of the Teutonic god of renewal, bursting powerfully forth in the spring of a New Day, cleansing the way for the German people to follow. My patient was shielded from any awareness of the inhumanity of the death camps. Like her fellow Hitler Youth, she had blinders on, and she idealized her Führer as the redeemer of Germany. When the truth was slowly revealed, she, like so many, had no way to conceive of anything so monstrous. Just as the calm of her city was shattered by the bombs that turned it to rubble, the framework of what she believed to be real was shattered as well. Her perception of reality had been compressed into so small a space that when she came to find that her deeply held truths were in fact lies, the miniature world she had been enclosed in began to fall to pieces. When she faced the fact that all of her trusted parental figures had betrayed her, and that any sense of purity she might have felt was irreparably poisoned, she was left only with depression and utter despair. All her adult life she carried the burden of shame and pain for all those nameless souls who were lost during the Nazi reign. She bore the shame of having been silent, or for not looking deeper for the truth. Mostly, she felt the pain of responsibility for all those who had shunned responsibility and who had no intention of ever accepting their share of blame.

We wondered together whether a feigned innocence might have been necessary at the time. Perhaps she did not want to know, for the sudden truth revealed so early in her life could have shattered her young and tender mind. But even a perfectly choreographed life, manipulated to dwell only in illusions of purity, goodness, and light could not prevent the eventual destruction of her one-sided reality. With all hell breaking loose just out of direct earshot, truth would come to her as nightmares, depression, panic, anxiety, intestinal problems, and guilt. The things she denied and silenced would find a way to show their faces, to bring balance and a deepening awareness to her of what she had left painfully unacknowledged in the unconscious. You might say that the depression and anxiety symptoms that carried my patient into therapy were what made her human—as the creations of her moral and ethical core. They were the fragments of herself that she needed to gather together, grieve for, and give new life to. When they could be symbolized in the form of thoughts and emotions, her overwhelming symptoms of depression and anxiety eased.

## Conclusion

Destructive narcissism can fix a man in sadistic senex attitudes, just as it can drive him in his puer flights "above life." Dashing any possibility of closeness with the other it compels his exile to the cold and lonely borderlands of psyche, or to moralistic extremism. It is both personal and psychohistorical in origin, pervading both contemporary culture and the individual psyche, and it assumes many forms. It can be recognized in the hatred of uncertainty; the revulsion against anything imperfect, impure, or bodily; the rage and violent retaliation against perceived attack, unbearable humiliation, and shame; destructive envy and the arrogant disregard for humble limits; the quest for knowledge and the superiority of reason and logic over feeling and irrational experiences; the evasion of vulnerability; the presence of self deception and the denial of the harm that one has done to others; the moral condemnation for those who do not share the same beliefs; and ultimately in the negation of love.

All through this litany we hear the fear and suspicion of alterity, both in the world and in oneself. Under its influence, the psyche is split and without cohesion, like a group of feudal kingdoms hostile to one another. If there is to be any hope of transcending narcissism, a man must learn to bear the ambivalence of differences and weigh the options between blind adherence to authoritarianism, and individual reflection. To do so requires what Andrew Samuels has described as a *moral imagination.*

Samuels posits that human conscience derives from the interplay between *original morality*—the traditional teachings of good and bad and right and wrong—and the *moral imagination.* On its own each is deficient, leaving one unable to lead to a moral life. Without its mitigating partner, Samuels writes, original morality, "can be experienced as harsh, vengeful, primitive, and cold. . . . [It can take] the form of a profound suspiciousness of others . . . [in which one can] rejoice in the other's misery when it seems deserved . . ."[70] The law is the law, the rules are the rules, and justice is both blind and cold. There is no mercy. On its own original morality leaves one alone with one's blame and guilt, providing only endless punishment for wrongdoings. Samuels describes its fatal flaw as a split between superiority and inferiority. In its severity it can edge dangerously close to that dark territory inhabited by the Spanish Inquisitor. Yet for a man lacking strength of character or will, the rules enforced by an original morality, with its black-or-white attitudes, may provide the boundaries needed to keep him on the straight and narrow. It may also provide moral outrage when he is faced with injustice.

Moral imagination, by contrast, forces one to face his shadow. Sometimes, Samuels says, it is "*morally permissible* to tell lies . . . [to] break promises. . . ."[71] "[A] weighing up of conflicting claims" may be required.[72] The Dutch household that protected the family of Anne Frank, who was secretly living in their attic, lied to and deceived the Nazis for years. These deceptions were not simply permissible but rather moral imperatives, in service to a higher order. In struggling with what is right or wrong, one must rely upon a reflective relatedness to steer one's course. Errors have consequences, and from them one learns where one's boundaries lie. Morals and ethics are always messy and never clear.

A man's own ethical and moral stance arises, not from some collective obligation to be good and to do the right thing because one is supposed to, but rather from the demand for justice that compels him—no—that transports him above and beyond the law of the day. In this stance he may be moved to rise up against the hypocrisy and tyranny of those who pass as the pure and righteous bearers of what is held out as the truth. This creative individual act is born of a confluence of the original morality and moral imagination in which, in Samuels' words, the former "guarantees the depth and authenticity of moral imagination" while the latter "enables us effectively to use original morality."[73]

## *Notes*

1 James Hillman, *A Blue Fire: Selected Writings by James Hillman*, "Father: Saturn and Senex", Introduced and edited by Thomas Moore, (NY: Harper & Row, 1989), 208. Originally published "On Senex Consciousness," *Spring* (1970): 146-165.

2 James Hillman, "Senex and Puer: An Aspect of the Historical and Psychological Present" (Zurich: Rhein-Verlag, 1968), an offprint from *Eranos-Jahrbuch* XXXVI / 1967, 325.

3 Hillman, *A Blue Fire*, 209.

4 Hillman, *A Blue Fire*, 209.

5 Rosemary Radford Ruether, *Gaia and God: An Ecofeminist Theology of Earth Healing* (New York: HarperCollins Publishers, 1992), 117.

6 Plato, "Phaedo," in *Great Dialogues of Plato*, translated by W.H.D. Rouse (New York: Mentor, 1956), 462–63.

7 The text here is my paraphrase from pages 3–18 of Apuleius, *The Transformations of Lucius otherwise known as The Golden Ass*. Translated by Robert Graves (NY: Noonday Press, 1951) 3–18.

8 Far from the philosopher's ideal state of transcendence of emotion through *apathea*, both the author and his protagonist's initiation into the Mysteries of Isis suggest the surrender of will, a form of psychological death, and a merging with the diety.

9 Apuleius, *The Golden Ass*, xxi.

10 For nine years in his youth, Augustine had adhered to the beliefs and practices of *Manichaeanism*, the Gnostic dualistic religion of Persia.

11 Augustine, Saint, Bishop of Hippo. *Confessions. Great Books of the Western World*, Volume XVIII (Chicago: Encyclopedia Britannica, 1952), 81.

12 Ruether, *Gaia and God*, 135.

13 Henri F. Ellenberger, *The Discovery of the Unconscious* (New York: Basic Books, 1970), 126.

14 Augustine, *Confessions,* Chapter X, Par. 41.

15 Neville Symington, *Narcissism: A New Theory* (London: Karnac Books, 1993), 58.

16 This was evidently the case, as well, with Saint Teresa of Avila, according to the *Encyclopedia Britannica*.

17 John Edward Longhurst, *The Age of Torquemada* (Lawrence, KS: Coronado Press, 1964; at http://vlib.iue.it/carrie_books/longhurst2/07.html, 88–90, accessed 12/26/2009.

18 Anthony Bruno,"The Hammer of Heretics", in "Torquemada and the Spanish Inquisition", 2, at http://www.trutv.com/library/crime/notoriousmurders/mass/torquemada/2.html, accessed 12/26/09.

19 Bruno, "Sangre Limpia", in "Torquemada," 2.

20 Bruno, "Predecessor to Hitler?", in "Torquemada," 2.

21 Machiavelli's classic work, *The Prince* (1513) advocated amoral, deceitful, and ruthless actions if these were needed to achieve power.

22 Opposing one another on the left and right pillars of the mystical Kabbalah's Tree of Life, in an area generally associated with the emotions, are the two *sefirot* of *Chesed*, meaning "mercy or loving kindness," and *Gevurah*, the place of "strength, severity and judgment."

23 William Blake viewed the serpent's role as one of initiation. The innocent couple was compelled to break out of the old and into the new, forsaking Eden through the conscious-making act that Blake named *orc*. In his "Proverbs of Hell" he boasted (perhaps ironically), "The road of excess leads to the palace of wisdom."

24  John Milton, *Paradise Lost* (Indianapolis: Bobbs-Merrill, 1962), VII (line 120). Cited in Roger Shattuck, *Forbidden Knowledge* (New York: Harcourt Brace, 1996), 65.

25  Milton, *Paradise Lost*, VIII (lines 172–78), in Shattuck, *Forbidden Knowledge*, 66. (My italics)

26  Michel de Montaigne, "Apology," in *Oeuvres completes* (Paris: Gallimard, 1962), 501, 588 (Biblioteque de la Pleiade), as cited in Shattuck, *Forbidden Knowledge*, 29.

27  John Beebe, *Integrity in Depth* (New York: Fromm International Publishing, 1995), 58.

28  Milton, *Paradise Lost*, XI (lines 1086–92), 264, as cited in Beebe, *Integrity in Depth*, 58–59.

29  *Mercurius*, the transcendent alchemical image that emerges from the *coniunctio* of the King and Queen (who are also brother and sister) is often perceived as evil from the orientation of the conscious mind. This is because of the ego's instinctive fear of the unconscious, and its reaction against the "immoral pull toward incest" and the incestuous images themselves, which are seen as abhorrent and regressive from the conscious standpoint. However it is precisely through this struggle of consciousness to bear the impact of the unconscious that the image of the Self emerges, namely in the person of Mercurius, who holds both the dark and the light. See *C.W. 16*, "Psychology of the Transference."

30  Shattuck, *Forbidden Knowledge*, 81.

31  Immanuel Kant recognized the Enlightenment as a time when man could begin to use his "own reason without the guidance of another." It was "due not to a lack of reasoning power, but to the lack of decision and courage to make use of it without the guidance of another. . . . Have courage to make use of your *own* reason! Is thus the motto of the Enlightenment." Immanuel Kant, 1784, as cited in Ellenberger, *The Discovery of the Unconscious*, 195. The urgent necessity for change that fueled the Enlightenment came out of a reaction to the bombastic era that preceded it. The Baroque Age had been a time of witch hunts and belief in demonic possession and torture. As it fell into decline, power had began to shift from the Baroque era's monarchs and their nobility to the rising social class of the *bourgeoisie*. The Enlightenment that followed reached its height between 1730 and 1785.

32  The Romantics, in turn, rebelled from the Enlightenment's search for reason and order in all things. The Romantic Age reached prominence in Europe between 1800 and 1830. The Romantics are discussed in Chapter Two.

33  Perhaps the great poet's work reflected elements of an age in great flux, where the fever for revolution and freedom in all things political, cultural, artistic, and scientific reset the bar to limitless heights. Freethinkers were at last unburdened from the shackles of blind subservience to moral traditions and sovereign authority. The late eighteenth century, from which Goethe emerged, wrought massive changes in philosophical thought and in the political arena. The American colonists liberated themselves from Mother England, while establishing a democracy in the romantic image of ancient Greece, and the French caught the fever as well. It "performed the double feat of liberating us from the domination of priests and kings and of creating a civil society based on law and representative democracy" Shattuck, *Forbidden Knowledge*, 231. As the nineteenth century loomed, the "rationalist spirit of the Enlightenment" had become deeply rooted, and was beginning to dispel the antique beliefs in such things as the devil in favor of a rationalist approach. Ellenberger, *Discovery of the Unconscious*, 18. With advances in technology and scientific inquiry, the iron horse of the industrial revolution chugged onward into nineteenth century Europe.

34  Johann Wolfgang von Goethe, *Faust: A Tragedy in Two Parts*, translated by John R. Williams (London: Wordsworth, 1999), 14.

35  Shattuck, *Forbidden Knowledge*, 82.

36  Goethe, *Faust*, 111.

37  Goethe, *Faust*, 447.

38   Shattuck, *Forbidden Knowledge*, 89–90 (my italics).

39   Goethe, *Faust*, 34.

40   Shattuck, *Forbidden Knowledge*, 81.

41   Shattuck, *Forbidden Knowledge*, 84.

42   Retrospectively, the memoir of Claire Clairmont, a self-professed victim of the Romantic experi-
ment in communal living, speaks for those teenage wives and lovers—some of whom attempted
and some that succeeded in their suicide attempts. She viewed the Romantic doctrine of free
love, not as a liberator of stifling and outdated institutions and mores, but as a damaging form of
predation upon the beguiled, the naïve and the innocent. Clairmont, a "devotee" of Lord Byron's
philosophical circle described the powerful spell cast upon her mind and heart by the charismatic,
central figure of the movement, who apparently accepted her advances and made her pregnant
at age seventeen. The hypocrisy, inconsistency, cruelty, and selfishness displayed by various male
proponents of a progressive ideology espousing care and relationality, can not be underestimated,
argues Daisy Hay, the author of the recent book *Young Romantics*. Daisy Hay, *Young Romantics:
The Tangled Lives of English Poetry's Greatest Generation* (New York, NY: Farrar, Straus and Giroux,
2010).

43   Shattuck, *Forbidden Knowledge*, 94.

44   In her critique of the dark side of science, which forever searches for ultimate knowledge and
power at the cost of mother nature, she was not alone. The same themes present themselves later
in Robert Louis Stevenson's *The Strange Case of Dr. Jekyll and Mr. Hyde* (1886), not to mention H. G.
Wells's *The Time Machine* (1894) and Jules Verne's *Twenty Thousand Leagues Under the Sea* (1873).

45   Beebe, *Integrity in Depth*, 59.

46   Herman Melville, *Moby-Dick* (New York: Signet Classic, 1998), 519.

47   Melville, *Moby-Dick*, 519-520.

48   Melville, *Moby-Dick*, 520.

49   Melville, *Moby-Dick*, 521.

50   Ellenberger, *The Discovery of the Unconscious*, 237.

51   Gottfried Benn, *Das moderne Ich* (Berlin: Erich Reiss, 1920). Cited in Ellenberger, *Discovery of the
Unconscious*, 235.

52   Prince Piotr A. Kropotkin, *Memoirs of a Revolutionist* (Boston: Houghton Miflin, 1899), p. 498.
Cited in Ellenberger, *The Discovery of the Unconscious*, 235.

53   From the ashes of Hiroshima a dawning realization arose that, for the first time in history,
mankind possessed a power so terrible that every living thing on the face of the earth could be
annihilated. American children growing up during the McCarthy era witch hunts or the Cuban
Missile Crises were exposed at some level to an emotional climate of collective hysteria or paranoia
based in our powerlessness at the perceived threat of attack by the Great Red Menace, which, it was
feared, would spiral us into war and inevitable world destruction. Much of the worldwide rebellion
by the Beat and Woodstock generations during the 1950s and '60s could be seen as young people's
reaction to this threat of obliteration.

54   Christopher Hauke, "Psychology and the Postmodern," paper presented at the Northwest Alliance for Psychoanalytic Study, Seattle, Washington, May 8, 2003.

55   Henry Picker, ed., *Hitlers Tischgespräche*, 1941-1942 (Bonn: Athenaeum-Verlag, 1951), 227. Cited
in Ellenberger, *The Discovery of the Unconscious*, 235.

56   Theo. L. Dorpat, *Wounded Monster: Hitler's Path from Trauma to Malevolence* (Lanham, MD: University Press of America, 2002).

57  Only two to three percent of all soldiers survived that long. In over fifty battles, he was wounded twice. Personal communication, Ted Dorpat, November 2002, prior to publication of his book, *Wounded Monster*.

58  Richard Raubolt, "Book Review: Wounded Monster," [review of *Wounded Monster: Hitler's Path from Trauma to Malevolence*, by Theo. L. Dorpat], *Journal of Trauma Practice* 3(3), 2004; accessed at http://raubolt.blogspot.com/2007/11/book-review-wounded-monster.html on December 18, 2009.

59  Ted Dorpat, personal communication, November 2002, prior to publication of his book, *Wounded Monster*.

60  Dorpat, *Wounded Monster*, 171.

61  Bee Wilson, "Mein Diat: Adolf Hitler's Diet," *New Statesman* (London) 127(4406): 40ff (October 9, 1998), at http://web.archive.org/web/20050321091219/http://www.findarticles.com/p/articles/mi_m0FQP/is_n4406_v127/ai_21238666, accessed December 19, 2009.

62  Dorpat, *Wounded Monster*, 172.

63  Dorpat, *Wounded Monster*, 247–48.

64  Nietzsche wrote *Beyond Good and Evil* in 1886. "[L]ife is *essentially* appropriation, injury, overpowering of what is alien and weaker; suppression, hardness, imposition of one's own forms . . . exploitation." Friedrich Nietzsche, *Beyond Good & Evil: Prelude to a Philosophy of the Future*, translated by Walter Kaufmann (New York: Vintage Books, 1966), 203. His powerful critique of the violent nature of the human unconscious was appropriated by the Nazi propaganda machine in order to enflame those frantic souls longing for an end to their desperate times.

65  Marie-Louise von Franz, Chapter 12, in *The Problem of the Puer Aeternus* (New York: Spring Publications, 1970), 4–5. [Only numbers for chapters]

66  The zeal of patriotism was fuelled by fear and hatred toward the Jews, and all non-Aryans, who were depicted as parasites, "Christ killers," and the chief villains responsible for contaminating pure bloodlines and keeping the German people down. Robert George Leeson Waite, *The Psychopathic God: Adolf Hitler* (New York: Basic Books, 1977), 308.

67  The September 11 attacks that shocked and wounded America, and the administration's "War on Terror" soon launched in retaliation, could indicate another example of this. September 11 precipitated what Donald Kalsched called a "rupturing of the security membrane" of the United States, a traumatic, unbearable wounding of its vulnerable underbelly. Despite a worldwide outpouring of sympathy and support for its loss, a grieving nation soon went to war on two fronts. While many innocents in the United States were scapegoated and marginalized (such as moderate Muslims), policies chillingly reminiscent of McCarthy's Committee on Un-American Activities were instituted, placing limits on personal rights to freedom and privacy, all in the name of Homeland Security. Journalists and critics were blackballed and fired for opposing views, and the country became alienated from and hated by much of the world community for the administration's unilateral military decisions. All these actions suggest an increasingly rigid need for institutional control in an attempt to manage a threatening and uncertain world. As history has shown, violence and retaliation often occur when traumatic and painful wounds, too shameful to bear, are narcissistically split off and deposited into scapegoats. As is true with both nation-states and heads of state, acknowledgement of one's own vulnerabilities is rarely the course taken in public policy. Interpreted as weakness to oneself or one's enemies, vulnerability leaves one subject to attack and potential annihilation.

68  Adolf Guggenbuhl-Craig, *Eros on Crutches* (Irving, TX: Spring Publications, 1980), 84, 108–09.

69  Ladson Hinton, "How Did We Become 'Modern'?", paper presented during training at the North Pacific Institute for Analytical Psychology, Seattle, Washington, October 16, 2002, 21.

70  Andrew Samuels, *The Plural Psyche*, "Original Morality in a Depressed Culture," (London: Routledge, 1989) 199.

71  Philippa Foot, *Virtues and Vices* (Oxford and NY: Oxford University Press, 1978) 186-7. In Samuels, *The Plural Psyche*, 202.

72  Samuels, *The Plural Psyche*, 204

73  Samuels, *The Plural Psyche*, 196.

## CHAPTER EIGHT

# CLEMENCY ON THE WAY TO THE GALLOWS
# TRANSCENDING TRAUMA AND DISSOCIATION

Torquemada, Dorian Gray, and Mr. Hyde are figures from history and literature, but cruelty like theirs lives in the darkest places of the psyches of men who are characterologically damaged. Such men rarely assent to an examination of their inner workings, nor do they offer an accounting of their actions. Through the son who bears the wounds a father has inflicted on him, however, we may come to understand the violent forces that drive them to perpetrate the crimes they commit. The patient we will meet in the extended clinical vignette that follows, victimized by his predator-father's extremes of pathological narcissism, perverse violence, and sociopathy, had spent a lifetime carrying components of the hated, tainted other for his father.

As a boy, my patient was the very symbol of innocence and purity, the chosen offspring onto whom his father projected a murderous hatred. I believe the father hated the damaged vulnerability he felt in himself and could not bear it, and that he both envied that part of his young son and wished to destroy it. From the time my patient was four and until he was twelve years old, his father both preyed upon him and abjected him through acts of traumatic sexual violence, terror, and deprivation. How the victim of such violence may survive it and even transcend its effects is a mystery. Such words as grace, courage, shared suffering, love, and faith may begin to approach it, but no matter what words we use to describe this ineffable process, somehow a gradual transformation occurred in the patient I am about to present.

My patient married very young, fathered two children and divorced after four years when he could no longer deny his homosexuality. He was the eighth "stair-step" child of ten born to a Catholic family, who came for treatment in middle-age. His father worked for a trucking company and his mother was a stay-at-home housewife whom he initially described to me as innocent and fragile. My patient attended Catholic school, which at first he perceived to be a safe and idyllic haven. He was an altar boy and was considering the priesthood, but when he saw boys being sexually groped in the shower by priests it spoiled the idea for him. Idealization turned to devaluation. His father had been abandoned and was raised in a Catholic orphanage, where my patient suspects he was subjected to extreme conditions of violence, neglect, and abuse.

The sadism and deprivation that his father most likely suffered from the time of his birth have a bearing on my patient's own lifelong obsessive thoughts and fantasies about death: *wishing to be dead, fearing he would be killed, deserving to die, being the willing sacrifice, believing he would die young, working himself to death, suffering and being left for dead,* and more. I believe that in his violent enactments the father had evacuated his own fantasies of death into his son, who then throughout his life carried the image of the "murderer-father" inside himself. In the internal object relations beneath suicidal fantasies, the vulnerable and innocent parts of the child-self may become the envied, bad objects that cannot be tolerated, and that evokes destructive impulses in this murderous part of the psyche. The homicidal internal object attacks the suicidal one.

At the core of my patient's obsession with death lies the binary complex of "saintly martyr" and "condemned criminal," in which ego-identification with either pole leads to fantasies of submission to death as a means of release and freedom from a lifetime of pain.[1]

My patient and I worked together in multiple-times-a-week psychoanalytic psychotherapy for over ten years. Prior to beginning psychotherapy with me "a thin veil" had covered his awareness of those early years of abuse. Toward the beginning of our work a dream fragment prompted a memory of being sodomized as a small child. He told me "It was as if the memory was always there," the veil had simply been pulled aside. In our work over the years I contained his unbearable memories as best I could as they emerged from split-off compartments of his mind and gradually became more integrated. The treatment was fraught with painful regressions but my patient's psyche became increasingly more cohesive.

His father, who passed away one month before my patient's wedding, was an extremely ambivalent figure for my patient. In the young boy's mind, he swung between the daytime caring dad and the nighttime monster. As a result he could disavow his father's monstrous side for periods of time, preserving him in his mind as the ideal father. At times he could feel like the "chosen one"—the object of his father's love and attention. This identification was probably based on incestuous fantasies of fusion of father and son, a state in which all human boundaries and limitations break down. In turn these fantasies evoke inflated, compensatory fantasies of the ego's omnipotence and "oneness" with the archetypal Father.

At other times, when the father's violence became unbearable, my patient wished that his father would just kill him and put him out of his misery. Those times would evoke other inflated fantasies, like that of being God's sacrificial lamb who paradoxically was being punished for disobeying His commandment to honor his father.

My patient never allowed himself to believe that his mother and siblings knew what he was going through, for surely, he thought, if they had, they would have tried to protect him. He decided, therefore, to maintain the secret and protect them by sacrificing himself. The ugly truth was that his mother had some inkling of what was going on but was too terrified to do anything. From early childhood my patient had conspired with his "innocent," "fragile" mother in the maintenance of split-off compartments of truth. Early in our treatment my patient dreamt that *his mother was walking through a pornographic video store with both hands up like blinders, shielding her eyes, pretending not to see where she was.* In this dream his objective psyche poignantly depicts the extent of both her denial and his own.

Once, as a child, my patient was seized by a sudden fantasy of crushing his father's head with a hammer. When the father injured himself shortly afterward, the boy believed he had magically caused the accident. This fantasy may have further reinforced his need to repress his sense of having inflated powers to do evil, powers he secretly feared he had inherited from his father. He could maintain his preferred identification as a saintly, wounded martyr only by disavowing his rage at the years of terror and abuse he had experienced.

My patient took two breaks late in our work. They corresponded to his emerging memories of the two episodes, occurring when he was ten and twelve years old, that are the focus of this clinical excerpt. In each instance his return to psychotherapy a year later initiated a period of shattering self-revelation that collapsed the complexes underlying both his preoccupation with death and his compulsive victimization at the hands of his internalized predator father, who had brought him to the brink of suicide countless times. In the dreams that followed we can see the emergence of long-repressed primal aggression that collapses his identification with the Lamb of God who sacrifices himself to protect his mother, whom he believes to be pure and innocent. His idealization of her crumbles with the stark realization of her culpability in his abuse.

Upon returning to therapy after one of these abrupt breaks, my patient shared a memory that he had wanted to protect me (as the ideal object) from—something that was too horrible for me to know about. He was ten and entering preadolescence, no longer the smooth-skinned androgynous child the pedophile father had tyrannized. After sodomizing him, his father, without warning, impaled him anally with a large instrument like a broom handle, perhaps out of retaliation for losing his preferred sexual object, the young boy. The boy passed out and awoke in the hospital, having barely survived the attack. He was afraid to tell the doctors or nurses who the attacker was. The father fabricated a story to explain his condition. His recuperation at home lasted months and was quite humiliating. He had to lie on the couch in the family living room, "a bloody mess," while his mother changed the towels underneath him. She grew weary of the task and started complaining that his draining wound would ruin the couch. He was filled with shame each time he needed her help. Subsequent psychotherapy revealed his mother to be in complete denial of his father's guilt.

During this same time in the psychotherapy, there was one further crime my patient left me to hold. At age twelve he was witness to his father's murder of a child he had abducted. My patient had accompanied his father on a trip to the railroad tracks where transients often congregated. The father lured a ten-year-old boy who was alone into their car. The boy was brought to the basement of a vacant house and kept captive there for a period of time. My patient could not remember how long. The father put a noose around the boy's neck and hung him. My patient was helpless to save him, being scarcely two years older than the boy. Later his father told him that he had "done away with the body." My patient remembers thinking that the boy was lucky. He was dead, but my patient had to endure living with the memory. Having exposed this darkest secret to me, my patient could not bear to think about it, and he left treatment.

## *Dreams*

When my patient finally resumed therapy a year had passed. Shaky from the side effects of antipsychotic medication, he appeared rigid and dissociated as he described the sleeplessness and the feelings of anxiety and self-destructiveness that had come up following a visit from his mother the month before. She had denied the abuse he had suffered, and he told me that he was successfully using prayer to keep the sin of despair—suicidal preoccupation—from taking over. He presented the following dream:

> I get sentenced to death for killing Mom's white horse. I know it's not my crime but I'm willing to go to the hangman. I'm on a cart being pulled by white horses that collapse and die suddenly. I can't make it to the gallows. What am I going to do now? I wake-up with a gut-ache.

The death of his mother's white horse reminded my patient of a recurrent dream motif from early life, the image of a "pure white virginal bride, a farmer's daughter," whom he had to protect from an evil man. This, he said, was the image of his young, beautiful mother before she was tainted by marriage to his father. He associated the white horse to his fondest memories of his mother, which stemmed from family visits to her childhood farm, where she would ride bareback across the fields, reliving her youth. He thought that was the only time she was really happy. Both the "pure white virgin bride" and the idyllic scene of his mother on horseback can be understood as images of the ideal internal mother object. This was the mother that his martyred child-part would sacrifice himself for in order for her to retain her purity and goodness and be safe from the persecutory "evil man" within himself.

The figure of the virgin bride that my patient had to protect is reminiscent of an aspect of Ferenczi's work with a trauma patient known as "R.N." During R.N.'s treatment, Donald Kalsched tells us, "a remarkable inner object . . . appeared in the patient's trauma experience and saved a seed of personality from total annihilation . . ."[2] My patient may have needed the fantasy of the unadulterated, "pristine child" to survive the violence and mortal danger of his childhood. Through projection he deposited it, for safekeeping, into the image of his mother as an innocent maiden who resided in his mind, far from harm's way.

Associating further to the dream, my patient's thoughts turned to the meaning of the dream gallows, which evoked the memory of the kidnapped boy who was hanged by his father. This brought up his own feelings of culpability for the crime, which in turn evoked his fantasy of hanging himself. In this complex dialogue different self states that he had never given voice to emerged: the guilty accomplice, the innocent martyr, the compliant child, and more.

During this period in our work my patient had great difficulty thinking symbolically about the boy's hanging. He told me that he hadn't tried to save the boy, and he admitted feeling relief that the boy had finally died. He had fantasies of turning himself in to the police for the murder and being sentenced to death—his just punishment. However, when I was able to contain his conviction of guilt, he realized that his dad had needed him as a witness who would *carry his* guilt. Here is an example of the father introjecting his own unbearable guilt into his son to carry for him—forever!

My patient recognized that the pillory cart on which he was being pulled to the gallows in the dream was like those once used to parade criminals through the streets in shame. He had, however, no associations to the horses' collapse while pulling him on the cart. He could only describe his feeling of panic and anxiety upon waking, owing to his uncertainty about "what to do next."

I believe that his uncertainty and panic were a response to his ego's threatened loss of stability. This is an example of John Mills' psychological reformulation of the death drive, in which the fantasy of death is a defense against engagement in life. I offered a tentative interpretation at this time. I wondered if the collapse of the white horses "driving" him to the gallows signifies the collapse of the "condemned criminal" and "martyred saint" complex. In perpetual, compulsive repetition, both poles of this complex led to the fantasy of death and sacrifice as a means of ridding himself of the massive guilt, grief, and unbearable pain his wounded internal child experienced. These were things no child should ever have to bear. The ego's loss of identification with this familiar complex might, I thought, be triggering his panic and distress about what to do next.

As my patient's complex showed signs of collapse, the underlying bitter truth—that his mother shared culpability for his abuse—began to emerge. The death of her white horse, I believe, signifies the loss of his belief in his mother's innocence and his idealization of her.

This too aroused great ambivalence, feelings of uncertainty, and panic in him. He admitted that she allowed him to go off with his father and never protected him. The gut-ache that he awoke with from the dream was perhaps a response to his recognition of her guilt.

With this violent blow to his obsession with death, anger and rage at his father and mother began to emerge. It had never been safe enough for these primal emotions to be consciously felt, and the result was tumultuous and terrifying to his ego-complex, because these impulses triggered fear of retaliation from the internal persecutor. My patient was frightened that his anger would turn him into his father and that his fragile mother would be destroyed by his rage. He would rather be dead, he felt, than to be identified with his father's violence. This triggered a suicidal depression.

The next dream was horrifying because it brought back memories of his impalement and the murder of the boy.

> I was on a respirator, but I was watching too as my adult self. [Perhaps this indicates some reflective capacity?] I am ten or twelve years old. It's happening again. Mom is put out, and she's being asked to clean up the mess, because I have soiled myself. Next to me in a bed is a fifty-five-year-old ethnic man. It's the murdered boy, all grown up. He's on life support and mom unplugs him. He convulses and strangles to death. Then a cleanup crew in armor and masks—like hazardous materials protective suits—come in and they are dripping with fluids. When they are done, one of the guys leaves the room and takes off the suit. Underneath he is wearing a cashmere sweater and its you [Ken].

Initially, my patient could not consider the dream symbolically. He took it as an injunction to kill himself. In my own response to it I felt a sense of relief at seeing the ruthless, deadly side of the mother finally unveiled. At the same time, I had thought that my patient had been keeping the murdered boy alive in his psyche as an aspect of himself, and that his mother had pulled the plug on him, as if to say "let him go." I thought of the unplugging in relation to the idea of the Self and its often violent impact upon the ego-complex and its identification with the complexes.

My patient was moved by the fact that the "dream Ken" was not afraid of dealing with the "bloody mess." This indicated, perhaps, that I possessed a sufficient enough "skin" (in the form of the protective suit) to tolerate the toxic process. Here Winnicott's idea of the infant's need for his mother to survive his aggressive attacks and to metabolize his unbearable pain came to mind. My patient's own mother could do neither. According to Winnicott, if the mother does not "survive," then she is not felt to be real.

With this awareness of my capacity to tolerate his turbulent psychic contents, my patient could begin to acknowledge how much he had idealized me and how much he had hated having to protect me over the years from his painful memories and his anger. "I treated you with kid gloves," he said. In his mind, I had become the fragile, virgin mother whom he needed to protect as a means of disavowing his own dependency upon me. He was beginning to see me as the bad object beneath the ideal one, a development that was accompanied by his expression of long-repressed, aggressive feelings that he experienced in the transference. My ability to tolerate them helped to normalize these feelings.

In my patient's next dream, he has become a "man-wolf," with the head of a wolf and the body of a man, who viciously attacks a young woman working in a hat store, ripping her throat, with blood spurting everywhere. He is naked and has an enormous erect penis. He realizes that he has killed her to protect her from being violently raped. My patient was terrified that the dream implied that he was identifying with his monstrous internal father and that he was not going to be able to stop himself from acting out violently. I thought it interesting that this "man-wolf" was protecting the girl from his phallic aggression by killing her. I wondered if his reaction signified his inability to differentiate between his own, potentially healthy phallic aggression and that of his internalized, sexually violent, predator father.

From the "man-wolf dream" ambivalent, unacceptable, yet pleasurable and potent sexual memories, related to later adolescence, emerged in him. These memories suggested the possibility of some *unknown third thing*—what Jungians call the "transcendent third"—that threatened the ego's identification with the masochistic complex underlying his abuse history. But when these potent sexual feelings became too much to bear he split them off. He went to the bathhouse and acted out the familiar role of the sexual victim. Taking the submissive role triggered post-traumatic memories of his being impaled when he was ten, reinforcing his feeling that it would be too dangerous to own his own phallic power.

When the Lenten season arrived my patient immersed himself in prayer. As he described them, his prayers had an ecstatic, manic quality. He came to our session just before Easter announcing that this would be our last time together. He had realized, he said, that his memories of the abuse were all lies. He asked for my forgiveness and assured me that his Hail Marys and his prayers would keep him safe from the sin of suicidal despair. I expressed my concern that he had swung back into identification with the "saint," and I worried about the condemned boy. He promised to call if his suicidal feelings returned. He had taken flight into the ideal of purity as a manic defense, using prayer to put away the man-wolf inside of him.

Three days later, deeply depressed by a violent dream in which his mother had died, he called to reschedule. In this dream, he did not wish to face his family at the funeral and went to his sister's house afterwards. He started firing her semiautomatic pistol, and the trigger got stuck. He was shooting blindly, putting holes in the ceiling. Everyone was ducking in fear. He noticed me crouching behind a couch.

This dream led him back into making suicidal plans, but his concern for me and his recognition of how deeply his loss would affect me prevented him from carrying them out. Yet with suicide not an option he became deeply worried about his powerful and violent feelings getting out of control with his family and with me. He joked about "almost wing-ing me" with the Uzi semiautomatic. He feared that I would hate him and send him away if he hurt me.

His suicidal thinking then began to subside. Easter marked an important renewal time for him. He looked forward to coming in to therapy because he was no longer mad at me. He was beginning to see me in a more ambivalent way, as someone "good-enough," in Winnicott's phrase, who he could fight with and get angry at. This was something new for him.

The last dream I will recount continues with the theme of violence.

> My ex [a man he had lived with for over ten years] is walking our old female rottweiler. I'm mad at my ex. She has chomped a chihuahua and killed it. I have always associated my mother with chihuahuas. I think it's her that my dog has killed. Then my old dog turns on my ex and kills him, too. I fear for her safety. I was trying to protect her from being put to sleep.

My patient associated chihuahuas with being tiny, neurotic, helpless, and fearful, just like his mother. In the dream he wasn't concerned about his dog's violence, but he feared reprisals from the authorities for her aggression. The repeated theme of his fear of being met by retaliation for his aggression is present here. It is interesting that he was afraid of her being "put to sleep," which is how he imagined his suicide. But now he was protective of his beloved animal—his internal instinctive power—and would fight to keep her safe from harm. This may speak to the renewed life-giving capacities that were fueling his increasing sense of agency. The destruction of the chihuahua represents the negative aspects of the mother that he had dislodged from their dominant place in his psyche, thus opening up the possibility of retaining the parts of his internal mother that are viable, loving, and free of the negative complex.

In my patient's repetitive fantasies, death is the unconscious representation of relief, certainty, and freedom from a life of pain. These fantasies emerge in reaction to the internalization of his father's primitive destructiveness, which aims to enslave and annihilate him. His role as perpetual victim of his father's predations has taken the ego-syntonic form of the privileged "saintly martyr" who sacrifices himself to protect his idealized mother. It is she upon whom he unconsciously projects vestiges of his pristine child-self so that something of himself may survive. As Kalsched writes, "the archetypal world functions to defend the traumatized psyche against further trauma."[3]

In the process of analysis the internal, abject part of my patient that we know as the "condemned criminal" emerged through memories of his perceived role as accomplice in the unknown boy's abduction and murder. As the truth slowly dawned upon him, his illusions of his mother's purity and innocence could not be sustained. As his ego became more integrated and he became more able to bear the conjunction of the two irreconcilable opposites of martyr and criminal, we began to glimpse the transformation of his aggression into assertiveness and intentionality.

Like Echo, my patient had surrendered all his power to the colonizing father, and as with Dorian Gray's lover, Syl, thoughts of suicide and the fantasy of relief from pain that accompanies it were his only relief from abject suffering. He was subject to the insane swings of his father's Jekyll and Hyde personality, he resembled the Jew that Torquemada violently denied in himself, and he was entrapped like one of the four hundred maidens hoarded by Clinschor in his Castle of Wonders.

But in contrast to all these figures, in my patient a third, new way emerged from within, through a momentous struggle to transcend his condition. Two years after we terminated analysis, my patient reported that he was doing well. He had returned to the Church, made his first confession since he was twelve, and received his first communion. He was in a serious relationship that had begun a year earlier, with a man he was engaged to be married to. The memories of his wounds are always with him, but rather than bursting in upon him without warning like ghouls from some dark place in his soul, now they form only a part of the continuum of his existence.

• • • • •

How can love find a way when a lifetime is spent in concealment, and when the trauma of one's wounds, grief, humiliation, and shame is so violently disavowed? Often, a silent but stony hatred grows toward one's own interior vulnerability, a vulnerability felt with such intensity that it must be ejected and deposited into another. The other then becomes the hated object to which all links are ruthlessly severed.

In other scenarios, secret abuses are perpetrated upon once-idealized and now debased scapegoats—in retaliation against the taint of humanity that threatens to breach the clean-rooms of the mind, as one of my patients put it. In some men a saccharine goodness and submissiveness hides a split-off chamber of fantasied sadomasochistic horrors. In others, aesthetic ideals and feelings of fundamental righteousness and intellectual perfection elevate and inflate the subject, who sunders heaven from earth in his own being. Yet at the same time he exterminates the marginalized, the abject, and the unique—destroying all differences. These are the primal acts of destructive narcissism that isolate and encapsulate one's being.

In the rare cases that defy the odds, something other, something violent and decentering, may come to affect the life of the individual, demolishing the ego's embedded narcissism and confronting the individual with his long-disavowed grief and humiliation. In these rare moments, love may find a way.

## *Notes*

1 The re-visioning of Freud's death drive, and the process of repetition compulsion that lies at its heart, hypothesize regression to fantasies of a preanimate existence in which the ego is encapsulated in a perpetual, pain-free state. In this fantasy the ego assumes that it can know and understand the incomprehensible as a way of disavowing memories of unbearable agony. The concepts put forth in Melanie Klein's *paranoid-schizoid position* and in Kalsched's description of the encapsulation of the wounded and aggressive internal child objects in the *self-care system*, further elucidate this stabilizing yet agonizing repetition. Klein's paranoid-schizoid position describes a form of splitting which can be viewed in Jungian terms as the ego being possessed by complexes. Kalsched's self-care system is comprised of persecuting and protecting "archetypal defenses," that defend the ego-self against the threat of re-trauma.

2 Donald Kalsched, "Trauma and Daimonic Reality in Ferenczi's Later Work," *Journal of Analytical Psychology* 48(4) (2003): 479.

3 Kalsched, "Trauma and Daimonic Reality in Ferenczi's Later Work," 48.

# PART THREE

# THE SHATTERING GAZE

*While she clung to him, utterly bewildered with delight, the lamp which she was still holding, whether from treachery or from envy, or because it longed as it were to touch and kiss such a marvelously beautiful body, spurted a drop of scalding oil on the God's right shoulder. What a bold and impudent lamp . . . so to scorch the God of all fire! Cupid sprang up in pain, . . . spread his wings and flew off without a word.[1]*

## *Introductory Remarks*

On this fateful night, when Psyche burns the sleeping Eros with the oil from her lamp, one lover dares to break the spell and bring about the end of her state of dark union with her mysterious lover. Desire drives Psyche to finally glimpse the face of the other. As the light of the *lamp's scalding oil* opens the night to bring the truth to awareness, the penetrating energies spilled by Psyche's trembling hand illuminate the darkness. This in turn reveals the true agent of this soul awakening—her shattering gaze. Psyche believes Eros to be a viperous serpent, and she is prepared to cut off his head with the *knife* she wields. This is a tool of discernment that can sever her from their erotic fusion. Beneath her obsession lies the accusation that exposes the monstrous narcissism of Eros, a narcissism that must possess and devour his erotic objects. In a wounding both provoked by and for the sake of the Other, Psyche's violent act of consciousness shatters the more subtle and endless violence of sameness that Eros has imposed.

Beholding the face of Love in the lamp's light Psyche is startled. She spills the oil upon the bare shoulder of Eros. The perfect skin of the young god is burned, wounding him deeply. Awakened, he springs up and flies from the scene, admonishing his bride for spoiling their secret love tryst. He scurries back to his mother Venus so that she can nurse his wound.[2] The consequences of these events lead to the couple's separation, suffering, and trials, and then to transcendence when Psyche and her Eros find one another in a new way.

Through the wounding of Eros the lovers sacrifice the sentimental patina that surrounds the paradise of their immature, romantic love with its fiery passion and blind possession. Until then their passion has melted away time and boundaries, leaving them withdrawn from life in a twinned state of fusion. Shattering the limited dimensionality of the romantic love dyad requires a third element. In this instance it is the jealous sisters who are the agents of a cataclysmic change that enables the emergence of a third dimension. A cleavage of the original unreflected state must occur for the lovers to avoid the dark fate of Narcissus, who is unwittingly transfixed by a reflection of his own beautiful appearance, and then consumed in a perpetual state of paralysis until he fades away.

The sisters' destructive envy compels them to poison Psyche's mind with distrust for her husband, whose face she has never beheld in the light of day and who they claim is a monster. The ego often regards new truth as monstrous, and it initially seems impossible to assimilate. Psyche, however, courageously seeks to know the truth in all its monstrosity, whatever its catastrophic effect upon the ego's illusions.[3] The Greek word for truth, *aletheia*, captures this moment of unveiling or unconcealment. *Aletheia* often has an uncanny aspect that may arise from the negative as it does in Psyche's sisters, so that the apparent shadow contents also serve the function of truth.

The illumination that Psyche glimpses here also has to do with becoming distinct, *one in relation to an other*, as opposed to being what Neumann calls a "languorously ensnared being."[4] By her act, Psyche brings into being a moment of consciousness that disrupts her state of archetypal inflation. Psyche, who signifies *the psyche* as such, finds the truth overwhelming. She cannot grasp it because she is too weak and immature to contain it. Eros' sudden flight to Venus can be seen as the ego's further regression to the mother complex and its protective envelope.[5] We can understand his regression as resulting from a splitting process in the male psyche in which the ego's inability to bear life's intimate, emotional encounters has produced traumatic symptoms. These symptoms are represented by Psyche's compulsive suicide attempts as she wanders alone and aimlessly throughout the land. Psyche's suicidality reflects the repetition compulsion inherent in the death instinct, as we have seen in Chapters Two and Eight; that is, the impulse toward annihilation envisioned as relief and freedom from life's suffering and hardships.

Interpersonally, Eros, as a mother-bound man, is "mother's little god." He is enthralled with an erotic object of desire who is his to possess in body and mind. But in this inflated state his ego suffers a sudden narcissistic wounding that severs the death coniunctio. The wound is only skin deep, but it exposes how close the ego's vulnerability is to the surface. It presents Eros with a dimension he cannot bear to see. Psyche's act signifies, as Levinas puts it, a stripping of the ego of "its pride and . . . dominating imperialism. . . ."[6] Both Eros' withdrawal and Psyche's suicidal gestures demonstrate the ego's initial reactions of avoidance, denial, and resistance to the shattering of its defenses. Flying away in a retreat to apparent safety within the mother complex, Eros attempts to restore himself through Kalsched's notion of the "archetypal defenses of the self-care system."[7]

Apuleius' allusions to the lamp oil's "treachery or envy" in scorching Eros' tender shoulder point to the darker aspects of the fires of erotic passion that are sacrificed through Psyche's light-bringing act.[8] That divine madness compels lovers to betray, to kill, to covet, or to obsess about an unobtainable desire, all in the name of Eros. But the fantasy of an ultimate satisfaction so typically sought in obsessional erotic pleasures never achieves the definitive escape from ordinary life it envisages. Instead, only drowsiness and sleep arrive, or even the sadness that overtakes one post coitus.[9] The escape is flawed and only momentary. In the terrible deflation that ensues after the wounding and withdrawal of the god of fire, Psyche too experiences a separation from her unconscious identification with a dark, erotic obsession that was consuming, blinding, and momentarily self-gratifying. In the narcissistic psyche such a moment brings the possibility of awareness of the split between intimate love and predatory sexuality.

Following her expulsion from the lovers' paradise, Psyche undergoes the four difficult and at times near-fatal trials Venus puts her through. Psyche longs to restore, at a new level, the lost union of the lovers.[10] Psychologically, these tasks represent the slow and gradual process of integrating what the psyche could not fully know or hold in the shock of love's momentary illumination in the bedchamber. The compulsive symptoms of suicide are gradually transformed into the symbolic death and rebirth of initiation.

In this aspect, Psyche symbolizes the *anima*'s differentiation from the taint of the maternal complex, a process originally set in motion in this tale by the work of the shadowy sisters. As each task is accomplished the nascent agency of the psyche gradually gains the resiliency and cohesiveness needed to bear the vicissitudes of life and relationships.[11] But in completing the last undertaking Psyche disobeys Venus's command that she return Persephone's ointment of eternal beauty to the goddess.[12] Psyche's disobedience may signify the psychic intentionality of *psyche-anima-soul* that is beginning to separate from the rigid and habitual patterns characteristic of the maternal complex. Psyche then falls into a "death-like sleep" that somehow allows new capacities for love to emerge from her "sacrifice."

Psyche's "death" is an initiatory one, leading to reunion when Eros comes to her side. Like his initial withdrawal, his eventual return to Psyche is set in motion by his shattering awakening in the bedchamber. This awakening calls Eros to his responsibility, despite the ego's futile efforts to deny its burning torment and shame through a short-lived return to the mother. Here Eros, transformed through the fire, signifies a moral subject, a self steadfast and differentiated enough to break free of his maternal narcissism, who then comes to Psyche in a heroic way, as Hillman says, to awaken the slumbering soul through love.[13] His transformed selfhood is predicated upon a sense of being-for-the-other and an intent to live in awareness of this truth. *Love is hostage to Other*! It is Eros' turn to induce Psyche's awakening from her complacent slumber. This awakening evokes an "insomnia" in the psyche, that never rests from the awareness of the responsibility it assumes toward the Divine recognized in the face of the other, a divinity that is described by Levinas as a "saying prior to anything said . . ."[14]

Psyche has gone through death for the sake of Eros, sacrificed herself for the other. In Levinas's *Totality and Infinity* he writes, "Death, source of all myths, is *present* only in the Other, and only in him does it summon me urgently to my final essence, to my responsibility."[15]

The mythic couple then ascends from this world, not in death as such—far from it—but to the heavenly hall of the Gods, where Psyche drinks the ambrosia of eternal life. She undergoes an *apotheosis*—the transformation of mortal into god. The child born to the two of them is called *Voluptas*. Upon the lover's transformation of her material substance into spirit the *third* emerges from the *two*. This is known theologically as *transubstantiation*—as in wafer and wine becoming the body and blood of Christ. Yet despite the temptation to view her ascendance as a transcendence of the symmetry and fusion of erotic love, Psyche's abandonment of all earthly limits prompts the nagging suspicion that love will always be searching for some mystery to be found only in the far, far beyond—a beloved that can never be grasped or embodied in a good-enough life in the here and now.

Perhaps one could view this process as cyclical, with an expectation that it will recur on another level. But we cannot transcend time and earthly existence, and this lesson has to be learned over and over again. Is the final apotheosis itself another level of narcissistic illusion? If so, it bears a resemblance to the courtly romances in which star-crossed lovers can only hope for union in Heaven, because there they may find or experience (the illusion of) wholeness and finality through a spiritual love.

And yet Eros and Psyche's child is called *Voluptas*—Latin for voluptuousness—filled with *earthly* pleasure and sensuous delight. Her birth to the awakened and "ascended" lovers may present an inkling of Love—unbound from narcissism—that is ambiguous, paradoxical, transcendent—the Erotic and the sacred Beloved. Such love is both passionately self-gratifying and compassionately for the other. Enduring love calls for interpenetrating boundaries and at the same time for autonomy, acceptance of difference, and the placing of the other before self. As we proceed, the meaning of these paradoxes will be further considered.

· · · · ·

The *burn that wounds* Eros leads to an initiation into a greater story, a symbolic searing open of the narcissistic skin surface, a disruption of the illusion of calm, superficiality, and sameness that is prompted by the overwhelming need for control. Here in Apuleius' story we glimpse a hope for transcendence of the narcissistic currents within a man. As psyche matures, coalesces, and gains resilience, love's capacity is no longer bound, either to the puerile patterns of maternal narcissism or to the allure of the *elemental Eros* that can be described as a form of darker erotic fusion.

With the wounding that pierces the ego's grandiosity, the suffering psyche—stricken, outraged—is exposed to the shattering call of the Other. In its wounding by the Other the psyche is loosened and released from its identity with the Same. In the language of Levinas, "the psyche in the soul is the other in me."[16] The Same, now a psyche that denies its own self-importance for the sake of the other, has entered into service to the other.

In this context, Jung's notion of the *Self* appears in a different light. I believe that his description of the ineffable, enigmatic Self borders on a religious or philosophical—rather than psychological—idea that transcends the psyche and might be better described as the *Self akin to Other*. Although Jung tends to qualify his "non-psychological," theological discussions as merely personal speculation, he does write that the concept of the Self is "a construct that serves to express an unknowable essence which we cannot grasp as such, since by definition it transcends our powers of comprehension. It might equally be called the 'God within us.'"[17] Yet even his consideration of such an inward, underlying "essence" and its indwelling nature as a "God *within*" restricts the larger possibility that what he is describing may also, in fact, *transcend* psyche.

The Self may initiate a violent wounding of the psyche through its shadow agents, as Lucy Huskinson describes. Its effects are not always benevolent nor do they always serve a higher purpose. Trauma and tragedy can evoke useless suffering and even shatter a fragile psyche that cannot bear it. Or, the impact of the Self may rend asunder the fixed orientation of the narcissistically bound ego. In the words of Simon Critchley, the violence of the Self as an unknowable Other may bring trauma that "tears into my subjectivity like an explosion, like a bomb that detonates without warning, like a bullet that hits me in the dark, fired from an unseen guy and by an unknown assailant."[18]

Traces of the Self may emerge from primary, unconscious processes like dreams, or they may impact our lives through the traumas we suffer in the relational world. The destabilizing of the ego comes about through these enigmatic processes, accompanied by the feelings of grief and loss that follow. New and imaginative possibilities may then emerge— retranslations of the enigmatic experience that I feel are akin to what Jung would describe as the work of the transcendent function.[19] It awakens an emotional aliveness that transcends and is untethered by the repetitive malice of the complexes.

Like the Other, Jung's Self, understood more deeply in this way, transcends the traditional, constructed dualism that views 'inner' and 'outer' as if something is either actually inside one's head or outside only as another person in some concrete sense.[20] For example, the powerful impact of the Self may be felt within from the big dream or outside in the shattering human encounter or trauma. In my view, however, it transcends both psychic process and physical phenomena. Like the Other the Self is "exterior" to both inner and outer and should not be taken too literally, for it is not spatial nor can it be measured or represented. Certain contemporary ideas in philosophy question this distinction between inner and outer, as well. Lacan's paradoxical term *extimetée*, for instance, speaks to this by conflating exteriority with intimacy. The external is also and at the same time the most intimate. In this regard, Jung's concept of an enigmatic, unknowable Self bears a resemblance not only to Levinas's Other, but to the Torah's religious idea of YHVH—*I AM*—the unspeakable name for the Holy One of Being, whose infiniteness can never be encompassed by any human concepts or understanding.

In Levinasian thinking, our subjectivity comes into existence through the impact of the primacy of the Other, which *precedes* our own being, and to which we are responsible before all else. This is what Levinas calls his First Philosophy. Here the Other is regarded as something outside the bounds of what we conceive to be our internal subjectivity. Laplanche corroborates this with his idea of the "decentered self." Our subjective core develops only within and through a relationship to an "other," like the earth around the sun, or a baby to its mother.[21]

Levinas's existential phenomenology would view the *self* ontologically, in line with the more limited, traditional definition—that is, as an inner essence or internal Being, that is at the core of the psyche's totality and *not* transcendent to it. Levinas would consider anathema any notion that a subject might be filled by "grand truths," when these are imparted by a self that places personal development above responsibility to others.[22] The subject Levinas envisions is instead a humble one. Having witnessed cases where a man's humble self awakens, I recognize the importance of his idea, because in its achievement, narcissism is transcended.[23]

The Levinasian critique of the *self* as the center of one's being, however, does not consider the deeper conception of the *Self* as transcending the psyche and its totality, decentering the ego, and ushering a humble subjectivity into being. This contemporary concept has not found its way into Levinasian scholarship. It is understandable, then, that this argument will raise questions among readers familiar with Levinas's ideas, who might take issue with the correspondence of Self with Other, and Ego with Same.

As I see it, the Levinasian view of the *self* as an inner essence at the core of the psyche's totality—and not transcendent to it—describes Jung's subjectively experienced *psychological self*.[24] It fails to encompass the more radical and contemporary Jungian view of the *Self*, informed by exploration of Jewish mysticism and Levinas's own philosophy. This contemporary view describes the Self as an enigma, a radical Other, an infinite mystery that cannot be reduced to origins in the psyche, that shatters sameness as the sine qua non of self experience, and that draws the subject into an ethical relationship to the world in which the infinite obligation to the other is recognized.

Analytical Psychology's contemporary view of the Self corresponds not to Levinas's conception of the ontological self but to Levinas's First Philosophy. It is his First Philosophy which will be crucial to the creation of a *unifying theory of the transcendence of narcissism.* Part Three will be concerned with this issue. It is my considered opinion that only something transcendent and utterly other than oneself can shatter a man's narcissism, forcing him out of what has enclosed him and out of what he has defined himself to be. It does not matter what name we give to this agent of change, whether we call it the Other, the Self, the Hand of God, or the trauma that crosses my path, but from its decentering of the self, the nascent beginnings of a humble, resilient being may appear.

Others in relationship with this more resilient subject can then be recognized not as objects to be colonized to serve one's needs, but rather as presences with whom one feels a sense of the sacred and the vulnerable. This may suggest a new perspective on the ineffable nature of the mystic's surrender to the Beloved. In this surrender one might glimpse a trace of God, not as an idea or an inner vision of oneness that draws one away from the human cry, but as the awakening of one's responsibility for others. This responsibility remains at times a torment, a burden one might wish to be relieved of. It may be felt but remain unclear. When faced with the shattering gaze of the most naked and fragile other, one may not know what to do or how to respond.

What I am suggesting is that beyond the satisfaction of one's need for private personal relationship,[25] a new orientation may arise, leading to expressions of love of a different nature. This may be akin to the welcoming of a stranger, the offering of charity, compassion for the suffering of others, or the love of justice for all. These wider possibilities for love are the antithesis of the narcissistic option.[26]

* * * * *

Part Three delves further into the processes that can awaken a man encapsulated in the modes of narcissism described earlier as defensive and destructive. What the open wound reveals is a man who is broken—whose psyche is split and who cannot love. In the fortunate case, the catastrophe of this wounding initiates the analytical work necessary to expose and renounce the illusions projected by the light of romantic love. This may also bring to an end the man's need to triumph over emotional deprivation. A good-enough kind of loving—mutual, intimate, mature—can emerge from a resilient and more cohesive psyche, made so through the work of the transcendent function. These qualities are crucial to one's ability to bear separation, frustrated longing, and closeness in relationships. In addition, the tempering heat of analysis can participate in the psyche's development of the resilience it will need to survive its ongoing shattering by the traumatic Other in the endless challenges of life.

In the first two parts of this book I have drawn primarily on the theoretical formulations of analytical psychology, object relations, and contemporary psychoanalysis because they are useful lenses through which to explore narcissism's overwhelming engulfment of the individual ego. The ego that is caught and must remain *at the surface* defends itself against shattering incursions from internal emotional states and the relational world. In contrast, Part Three of this book attempts to translate Levinas's thought into a "psychology for the other." While that may go beyond his own intent, my feeling is that this approach nevertheless offers possibilities for the transcendence of narcissism. Thus you will notice a shift in focus from narcissism's pathology of self-isolation to a psychology of exteriority rather than interiority, along with the introduction of psychoanalytic ideas that privilege intersubjectivity and relationality. The three chapters that comprise Part Three are summarized below:

**Wounded by the Other**. A humble subject emerges from the violent encounter and incursion by the Other that shatters the ego's entrenched narcissism. Often it is tragedy, crisis, or loss that provokes this traumatic awakening and decentering of the psyche and arouses one's ethical sense of responsibility for the other. An emotional depth may emerge from the enigmatic core of one's being, bringing greater dimension to consciousness and reopening links to interpersonal relationships. This wounding process can best be described as the *shattering gaze of the Other*.

**Emergence of the Father**. The ego's calcified attitudes break down when confronted by the truth, as revealed by the violence of the shadow, which is then allowed to bring new qualities to the psyche, qualities of resilience, agency, and a sense of care for the other. An ethical subjectivity appears, tempered by suffering and the bearing of shame, as the *Father Principle* emerges.

**The Capacity to Love: Transcending the "Heat-Death" of Eros**. The work of the transcendent function awakens a *transcendent relationality* in the humble subject. Through this experience he may develop a capacity to bear the tensions in love, produced by conflict, separation, suffering, and loss. The intimate surrender that reveals the man to his lover, and his new acceptance of the needs and human limitations of the other, inescapably affect him and those with whom he is in relationship.

### Notes

1  Apuleius, *The Transformations of Lucius otherwise known as The Golden Ass*. Translated by Robert Graves (NY: Noonday Press, 1951), 118.
2  In a sense he transits from one "good mother" back to the other "good mother" as the lover's paradise and the mother's nurturing embrace both represent aspects of regression within the mother complex.
3  Richard Kearney, *Strangers, Gods and Monsters* (New York: Routledge, 2003).
4  Erich Neumann, *Amor and Psyche* (Princeton, NJ: Princeton University Press, 1956), 78.
5  I suggest a "further" regression, for indeed the lovers were "there" from the beginning.

6  Emmanuel Levinas, *Otherwise Than Being: Or, Beyond Essence* (Pittsburgh, PA: Duquesne University Press, 1998), 110.

7  Donald Kalsched, *The Inner World of Trauma: Archetypal Defenses of the Personal Spirit* (London: Routledge, 1996), 12.

8  Perhaps the "treachery and envy" could also be viewed as the ego's judgment of the painful process of deflation of the death coniunctio state, which cannot contain the "fluidic energies" of the lamp's oil.

9  After love all animals are sad. Whence this sadness? From the Latin proverb.

10  We see here the ambivalent nature of the archetype, as Venus is both the "regressive Mother" as well as the one who sets the tasks before Psyche that lead to psychic transformation.

11  In each of the tasks, Psyche is either aided by or must confront dangerous masculine figures, so that she might develop positive *animus* qualities. See Neumann for more details.

12  Psyche selfishly keeps the beauty ointment for herself to enhance her own beauty in the eyes of Eros.

13  James Hillman, *The Myth of Analysis* (Evanston, IL: Northwestern University Press, 1972), 55. Eros' heroic act signifies the prefiguration of the self.

14  Levinas, *Otherwise Than Being*, 145.

15  Emmanuel Levinas, *Totality and Infinity*, translated by Alphonso Lingis (Pittsburgh, PA: Duquesne University Press, 1969), 179.

16  Levinas, *Otherwise Than Being*, 68–69.

17  *C.W. 5*, 238.

18  Simon Critchley, *Ethics–Politics–Subjectivity: Essays on Derrida, Levinas, and Contemporary French Thought* (Brooklyn, NY: Verso, 1999), 190.

19  Ladson Hinton, "The Enigmatic Signifier and the Decentred Subject," *Journal of Analytical Psychology* 54(5) (2009), 641.

20  Jung actually held that the psyche is not to be found inside us, but between us and everything else we experience, so that in effect psyche exists in everything. Intuited from the beginning in his thinking was the idea of a non-dualistic experiential relationship between psyche and outer reality, with the subject already immersed in an empathic relation with the object. In *Psychological Types*, (*C.W. 6*, 46-64) he calls this *esse in anima*, to be in soul, which applies to everything the psyche experiences. His idea of the analytic transference as a shared psychological field between analyst and patient was a clinical instance of this, and served as a precursor to contemporary understandings of intersubjectivity as the key to what enables psychotherapy to proceed. See *C.W. 16, The Practice of Psychotherapy*, "The Psychology of the Transference," 211-235. His theory of synchronicity attempted to explain the uncanny connectedness between emergent states of mind and developing realities in the physical universe. It led to his development of the medieval idea of *unus mundus*, the world's latent unity, (*C.W. 14, Mysterium Coniunctionis*, 533-543. ) meaning that the unconscious can become apparent to the psyche through its manifestations in the world. The seeds of these ideas seem to have come through Jung's life experiences, two of which I will share here. In his lonely early childhood, Jung was not in a position to share much of his emotional life with his parents, but his dissociation from human self objects was healed through fantasy and play, where he endowed outer objects like rocks, fire and a carved wooden manikin with great meaning, treating them as extensions of himself and deriving solace from them. As he would have put it later, his personality extended into these objects through identification with their archetypal meanings. In midlife, he detailed a strange encounter with what he described as an assembly of spirits, ghosts of Anabaptists who appeared in various poltergeist phenomena, such as the ringing of the front

door bell of his house in Kusnacht, not only to his perception but to that of other members of his family. In a mediumistic style of automatic writing, Jung induced his alter-ego Philemon to preach to them and what he found to say curbed the spirits' restlessness. The resultant "Seven Sermons of the Dead" now definitively published in the "Scrutinies" section of *The Red Book*, reveals the degree to which Jung's psychology was his effort to deal with what he felt he owed the dead, who would literally otherwise not have left him alone. For further details refer to C. G. Jung, *Memories, Dreams, Reflections* (New York, NY: Vintage Books, 1965) & *The Red Book: Liber Novus*, edited by Sonu Shamdasani, translated by Mark Kyburz, John Peck, and Sonu Shamdasani (New York: W.W. Norton & Company, 2009).

A significant contemporary contribution that furthers the notion of a nondualistic relationship between psyche and outer reality may be found in the work of the Brazilian Jungian analyst Roberto Gambini, *Soul and Culture* (College Station, TX: Texas A&M University Press, 2003).

21   Hinton, "The Enigmatic Signifier," 639.

22   Most Western philosophical and psychological traditions have long denied this radical notion of the primacy of the Other's exteriority. Ontology—the nature of being—is viewed by Levinas as solipsistic, meaning that the self is the only reality and the only thing that can be known. Levinas's project of responsibility to the Other is a radical and much needed departure from what he believed to be ontology's inherent egoism, self-absorption, and violence, which privileges being and the needs of self before the other. See Brian W. Becker, "Self as Other? A Levinasian Analysis of Carl Jung's Concept of the Self-Ego Relation," paper presented at Psychology for the Other Seminar, Seattle University, Seattle, Washington, October 16, 2006.

23   Despite Levinas's general critique of psychoanalysis and its inward focus on unconscious states of being that turn the subject away from the other, he does make exceptions. "[I]f the concept of the unconscious were to signify a lived mental experience which is *not reducible to re-presentation* and to the present, [my italics] thus giving it all the significations of temporality, then it suits me fine." *Is It Righteous To Be: Interviews with Emmanuel Levinas*, Edited by Jill Robbins (Stanford, CA: Stanford University Press, 2001), 118. The unrepresentable unconscious experience he describes begins to approach my definition of the ineffable Self whose temporality, like the Other's, is recast as infinity.

24   Papadopoulos considers that there is an implicit conception of the Other throughout Jung's entire opus. This Other is not equivalent to the Levinasian Other but is constituted by the experience and recognition of the autonomy and reality of the psyche, which refuses to obey ego expectations. This Other can be thought about as creating a dialectical process with the part of the psyche that is aligned with the ego. In Jung's youth the Other took form and spoke to him through his #2 Personality, a much older, wiser voice that countered his normal conscious thoughts. His doctoral dissertation studied the separate personalities that came through a young medium during séance trances. This study led to his idea of the Other as a whole series of autonomous, personalities in the psyche—the complexes. As he attempted to expound upon collective Otherness in dreams and imagination he amplified the phenomenology of the Other with symbols he found in mythology, creativity, national symbolism, and the history of language. After his break with Freud and the publishing in 1912 of *The Psychology of the Unconscious*, (which was later revised in 1954 and renamed *Symbols of Transformation*) Jung underwent a period of inner fragmentation, where he encountered *Philemon*, the inner image of an ancient man of great insight who emerged in his work with the unconscious. Through this image and the meaning derived from their inner dialogue, one could suggest that he experienced a glimpse of the personified self. Jung's work culminated in this conception of the self, the symbol of a movement toward *psychological* wholeness. It was, paradoxically, both the symbol that transcended all opposites in the psyche and the central core of the personality. This Other in Jung's psychology, then, remained largely a *psychological self* that

transcended and expanded the confines of ego. His ideas, however, did not encompass a vision of the self that transcended the totality of the psyche, as contemporary thinking about the Self now imagines. Renos K. Papadopoulos, "Jung and the Concept of the Other," in *Jung in Modern Perspective*, Edited by Renos K. Papadopoulos and Graham S. Saayman (Bridgeport, UK: Prism Press, 1991).

25  Levinas's evolving view of the Other is not personal or psychological, but social and philosophical. He avoids viewing the relation of the Other to the subject in any second person relationships—the closed "society" of romantic love, friendship, or the "I–Thou" of the lover and Beloved. But earlier in his work the second person was the first and original other—the naked other, neither lover or friend, without qualifications other than his otherness. In later reflections the Other as "God" is located in the law of justice, which is non-intimate, the "third." We do injustice to the third and to all peoples, he contends, if we abandon ourselves to the "dual privacy of love." The beloved is "too intimate" to be called Other, for the Other is ineffable and infinite. See Adriaan T. Peperzak, and Emmanuel Levinas, *To the Other: An Introduction to the Philosophy of Emmanuel Levinas*. (West Lafayette, IN: Purdue University Press, 1993), 176–77. Intersubjectively, I am of the opinion that the trace of the Other in its infinitude, may be glimpsed in the beloved, not in love's fusion, but in both the lover's painful recognition of their separation, and in his welcoming of the beloved's ineffable and distinct otherness.

26  Hasan Rafeeq, *Aporia: Divining the Divine: The Role of God in Levinasian Ethics*. At http://humanities.byu.edu/philosophy/aporia/volume/vol.112/hasanto.html, p. 2 (accessed 3/23/05), 2.

## CHAPTER NINE

# WOUNDED BY THE OTHER

A man's encounter with tragedy, illness, trauma, or loss may deeply wound his narcissism and awaken him to revelations that will change his life forever. This is the shattering encounter with the Other, and it may originate from the impact of an event, or a person, or the unconscious. The gaze of the Other is enigmatic and violent to the ego and its syntonic complexes because it leads to their painful deflation and to the collapse of the false self and its defenses. A terrible vulnerability, rarely felt before, may be sensed as inescapable. Some aspect of the Other is calling the tormented being to its responsibility. The outcome of the matter may remain in doubt, but in the more fortunate cases an immense grief and shame for past wrongdoings are followed by states of humility, acceptance of one's human limitations, and a restored heart that places others before the self. A gratitude for simple moments of grace and modest achievements then takes a privileged position in one's life.

In this chapter, ancient myths, modern films, a case vignette, and a dream are presented, each replete with the symbolic theme of a new consciousness arising from the shattering of old, fixed attitudes and orientations of the ego. At heart, each of these are *love wounds*, in all their vicissitudes. The philosophy of Emmanuel Levinas informs my commentary, particularly when I discuss the biblical tale of Jacob's wounding by the Angel and his humble encounter and reconciliation with his aggrieved brother.

• • • • •

The initiation that wounds a man mired in narcissism does violence to his states of fusion, drivenness, and inflation—his alleged merging with totality. The narcissistic character often lacks internal or external boundaries, and in many cases the ego is infused and overflowing with what Jung called *mana-personality*. The ego identifies with an omnipotent mask that cuts its wearer off from adaptation to reality.[1] Contact with the enigmatic element that shatters the ego gives rise to a deeply felt separation and a profound loss of grandiosity. The subject is decentered from his illusion of being at the hub of the world. Such loss evokes the human emotions of grief, shame, and dependency, as well as the distressing realization, during this tumultuous process, that the presence of another, often (but not only) the analyst, is of the deepest importance to him.

In an early Greek myth, Prometheus was punished by Zeus for stealing fire and giving it to man. His penalty was to be chained to a rock where a vulture would come and tear out his liver each day. Because he was an immortal, however, his liver would heal during the night and he would be subjected to repeated suffering the next day. Prometheus' endless pain stemmed from a never-healing wound that severed him from the original unity. It signifies the painful cost we pay for consciousness as we attempt to break the ego's identification with its primal, unconscious core. The story is similar to that of Adam and Eve. Their disobedience in stealing fruit from the Tree of Knowledge of Good and Evil, their expulsion from the Garden, and their endless labor upon the hard, dry earth represent a similar form of wounding.

In another Greek myth, Actaeon was a hunter who gazed, hidden and unseen, upon the virgin huntress and moon goddess Artemis while she was bathing. In reprisal for his trespass he was changed into a stag, whereupon his loyal hunting hounds tore him to pieces. At one level, violent consequences like these signify the ego's Dionysian-like initiation and dismemberment for attempting to "know" something that is unknowable and ineffable. Gazing hungrily upon the virgin in her nakedness provokes a terrible side of the Other, which violently obliterates the inadequate consciousness that seeks only to appropriate— to *hunt down* the other. The merciless attack is incited by the ego's inflated and misguided assumption that it can steal more than a glance at the divine without dire consequences.

King Oedipus's tragic, self-inflicted blinding, acted out in the anguished moment when he could no longer deny who he was, came as a consequence of his arrogant disregard for his human limitations. These were signified by his incestuous union with his mother, the murder of his father, and his egotistical claim that only he could solve the riddle of the Sphinx—that embodiment of the dark, enigmatic, feminine mysteries that no man could truly know.

In each of these timeless stories a terrible deflation of the ego occurs. In three of them— Prometheus, Adam and Eve, and Oedipus—the wounding of the characters opens them to a deeper awareness through the trauma of sacrifice and suffering. In one, the story of Actaeon, the theme of death may signify the dissolution and violent transformation of the ego.[2]

The narcissistic man appears to merge unencumbered with the free flow of life. To the observant eye, however, what seem to the narcissist to be grand and magical encounters are in fact a superficial skipping from object to object, an attempted compensation for the fear of staying in one place and being truly engaged in life. Like Prometheus, chained to the rock for years, the narcissist's freedom and autonomy are constricted when the trauma of the Other disrupts his splendor. His questionable endless freedom brings to mind Levinas's discourse on freedom. Levinas understands "freedom" as the living out of a spontaneous (unconscious) and independent life as "the center of a universe . . . defined . . . [only by one's] needs and satisfactions . . . . a practice of the Same . . . a cynical behavior reducing all otherness . . ." In his freedom, the subject is not impacted or determined by anyone else. The other is turned into nothing more than an object that is appropriated to maintain the subject's freedom. In this sense Levinas sees a "moment of violence" as "inherent in every human individual's freedom."[3] When such a man suffers the shattering of his boundless freedom and inflation he is humbled and his energies are curtailed.[4] Yet from this suffering he may learn to relate to the other differently. Through bearing pain and difficulties his psyche may develop an emotional resilience permeable enough to bring forth what is within him and to affectively engage the core of his own being.

## *The Natural*[5]

*The Natural* (1985), is a classic baseball story, Hollywood's own Wagnerian hero myth, set in the Midwest during the period from the early 1920s to 1939. Robert Redford stars in the film, playing Roy Hobbs. As a boy, Roy's father teaches him everything there is to know and love about America's favorite pastime. He learns to pitch and to hit. He is a "natural," destined for stardom. On the night after his father collapses and dies at the foot of their old oak tree, a furious storm comes and a lightning bolt strikes and splits the great oak. The next morning Roy takes a piece of its trunk and fashions a bat. On its barrel he carves a lightning bolt and the name "Wonderboy." Years pass, and at nineteen years of age the young man receives word that the Chicago Cubs want to take a look at him to determine if he has the talent to play in the major leagues. He leaves behind Iris, his childhood sweetheart (Glenn Close), promising to send for her and marry her, and boards a train with the old scout who discovered him.

A mysterious woman named Harriet Byrd (Barbara Hershey) boards the train at one of the stops. She quickly attaches herself to a famous, larger-than-life, home-run-hitting ballplayer named "The Whammer," widely regarded as "the best there ever was," who was traveling to Spring Training with a noted baseball writer (Robert Duvall). The train stops at a fairground where the two men are pushed into settling a wager, goaded on by the beautiful woman who loves heroic tests of skill. To the amazement of all who witness it, Roy strikes out the slugger on three straight pitches. At this moment a myth is born, the sportswriter envisioning the storyline of a young David who slays the mighty Goliath with just three pitches. The femme fatale turns away from the defeated warrior and sets her eyes upon her new prey, the young hero, himself filled with the hubris of youth and dreams of becoming the best there ever was. Over a long dinner and drinks she seductively toys with the simple farm boy and he cannot resist her charms.

The next day the train arrives in Chicago. As Roy is about to head to the ballpark the woman calls and invites him up to her hotel room. When he enters she is standing, veiled in black, and she asks him, "Roy, will you be the best there ever was in the game?" "That's right," he boasts. She holds up a gun with one silver bullet in its chamber and shoots him. Then she turns to the open window and leaps to her death.

Sixteen years later, a wounded, humbled man walks back into the baseball stadium, having been away from the game all that time, in hopes of being given another chance. The bullet wound to his stomach has never fully healed, so his days as a pitcher are over. But he has nursed a deeper wound throughout those aimless years: his unbearable shame. He has betrayed his childhood sweetheart (and, although he does not know it, the mother of his son), and shame has prevented him from returning to face her. He has failed everyone—his father, the old washed-up scout who had believed in him, but especially himself. His inflated need to be recognized by the world as baseball's greatest has left him susceptible to the tempting seductions of the death mother, followed by the deflation and shattering of his omnipotence. Like Prometheus' wound, the silver bullet that lodges in his belly destroys the ego's inflation and its unconscious identification with the primal core of the self.

A lowly wisdom has emerged in Roy through the long years of suffering and sacrifice. With the aid of the old trusted bat he had carved himself on the night his father died, he brings renewed hope to a last-place team that has lost its way. His team, the New York *Knights*, starts to win and the players begin to believe in themselves, but sinister forces are at work to try and undermine Roy. The "Judge," the team's disreputable majority owner is in league with a shadowy gambler, and they stand to take total control of the team and force "Pop," the gruff but kindly old manager, to sell his share in it if he doesn't win the pennant. When bribes don't work on Roy because of his loyalty to Pop, they send a beautiful seductress named Memo (Kim Bassinger) to distract Roy with her charms. The scheme works and he falls into a terrible slump, her allure draining him of power. But in his last at bat during another losing game, at a point where he has fallen completely under Memo's spell and sunk to the lowest point, he sees a woman stand up in the crowd, dressed all in white, illuminated by the sunlight. Seeing this mysterious vision his energies are replenished and he belts the winning home run. Soon afterward he discovers that the woman is Iris, the girl he left behind, now a grown woman and the mother of his son. Her unwavering love for him, despite all the years of separation, renews his faltering strength.

Before the last few games of the season, with the pennant race hanging in the balance, the team has a big party and Memo offers Roy a poison *éclair*. He falls ill and without him in the lineup the team loses its final games and ends up in a tie for first place. The doctor pumps his stomach and discovers the last remnant of the silver bullet still lodged there and removes it. The doctor warns him that the bullet has caused his stomach lining to deteriorate over the years and that he may die if he continues to play baseball. Regardless of his weakened condition, Roy's loyalty to Pop impels him to play in the final play-off game the next day. Despite the great pain that has sapped his power, and with blood soaking through his jersey from the old wound that has torn open, he stands at the plate and summons up one last bit of strength. As lightning flashes overhead, he hits a tremendous home run that wins the pennant. The ball flies high over the fence and above the right field roof, crashing into the stadium's night lights, and sending showers of sparks of light down upon the field. The jubilant scene fades to black, and the final image on the screen depicts Roy playing catch with his son in an idyllic grassy field. In an ending typical of myths, he is happy to return to his old boyhood farm with his new wife and son, in the place where he had first discovered a simple peace and contentment.[6]

Roy Hobbs is a modern day solar hero in the mould of the Biblical Sampson or the legendary knight, Sir Gawan. His team is called the "New York Knights." The wondrous powers of King Arthur's sword, Excalibur, are embodied in Roy's bat "Wonderboy," which he hewed from the old oak split by lightning on the day his father died, just at a time when Roy was coming of age. Both oak and lightning, associated with the mythic figures of Zeus, Odin, and Thor, are symbolic of the father and of strength and solidity. The team's manager and owner, "Pop" and "The Judge," respectively, are also allusions to the father. The loss of the father, and the son's development into a father in his own right, is a powerful theme in the film.

The boy's strength and prowess as a baseball player grows, but without his father's steady guidance and cautionary restraint, Roy's hubris and inflated aspirations grow out of bounds. They leave him susceptible to the seductions of the femme fatale whose betrayal and wounding deflates his ego and humbles him. His shame banishes him from Iris, his first love, and from baseball, his second love and true calling.

The theme of light and darkness that pervades the film is evident in Roy's relationships to Iris and Memo/Harriet. The two types of women seem to reflect the typical split between the light bringer and the dark feminine. On closer examination, however, the dark feminine serves the function of initiator of truth and bringer of light, but her light often betrays the hero and wounds his omnipotence. *Aletheia*, the unveiling of truth, as we recall, often arises from the psyche's uncanny and shadowy contents. Memo, with her poisoning of Roy with the éclair, parallels Psyche's sisters' poisoning of Psyche's mind, that brings about her enlightening revelations, the wounding of Eros, and the destruction of his monstrous narcissism. Like Psyche's lamp in the bedchamber, the *éclair* too is a symbol of light, for it means "lightning flash" in the French.

Young Roy's own monstrous narcissism is destroyed by the silver bullet from Harriet Byrd's gun, her violent act a reaction to his hubris. The wound that never heals parallels the Grail King's wound by the poison lance that pierces his side in the Parzival legend. It is said that the king's endless suffering comes as a result of his youthful lust and arrogance.

From the poison comes the cure. The "silver bullet" is an old adage for the magic cure. Silver has been used worldwide as an antibacterial and antiseptic for wounds prior to the advent of antibiotics. The silver bullet is the only weapon in vampire lore that can destroy the beast in the man and release the soul's purity from captivity. Electric fields have long been known to enhance the antibacterial qualities of silver, (as the use of electrodes covered by silver nanorods have proven.) This connection between silver and electricity is present in the film, as well, with its prominent use of lightning storms.

Lightning heralds the hero's loss and triumph: The first lightning storm comes on the night of his father's death, while the last one signals the hero's triumph over darkness. The silver bullet wounds and imperils the life of the hero, yet silver's healing properties are legendary. The dark feminine in the story is also a harbinger of light and sacrifice. These three symbols appear to carry both life-giving and destructive meanings and may allude psychologically to divisions in the psyche beginning to resolve. If their paradoxical nature can be held consciously, they can hint at the growing cohesiveness among the psyche's fragmented parts. This is the function of the living symbol that brings new and transcendent possibilities into awareness.

Roy's redemption comes when he returns to the game as a renewed and humble subject. Perhaps he carries the pain of the silver bullet as a constant reminder of his need for humilty and humanity. The doctor's surgery reveals the hidden remnant of silver and he removes it, reminding Roy that he must find his own capacities for love and responsibility. By the film's end the boy who lost his father has learned to become a father, one whose wound is with him always. He has come full circle. Bearing the wound of the dark feminine has brought wisdom that he could not have gained had he not suffered the betrayal and wounding. But it has also taught him to recognize the futility in his longing for oneness with the temptress, and to let her go. For lying beneath his attraction to this kind of woman is the death mother who brings fragmentation and loss of integrity to the self.

Instead, Roy is given a second chance to be with the woman who has always loved him and who is the mother of his son. From a psychological perspective, the narcissism of an ego that splits off from emotional life by retreating into fantasies of the death coniunctio is transcended through the emergence of a man's capacities for mutuality and intimacy in relationship, born of sacrifice and suffering.

### The Family Man[7]

In *The Family Man* (2000), Nicholas Cage, as Jack Campbell, a rich, success-driven womanizer, undergoes a similar transformation when a Mephisphelean angel (Don Cheadle) gives him a long "glimpse" of what his life would have been like had he married the girl (Tia Leoni) he left behind to pursue his career. Jack awakens on Christmas morning in a strange bed in a house in a middle-class suburb of New Jersey, his perfectly manicured former life spirited away by the angel. Cast unwillingly into the role of a husband and father who works as manager of a tire company, Jack's narcissistic omnipotence falls away with the first load of dirty diapers that needs washing. The man that his wife and children knew and adored is a stranger to him, yet over time he begins to see himself through their eyes. This family man knew how to love and give of himself in a way that is foreign to the power broker, who knows only sexual conquests and how to remove himself when things get too intimate. His wife, who has grown more beautiful than the coed Jack remembers, will not let him touch her until he tells her how much he loves her. Finally, when the glimpse of their possible life is nearing an end, Jack recognizes that the angel has brought him here, wounded his omnipotence, and laid him low for just one purpose: to teach him the meaning of love. The things most important to him are no longer billion-dollar deals but rather the plain, everyday things that graced his life in the vision the angel showed him, like the pride and devotion he felt for his children and the love and intimacy he felt with his wife.

Most of us react to these words as if they are obvious or corny, not knowing what this experience would mean to a man who has never known such a level of vulnerability and intimacy before. When he awakens from the dream Jack is in grief. But the angel had promised him only a *glimpse* of what might have been had he chosen the other path in life. This is perhaps all we ever get, or perhaps all we ever need—that tiny glimmer or awakening of something beyond us that finds a way to shatter our omnipotence and isolation.

In the film Jack seeks out the woman he had grown to love in that other lifetime. She is of course more than a bit skeptical when he proceeds to tell her the story of their life together. He somehow finds a way to touch a place in her heart that she had buried a long time ago, at least enough to convince her to put off her scheduled flight to Paris, where she was planning to move. In the crowded airport terminal he blurts out something to her that she had once said to him in their "other life," something that spoke of her willingness to put others before her at important times, to sacrifice her own personal wants because of her love and devotion to him and their family. In this supreme act of surrender to the other she had said, "I choose us." When he speaks these words to her in the crowded terminal they stop her in her tracks. The film ends without resolution, but with hopefulness, as the two sit and talk through the night in a coffee shop at the airport. Is this the nature of life? To what extent are we endlessly poised between these opposites of coming and going, love and loss, certainty and the unknown? Is maturity the acceptance of the suffering in between?

### *Reign Over Me*[8]

In this 2007 film the audience is witness to the senseless suffering of a man whose life has been violently pulled apart by tragedy. Compelled by the depth of his trauma, this lost soul floats aimlessly above life as if suspended in time, seeking refuge in activities similar to those he pursued at a much earlier period in his life. He enacts the same compulsive rituals and behaviors over and over again in order to insulate himself from the unbearable loss of his wife and three young daughters, who were aboard one of the planes that went down on September 11.

The opening credits of the film show Charlie Fineman (Adam Sandler) as he speeds along the empty streets of New York City on his motor scooter in the small hours of the night. His headphones blare, blocking out all exterior influences. Other compulsive defenses take the form of addiction to video games, playing drums in mind-numbing punk-rock bands, a constant barrage of loud rock music on his headphones, and ongoing kitchen remodels that he tears out as soon as they are complete.

Then a chance encounter rekindles a friendship with his former dental college room-mate, Dr. Alan Johnson (Don Cheadle), who has not seen him for years. Their odd reunion slowly reawakens Charlie's need for a companion that would bridge the gap from his dissociated state. But all attempts by Johnson to broach the subject of Charlie's family or his past are met with rejection. Charlie reacts with paranoia, angry retaliation, and violent splitting whenever it appears that his psychic skin is being impinged upon.

After repeated nudging, Charlie finally comes to the realization that his life would be easier if he did not have to "think about certain [troubling] things." He asks his friend for help in finding a therapist. Johnson knows a woman in his medical building. He accompanies Charlie to his initial therapy session and to each of the following ones. In work fraught with regressions and stalemates, Charlie begins a one-step forward, two-step back approach to his traumatic memories, guided by the caring, sensitive, yet inexperienced young psychiatrist, Angela (Liv Tyler). After weeks of frustrated attempts to get her patient to discuss his family, Angela commits a misstep that could have punctured the analytic container, had this been an actual therapy. She appears impatient with their impasse and gently confronts Charlie's avoidance, inadvertently pressuring him to open up before he is ready. He ends the session after only five minutes, and as he heads for the door Angela says to him, "Look, the fact is you had a family, and you suffered a great loss. [He turns the volume up to maximum on his headphones as he faces her]. And until you can discuss that and we can really talk about that, this is all just an exercise. I can be patient, Charlie, but you need to tell someone your story. It doesn't have to be me. But someone." Without a word or gesture, Charlie turns and leaves the room.

Johnson, the principle in a highly successful New York dental practice, is sitting in the waiting room, engrossed in one of Charlie's superhero comic books. He makes an inane comment to Charlie about the comic, and, without intending to, Johnson literally stops him in his tracks with his simple, stupid guy talk. Without pretense, and asking nothing from him (in part because neither man has any idea how to communicate at any depth), Johnson has somehow been able to reach him. Charlie proceeds to sit down next to him and launches into the memories that he has not spoken about for five years. With tears in his eyes, Charlie begins, haltingly, to tell his story.

He speaks of his three daughters—five year old Gina, seven year old Jenny and his eldest, Julie, who was nine. His wife was named Doreen, or "DT"—Doreen Templeman. They had a dog, Spider. At this point, Angela comes quietly to the door that is cracked open, and listens in to Charlie's story. He recalls to Johnson how he'd wake up on Saturday mornings to the four of them singing Beatle songs, in harmony. "So cute, so cute," he says, lost in the tender memory. Charlie speaks of how Doreen never nagged him as some wives do. All she asked of him was to take off his shoes when he came home from work to keep the carpet clean. They were all so very female, while he was the oddball, "Mr. Man." But he knows they all adored him. Tears begin to fall.

Charlie goes on to talk about each girl's beautiful long, brown hair, all except the youngest, Gina. She kept her hair short because she prided herself on being different. "She had a birthmark, too. Looked like a *burn*, but it wasn't." (My italics.) The doctors had told them it would go away but it never did. The middle daughter, Jenny, wanted to be a gymnast. "She was such a klutz, though. I didn't have the heart to mention it as a problem." They had gone to visit Doreen's sister in Boston and they took the dog with them because Charlie had to work. They teased him that he'd forget to feed Spider. Their plan was to all meet a few days later on the West Coast for a family wedding. The girls wanted to go to Disneyland and he felt bad about having to say no, because they were already missing several days of school. Charlie's story continues.

> So I go on to meet 'em in Los Angeles, and on my way to JFK I'm in the taxicab and I hear on the radio . . . I get there and some guy tells me the plane's from Boston . . . Some other guy says there are two planes . . . Then I go inside the airport and I'm watching on the television and I, I, I saw it. I saw it and I felt it at the same time. I thought about Gina's birthmark . . . and I felt them burning . . .

Charlie has revealed himself to his friend, and in that moment Johnson gazes upon his nakedness, the burning wound—raw, gaping, horrific, never before spoken aloud. The Other is revealed in the indelible image of the face of his fragile child—in the tortured instant he shares with her, and then as if a wave has passed over him Charlie falls silent. After a long pause he says, "I'm going now. I'm going home now. I don't like this . . . I don't like doing this, remembering. I don't like remembering." Remembering has returned him to his utter, unbearable helplessness. As Charlie turns to leave, Angela waves goodbye to Johnson, deeply moved by what has just unfolded.

Surely a senseless violence had rained down upon Charlie on that morning in September of 2001, splintering apart his life and his heart. He was cast adrift in madness and useless suffering for his family—innocent victims of crimes of hatred and violence. And yet, as he speaks to Johnson of his love and grief, the truth flays him open, revealing his vulnerability and nakedness that tears him apart once again.

Having witnessed an opening much like this, a therapist versed in trauma work would probably have instructed Johnson to keep vigil with Charlie and not leave his side. It would be natural to anticipate violent repercussions from Charlie's narcissistic defenses in retaliation for this threatening exposure. In the film, however, Charlie goes home alone to contend with his demons, unable to block out the memories of the tragedy. Obsessional thoughts of suicide take possession of him. Violent, suicidal fantasies and impulses are typical means used by the persecuting internal objects of the self-care system to "protect" the traumatized individual from unbearable pain. The inner persecutor will choreograph the individual's plans for suicide, in order to escape the merciless, unyielding memories that subject the individual to threats of retraumatization. Death is the ultimate protection against the pain of life that is too great to bear alone. These were the obsessional thoughts that took possession of Charlie.

In despair, Charlie finds an unloaded revolver and searches frantically for bullets, to no avail, as hallucinations of his wife and children haunt the hallways. He then flees into the night, noticing a pair of cops in a diner across a street. He steps into the street directly in front of an oncoming taxi which screeches to a halt. The cabbie jumps out and they get into a screaming altercation, whereupon Charlie pulls out his unloaded gun in clear sight of the two officers, who jump into action. One draws his firearm and orders Charlie to drop his weapon, while the other circles around. Under his breath Charlie pleads with the cop to pull the trigger. "Come on, do it! Do it!" Meanwhile the other cop comes up from behind and tackles him. The two police officers beat him badly and haul him off to jail. We might conjecture that this encounter with the policemen can be understood as Charlie's failed attempt to induce the officers to enact the roles of his internal murderers.

In the film, the state sets a hearing before a judge (Donald Sutherland) to commit Charlie involuntarily to the state mental hospital for up to a year. The motley collection of people who have come to care about him rally around and fight for his release. Johnson comes to court every day. Angela testifies. She tells the judge that he needs to find his own way, in his own time, and that he will find people who will fill his life again. She is right and, as it turns out, the "re-collecting" of his shattering memories begins to bring about small but important changes in Charlie's life, supporting his capacity to tolerate degrees of emotional closeness.

The various people who have traversed Charlie's life are damaged and helpless, each in his or her own particular way. Johnson is cut off and stifled by convention and expectations; Angela is awkward and insecure; Angela's patient, the beautiful but emotionally unbalanced divorcée Donna (Saffron Burrows), takes a shine to Charlie because she understands the wound he has suffered. The wound is one that she shares as well: a broken heart. They have all found one another and are better off for it. Called by their feelings of responsibility to this marginalized stranger, these human others can welcome him and 'hold his gaze.' The violent encounter with the Other comes as a result of the unconcealment of his memories, and from that point signs of erosion in his narcissistic encapsulation begin to appear. Enslavement to the repetitions of a solitary soul's lament and its silent monologue begin to give way to tender moments of *saying*, of *touching*, of *seeing* the face of another. This speaks to Levinas's basic principle, which lies in "the most ordinary, simple, and everyday fact of another facing me."[9]

Pete Townsend's song, "Reign O'er Me," is the musical inspiration for writer/director Mike Binder in the making of this film. The songwriter substitutes the word "reign" for "rain" in his lyric, describing how love is the only thing that could make it "reign." He longs for love to reign over him. In bridging the deepest chasms of the soul, wrought by the most agonizing losses, it is love that reigns supreme over us all, is it not?

Something sovereign, utterly infinite and enigmatic, reigns over the course of our lives. The incursions of a terrible and overwhelming side of the Other may demolish our fortresses of granite or dissolve our fragile castles in the sand. The trauma of this encounter with incomprehensible otherness—violent and final—may send some of us reeling far away, into the most remote recesses of the mind. A few who are fortunate or resilient enough may return again, called to their human responsibility. Perhaps they return for the sake of the memory of those closest and dearest to them—those suddenly torn from all human embrace, or stolen long before life could be imagined without them.

These ancient and modern dramas are the artistic representations of human suffering and renewal, based at least in part, we assume, on the revelations of their authors. Their common themes are reflected in the following case vignette.

## Clinical Vignette

Deep wounds resulting from infidelity are explored in the case described here. Viewed clinically and dispassionately, acts of this kind may inadvertently, at times, precipitate the incursion of a violent *third* that tears apart the false ties that keep a man tethered to the security of a relationship. The perpetuation of its hollow rituals suddenly come to an end, as well as his tyranny over his objects.[10] To the great misfortune of all, in the destruction of its false edifice the young innocents can often not escape the greatest suffering and harm.

In the case of my patient, the "adulteration" of his twenty-year marriage with another woman was experienced by his wounded partner and children as a life-changing violation and an unbearable betrayal of the heart. The impact of this violence upon them penetrated his narcissism, precipitating the ego's unraveling in the endless challenges of the enigma, from which a deep sense of shame, loss, and grief ushered forth. These *enigmatic signifiers*, thrown up from the unconscious core of the patient, became the source for the emergence of new and creative possibilities.

Since enigmatic signifiers have been discussed in Chapter One, a brief description here will suffice. As primal fantasies they originate from the mother's unconscious affects that flood her helpless infant, whose only recourse is to repress them. As in the example of my patient, these repressed fantasies emerge throughout life from the gap between the unconscious core and consciousness, their enigmatic meaning disrupting and decentering the ego's fixed orientation.

For two decades my patient had lived a provisional life as a husband and a father of two, having never fully committed himself nor engaged in the raising of his children. An only child, he did well enough through his school years and achieved moderate success as a partner in an architectural firm. In our work he often mooned for the easier time in his life, before he became saddled with marriage, family, and work responsibilities. Over time, he came to devalue his wife, who in her younger years had embodied his image of the ideal woman. She was seven years his junior. As their sexual passion and intimacy dwindled and disappeared, he began to seek aesthetic escape in erotic and romantic fantasies like those of his youth. He would envision in a very precise way the perfect girl or woman who would desire him and arouse and enthrall him in ways that would temporarily restore his sense of himself. His perfectionism and his criticism of his wife's body, which had changed from childbirth and natural aging, gave him the alibi he used to justify his dissatisfaction with her. But this attitude, I believe, was merely a cover-up for a deeper terror of emotional intimacy originating in his early life.

Intimacy with his wife, my patient feared, represented submission to a maternal influence that would engulf and obliterate him. He would often experience the moments preceding intimate sexual encounters as too threatening and impinging. Such closeness evoked feelings of helpless, infantile dependency in him, along with fears of being devoured—and then discarded—by a needy and controlling mother. To manage these unbearable feelings he found ways to distance himself from his wife. For instance, he would inject his poisonous criticisms into her in their most vulnerable moments, almost irreparably damaging her spirit and her sense of her own native sensuality. In those instances it was he who became like the obliterating mother, while his wife became the helpless and abjected child that he detested in himself and therefore projected onto her.

Although his mind increasingly turned toward fantasies of other women, he had never acted on any of these feelings for fear of exposing dark impulses that might tarnish his persona of goodness. But over time a dark abscess of resentment and hatred toward his wife grew in him, perhaps evoked by his internalization of his own mother's desire for the complete and total perfection of her son. This set the stage for a premeditated hunt for a woman who would give him freedom from the pain of a passionless, conflict-ridden relationship. When he found the woman, their sexual encounter lasted for several months before he broke it off, feeling that she wanted more than he wanted to give.

He entered psychotherapy shortly afterward, uncertain of whether he wanted to leave the marriage or stay in it. Would it be possible, he wondered, to hide the affair and simply go on as before, perhaps until another opportunity presented itself? Deeper questions soon surfaced: Would it even be possible to conceal such a terrible secret? For everything had, in fact, changed forever, both for him and his wife, regardless of whether she was conscious of it. Would the man that he had hoped one day to become have any possibility of emerging in his life if he buried the truth from his family or ran away from them? He had come to a moral and ethical crossroads where his integrity and authenticity as a man were at stake— qualities he knew relatively little about. The crisis had brought something to light in him: a terrible, unsettling recognition of a lifelong cowardice and inability to love. And yet if he were to reveal the truth, a long and arduous process would stretch out before him, one that would shatter the false mask he showed to the world. It would be a "death blow" that would become, as we came to realize, a "life blow."[11]

The shattering of my patient's false self began on the morning that he shared with his wife what he had done. Initially she was emotionally devastated and deeply hurt by his betrayal. Her continuing emotional avalanche seemed unending to him. It became "too much" and too exposing for him, prompting in turn his attempts to minimize and skirt the truth. The more he clung to mind-numbing denials over the days and weeks, the more her pain turned to blind rage, and then to emotional collapse. He was ill-prepared for the splintering of his wife's fragile world, brought about by his betrayal. She became a vulnerable and frail being, standing naked before him. The dawning recognition of the violence he had perpetrated upon her over the course of their marriage demolished the illusions he had maintained of himself.

This was the "dropping down point," the place of initiatory descent for our analytical work. My patient felt like he was falling apart. Over many months a steep regressive process ensued that we contained by meeting multiple times a week. Dreams, memories, and primal affects emerged that we could connect to early and deeply ambivalent childhood relations to his mother.

Our exploration led us to his mother's traumatic origins as a Jewish refugee who emigrated with her family from Lithuania to escape persecution at the age of two. My patient and I came to recognize the subterranean wells of terror and instability within her that had permeated the world of mother and infant. The mother's emotional needs—unmet by a husband whom she kept at a distance—may well have found expression in unconscious erotic and seductive communications with her baby boy. At times in his childhood my patient had felt intensely desired by his mother—as if he were the center of her world. But then, without warning, his mother's black, depressive moods would descend. Then she would sometimes sear him with her rage and at other times turn away from him coldly, as if he were a base thing.

We came to understand the fantasies underlying my patient's marriage difficulties as translations of these original configurations. For instance, when his wife grew irritated with his selfish behavior he projected the "rejecting mother who wanted nothing to do with him" onto her, whereas he envisioned the "other woman" as the "one who wanted and desired him."

At the depth of his regressive process in analysis, he drew an enigmatic image that had emerged from an active imagination, the image of *a mother's blood-red, gaping mouth with razor-sharp teeth, in which, as his associations made clear, he conflated the vaginal and anal openings.* It was an uncanny, enigmatic maw—a maternal container both horrific and erotically alluring that evoked in the infant-part of himself not only terror, helplessness, and rage, but also excitement. Similarly, Julia Kristeva speaks of the ambivalent desire in the infant's fantasies of reentering the body flesh of the mother as combining both terror *and* the longing to merge.[12]

Laplanche's psychoanalytic theories provide considerable insight into my patient's strange image. In speaking of the mother's fantasies and their impact upon the unformed psyche of the infant, Ladson Hinton explains, "Laplanche uses the term 'seduction,' to include not only erotic fantasies, but also . . . a sense of provocation, charm, allure, and stimulation." This, Hinton stresses, is not psychopathology but the "usual state of things."[13] The erotic feelings evoked in the mother in the course of breast-feeding, caressing the baby's naked body, and in soothing him vocally, are all largely unconscious and they fill the infant's unformed psyche with enigmatic affects.

These and other more penetrating and disturbing maternal affects that flood the baby at times will arouse its dread and deep anxiety. In the case of my patient, these were states of mind identical with those that besieged his depressed mother throughout her life. Such states require the infant's creation of narcissistic defenses that trigger its primal repression of the overwhelming affects. According to Laplanche, it is this repression that is responsible for the creation of a "gap" between the self and the otherness within. As Hinton writes, "The impact of the enigma may create a kind of opening, a gap, a crack, a cleavage plane in the ordinary . . . process of things. If not for the enigma there would be no . . . dismantling of old patterns."[14]

My patient's regressive process, set in motion by the drama unfolding in the relationship to his traumatized wife, was marked by an upwelling of these long-repressed, enigmatic signifiers—the image of the gaping mouth, for example—and they loosened the grip of his narcissistic defenses. Deep wells of primal rage found expression, rage that he related to a lifetime of placating and pretense—defenses through which he hoped to protect himself from his mother's unpredictable and devouring, penetrating affects. We were at sea for many months with these turbulent emotions that wore away his false self.

Gradually my patient became more porous and vulnerable. At times his resistance and defensiveness melted away, leaving in their place a deep sadness and receptivity. Often he would swing back and forth from fragmentation to an exposed vulnerability that became too much for his thin skin to bear. This would give way to brief but repetitive attempts to reassert and restore his defensive shell through emotional attacks on his wife or on me, but these were mostly short-lived episodes. Something was beginning to emerge from the breakdown of his ego orientation that he had never before touched in himself. Nor was it anything his wife had ever seen in him. Nonetheless, it helped him stay in the fire with her, bearing her rage and her anguish as she tried to return from her own nightmarish journey—her own shattering. The wounded couple were seeing the first glimpses of a humble man, resilient and *unconcealed*. Though it would entail many, many years of work before he would embody it, he had begun to comprehend what it would mean to live his life *for the other*, and to know a freedom that comes from responsibility.

In the enigmas of life we are endlessly trying to answer the question that the infant asks: "What did my mother really want?" Did she want my patient to be the abject creature, or the good baby? Beneath the question is the infant's utter dependency upon the other. In the question lies the unrealistic hope that there can be an answer that will forever resolve the gap. The gap is in fact, the source of our freedom, because it can never be known. It is infinite, enigmatic, Other. The difficult process of analysis brings us to the conscious recognition that the *mystery* of life, the ultimate answers, can never be found.

Two years after the beginning of his treatment, my patient reported a dream of sublime quality. Given his porous emotional state, it might seem to have emerged prematurely, yet it appeared to speak to this endless, ineffable, and transcendent mystery.

> I'm driving along near a military development. Fighter planes are lined up behind chain-link fences. I realize that I am about to witness an epic reckoning that is going to occur—like a meeting from Heaven, or an extraterrestrial materialization, or some great astronomical event is coming down to earth exactly on one place. The meeting will take place between two military bases, the site being over a great, ancient, rectangular Jewish temple.

In this vision my patient is witness to the anticipated encounter with an enigmatic Other, whose descent to earth would bring a great change to the world. Its mere trace dwarfed and humbled the illusion of his singular isolation in the world.[15]

During most of his adulthood my patient lived a secular life as a Jew. In this period of fragmentation, however, he turned back to his religious roots to try to achieve some sense of stability and comfort. Sometimes he would awaken in the middle of the night from nightmares or anxiety and find that the only means he had to quiet his racing thoughts were prayer and meditation. He began to observe Jewish holidays again and to attend synagogue. In particular, his first High Holy Day services for *Yom Kippur*—the Day of Atonement—had an unexpected, deeply emotional, and transcendent impact on him. For him they were truly Days of Awe, as they are traditionally referred to. He was drawn to explore the mystical traditions of Judaism through study of the *Torah, Kabbalah*, and the image of the Tree of Life.[16] These were areas of interest not unfamiliar to me given our shared heritage as first generation American Jews.

At one level, the dream's images relate to my patient's conscious studies of *Kabbalah* and the meditation practices that he had been engaged in. From this it would be easy to reduce the dream's "meaning" to his associations to his inner, spiritual work. On its own, however, an interpretation that attempted to provide a sort of final understanding would have little value beyond an intellectual one. It could even cause great harm, for in our need to know we may be risking the perpetration of a kind of violence upon the ineffable and infinite mystery at which the dream may be hinting. With this in mind, we began to elaborate on the dream's prominent images, amplifying them through associations. To give the reader a sense of the dream's richness, I have embroidered upon it through references to scholarly and religious texts, both here and in the endnotes.

My patient's initial thoughts about the great cosmic event above the temple led to our shared associations to the *Ruach Ha Kodesh*—the Divine Spirit. This was known to the ancient Hebrews wandering in the wilderness as the Glory of God, hidden in the midst of a great wind or storm or fiery cloud, as in Ezekiel's vision.[17] A "cloudy pillar"[18] was said to have descended upon the place where God spoke with Moses. This was the tent— the inner sanctuary or *Holy of Holies*—that housed the Ark of the Covenant in which the Ten Commandments dwelt.[19] The Temple of Jerusalem was built to house this same Holy of Holies that contained the Ark, and the *Shekhinah's* Divine Presence was said to have hovered over it. *This, my patient realized, was the great Temple that had appeared in his dream.*

In his study of Kabbalah, my patient had come to understand the *Shekhinah* as inhabiting the root of the Tree of Life, called the *Kingdom*. "In it the Divine Lightning Flash is earthed. It constitutes the *Shekhinah*, the Presence of God in Matter," Z'ev ben Shimon Halevi tells us.[20] For the mystic, the base of the Tree would also act as a gateway to ascend the ladder of perception of the Divine mystery. Although God is infinite and unrepresentable and cannot possess form,[21] some early mystic teachings ascribed form to "the Glory," which they called *guf ha-Shekhinah*, or the "body of the Divine presence."[22] The "Divine Glory" and the "Glorious Kingdom" both refer to the *Shekhinah*, which Gershom Scholem paradoxically describes as the Glory *revealed* and *hidden* without form.[23] Early Kabbalistic traditions surrounding the Sabbath concern the return of the Sabbath Bride and the meditations upon the Beloved in the Song of Songs, which viewed the *Shekhinah* in her aspect as God's mystical bride.[24]

## Emmanuel Levinas

Levinas, as well has spoken of the "Glory of the Infinite." But his views are quite different from the mystical experience described in the previous paragraphs. He believed that these numinous experiences (like those in the case of enthralled lovers) do a kind of violence to the Other by elevating the human subject and transporting him into some type of ecstatic inflation. He writes, "The numinous or the Sacred envelopes and transports man beyond his power and wishes, but a true liberty [responsibility to the other] takes offense at this uncontrollable surplus . . ."[25] Throughout his writings Levinas privileges a *proximity* of relation to the human other, in which only a kernel of the Infinite is revealed, over a mystical oneness and ascent that result from the dissolution of the subject into the Object.[26]

The work of Levinas, like that of Laplanche, suggests that narcissism is transcended when something other than ourselves breaches our fixed ego state. In his dream, my patient bears witness to the Glory that is about to descend upon the Temple—an event that seems to transcend psyche—yet this appears through the interiority of the dream image. In the *imaginal* process of dreams the Infinite, that cannot be represented, is nevertheless signified! How can this be?

Glory as a trace of the Infinite, Levinas contends, could become a phenomenon by entering into conjunction with the subject as an indwelling presence. For this to occur the subject must not have closed itself up in finitude or immanence.[27] Its *content* may appear only when the ego has been "stripped by the trauma of persecution of its . . . imperialist subjectivity."[28] When this occurs, the subject becomes witness to the glory of the Infinite, belongs to it, and, as witness, gives voice in praise of it. Levinas's understanding of the Glory of God always returns us to the humble recognition of our obligation to the Other. Through "transcendence" of our egotistical subjectivity, he says, we "can receive a content from the dimension of height," from our experience of the "glory of the Infinite."[29]

## Jung

While differing from one another in their approaches to the enigma that transcends the psyche, both the mystical traditions and Levinas's philosophy of the Other differ from Jung's understanding of mystical symbols, which he conceives of as psychic phenomena. Jung viewed the living symbols that emerge from the totality of the psyche's depths as *inner* transcendent factors. The descending Other in my patient's dream appears to express just the opposite idea: that the Other is not a creation or construction of his psyche. Rather, the psyche glimpses a "trace" of the Other, which it expresses through the imaginative process. The image in the dream is better described by Hilary Putnam who paraphrases Levinas:

"my encounter with the other is an encounter with a *fissure*, with a being who breaks my categories. . . .a violator of [my] mind . . ."[30]

As a psychologist, Jung contended that all knowing—*gnosis*—arrives by way of psychic images. Jungian analyst Steven Joseph describes Jung's understanding of Divine Presence as "experience-near, not distant, abstract and metaphysical." Jung knew that God-*images* existed, but he did not profess to know "what [might] lie . . beyond . . images of divine presence."[31] Except as they manifested through psychic images, Jung left the unknowable and unspeakable to the theologians. In his studies of Hermetic and Gnostic symbols, Jung likened the kabbalistic *Shekhinah* to the Gnostic *Sophia* or the alchemical *Sapientia.* If Jung were consistent he would have considered these sacred images to have their origins in the realm of the Infinite and unknowable beyond the psyche. Instead, he saw these as *inner* transcendent factors pertaining to wisdom and arising from the psyche's depths in dreams or in the imagination, through the work of the transcendent function. The origin of these sacred images is not, then, an unknowable, unspeakable place that lies in the infinite beyond. Jung here stays within the bounds of psyche and its symbolic depths, relegating the images emanating from an infinite Divine Presence to a product of psyche.

The Kabbalah, Joseph continues, also employs a rich array of symbolic content, but, unlike Jung, "uses the materials of the *imaginal* for a specifically *noetic* intent." He defines "noetic" as "an immediate, experiential knowing, [an] embodied *gnosis*."[32] While the Kabbalists recognized the finiteness and inadequacy of their *noetic* insights into the endless and enigmatic mystery, they nevertheless found it possible to glimpse traces of the Infinite through their "*noetic* intuitions."[33] A passage from *The Zohar*, the classic thirteenth-century mystical text, intuits the presence of an unseen and ineffable Divine Being, impossible to reach or to know, that the mystic longs for nonetheless. "[F]or He is hidden, concealed, transcendent, beyond, beyond."[34]

To bring greater clarity to this, Joseph makes reference to a passage in *Proverbs* 31:23: "Her husband is known in the gates when he sits with the elders of the land."[35] The Biblical verse refers to "a woman of valor."[36] It is understood by the Kabbalists to be a hymn to the *Shekhinah*, the Beloved and wife of the blessed Holy One.[37] *The Zohar*, comprised of commentaries by the great Kabbalistic minds living in Spain at that time, elaborates on this passage:

> All beings above and below cannot grasp, till finally they declare: *Blessed be the glory of YHVH from his place!*[38] [YHVH refers to the unspeakable name of God, and the phrase implies that no one *knows* His place] . . . For He is unknowable, no one has ever been able to comprehend Him. Yet you say: *Her husband is known in the gates?*
>
> But indeed, *Her husband is known in the gates*—the blessed Holy One, who is known and grasped to the degree that each one opens the gates of *imagination* [my italics], according to the capacity to attain the spirit of wisdom. As one

fathoms in his mind, so He is known in his mind. So He *is known in those gates.* But can He be known accurately? No one has ever been able to grasp and know Him.[39]

Despite the limits of knowing, Joseph adds, "the *Zohar* teaches [that] the imaginal *experience* is the gateway through which one enters to attain true knowledge/*gnosis* of God, the *noetic* reality."[40] In other words, the noetic reality can never be more than a glimpse of the Infinite which lies exterior to psychic processes. *Zohar* Commentator Daniel Matt concludes that "Imagination enables the human mind to fathom God—though, as Rabbi Yehudah goes on to say, all imaginative representations fall short of true divine being."[41]

In my patient's dream, the presence of *Shekhinah*, a content of the Infinite, had come down from the heights to dwell upon the Temple. This could be conceived of as the lightning bolt from Her *Glorious Kingdom* that was "earthed" upon the Temple that houses the congregation of humanity. In a similar way, the shattering gaze of the Other had broken through my patient, who now stood unconcealed before his wife and children. He spoke again of his experience on the Day of Atonement, when he had become so overwhelmed by the weight of his acts. In those moments he felt his heart crack open from the profound revelations and the compassion he had begun to feel through his own suffering, shame, humiliation, and grief. He even sensed forgiveness. Nothing ecstatic or earth-shaking emerged from these meditations, simply deep reflection and a sense of gratitude for his life, for his second chance. As for the war planes that stood balanced at both ends of the Temple, they stirred opposite emotions in him. They reminded him on the one hand of the vigilance needed to face the continual presence of his violent narcissistic defenses against the shattering impact of the Other. On the other hand, these war birds, standing ready to defend the nation, embodied the symbol of the Father and protective guardian that he was trying to become. Both interpretations were true.

The experiences of wounding depicted in my patient's story involve a painful excursion into pathos—suffering and compassion—where the anguish and humiliation is enormous. The suffering of my patient enlarged the boundaries of what he imagined he could bear. Yet the same shattering revelations that broke him wide open led to a larger sense of what his life could become.

## Jacob and the Other

Humility and gratitude for the simple graces that are afforded to us in life emerge from the wounds that pierce the inflation and grandiosity of the narcissistic defenses. These are the values that come to assume a place of greater importance within us. I would like to conclude with the story of the wounding of Jacob by the Angel, described in the *Book of Genesis*. To me, no other story describes as richly the values I wish to convey.

*Genesis* depicts a pensive Jacob, standing alone on the evening before the day he is to meet his estranged brother, when a mysterious and unknown being—some say an angel, others a demon—suddenly appears and engages him in a fierce struggle. They wrestle throughout the long night, neither gaining the upper hand. Finally the nighttime spirit wounds Jacob in the hip, dislocating the bone. As dawn approaches the shrouded adversary bids Jacob release him before the light of day. Jacob refuses. "'I will not let you go unless you bless me.' It is then that the angel declares, "No longer will it be said that your name is Jacob [the "supplanter"] but Israel, for you have striven with the Divine and with man and have overcome.' . . . And he blesses him there. Jacob calls this place Peniel. 'For I have seen the Divine *face to face* yet my life [has been] spared.'"[42]

The next morning Jacob, lame and hobbled, comes to meet his brother, *face to face*, bowing seven times as he approaches. Jacob does not know what the outcome of their encounter will be. The aggrieved older twin had lost his birthright and his father's blessing many years before, both through his own greed[42] and through the trickery of his mother and brother. Will he be there with his armed force ready to slay Jacob and his family, or will he meet him with open hand and heart? As the story reveals, Esau welcomes his penitent and wounded brother with compassion and charity.

Over the millennia, this passage from *Genesis* has been understood in countless ways. In my reckoning, before all else, the angel who wounds Jacob signifies the enigma of the Other, that trace of the Infinite that hobbles the ego. Penetrating and disturbing, it burns through the psychic skin of the fixed attitudes and orientations that we feel we must fit into and hold fast to.

Jung speaks of God as the trauma that we must face, "a factor unknown in itself." His idea of God is not something inaccessible, but one that confronts us directly. Jung writes, "This is the name by which I designate all things which cross my willful path violently and recklessly, all things which upset my subjective views, plans, and intentions and change the course of my life for better or worse."[44] This is the unknown being that each of us must wrestle with, like Jacob, when trauma or catastrophe shatter our world.

The Spanish mystic Saint Teresa of Avila speaks paradoxically of her soul's wounding and penetration by her Beloved—God—as like a "rushing comet or thunderclap . . . Although no sound is heard."[45] Levinas asks at what moment the word of God is heard. He answers, "It is inscribed in the *Face of the Other*, in the encounter with the Other."[46] We recall Levinas's notion that the Face is an enigmatic signifier denoting the trace of the Infinite that is unknowable, beyond existence and without end, glimpsed in the presence of the human other. This is where Jacob's gaze rests, upon the face of his brother. This is the face that the newborn first sees, already there, before all choice.[47] Beyond its obvious religious implications, the exteriority that transcends one's individual being has profound psychological and philosophical meaning. From the ego's fixed perspective, the encounter with the Other is violent because the ego's requirements for stability call for things to remain the same. Simply put, Sameness and uncertainty are incompatible. As Jungian analyst Lucy Huskinson puts it, "The encounter with the Other causes the Same to realize its impotence; it creates a surplus value of infinity within the Same which then disrupts the totality and self-containment of the Same."[48] Jacob approaches the momentous encounter with his brother without certainty or knowledge of the outcome. Bearing the unknown in this way, he glimpses a trace of the Other beyond the finiteness of existence in a way that can neither be conceived of nor reduced to fit into the sum total of all that is known.

Jacob approaches his brother naked, bowed low, humbled, not in the service of his own desire, but for the sake of his brother, who is, in a sense, everyone. Jacob signifies a man whose egotism has been stripped from him and who has offered himself unreservedly to the other, as implied in the simple words, "I am here." Levinas considers this our fundamental, ethical *obligation* as human beings. It is not because of overwhelming feelings of sympathy or convictions of great understanding for the predicaments of others that we offer ourselves, but simply because this is the basic stance that one human being *must* take with another. If we are ever to evolve beyond our inhumanity toward each other, our ethical responsibility begins here.[49]

The penitent Jacob bows before his brother, willing to stand and be judged for his acts against him. He sees in his brother "the face of a Divine being," which Rabbi Elie Munk explains as a signifier of the principle of *supreme justice*.[50] This verse transcends the closed dyad of the personal or familiar and brings to mind Levinas' understanding of what we call God as being located in the *law of justice*. This divine law sees that justice is provided for all people—the stranger, the widow, the orphan. He believes that "The enigma of the face . . . functions as a bridge to the third party [the non-personal], to the claim to justice, [and that] proximity to the other's face is the source of justice."[51] Levinas unfailingly brings us back to our responsibility to the one who crosses our path and who stands before us: Beyond the narcissistic actions that serve our own needs, he writes,

> There is human nakedness . . . it cries out the shame of its hidden misery, it cries out "with a grieving heart" . . . it calls upon me from its weakness, without protection and without defense, from nakedness. But it also calls upon me from a strange authority—imperative, disarmed—the word of God and the verb in the human face. Face, already language before words . . .[52]

Levinas speaks out here for the grieving, for the long history of human suffering, and for the wounded soul of the world—that they be seen, remembered, and placed before the self. This is the ethical standpoint that challenges pervasive narcissism in a man and that has the potential to reverse it.

The trauma of Jacob's encounter with the Other has wounded him and "grieved his heart." The experience of this transforming encounter is a point where Jung, Levinas, and the Kabbalists all come together, despite their differences: This experience, Jung tells us, is the transcendent human achievement of anyone who has suffered the incursion into consciousness of what analytical psychology would call the Self. One comes away from the encounter, he writes, with "at least a scar if not an open wound. . . . The wholeness of his ego personality has been badly damaged, for it became obvious he was not alone; something which he did not control was in the same house with him." With this wounding comes a "fatal blow to his own monarchy."[53] Here Jung acknowledges that our omnipotence and egotism cannot exist in the same space with such a transcendent possibility as the Self in its infinitude. As each of the stories recounted here has shown, our wounding may bring destruction to our "nation of one," but in so doing it may open us to something far greater than the achievement of self-satisfaction—a humble glance into the face of the Other, calling us to our responsibility.

## Notes

1　See Ladson Hinton, "Narcissism, the Unknown, and the Passion for Being," paper presented to the Jungian Psychotherapy Association, Seattle, Washington, September 22, 2001.

2　Edward Edinger, *Ego and Archetype* (Baltimore, MD: Penguin Books, 1972), 24.

3　Adriaan T. Peperzak, and Emmanuel Levinas. *To the Other: An Introduction to the Philosophy of Emmanuel Levinas* (West Lafayette, IN: Purdue University Press, 1993), 176.

4　Hinton, "Narcissism, the Unknown, and the Passion for Being."

5　*The Natural*. 1985. Screenplay by Roger Towne and Phil Dusenberry, based upon Bernard Malamud, *The Natural* (New York, NY: Farrar, Strauss and Cudahy, 1952), Directed by Barry Levinson.

6　In Bernard Malamud's 1952 novel, *The Natural*, from which the screenplay was derived, Roy Hobbs strikes out at the end, and newspaper headlines accuse him unjustly of taking bribes to throw the big game. The book ends when a boy asks him in the street if this was true, and Roy covers his face in his hands and weeps bitterly. This may allude to the sacrifice of the egoic hero.

7　*Family Man*. 2000. Screenplay by David Diamond and David Weissman. Directed by Brett Ratner.

8　*Reign Over Me*. 2007. Screenplay by Mike Binder. Directed by Mike Binder.

9　Peperzak, *To the Other*, 19.

10　This brings to mind Psyche's jealous shadow-sisters whose poisonous lies destroy the dark fusion that encompasses Eros and Psyche.

11　"A death-blow is a life-blow to some

　　Who, till they died, did not alive become;

　　Who, had they lived, had died, but when

　　They died, vitality begun."

　　Emily Dickinson, "A death-blow is a life-blow to some."

　　http://www.bartleby.com/113/4046.html. (Accessed 3/6/2011).

12　Julia Kristeva, *Powers of Horror: An Essay on Abjection* (New York: Columbia University Press, 1982), as cited in Mark C. Taylor, *Altarity* (Chicago: University of Chicago Press, 1987), 161–67.

13　Hinton, "The Enigmatic Signifier and the Decentred Subject," *Journal of Analytical Psychology* 54(5) (2009): 642; and Jean Laplanche, *Essays on Otherness* (New York: Routledge, 1999), 227.

14  Hinton, "The Enigmatic Signifier," 643 and Jean Laplanche, *New Foundations for Psychoanalysis* (Oxford, UK: Blackwell Publishing, 1989), 160, and Laplanche, *Essays on Otherness*, 228–29.

15  Over the entry to Jung's home is written, "Bidden or unbidden, God is here."

16  See Areh Kaplan, *Meditation and Kabbalah* (York Beach, ME: Samuel Weiser, 1982) and Z'ev ben Shimon Halevi, *Kabbalah: Tradition of Hidden Knowledge* (London: Thames & Hudson, 1980).

17  From Ezekiel's vision: "I saw, and behold a stormy wind came from the north, a great and flashing fire, and a Glow round about and from its midst was the likes of the Speaking Silence, in the midst of the fire." Book of Ezekiel, 1:4, from Areh Kaplan, *Inner Space* (Jerusalem: Moznaim Publishing, 1990), 147. This "Speaking Silence" is reminiscent of Saint Teresa's paradoxical image of her Beloved as a "thunderclap with no sound."

18  Exodus 33:10, from *The Jerusalem Bible*, English text revised and edited by H. Fisch (Jerusalem: Koren Publishers, 1992), 104.

19  "He told Moses, "I will commune with you, and I will speak with you from above the ark-cover from between the Cherubs [the golden angels carved on the ark-cover], Exodus, 25:22. This place between the cherubs was believed to be "an opening into a spiritual dimension. In concentrating his thoughts between the Cherubs on the ark, a prophet was able to enter the prophetic state." Kaplan, *Inner Space*, 32.

20  Halevi, *Kabbalah*, 7, 8.

21  "In Kabbalah, God the Transcendent is called *AYIN* . . .'No Thing', for God is beyond Existence . . . absolute Nothing. . . . [Whereas] *AYIN SOF* means 'Without End' . . . God Who is everywhere. . . . *AYIN SOF* is the Absolute All . . . the One to the Zero of *AYIN*. . . . *AYIN SOF* has no Attributes, because they can manifest only within existence, and existence is finite. Halevi, *Kabbalah*, p. 5.

22  Gershom Gerhard Scholem. *Kabbalah* (Jerusalem: Keter Publishing House, 1974), 17.

23  Scholem, *Kabbalah*, 40.

24  Scholem, *Kabbalah*, 195.

25  Emmanuel Levinas, *Difficult Freedom: Essays on Judaism*, translated by Sean Hand (Baltimore: Johns Hopkins University Press, 1990), 11–23.

26  As an orthodox Jew he drew much of his philosophical thought—which he insisted was not religious but ethical—from universalized Judaic themes. He was from Lithuania (the same area as my patient's mother's family), an area of Jewish learning in Eastern Europe that prided itself on rigorous argument while eschewing the charismatic, mystical experience as instanced in Hassidism and Kabbalah. See Hilary Putnam, "Levinas and Judaism," in *The Cambridge Companion to Levinas*, edited by Simon Critchley and Robert Berasconi (Cambridge, UK: Cambridge University Press, 2002), 46. Hassidism is a charismatic, mystical, orthodox sect, founded in the eighteenth century in Poland by the Ba'al Shem Tov, that worshipped God through contemplative prayer, song, and dance.

27  Emmanuel Levinas, *Otherwise Than Being: Or, Beyond Essence*, translated by Alphonso Lingis (Pittsburgh, PA: Duquesne University Press, 1998), 144.

28  Levinas, *Otherwise Than Being*, 146.

29  Emmanuel Levinas, *The Levinas Reader*, edited and translated by Sean Hand (Oxford, UK: Basil Blackwell, 1989), 70.

30  Putnam, "Levinas and Judaism," 42.

31  Steven Joseph, "Jung and Kabbalah: Imaginal and Noetic Aspects," *Journal of Analytical Psychology* 52(3) (2007): 324–25.

32  Joseph, "Jung and Kabbalah," 325–26.

33  Joseph, "Jung and Kabbalah," 326.

34  1:103b, from *The Zohar*, translation and commentary by Daniel C. Matt (Stanford, CA: Stanford University Press, 2004), 133.

35  Proverbs 31:23, from Rabbi A.J. Rosenberg, translator, *The Book of Proverbs* (New York: The Judiaca Press Inc, 1993), 202.

36  Rosenberg, *Proverbs* 31:10–31, 200.

37  *The Zohar*, 133.

38  Ezekiel 3:12, in Rabbi Moshe Eisemann, *Ezekiel*, translation and commentary (Brooklyn, NY: Mesorah Publications, 1988), 101–02. In his vision, Ezekiel had been lifted up by the wind, suspended above the earth, and heard the sound of the angelic wings. One commentary described it as the "song of glory" that "emanates from the whole earth."

39  *The Zohar*, 1:103b.

40  Joseph, "Jung and Kabbalah," 325–26.

41  *The Zohar*, 133.

42  Genesis 32:26–31 (my italics); see also Rabbi Elie Munk, *The Call of the Torah* (Brooklyn, NY: Menorah Publications, 1994), 445–47.

43  Esau impulsively sold his birthright to his clever brother for a bowl of lentil soup, after returning famished from the fields.

44  E. A. Bennet, *What Jung Really Said* (London: Macdonald, 1966), 168.

45  Teresa of Avila, *Interior Castle* translated and edited by E. Allison Peers (Garden City, NY: Doubleday Image Books, 1961), 135.

46  Emmanuel Levinas, *Entre Nous* (New York: Columbia University Press, 1998), 108.

47  For a psychoanalytic discussion of "the face," refer to Michael Eigen, "On the Significance of the Face," *Psychoanalytic Review* 67 (1980-81) 425-439.

48  Lucy Huskinson, "The Self as Violent Other: The Problem of Defining the Self," *Journal of Analytical Psychology* 47(3) (2002): 43–44. For Levinas, shame often comes when we see our own "drive" for sameness, as in erotic desire.

49  Putnam, "Levinas and Judaism," in *The Cambridge Companion to Levinas*, 39.

50  Genesis 33:10; see also Munk, *Call of the Torah*, 452–53.

51  Bernhard Waldenfels, "Levinas and the Face of the Other" in *The Cambridge Companion to Levinas*, 78.

52  Levinas, *Entre Nous*, 198–99.

53  C. G. Jung, *Nietzsche's Zarathustra Seminar: Notes of the Seminar Given in 1934–1939*, vols. I and II, edited by J. L. Jarrett (London: Routledge, 1989), 1233.

## CHAPTER TEN

# EMERGENCE OF THE FATHER

The making of fire, Jung has said, is a "pre-eminently conscious act" that breaks a man's "dark state of union with the mother."[1] Humankind's response to mother nature's overwhelming power and unpredictability, this dawning achievement signifies the birth of the ego, as the center of consciousness, out of unconsciousness. Analytical psychology sees in this act the ego's heroic battle for autonomy from its primitive identification with the mother complex, in which it has been mired from the beginning and with which it might well go on being identified into adulthood. In early child development, between two and three years of age, we see this consciousness-making act in the form of the aggression needed in the first attempts to separate from the mother's world—to say *no!*—so that adaptation to life outside the early charmed circle can progress. Yet so many men's fires have long been stamped out, their "births" stunted, and their lives frozen in destructive patterns of narcissism. As earlier chapters have illustrated, there are fortunate occasions where an enigmatic process has brought about a shattering of these calcified states, leaving a humble and awakened man in their wake. From this shattering new potentialities may arise. The one that is the focus of this chapter is the emergence of the Father.

Many mythic and legendary stories speak of a fatherless royal boy child who is raised under a powerful and controlling maternal influence. Out of such difficult beginnings a negative (or too positive) mother complex may fixate the male ego, which will then be identified with the negative *puer aeternus* in a destructive orbit around the complex.[2] Assimilation of *shadow* contents is then precluded. The *puer* remains deprived of the support normally afforded by the *senex*: the assertion of masculine energies needed for survival, maturity, and resilience. As the nascent ego, the young hero must be confronted by shadow contents—and be *wounded* in his fixed attitudes and orientation to reality—so that he may free himself. When the ego's limited mindset "dies" at the shadow's hand, another form of masculine consciousness can emerge.

The father emerges from a narcissistic *puer* psychology only after the ego's long and violent encounter with the enigma of the Self. The discussion that follows describes how difficult it is for such a true surrender to occur in narcissistic personalities. This problem is best described by Jung in the important distinction he makes between the hero and the *puer aeternus*, who lacks the gravitas and substance required to endure the violent impact of the shadow contents of the Self upon the ego. His deficiency then leads to swings between inflation, terror, disorientation, and fragmentation. The *puer* then insulates himself from the trauma of the Other by making a hasty withdrawal to the apparently safe confines of the mother complex.

The roots of destructive narcissism lie in projection of or unconscious identification with the disowned shadow. This can be detected through evidence of hateful attacks upon vulnerability in the man himself or in others. In Apuleius' *The Golden Ass* the possibility of bringing the shadow to light and overcoming this destructive process is exemplified by the heroic warrior *Tleptolemus*, who carries the shadow for young Lucius, himself something of a dandy. This warrior embodies a needed resilience, the capacity to endure suffering and difficulty, and the steadfast courage not to evade the experience of the shadow.

The Grail Legend of *Parzival* offers particularly rich and meaningful metaphors for solutions to this problem in masculine development. Analyzing the main characters in the legend reveals problems in *puer* psychology: narcissism, trauma, suffering, and depression. Such difficulties become ameliorated as the ego grows strong enough to bear shame and humiliation; it gradually gains resilience and humility, as well as strengthened capacities for love and care.

These literary amplifications also illuminate case material from my work with a man beleaguered by depression and a family history of alcoholism. Over years of work, the father principle gradually emerged within him, and in its train came a transcendent and heartfelt love for his young son.

## The Shadow of the Masculine

I turn to Apuleius' story of Lucius, who is initiated into the ancient rites of Isis, one of the first descriptions of the mystery of death and rebirth. "The gates of the Underworld and the guardianship of life are in [the hands of Isis,]" Apuleius tells us, "and the rites of initiation approximate to a voluntary death from which there is only a precarious hope of resurrection."[3]

Jung found in such *rites of passage* a metaphor for the death and rebirth of ego in its confrontation with the unconscious. In Jung's conception, the Self in an enigmatic and violent form akin to the infinite Other rips away the ego's self-important attitudes, fixed beliefs, and orientation to the world. From the ego's perspective this may feel like a complete obliteration, but in certain cases a new ego orientation emerges that is more creative in relation to the self, which is defined here not as the infinite Other but as the inner core and organizing center of the psyche.[4] Jung viewed ego and self as having equal importance, the ego being "the self's 'feet,'"[5] the embodied, conscious foundation for the self in the human dimension.

In narcissism, however, traumatic failures in mirroring and insufficient maternal containment may interfere with early infant development of self structures. There is a deficiency of mediation for the raw energies of the self, and tremendous anxieties arise when something affects this undeveloped, unarticulated core of the person. The ego lacks the capacity to process the primordial stuff of the self and flies along at the surface of life, subtly encased in its static patterns, as if in an eternal present, a space outside the blows of time.

As noted earlier, Narcissus' mother was told by the oracle that her son would live to an old age so long as he did not know himself. Similarly, the narcissistic man must disavow any attempts to know himself or to be known. If he were to know himself he would enter into time, into the turbulence of life, and into the certainty of death. Such narcissistic defenses as compensatory grandiosity and the hunger or demand for mirroring, foreclose on the individual's eventual development of a *transitional space* in which new psychic elements can emerge. The ego-self is unable to hold the tension of the tides of the unconscious, and it resorts to narcissistic defenses to guard against the terror of disintegration. Thus new psychic structures do not emerge and life must be borrowed or stolen from others.

In Jungian terms, the defenses bar access to the transcendent function from which living symbolism is born. Kalsched describes a "pathology of symbolic function" that occurs in such situations. He speaks of archaic (archetypal) objects that he calls "daimons of the inner world" (or the intermediaries between ego and unconscious) that "seem to lose their 'mediational,'" articulating and connecting "functions" as self structures. Instead they stunt normal psychic development through defensive attacks upon the links between the mind, the body and its affects, and the other.[6] In the thin-skinned narcissistic man these primitive complexes are triggered like narcissistic defenses when a rejection or personal slight occurs, prompting the threat of fragmentation and his withdrawal from emotional connections.[7] Repeated severing of such links results in the ego's encapsulation, a state that Kalsched describes as the "archetypal defenses of the self-care system."[8]

In the absence of early establishment of transitional space, owing to developmental failures in infancy, the narcissistic individual struggles to maintain his identification with omnipotent and grandiose phantasies, relying on these far beyond the normal period for mirroring.[9] The inflation and omnipotence are a compensation for his lack of self-worth. They offer a means through which he seeks to procure admiration and feelings of specialness from others in order to restore himself. When his stability is threatened he evacuates his toxic energy into others whom he abjects and deems inferior to his grandiose self.[10]

The compulsive patterns of the *puer aeternus* reflect a specific form of narcissism, marked by the individual's constant search for ecstatic fusion which is then followed by traumatic loss or disavowal of the other. This in turn leads to hasty and repeated retreats to encapsulation or grandiosity. These continuing enactments reflect a profound ambivalence of the early ego in its interactions with a highly primitive maternal complex. In this case, the infant's overwhelming anxiety may be linked to his traumatic but unsignifiable loss of the *mother's body* and the *maternal affects*, triggering narcissistic defenses that disavow his loss. Yet owing to its archaic nature the maternal complex remains unarticulated to consciousness, so that there is a longing for the maternal source followed by a terror of its reality.[11]

The *puer*'s endless searching and longing for integrity is therefore followed by swings between defensive encapsulation and attempts to restore, in fantasy, the paradisiacal union of mother and infant. Throughout his life the image of the mother, in her myriad forms, is the constant companion of the *puer aeternus*. Returning to the stories of antiquity, the son/lover in the myths is like a god who succumbs helplessly to the seductions of the mother/goddess in all her forms. He is enveloped in her orbit first as her divine concubine, then as her sacrificial victim.

### *The Graduate*[12]

To give an example from contemporary American film, the young college graduate in the classic 1967 movie is faced with a similar dilemma. Benjamin, played by Dustin Hoffman, represents the iconic lost youth of the post-Hiroshima, 1960s generation, alienated from a hollow and materialistic society. The opening credits roll to the plaintive cries of Paul Simon's "Sounds of Silence," as Ben is passively carried along by the electric walkway in L.A. International Airport, having just flown back home from college. Unable to face reality in the form of his family's expectations, he withdraws into depressive isolation, as depicted in the scene where he sinks to the bottom of the family swimming pool, gazing up at the surface through his scuba mask. His existential isolation is soon broken, and he is brought back to life when he succumbs to a beautiful but unhappy older woman's relentless pursuit of him. Mrs. Robinson, (Anne Bancroft) the wife of his father's business partner, tolerates an empty marriage of convenience and security with the help of alcohol and affairs. "Mrs. Robinson, you're trying to seduce me." Yes, she is, Ben, and she does quite a good job of it, too. The romantic young man creates a tempestuous triangle when he becomes helplessly enthralled a second time, this time by the alluring innocence of the woman's beautiful daughter, Elaine (Katharine Ross). Though she keeps running from him he pursues her like a madman until their fairy-tale rescue and escape at the end of the film.

If we deconstruct that romantic ending, let's imagine their relationship three months later. Elaine has come to her senses and goes back to her safe, well-manicured life. Ben is back down at the bottom of the pool again, looking up at the world through his scuba mask, symbolizing his return to a depressive, narcissistic encapsulation. In an alternative outcome, if we wax a bit morbid, perhaps the loss of love's ideal is simply too much for him and he winds up at the bottom of the pool again, but this time face down and lifeless. Here the *puer* has succumbed to another kind of fusion, in this instance the death mother.

In the inflation of narcissism the ego does indeed prove to be the "self's feet," but these feet are made of clay and are simply too weak to bear the weight of the unconscious. In this case, the enigmatic Self can do terrible damage to the inflated ego. There is no creative rebirth here.

⁕ ⁕ ⁕ ⁕ ⁕

When the ego is inflated and unconscious, the violent power of the Self can have a malignant effect upon it, closing off any possibility of rebirth or hope for the eventual awakening of the sleeping soul. This, Jung suggests, comes about when the "personality [ego] becomes so vastly enlarged [inflated] that the normal ego is almost extinguished."[13] The inflated ego evades any awareness of the shadow that could confront it and bring about its deflation.[14] In relating these developments back to the "Tale of Cupid and Psyche," we can see Eros' dark moments of ecstatic union with Psyche as alluding to this inflated ego state. The burning oil that brings consciousness and destruction to their union then represents the incursion of the violent Self. But so long as the ego can maintain its illusory paradise the shadow can be completely disavowed and then projected malignantly upon others.

This is what occurs in narcissism. When a man disowns his shadow he becomes capable of destructive and violent acts toward others as well as toward the vulnerable parts within himself.[15] Responding to real or imagined threats, the narcissist typically reacts with snake-like defensive strikes.[16] For example, Eros heartlessly spurns Psyche when she wounds and exposes him. He quickly retreats to his mother's palace. There he languishes in maternal captivity, hoping to recover and restore himself. The narcissist loads devalued objects with the inferior attributes he fears in himself and then attacks them. Ego control may be regressively restored by the sudden severing of emotional links to objects that threaten his stability. This severing is seen in Eros' retreat back to his mother and away from the pain and difficulty of ordinary human relationship.

In her analysis of *The Golden Ass*, von Franz seems to arrive at the same insight. She interprets the beautiful Charite as "the suffering feeling in the soul of Lucius," wounded by the brutality of a man's egotistical, disowned masculine power, as symbolized by the robbers who have stolen her.[17] When a man's masculine aspects are not integrated, one reaction is to become destructive and unfeeling.[18]

The disowned shadow can be detected in many a mother's good little boy, who harbors deep resentment and hatred for the mother because of his gross dependence on her, which devours both his freedom and his autonomy. At the same time, he can't openly express such feelings, because he is dependent on that same source of life. Such men may displace this secret contempt onto their unfortunate wives, who take over the role of the abject creature. Of course these men can never openly admit or express this. Instead, their repressed rage is cordoned off along with their feelings and compassion. They hide beneath grandiose masks of goodness, meanwhile encapsulating these dangerous feelings, which emerge only indirectly. This narcissistic adaptation destroys the capacity for real human connection and inner cohesion.

The analytic encounter with men identified with the *puer aeternus* is trying and challenging. Such men are extremely resistant to change (Narcissus will live to a ripe old age so long as he does not know himself). The human presence of the analyst is a threat that evokes a defense of grandiose contempt, punctuated by flights into thick-skinned encapsulations. In both instances the ego is threatened by profound anxiety based in the patient's fear of obliteration in the encounter with the threatening, unknown exteriority of the Other or the primordial stuff of the Self. The "trauma of the Self"—that is, the enigmatic, ineffable, and transcendent Self, which violently shatters the ego's firmly held notions of reality—is instead *evaded* by the narcissistic ego, as Lucy Huskinson explains. It does not experience the Self as transcendent to psychic processes—as Other—because it is already inflated by a primitive identification with contents of the self, in this case, with the unarticulated, archaic mother complex. In Levinas's language, the Self has been appropriated and made into the Same. In its fixity, the ego avoids the violence of the Self that would bring a new orientation and rebirth.[19] The analytical work too runs the risk of settling into the deadness of perpetual sameness that only maintains the fixed state in the patient's ego and does not threaten the status quo. This development is often due to the therapist's own fears of being attacked in the countertransference by these violent energies.

Symington's description of the way such a patient may swing from identification with "God" to identification as a "Worm" helps us further understand this deadness.[20] In the "Worm" state, the narcissist's exquisite sensitivity hampers the therapist's attempts to penetrate beneath his guarded outer shell. The defense is like a club he wields to keep prying eyes away, and it is highly resistant to change. At the same time, painful incursions from the unconscious—beneath the surface—may bring an upwelling in the ego of fear and shame at truly being seen. Typically, the shame is at first presented as so unbearable that it becomes a way to manipulate the treatment. How can the caring therapist possibly touch that awful wound, given how much the patient has suffered, and how mortified and ashamed he is? Fragility as well as over-sensitivity become weapons to keep people away.

The tendency in such a man, with his seemingly fragile ego, is to retreat behind the walls when the psychic skin gets even slightly singed, as a hedge against a fear of annihilation. This is an understandable fear in a man who at times feels identified with the worm, and it is best described as a fear of being squashed. Metaphors of shamanic initiation and mythic images of horrific dismemberment and death carry the same meaning. In this connection, Jung draws the distinction between the hero image as ego surrendering to initiation in service to the Self, and the *puer aeternus*, who is a would-be hero, unable to achieve full emancipation and rebirth from the realm of the mother because he lacks the vitality or the consciousness to free himself from the complex and fulfill his heroic task.[21] The puer lives life on the cheap and underneath feels unreal, or perhaps like a chameleon.

In the ancient stories, many sons and lovers have met their sacrificial end at the point of a razor-sharp boar's tusk, or from a poisoned lance while on the boar hunt.[22] In each, the *puer aeternus* is brutally killed by what von Franz calls the "shadow of masculine power."[23] "The shadow becomes fatal," Jung informs us, when the *puer aeternus* lacks ego strength and has too little consciousness and vitality.[24]

*Tleptolemus*, Charite's brave husband, meets a similar fate—a treacherous spear in the right thigh while out boar hunting.[25] Tleptolemus, however, is a true hero. As Apuleius' *shadow*, he carries the qualities that are woefully lacking in this aristocratic, soft-handed author of ours, as von Franz explains.[26] He takes action. He's not afraid to get his hands dirty.

For Apuleius, Tleptolemus is the part of his shadow that can teach him to endure suffering, to stand firm and not be bent and flattened by the powerful winds of disagreement and conflict, or by a mother's strong hand. It endows the ego with strength of heart and the capacity for sacrifice. Before the self can emerge, says von Franz, the shadow contents must first be confronted and suffered. Otherwise

> the ego is too weak and does not have enough substance to endure the inner process. One can compare it to catching a huge fish which one cannot land, and it disappears together with the hook. The more shadow aspects the ego can integrate, the more vital, substantial, and strong it becomes, so that at the decisive moment it can "land the fish." . . . Life itself, for instance bad fortune. . . . being tortured by people in one's surroundings, being persecuted by them, any kind of pressure, such as poverty, help to strengthen the ego (and integrate the shadow). I would say that regular work is the best remedy. Jung speaks of it . . . he says that work is the means by which to overcome the mother complex and avoid being overwhelmed by the unconscious.[27]

One may ask how the wounds from the shadow can be tolerated by a fragile ego when narcissistic options are compulsively chosen as a means of thwarting the unknown threats to its sameness. As Lucy Huskinson notes, for there to be rebirth, the ego must be endowed with enough substance to withstand the onslaught of the shadow and its deflations. How, then, does one muster up the inner substance needed to bear the wounding?

I believe that sufficient substance can be very gradually developed in the grain-of-sand by grain-of-sand work of analysis. Supported by the analyst's *ongoing human presence*, painful and humbling deaths and births occur again and again. By working through our suffering, something in us is revealed that we did not know we possessed, something that emerges amid the uncertainty and difficulties of life: an enduring *faith* in our continual rebirth.

## *Clinical Vignette*

My work with a 35-year-old male patient centered on his desire to overcome a penchant for short-lived affairs, pornographic addiction, and the eternal search for untouchable female perfection. His behavior was an indication of his psyche's domination by the maternal complex of virgin and whore, and of his retreat into narcissistic encapsulation. Four years into treatment he married. Violent shadow energies burst into his dreams:

> He dreamt that he was with two Afro-American adolescents, who were his brothers, "his family." The younger brother had killed someone and buried the bones in the dirt driveway of the mother's house. He and the dreamer had once tried to dig up the bones to remove the remains so that they would not be found out, but the mother had detected them. Now the older brother had dug them up and they must all try to escape. They can't open the gate. The mother is going to catch them. One obstacle after another slows their escape. He fears that if they dump the bones in the lake the police will only drain the lake and find them.

My patient awoke filled with anxiety and fear. His first comments centered on the voice of his mother who, as his conscience, had controlled his ego throughout his life. His Afro-American "brother" had committed "murder" and the three were trying to get the bones away from the influence of the mother, who had the characteristics of a devouring, *Baba-Yaga* type witch. My patient was uncomfortable with the possibility that the dream could be showing him an exaggerated aspect of his mother's protectiveness, entrapment, and aggression.

We were able to derive some general meaning from his associations to the main symbols in the dream. He saw his Afro-American brothers as representative of his otherness—his shadow. They dared to break the laws of civility and morality in order to get away from the mother. I thought this could represent the shadow's ruthless breaking of the bonds that tether the ego to the mother complex. First the brothers commit a violent murder; next, they unearth the victim's bones; and then they search for a new burial place. I wondered if the sacrificial victim represented a puerile aspect of the patient's ego-complex in relation to the internal mother. As victim of the shadow, this death could herald a separation of the ego from the complex. The bones brought to the surface suggest enduring essence and substance; since ancient times bones have been considered to hold the *mana*—the power—of the ancestors. They may indicate the emergence of a positive ancestral masculine power, one that is carried by the split-off self-states in his shadow, one that can free him from the realm of the devouring mother.

The dreamer associated his fear that the police would drain the lake with his lifelong fear of powerful, aggressive authorities and bullies. His own father was kindly but very passive, narcissistic, and life-avoidant. When my patient was only 3 months old, his father abandoned his wife and newborn baby for a period of six months because he "simply could not bear the weight of responsibility as a husband and father." Both my patient and his father lacked much of a sense of internal authority or agency. Such a deficiency encouraged my patient's overdependence on his mother. Perhaps the policemen in the dream are projections of his disowned inner authority which has assumed the negative character of a punishing internal superego. This superego will catch and crush him if he aggressively asserts his ego's autonomy. The dream suggests great resistance by his complexes to the powerful agents of change emerging at this time in his life.

As my patient's narcissism lessened, greater resiliency emerged. Increasingly, his ego could bear the encounter with the transcendent and turbulent elements of the Self. It is from this crucible that my patient's maturing manhood and potentials for fatherhood are being forged.

## *Parzival and the Grail King*

*Parzival*, Wolfram von Eschenbach's version of the medieval Grail Legend, written in the first years of the thirteenth century, is a tale of a royal boy child, fatherless at birth, who is subjected to an all-enveloping mother.[28] Recalling the story of his early life as told in Chapter One, Parzival's mother adores his purity as well as his phallus: she substitutes her child for the husband she has lost. Within the story are the seeds of transcendence of the mother complex and the emergence of masculine agency.

Here I will paraphrase selected passages from von Eschenbach's text that poignantly speak to the problem of masculine development.

> Nine months pregnant, Queen Herzeloyde, Parzival's mother, learns of her husband's death in battle and falls into suicidal depression and grief. She recovers just in time, but Parzival's birth is traumatic.[29] Fearing she will lose the fruit of her husband's love to the same deathly fate, she retreats to the forest with her loyal ladies in waiting to raise her son as a simpleton. He is coddled, overprotected, and adored in all ways. He is the personification of the *puer aeternus* who lacks all contact with the father, remaining under the complete influence of the mother's world.

When it lacks its opposite—the *senex*—the *puer* is largely negative, unable to bring gravitas to its labile moods. The loss of the father is profound and the longing to find the father is deep.

> By chance one day while out hunting, the youthful Parzival sees knights in full regalia galloping by on chargers. From that moment he knows his purpose—nothing that his mother could do or say could keep him from it. On the day that he leaves her to become a knight she dresses him in the sackcloth of a fool in hopes that King Arthur's court will think him a simpleton and scornfully send him home to his mother, unharmed. From a bridge, Herzeloyde watches Parzival disappear and then falls to the ground, "where grief stabbed her until she died."[30]

The King and the Fool are often cut from the same cloth. As Hinton notes, "In the same way that humor breaks the ice in a stiff group, the Fool prevents the King from becoming trapped in senex sterility, or a ritual from becoming constrained and lifeless. The Fool brings the fertility of the darkness, the fringes, the paranormal."[31]

It is the Fool who acts as scapegoat for human failures. In the mystery-cult rituals of antiquity he was even known to step in as the sacrificial substitute for his King.[32]

The King and the Fool lie in dynamic relation to one another. The King signifies the stability of known life at the center of consciousness and is the purveyor of established norms and attitudes. The Fool or jester is the link to the Great Unknown that, Hinton adds, "deconstructs the certainty of the King," often through insights disguised beneath pranks, bizarre humor, and foolishness.[33]

> A pivotal event occurs during Parzival's adventures.[34] While lost in reverie, his steed leads him to a lake where a fisherman invites him to his castle for supper and a bed. When he enters the castle everyone appears sad of heart, although "It seemed . . . to both old and young as though from him a new day shone."[35]
>
> Anfortas, his host, lies ill upon a cot facing a massive fireplace for warmth. He greets Parzival entering the great hall. A squire appears carrying a lance bleeding from its tip, and great sorrow fills the hall of knights and ladies as he circles its four walls. A solemn, mysterious procession of royal maidens follows, bringing in their midst the Holy Grail in the form of a stone and placing it on a precious garnet and hyacinth stone table before their host.[36]
>
> A marvelous abundance of food and drink of all kinds appears mysteriously in front of the Grail like a horn of plenty, and the four hundred knights assembled for this great feast are served in golden bowls.[37]
>
> In his youthful immaturity, Parzival fails to inquire into the nature of his anonymous host's wound. The feast ends, and the maidens and queen carry the Grail from the room. Parzival takes his leave and is escorted to a lavish bedroom where he readies himself for sleep. His dreams are agonizing and painful—like those of his mother before she learned of her husband's death. He awakes in

misery to an empty castle, the night's proceedings seeming like a dream. He
dons his armor and runs through the empty halls screaming for someone to
answer him, to no avail. The gates of the castle are wide open and he mounts
his horse and rides over the drawbridge and out of the Grail Castle.

Even the Grail, that very perfection of Paradise, through whose power the phoenix is consumed by fire so that it might rejuvenate again from its own ashes, cannot pierce the death
pall surrounding Anfortas, the King of the Grail Castle. In his cloistered life within the confines of the castle he languishes upon his cot in perpetual suffering, with only the same,
unchanging nightly procession of maidens by which to mark the endless days.

Anfortas' isolation from the world seems to mirror Parzival's engulfment by enveloping
maternal influences. The maidens' endless procession suggests the narcissistic encapsulation of a wounded and impotent man mired in the mother complex, who suffers yet remains safe in his perpetual sameness.[38]

Psychologically, a man may feel as if he is a pawn under the magical influence of the
dark mothering principle that keeps him safe but passive, wounded and unchanged, unable
to separate. In Parzival's case he is unable to ask the real question about Anfortas' wound.
Parzival's failure to question speaks to that aspect of narcissism that envelops a man in
passivity: the avoidance of shame and the fear of disrupting old rituals. If the question can
be spoken its truth will pierce the silent acquiescence and fixed repetitions of narcissism.
This is the trauma of the Other that pierces through our perpetual sameness, penetrates to
the core, and breaks the spell of mother-bound *Eros*. Because of Parzival's failed encounter
with the wounded king he betrays his own name, which literally translates as, "piercing
through the middle."

> As consequences of his failure to speak, shame and deep remorse soon become
> Parzival's constant companions. He journeys to the encampment of King Ar-
> thur where he is joyously accepted as a member of the Round Table for his
> valorous exploits upon the field of battle. His triumph is soon dashed by the
> arrival of Cundrie, the sorceress and messenger of the Grail. Confronting Par-
> zival before the entire Arthurian court, she publicly recounts all his failures,
> especially his failure to ask the question that would have released the Grail
> King from his suffering.[39]
>
> As Parzival stands alone, the narrator comments: "What help to him now
> was his brave heart, his manliness and true breeding? Still another virtue was
> his, *a sense of shame*. Real falsity he had shunned, for shame brings honor as
> reward and is the crown of the soul. The sense of shame is a virtue above all
> others."[40]

Parzival fails in his task because he cannot bear the shame of a superficial social im-
propriety. When confronted by Cundrie he suffers the deepest level of shame: failure of
integrity. As Hinton writes, "Shame was not seen as an inferior concern of conformists, but

a guide to the knight who is serving the most sacred purposes. . . . In thinking of shame as a teacher . . . [i]t is Parzival's assumption of the mantle of shame that leads to his redemption and transformation."[41] Parzival bears his greatest wound in that public shaming, which tears away his narcissism and arrogance, brings him to his knees, and sets him on a course to find meaning and to be of service in his life. In Cundrie's piercing truth Parzival is revealed by the gaze of the Other; this shocks the autonomy of the ego, placing it in question. As Peperzak adds, "[the ego's] ruthless spontaneity is converted into shame and conscience is awakened."[42]

> Feeling far too ashamed to stay another minute with Cundrie's admonishment still stinging his ears, Parzival rides forth from Arthur's encampment to seek the Grail. He prays to God to guide his steed. He comes upon a holy man living in a cave, a man who has renounced all sensuous pleasures. Parzival learns that this holy man is the brother of Anfortas, Lord of the Grail Castle, and that the two are Parzival's uncles (and his mother's brothers). Parzival listens spellbound to the sad tale of his uncle's wounding.
>
> Anfortas, the successor to his father as King of the Grail Castle, strayed from the path of sanctity in his youth, choosing to serve the beautiful Orgeluse, whose name means pride or arrogance. As von Eschenbach writes, "Amor was his battle cry," for he desired love "beyond all restraint and bounds."[43] He adds, "Love's desire compelled him to it."[44] During a joust he was wounded by a heathen knight with a poisoned spear, pierced through the testicles. The iron remained embedded there.[45] Stricken, he was brought to the Grail. Through its grace Anfortas staved off death. But he endured endless suffering. The wound had festered and no cure could ease his pain.

Through the hermit's tale Parzival learns that his destiny and that of the mysterious Grail King are inexorably linked.

Jung discovered the theme of the old poisoned king who is reborn as the royal boy child in the arcane philosophy of medieval alchemy.[46] Mythic imagery and dream language frequently show an old man and young son as one flesh, as they are simply different stages or aspects of the archetypal process of the self. When the old king is dissociated from his life-giving child, the psyche bears his sickness. According to Hillman, "[T]he negative senex is the senex split from its own puer aspect. He has lost his 'child.' The archetypal core of the complex, now split, loses its inherent tension."[47]

The old hermit reveals "Love's desire" as the sole cause of King Anfortas' castration wound. In the German, the author is referring to *liebe*—erotic desire, or what I call *elemental eros*. (It differs from courtly love—*minn*—which is of a more refined nature and of a quality that I refer to as *relational eros*).[48] Metaphorical images abound in the next passage that unmistakably point to the *elemental* realm of Eros and the dark feminine as the source of the king's sickness *and* his cure. The holy man describes the Grail attendants' desperate but failed search for a *homeopathic* remedy for their master. In an attempt to fight fire with fire, they try ancient and mythical cures to heal the king using talismans, herbs, and gems. All of these attempts prove to be unsuccessful.

> The Grail attendants seek out the sacred bough of *Aeneus*. It had overcome the hellfires of the underworld, and perhaps it could quell the "poisonous fire's passion" within Anfortas as well. The cure for "snakebite" is administered next. (This calls to mind Eros, who, when armed with bow and arrows, is described as "viperous and fierce"[49] by Apuleius.) A garnet is then taken from beneath the magical horn of a slain unicorn. The feigned innocence of a pure virgin beguiled and betrayed the fiery, untamable beast. Even the murdering of the animal's primal instinctive life cannot cure poor Anfortas. Next, they use the dragon-wort plant to cool the heat of his love-wound. It grows from the blood of a slain dragon (another allusion to Eros, "fierce and wild and of the dragon breed" who swoops down "on airy wing" to do his "harvesting"[50]). As with the wild unicorn, they make the sacrifice of that which harms so that it might heal.[51]

Eros and Saturn, dragon and king, are of the same kindred blood, as Jung points out in his analogy to the alchemical rebirth. von Eschenbach, who portrayed the Grail as a stone rather than a cup, was also apparently familiar with alchemy and its Philosopher's Stone.[52] "The dragon as the lowest and most inchoate form of the king is, we are constantly told, at first a deadly poison but later the alexipharmic itself."[53] Jung speaks here of the paradoxical nature of the dragon as first a poison and then a cure. The *elemental Eros* is a venomous dragon, one that consumes the narcissist in insatiable drives and desires. With the union of *senex* and the royal boy child, the *relational Eros* emerges from the ashes as the king reborn, and he and the land are made whole and healed again. Psychologically, from the conflict of opposites a new thing is created from within the space of the transcendent function. These sacrifices of the unicorn and the dragon suggest that the primal energies of the self may be coming into contact with the human dimension, as Parzival and Anfortas move toward their ultimate reckoning and resolution.[54] As Jung says, "It is not man who is transformed into a god, but the god who undergoes transformation in and through man."[55] The *elemental* Eros that brings us to ecstatic and inflationary moments of oneness gives way to the human dimension of Eros as *relatedness*, in much the same way that Eros must renounce his incestuous fusion with Venus the goddess to be with his human bride Psyche.

A further detail in the hermit's story points to the transformative nature of the *new moon* and its embodiment of dark, ineffable, and volatile energies that break down narcissistic fixity in the senex.

> Anfortas' suffering is greatest when Scorpio is in ascendance in the night sky during the time of the new moon.[56]

The new moon in the text signifies, as von Franz and Emma Jung write, a "dark feminine element at the back of the Grail King's wound."[57]

We know that the moon, its phases, and the effects it has upon tides, planting, and even the emotions (lunacy!) has long been associated in all times and places with the cycles of nature.[58] In the words of the sixteenth-century Hermetic scholar Blaisius Vigenerus, "in her conjunction when [the moon] is totally darkened for us, she is fully illuminated on that side which faces the sun. This should teach us that the more our intellect descends to the things of sense, the more it is turned away from intelligible things."[59] What we cannot apprehend with our senses may be, in fact, brightly illuminated from a transcendent perspective that we cannot understand because it does not exist in our frame of reference. Jung adds, "The moon, standing on the border of the sublunary world ruled by evil, has a share not only in the world of light but also in the daemonic world of darkness."[60] The two must be kept in relationship—one unchanging, the other changing.

Marginalizing and disavowing the things on the fringes that a man fears or does not understand reinforces the psychic split brought about by his wounded and deadened *senex*. His disavowal divides him from his *eros* and the mercurial nature of the anima's feeling. Their presence threatens to break down *senex* attitudes in the ego so that something new and unimagined may emerge. In this way the darkness of the new moon may be perceived as destabilizing to the fixed sterility of the *senex*, who recoils from the "wickedness" he believes to be inherent in the dark feminine, so that he can maintain his life of unchanging sameness.

> The old hermit divulges one last secret concerning the king's wound. His pain is intolerable when the planet Saturn is at its zenith point in the starry heavens, when the moon is new. At these times his body becomes as cold as ice and only the hot poison from the spear tip, lying in the wound, can draw the cold from him. Here again the Grail attendants use the very thing that harms the king to try to ease his unrelenting pain.

The wounded king, we learn here, lies stricken by unbearable cold due to the influence of the ruling planet Saturn, which signifies the ego's embeddedness in cold and calcifying attitudes that cut off consciousness from the vitality of life.

Hillman speaks directly to this Saturnian malaise that grips the psyche in a deadening complex: "the senex spirit . . . appears . . . when any . . . attitude we have . . . begins to coagulate past its prime. It is the Saturn within the complex that makes it hard to shed, dense and slow and maddeningly depressing—the madness of lead poison—that feeling of the everlasting indestructibility of the complex. It cuts off the complex from life and the feminine, inhibiting it and introverting it into an isolation."[61]

If we imagine the old king's plight and the degree of his isolation and hopelessness, we see before us a deeply depressed man.[62] Anyone who knows a person suffering from chronic pain, as Anfortas is, knows that the steady companion to his suffering is depression. To the medieval mind lead was the metal associated with the planet Saturn. "[I]n certain depressions," von Franz writes, "one feels literally like lead . . . In a heavy depression one feels unable to get up from one's chair, or even open one's mouth to explain that one is depressed."[63]

von Franz speaks of Saturn as the god not only of mutilated people and cripples, of which Anfortas is one, but also of artists and creative people. Depression, that is, may also function as a creative process that allows new aspects of the unconscious to emerge. Sometimes, von Franz says, the "real energy of life" is pressed down into a deeper layer of the psyche and can be reached only in a depression. So in certain analytic situations she encourages following regression down to the "bottom" in depressive states until an "impulse for life and creativeness" appears.[64]

Jung writes of Saturn's ambivalence as not only a malevolent planet but a harbinger of light as well. "[A]lthough astrologically Saturn is a malefic planet of whom only the worst is expected, he is also a purifier, because true purity is attained only through repentance and expiation of sin."[65] The appearance of Saturn at this stage in the development of the story line, then, alludes to the "coagulation past its prime" of the negative senex attitudes. This is then followed by an enantiodromia, the process in which the over-abundance of a force inevitably produces its opposite. Saturn's appearance foreshadows union and resolution.[66]

> The hermit's long tale comes to completion and Parzival takes his leave from the old man. Late in the story Parzival is confronted with his shadow-other, an unknown and majestic heathen knight who turns out to be his long-lost half-brother of Middle-Eastern origin, Feirefiz. They meet in an evenly matched joust and declare a truce in which each reveals his identity. The brothers embrace and kiss one another as two missing parts made one again. The brother's appearance is uncanny; his face is described by von Eschenbach as having the markings of the magpie, "black and white and all mixed up."[67]

The shadow is often the carrier of desperately needed masculine qualities that a man requires to free himself from the negative bonds of the mother. This is particularly true for a man who has been raised under the sole influence of women.

It is important that this shadow companion is Parzival's *older* brother, both dark and light, who carries the missing father in his blood. All along it is the Father Principle that has been missing in Parzival's story, and Parzival has come upon it through the confrontation with his shadow. It is the ego's heroic struggle with the shadow that brings the principles of manhood, maturity, and humility into being. Parzival is now ready for his final test.

> After a short time Cundrie comes to their encampment to escort Parzival and his brother to the Grail Castle to be its new King. Entering the castle they are

met by joyful throngs. They make their way to Anfortas straightaway. In his presence Parzival rises to his feet and says, "Uncle, what is it that troubles you?"[68] The words from the lips of the wiser, battle-weary warrior—no longer a simpleton—instantly heal Anfortas. The succession of life begins anew as the old king steps down and the new king ascends to guardianship and Lord of the Grail. His beloved wife Condwiramurs, whom he wedded early in his long quest and who bore him two children, joins him there.[69] Parzival reigns with humility, and his son after him, so the story goes.

Underlying the reunion of Parzival and King Anfortas is the psychological union of *puer* and *senex*. Recalling Hillman's quote from Chapter Seven, "Negative senex attitudes and behavior result from this split archetype, while positive senex attitudes and behavior reflect its unity; so that the term 'positive senex' refers merely to a transformed continuation of the puer."[70] *Senex* needs the youthful spirit of *puer*, and *puer* needs *senex* to provide order and substance, their continuity signifying the psyche's cohesiveness.

No magic talismans could heal the wound of Anfortas. As with narcissism, no grand, ecstatic, or otherworldly encounter could help him. Only in the presence of a humble being could Anfortas be saved: *he was healed by human care* and compassion from a soul who had learned to bear his own suffering and shame, and who had made shadow his companion. Parzival had awakened to his endless responsibility for the other and had thereby become a man worthy of being king. The transformed eros leads us to the mystery of the Other.

## *Clinical Vignette*

My work with the patient described below evoked in me vivid images from von Eschenbach's *Parzival* and the transcendent nature of the Grail Legend. Their shared symbolic themes of the *eros wound, shame that deconstructs omnipotence and narcissism*, and the *reunion of son with father* (or nephew with uncle) are illuminated in what follows.

The depressed, 40-year-old son of an alcoholic father, whom the patient described as a "pathetic and helpless old man," came into a session awash in a hateful mood, his waspish rage directed at a woman he felt used and slighted by. In the previous week we had spoken about his deceased grandfather, from whom his own father had been bitterly estranged. As a result my patient had never gotten to know this man, who might have been a strong male presence in his life. The grandfather had owned a long-established machine shop in Montana, and the great-grandfather had been a blacksmith before him. My patient's own father had always worked for others in menial positions and never provided adequately for his family.

My patient ranted on in the session, his disdain dripping from each word like poison. I commented how on occasions such as this he seemed to be so thin-skinned. Reacting to the slightest criticism, he would defend himself from any feelings of impingement through his loathing and tirades. Agreeing, he wondered painfully what it might be like to be free from these rages, to not be so thin-skinned. I suggested he go into that fantasy, and closing his eyes, he quite spontaneously imagined himself to be like a medieval warrior who roamed the countryside all alone, offering his sword to help villagers in need.

As my patient described this fantasy I was flooded by a powerful image of his great-grandfather at the forge, the fire blazing as he brought his hammer down on a red-hot blade on the anvil, sparks flying. I shared the image with him, and just as I finished, a story from his troubled adolescence came spilling out of him. These were years filled with great confusion around his sexual identity and his parents' divorce, which he coped with through drug use and deviant sexual acting-out. Concurrently during this painful period he became immersed in the Dungeons and Dragons fantasy games and in medieval re-enactments, both as self-admitted forms of escape. In metal shop he had begun a project of fashioning chain mail (mail/male?)—a project he never completed. He described the chain mail as woven, permeable armor. My unspoken interpretation was that this was the symbolic fortified skin he so needed as a youth (a substitute for a protecting and guiding father) to help him bear the pain and difficulties of life. This powerful symbol of masculine boundaries and protection had come back to him in the here and now.

My patient had come into the session possessed by the kind of negative mood one finds in a little boy feeling enraged and powerless at being ejected from the precinct of a mother he has endowed with the power to grant or deny his very existence. Analytical psychology calls this negative frame of mind an "anima mood." My patient began to move out of this poisonous state when he could begin to think about my interpretation without defensiveness, and consider the idea that his hateful feelings were manifestations of his thin-skinned vulnerability. This enabled him to stay in touch with the deep regret and pain that lay beneath his defensive rage.

Something creative could then emerge in our shared, intersubjective analytic field, embodied in my patient's fantasy of the heroic knight, followed by my image of his great-grandfather tempering the blade at his forge. I associated my patient's memory of the chain mail to skin permeable but strong enough to bear the difficulties of life. These imaginal links brought him into conscious relationship with his patriarchal roots. In the conflict of conscious and unconscious the image of the chain mail arose as a *third or unknown thing*, emerging in the space of the transcendent function and signifying the coming into being of the *Father Principle*.

In this process my patient seemed to have transcended his negative state. As a result, his thin-skinned foul mood in the analytic hour dissolved, his anxiety transcended. In their place was a feeling of calm reflection. Over time, my patient looked back on that session as a course correction. He felt a renewal of energies to move forward with his life. Soon he began envisioning things that had in the past felt impossible to even consider. One of his greatest fears had been dying alone like his dad, a crotchety old man who was afraid of getting too close to anybody. Now he and his wife had just bought a new home. He had begun to glimpse the Father-part emerging in himself, and six months after this session his wife became pregnant with their first child, a son.

My presence as an affirming, but boundaried and steadfast older male likely played a part in my patient's transition from the shadowlands to the emergence of the Father imago within himself. Early on in our work he experienced my limit setting as an unkind and sadistic rejection that led to feelings of abandonment and to his abrupt termination of treatment. He returned, however, and in working through the transference he could experience the care beneath my concern for clarity and boundaries. Coming from a man, these ways of relating were foreign to him. In our long association he could experience my ongoing presence and acceptance of him, as well as my capacity to tolerate and contain his rages and black moods without (for the most part) resorting to my own enactments of retaliation or abandonment. These were qualities of relation sorely missing between him and his brittle, wounded father. As I think of it now, the image of the forge that emerged from my vision could be seen as representing the consistent, hard work of our analysis.

Surely our role in the analytic relationship is to help lay to rest the ghosts who haunt the unconscious of our patients and feast upon their life's blood through symptoms and defenses. Our task is to release them, Hans Loewald writes, so they may become the ancestors whose power is "transformed into the newer intensity of present life" as our patients' own embodied presence and life's blood, that "lives forth in the present generation."[71]

Eighteen months after the birth of his son my patient was beset by a cascade of memories and emotions surrounding his own deprivation during the same period in his own early life. His frantic young father had squashed his son's childhood grandiosity, owing perhaps to his own narcissistic envy and hatred.[72] Through my patient's love for his own son he could better tolerate in his child what his father had hated in him—that beaming, grandiose look on the boy's face that declared "I'm the center of the world!" Tears flowed from his eyes as we spoke of his pain and his gratitude. Remembering the deprivation he had suffered at the hands of his wounded father brought into clear relief his longing and his grief, but also the recognition of the father he was becoming to his son as he developed the patience and kindness he himself had not received in his early life.

· · · · ·

In this chapter I have described in many ways the often violent confrontation of the shadow, as the carrier of the potentialities of the self, with the narcissistically bound ego, a contact that shatters the ego's inflation and its identification with the mother complex. Through the ongoing presence, containment, and holding that the analytic relationship provides, the ego, wounded by the violence of the shadow, gradually learns to better tolerate the collapse of its perceptions of reality without resorting to its habitual splitting and reliance on narcissistic defenses. The wounding is just as likely to occur within the analytical transference, in the form of the analyst's disruption of the patient's calm fixity, either by intent or simply through the analyst's own human presence. In both cases the ego's orientation is first deflated and then enlarged as the missing parts of the father within him, such as agency, resilience, and self-sufficiency, emerge. This is a process that allows a greater cohesion in the psyche as well as an increased capacity to bear the vicissitudes of inner and outer life, love, and relationships. This violent and deathlike initiation requires a special degree of endurance, courage, and steadfastness on the part of both analyst and patient.

## Notes

1  *C.W.* 5, 211.

2  Beneath the too-loving "good mother" there may exist a negative shadow that sucks away all of her son's initiative.

3  Apuleius, *The Transformations of Lucius otherwise known as The Golden Ass.* Translated by Robert Graves (NY: Noonday Press, 1951), 277.

4  In *Two Essays on Analytical Psychology*, Jung said that the outcome is either of three things: a "regressive restoration of the persona," psychosis, or individuation. *C.W.* 7, 163, 173.

5  C. G. Jung, *Nietzsche's Zarathustra Seminar: Notes of the Seminar Given in 1934–1939*, vols. I and II, edited by J. L. Jarrett (London: Routledge, 1989), 978.

6  Donald Kalsched, "Daimonic Elements in Early Trauma," *Journal of Analytical Psychology* 48(2) (2003), 152.

7  The psychic "thin skin" is in binary opposition to the thicker "second skin" that serves as an autistic-like encapsulation where nothing can penetrate the defenses. Both states are polarities of the complex that the narcissist maintains by repeated swings between the two.

8  Donald Kalsched, *The Inner World of Trauma: Archetypal Defenses of the Personal Spirit* (London: Routledge, 1996), 12.

9  According to Kohut, the early infant's internalizing of omnipotent parental self-objects is considered a "healthy" form of narcissism.

10  In certain circumstances, the analyst must meet the patient's omnipotent illusions in a playful, open way, as opposed to providing interpretations in service to reality. If his grandiosity is the patient's attempt to restore a damaged self-worth from maternal insufficiency during infancy, then the analyst's holding of his illusions can be a form of healing through the transference, a regaining of a sense of specialness in the eyes of the analyst/mother. In time a rapprochement with reality will naturally occur.

11  See the work of Julia Kristeva.

12  *The Graduate*. 1967. Screenplay by Calder Willingham and Buck Henry, based upon Charles Webb, *The Graduate* (New York, NY: Washington Square Press,1963), Directed by Mike Nichols.

13  *C.W.* 16, 263.

14  Jung, *Nietzsche's Zarathustra Seminar*, 1174.

15  Lucy Huskinson, "Self as Violent Other: The Problem of Defining the Self," *Journal of Analytical Psychology* 47(3) (2002), 447.

16  These attacks are snakelike because they are often subtle but devastating; frequently the other does not know what has struck or invaded him.

17  Marie-Louise von Franz, *The Golden Ass of Apuleius* (Boston: Shambhala, 1970), 76.

18  Charite's character in *The Golden Ass* is discussed in some detail in the Prologue and in Chapter Nine.

19  Huskinson, "Self as Violent Other," 447.

20  Neville Symington, *A Pattern of Madness* (London: Karnac Books, 2002), "God" 91-108. "The worm" 122-127. Goethe describes the struggle within Faust's nature between his godlike striving and his accursed wormlike state.

21  *C.W.* 5, 259.

22  For instance, Osiris is killed by Seth in the form of a boar in one of the Egyptian versions of the myth; the Greek Attis is gored in the testicles while on the hunt, and the hero Siegfried of the Nordic Ring Cycle in one version of the myth is traitorously murdered—pierced in the back by a lance in the only vulnerable part of his body—while on the boar hunt.

23  von Franz, *Golden Ass*, 142.

24  *C.W.* 5, 259.

25  See Chapter Nine.

26  von Franz informs us that the name *Tleptolemus* derives from "the warrior who can withstand or endure through war." von Franz, *Golden Ass*, 73.

27  von Franz, *Golden Ass*, 143.

28  Wolfram von Eschenbach, *Parzival*, translated by Helen M. Mustard and Charles E. Passage (New York: Random House, 1961).

29  See Chapter One for a more detailed description of Parzival's birth.

30  von Eschenbach, *Parzival*, 72. Characteristically, Parzival remains largely unaware of the pain he inflicts.

31  Ladson Hinton, "Fools, Foolishness, and Feeling Foolish," *Psychological Perspectives* 12(1) (1981), 44.

32  See Jack Tressider, *Dictionary of Symbols* (San Francisco: Chronicle Books, 2005), 48.

33  Ladson Hinton, "The Fool," presentation to the North Pacific Institute for Analytical Psychology, Seattle, Washington, October 31, 2003.

34  Many exploits follow, too lengthy to detail here and not directly relevant to our discussion, so a brief description must suffice: Parzival arrived at King Arthur's Court looking like a dummling; upon Arthur's prompting he defeated the Red Knight (in a less-than-knightly way) and donned his armor; he was tutored on knightly combat, chivalry, and honor by the old Lord Gurnemanz, who warned him not to ask too many questions; he freed the besieged lands of the beautiful Condwiramirs, who he took as his bride; with great pain of separation (though at this juncture he was rather obtuse to the impact of his actions), he left his new bride to visit his mother, unaware of her death.

35  von Eschenbach, *Parzival*, 172.

36  The dreamlike procession of Grail maidens and their queen that passed before young Parzival's eyes has been compared by scholars with the procession at the culmination of *The Golden Ass* in honor of the Goddess Isis. See Henry and Renée Kahane, "Proto-Perceval und Proto-Parzival," in

Emma Jung and Marie-Louise von Franz, *The Grail Legend* (Princeton, NJ: Princeton University Press, 1960), 72. In the procession, the squire carrying the bloodied lance was preceded by two maidens with burning candles in golden candlesticks who were followed by two ladies carrying two ivory stools that were placed in front of the host. Four ladies carried tall candles and four more bore a precious stone of garnet hyacinth that was cut as a tabletop. The four placed the table atop the stools, bowed, and returned to stand with the others. Then two more ladies came bearing silver knives, bowed, and laid them upon the table, then four more maidens "of a purity free from reproach" (von Eschenbach, *Parzival*, 128) carried more candles. Six more in silk and golden garb approached followed by the Queen, Repanse de Schoye. "So radiant was her countenance that everyone thought the dawn was breaking. . . . Upon a deep green achmardi she bore the perfection of Paradise, both root and branch. That was a thing called the Grail, which surpasses all earthly perfection. . . . Such was the nature of the Grail that she who watched over it had to preserve her purity and renounce all falsity." (von Eschenbach, *Parzival*, 129). Six great glass vessels burned balsam which illumined the Grail as the procession approached. They bowed and the bearer of the Grail placed it before the host. They joined the other women, twenty-five in all with their queen in the center.

Many knights and their squires assembled in the hall and servants brought golden basins of water for washing before the great meal. Priceless golden vessels on four carts were drawn around the four walls then offered to each of the knights and four then placed them on each of the tables. (Fourfoldness abounds in these images, connoting the mandalic structures of wholeness and completion found in images of the self.)

37  The Grail is depicted as a sacred stone rather than the vessel of the Last Supper that Chretien de Troyes describes in his earlier version of the legend. For analytical psychology's address of the Grail Stone as a transcendent feminine symbol and as a uniting symbol of the self, see E. Jung and von Franz, "Grail as Stone," in *The Grail Legend*, 142–60.

38  Here one may find a resemblance to the suffering Narcissus eternally frozen to the spot, gazing longingly at his mirrored reflection on the pond that never responds, or to Eros in Mother Venus's chambers, languishing from his own burn wound, suffered by love's awakening.

39  "The Round Table is ruined; falsity has joined its ranks . . . now that Sir Parzival has joined its company . . . why don't you speak and tell me why, as the sorrowful fisherman sat there, joyless and comfortless, you did not release him from his sighs? He showed you his burden of grief. Oh faithless guest! You should have taken pity on his distress . . . your heart is empty of feeling! You are destined for hell, in Heaven before the hand of the Highest, and also upon this earth." von Eschenbach, *Parzival*, 170–71.

40  von Eschenbach, *Parzival*, 172 (my italics).

41  Ladson Hinton, "Shame as a Teacher: 'Lowly wisdom' at the Millennium." In M. Mattoon, editor, *Proceedings of the 14th International Congress for Analytical Psychology* (Einsiedeln: Daimon Verlag, 1998), 15–16.

42  Adriaan T. Peperzak and Emmanuel Levinas, *To the Other: An Introduction to the Philosophy of Emmanuel Levinas* (West Lafayette, IN: Purdue University Press, 1993), 164.

43  von Eschenbach, *Parzival*, 253.

44  von Eschenbach, *Parzival*, 253.

45  As in all fertility myths of which this is an example, with the king's castration the earth ceases to grow, as his fructifying powers are lost. The king and the land are one.

46  *C.W.* 14, 334.

47  The split complex, Hillman continues, "is just dead in the midst of brightness which is its own eclipse, as a negative *Sol Niger*." (The *Sol Niger* is the alchemical "Black Sun," referring to a subter-

ranean or unconscious sun that rises from out of the earth and is associated with a consciousness within the darkness of the "lunar feminine," as opposed to a "solar/masculine" consciousness. It may also speak to the *nigredo* or the stage of the alchemical process where the ego consciousness undergoes a death; see *C.W.* 14, 95.) "Without the enthusiasm and eros of the son, authority loses its idealism. It aspires to nothing but its own perpetuation, leading to tyranny and cynicism; for *meaning cannot be sustained by structure and order alone*. . . . Sexuality without young eros becomes goaty. . . . Cut off from its own child and fool . . . [f]olly and immaturity are projected onto others. Without folly it has no wisdom, only knowledge – serious, depressing, hoarded in an academic vault or used as power. The feminine may be kept imprisoned in secret, or may be . . . a moody consort, as an atmosphere emanating from the moribund complex, giving it the stench of Saturn. Or, to awaken the puer side again there may be a complex-compelled falling in love. (Venus is born from the imaginal froth in the unconscious out of the dissociated sexuality cut off through Saturn.)" James Hillman, "Senex and Puer: An Aspect of the Historical and Psychological Present" (Zurich: Rhein-Verlag, 1968), an offprint from *Eranos-Jahrbuch* XXXVI / 1967, 322–23.

48  von Eschenbach, "Introduction," *Parzival*, vii-lvi.

49  Apuleius, *Golden Ass*, 100.

50  Erich Neumann, *Amor and Psyche* (Princeton, NJ: Princeton University Press, 1956), 7.

51  "If, in the case of Anfortas and the union of spear and Grail, only the sexual problem is discerned, we get entangled in an insoluble contradiction, since the thing that harms is also the thing that heals." *C.W.* 6, 219–20.

52  E. Jung and von Franz, *The Grail Legend*, 152.

53  An alexipharmic is "a medicine to ward off," from the Greek. *C.W.* 14, 335–36.

54  Similarly, in the *Book of Lambspring*, an alchemical series of woodcuts, the dragon that is first encountered by the warrior is slain. It corresponds to the primeval chaos of the self, the undifferentiated unconscious that is too overwhelming to the ego. It must be "killed" so that the ego may "face the unconscious without being swept away" and can then effect changes in the unconscious. Jeffrey Raff, *Jung and the Alchemical Imagination* (York Beach, ME: Nicholas-Hays, 2000), 98.

55  *C.W.* 5, 337–38.

56  Astrologically, Scorpio rules the genital region of the body. Since antiquity Scorpio has been identified, as has Libra, with the astrological constellation of the Red Dragon, with both Scorpio and the dragon alluding to sexuality and eros.

57  E. Jung and von Franz, *The Grail Legend*, 201.

58  Christianity's achievement of consciousness has in turn led to "a deadening and violation of nature, which imply a tremendous loss of soul. . . . The feminine symbol of the Grail . . . point[s] to a compensation originating in the unconscious, by means of which the feminine and the soul of nature may once again achieve recognition." . . . "In view of all this, it is not surprising that the moon, as a symbol of feminine consciousness and of the anima, should be connected with the suffering of the Grail King." E. Jung and von Franz, *The Grail Legend*, 205.

59  *C.W.* 14, 24–25. He does not suggest a dualistic prohibition against the sensory world. Rather, the darkness of the moon, to which we must submit, confronts us with the ineffable that cannot be named or understood. The moon may appear dark and unknowable from one side, but provides a source of illumination in her conjunction with *Sol*. She is the uniting symbol between the world of sense, body, and emotion, and that unknowable world some call "spirit."

60  *C.W.* 14, 25.

61  Hillman, "Senex and Puer," 323.

62   This describes Hillman's earlier allusion to Saturn, severed from his child, as a "negative" *Sol Niger*. Julia Kristeva, the French psychoanalyst, speaks to the "Black Sun" in her book of the same name as an empty and dead presence within the depressed person, described as a "light without representation." This deep, melancholic sadness she explains as "the most archaic expression of an unsymbolizable unnamable narcissistic wound." Julia Kristeva, *Black Sun: Depression and Melancholia* (New York: Columbia University Press, 1989), 13, 14.

63   Marie-Louise von Franz, *Alchemy: An Introduction* (Toronto: Inner City Books, 1980), 102–03.

64   von Franz continues, "[I]n a depression the person is pressed down, compressed, usually because a part of the psychological libido is below and has to be fetched up; the real energy of life has fallen into a deeper layer of the personality and can only be reached through a depression. . . . a depression should be encouraged and people told to go into it and be depressed – not try to escape . . . [you] go deeper and deeper until you again reach the level of the psychological energy where some creative idea can come out and suddenly, at the bottom, an impulse of life and creativeness . . . may appear." von Franz, *Alchemy: An Introduction*, 103–04.

65   *C.W.* 14, cit. 288, 335.

66   Nothing upon this earth could ease the pain of the sorrowful fisherman. When all hope was lost and all that remained were prayers before the Grail, their pleas were at long last answered. Appearing mysteriously upon the Grail were writings foretelling the coming of a knight who would ask an unbidden question that would bring an end to all their sorrows and suffering. Then Parzival shamefully confessed that it was he that had once visited the Grail Castle but had failed to ask the question that would deliver his uncle from his endless suffering. He begged for the old man's forgiveness and it was granted.

67   von Eschenbach, *Parzival*, 751. They ride off together as comrades and meet up with King Arthur and his Knights of the Round Table.

68   von Eschenbach, *Parzival*, 414–15.

69   His brother, Feirefiz, only after receiving Christian baptism and the renouncing of his gods, was wedded to the beautiful Guardian of the Grail, Repanse de Schoye, who accompanied him on his travels to the East.

70   Hillman, "Senex and Puer," 325.

71   The statements here are from Hans Loewald, as cited in Stephen A. Mitchell, *Relationality: From Attachment to Intersubjectivity* (Hillsdale, NJ: Analytic Press, 2000), 24–25.

72   Neville Symington, *Narcissism: A New Theory* (London: Karnac Books, 1993), 74–75.

## CHAPTER ELEVEN

# THE CAPACITY TO LOVE TRANSCENDENCE OF THE "HEAT-DEATH" OF EROS

With the disruption of the ego's narcissism and the giving way of its frozen state to the flow of time and the opening of space, a new orientation in the psyche has occurred, one that signifies a major human achievement. The shattering of narcissistic encapsulation breaks up the repetitions of the past that seize hold of the present and doom the future to replicate what has already happened. The flowing of life indicates a process of cohesion taking place in the psyche, a process through which new possibilities emerge from the conflict between consciousness and the unconscious. This is the work of the transcendent function. While the emergence of the Father, as we saw in the last chapter, is critical in this process, of equal importance is the awakening of *capacities to love*, signified by the emergence in the psyche of images of a transcendent eros.

What does the capacity to love look like? In the initial chapters of this book we have discussed the enduring romantic ideal of love that longs to reunite the two halves of one being, characterized throughout Western literature from as early on as Aristophanes' myth in Plato's *Symposium*. Throwing over these old idols—these fixed romantic notions, will not be easy. When a man has attained this major human achievement of decentering his narcissism, he is no longer under the sway of a magical other with whom he seeks fusion. In moments of clarity, he may experience a diminishing of his defensiveness toward the world and an opening of feelings of being-for-the-other. Love may then show itself more impersonally, as, for example, charity (*agape*), welcoming of the stranger (*xenia*), recognition of those that society marginalizes, compassion for the suffering of others, or concern for the justice of all—in other words, in desire that is not based upon personal satisfaction. Such love understands the Other's transcendent *height* and *distance* from self, as opposed to the closeness, familiarity, and symmetry of intimate love.

But what of love between intimate partners, where eros, tenderness, surrender, passion, and compassion play a part in creating a love that can last? Does not "being in love" have the capacity to heal and to transcend one's deepest alienation, narcissism, and suffering, even if only temporarily? Doesn't our only access to the divine move through the sphere of human love and relations, as Martin Buber and Emmanuel Levinas contend?[1] Is it the fate of intimate love to become merely an abandonment to "dual privacy," as Levinas describes it? I think not.

The intimacy of love does present us with paradox and conundrum. Love is the unsignifiable density of passion and compassion.[2] It is marked by a *desire* for the transcendent Beloved, and an inherent *need* for self-satisfaction. In love a humble subject glimpses a trace of the Divine in the other, yet succumbs to passionate and erotic moments of pleasure. Lovers' intimate penetration increases the chances for suffering when faced with inevitable distance and separation. In this gap between the divine and the personal, love—unencumbered by narcissistic needs—can go, as Levinas writes, "beyond the beloved."[3]

We begin this chapter by exploring the ambiguities of the erotic and beloved—that is, one's need for pleasure and one's compassion for the other. Both the erotic and beloved have been personified throughout Western history in projected feminine forms as iconic representations of constructed cultural and religious development. *Eve*, *Helen of Troy*, *the Virgin Mary*, and *Wisdom* or *Sapientia*, drawn from the pages of Goethe's *Faust*, are described by Jung as four "stages of development" in Western man's eros.[4] I view these iconic images of eros not as stages of development but as cultural signifiers of ever-present polarities that illustrate the complexity and paradoxes in love. The contemporary counterparts of these historical, cultural, and religious images take the form of psychic images, whether arising internally in dreams and imagination, or projected onto objects of desire. We imbibe their positive, culturally held attitudes and meanings, and reify or split off their terrible aspects when their truth becomes too much to bear.

Next, we revisit Apuleius' character Lucius who swings between two women who embody this same polarity, epitomized by the conflict between eros and *agape*. I then present a clinical vignette to bring contemporary relevance to these ideas. I describe a patient who has suffered unbearable loneliness and shame and who splits off these emotions through manic swings between prostitution (Eve) and religious piety (Mary). Through the transcendent function, an original, *third thing* emerges in his analysis that resolves this splitting, bringing cohesion to the multidimensional parts of the self and transformation to the patient's capacity to love.

From these ambiguous feminine images arising in the reflecting, fluid, and cohesive psyche, the capacity for what I call *transcendent relationality* may emerge through the workings of the transcendent function. In love that lasts, partners with eyes wide open gaze upon one another's tormenting limitations, the anticipated suffering that accompanies their disappointments, and the recognition of the inevitable loss of the other. *High Fidel-*

*ity*, the Nick Hornsby novel adapted to the screen, grapples with these problems, as do the Persian tale of "Scheherazade" and the contemporary film *Eternal Sunshine of the Spotless Mind*. In these last two stories, one lover must face threats of violent obliteration and reach beyond the narcissistic repudiation of grief and mourning to bring lost love back from an empty wasteland.

I end the chapter with Nietzsche's metaphor of the "tragic man who builds his castles in the sand," which describes the transcendence of narcissism. His metaphor speaks to the acceptance of life and of love's inevitable losses and the courage to live wholeheartedly in spite of everything.

### *Four Faces of Eros*

As noted above, Jung described the four stages in the development of a man's eros. *Eve*, primeval Mother of All, signifies the biological necessity of instinctual love, the bite of the apple of desire. The mother-bound man can be lost in the shadow side of Eve—that is, in the sensual and sexual addictions, so-called perversities, and dependencies she elicits. In his fantasies she promises instant gratification and a return to the Garden of Eden, free from struggle.

The divine beauty of *Helen of Troy* inspires a romantic love so profound that men will die for her or create works of art in homage to her; negatively, she can be the idealized object of desire, arousing jealousy and murderous rage in those who try to win her. She is too powerful for men ever to possess. Romantic poets tell of her fickle heart that has caused many a poor and sensitive young man to pine away and die from the weight of her loss.

*Mary* is the Virgin Mother of God, embodying the suffering, sacred heart of divine love and compassion. She is embraced by folk peoples, offering a love that transcends the everyday. The belief that Mary has no stain may in fact be her shadow. She is too good. Upon her is projected the ideal of purity and light, the Sacred Mother too perfect to be tainted by human desire. Possessed by this idealization of Mary's purity and perfection, distorted zealous minds have displayed the most heinous religious fanaticism.

Last is the most enigmatic face of eros, one that may lead beyond eros, that of *Sapientia*—Wisdom. Unlike the previous three feminine images, she is not mortal born but divine. She is known, under many guises, as the Beloved. In King Solomon's *Song of Songs*, she is called the Black Shulamite, and in *Proverbs* Wisdom, there at the beginning, before creation, Spouse of God. To the Gnostics and the alchemists she is Sophia.[5] As in da Vinci's *Mona Lisa*, her knowing smile seems to embody both the earthen and the heavenly guises of eros, creating an image that transcends instinctual, romantic, and spiritual loves. The suffering mystic longs to "die" to become one with God, his Beloved, to whom he gives the name Wisdom. This death refers to the ego's death, the surrender of the personal identity and its merging with the Infinite. By holding love's pain as well as its ecstasy, the sensual and the sacred, the mystic overcomes and transcends the opposites, embodying a psychological movement toward wholeness. For that reason, Sapientia is venerated and privileged by Jungian and mystical traditions as a paradoxical and transcendent form of eros.

Because of Sapientia's multidimensionality, from which awareness of both darkness and light can emerge, it may be difficult to consider that she has a shadow. But her shadow may appear in the numinous and ineffable dimension her presence evokes, engendering in the ego irrational fears of uncertainty and loss of control. In their fear of madness, of falling into the abyss, of loss of self, dissolution, death, and all things construed as evil or dark, some theologians and philosophers feel compelled to spiritualize or intellectualize Sapientia's erotic, mysterious, and numinous qualities. The ego's illusion that it is possible to integrate such an enigma is an attempt to delimit or skip over overwhelming truths that could threaten its fixed and secure beliefs.

When we fear what we do not know, or need to control the mystery and uncertainties of what we do not understand, we prevent the emergence of new and unknown elements. These are the contents that can come into being through the work of the transcendent function, and they may be announced by the appearance of images evocative of Sapientia. These elements are key to analytical work, and they signify the stirrings of a self that has gone through the fires and returned. Yet with these images a backlash can ensue that is far worse than the fear and control that shut off growth. As in Mary's case, we find elements of this kind in the most severe forms of fundamentalism, where all dimensionality collapses into the need for concrete and one-sided certainty. Suicide bombers are true believers. Seized by an absolute faith in their righteous causes, they love their god. In literally sacrificing their lives they adhere to the certainty that they will be joined for eternity with their god in paradise. Here the mystery of symbolic "death and oneness" with the Beloved is both debased and reified, bearing no resemblance to the function of transcendence that opens us to something original.

Despite their significance, I do not wish to privilege the later historical, more developed forms of eros over the earlier, more natural ones. As we see, each carries its own shadow for a man, a shadow he may split off and project or be utterly possessed by. Eros in all its vicissitudes impacts us all, each reflecting what love and the pain of its loss inflict upon us, demand of us, and call us to do. I believe that, from the first to the last, each form of eros contains a multiplicity of dimensions, as well as the seeds of the forms that follow or precede it. Paradoxically, within each one is its opposite, and each is contaminated by all the other elements of eros in the psyche. The Great Mother Goddess of the ancient agricultural civilizations, for instance, is both suckling mother and seductress to her son/lover. And the seductive innocence of a beautiful and virginal maiden can arouse feelings in a man either of great erotic desire or the fantasy of an ideal love too pure to adulterate with human hands. Psyche is an example of this. A more contemporary illustration is the cheerleader in the film *American Beauty* (1999).

We can observe a certain symmetry and antinomy in the two sets of opposites as well: Eve and Mary as *Mother*, Helen and Sapientia as *Beloved*. A badly split man may find himself moving torturously between the polarities of mother and *anima*, or dutiful wife and bewitching mistress. These phenomena were described more fully in Chapter Three. At their best, Eve and Helen, respectively, can embody a man's natural connection to life, and the inspiration and beauty that stir human love. Mary and Sapientia may evoke an inner, spiritual love—for Mary's compassion that transcends the everyday, and Sapientia's reflected wisdom and faith in the mystery. In a reflective, cohesive psyche, these dimensions of love, compassion, and wisdom draw us into passionate life and help mediate between ego and self as functions of intuition and relationship. Love that lasts becomes possible. At the same time, our unconscious projections into the concrete world, and the overwhelming moods that take us captive, also contain the shadow and destructive aspects of these four facets of eros.[6]

These four feminine forms must be brought down to earth, in much the same way as Mother Mary is brought down into the lives of the peasant folk that still throng to her shrine beside the healing waters at Lourdes, in search of her compassion and mercy. Numinous images of the dark feminine, seen in such venerated and mysterious guises as the Black Madonna, parallel our contemporary fascination with the myth of Mary Magdalene as Jesus' lover, whose womb, it was believed, was the *actual* Holy Grail that carried his offspring and the royal bloodline of Jesus. Both the Black Madonna and the Magdalene bring the iconic feminine into the human realm while deconstructing what some may rigidly adhere to as *the* Truth about Mary. Often it is in the in-between, marginal places of uncertainty that the seeds of new and creative possibilities may emerge, possibilities that transcend our conscious attitudes and the limitations of our sameness and constrictions. In these gaps between mother and beloved, and the erotic and the spiritual, the transcendent function can emerge from the conflict between the conscious and unconscious polarities reflected in the four faces of eros, bringing something new into creation.

If we consider these historical Western symbols as points of departure rather than as fixed truths, they may prove helpful in imagining the developing emotional and psychic landscapes of patients seen in analytic treatment. Each image, within its context, is experienced as ambivalent, complex—dark and light—and the emotions associated with these images can be contaminated and mixed up with other emotional states of mind. In a narcissistic man driven by these energies however, one aspect of eros in its shadowy form often struggles with its split-off opposite for dominance over the ego. One eclipses the others, while collapsing the dimensionality of the psyche into polarized and often obsessional emotional patterns and complexes.

## Eros and Agape

Early Christian luminaries and the Patriarchs of Judaism set their jaws firmly against the instinctive and erotic call of the Great Mother and her seductions. Aside from the mandate "to be fruitful and multiply," the Hebrews, in their allegiance to their desert god, shunned the entreaties of the Mother who would keep them orbiting endlessly round her like the other peoples in their world, who worshipped her through fertility rites honoring the *hieros gamos*, the sacred marriage of Divine Mother and Son.

The Christian archetype, two thousand years ago, was more differentiated than the ancient myth of the son/lover of the Great Earth Goddess, even though it annexed the same sacred imagery of divine son and virginal mother. It represented a numinous and living idea whose time had come. How else can we explain how powerfully the myth of the dying and resurrected Christ has affected so many civilizations for the past two millennia?[7]

The architects of Christianity, including Saint Paul and Saint Augustine, turned their thoughts upward, toward heaven, away from the sinful Eros who roamed the earth plane. This raises the age-old religious question of the renunciation of *concupiscence*—desire, a question that the Hebrew Patriarchs to the Platonists, the Augustinians to the Cathari, have all labored to resolve. Perhaps an old, cloistered theologian, far removed from succumbing to the scent of a woman, might advocate the simple amputation of all things earthy and sensuous. In this book we have heard enough of the Church's fanaticism, from its medieval crusaders to its celibate priests, who serve Mary, the Queen of Heaven as the pure and ideal vessel of God. In the depictions of medieval theologians the Mother of God is so untainted by nature that they portray her without a womb. Unless we cut off the desires, these theologians might argue, we remain nothing more than despised beasts of burden, possessed by and trapped within the spell of the destructive maternal complex that devours boys' will. This is surely the realm of Eve in her negative form.

The same theme is evident as we return to the text with which I began the book, *The Transformations of Lucius, otherwise known as The Golden Ass.* You will recall that Lucius the Ass is befriended by *Charite*, the young woman who has been stolen away by robbers on the eve of her wedding. *Tleptolemus*, Charite's betrothed, was a cousin to her, beloved since childhood. A lifetime of affection had finally blossomed into passion and longing for one another. Just before their love could be consummated, poor Charite was abducted by the robbers and held for ransom. Yet after her hero, Tleptolemus, managed to rescue her, their story became a tragic one. While hunting, he was ruthlessly stabbed in the thigh and slain by a jealous and cowardly suitor of Charite, who made the murder appear to be the work of a ferocious boar. This left the poor girl with nothing to live for, and she soon joined her husband in death. In the story of Charite and Tleptolemus Apuleius has left us with an early version of the *Liebestod*—the story of fatal love, the union of the soul with its Beloved in death, sung by troubadours throughout the Courts of Love in medieval Europe. In life, these two suffering bodies could never be as united as their two souls would be in death. Their earthly love is doomed while their heavenly union holds the promise of eternity.

If we take Apuleius' story of Lucius to be like the text of one of the author's own dreams, then his characters would signify the unlived parts of his own inner life, given animation through the creative process. Lucius is the writer's "dream-ego," Tleptolemus his shadow, for the warrior's heroic nature is foreign to him. Perhaps Charite is his pure, spiritual love, that aspect of his anima he eternally longs for but is too pure to exist in this world.[8] The chaste Charite might suggest how one-sided and out of touch the author might be with the kind of earthy relatedness that could infuse his heroine with flesh and blood, and the will to live. She becomes the icon of the suffering maiden whose unconsummated longing for her narcissistic twin could only end in fatal love.[9]

At this personal level, Charite, wounded as she may be, embodies an ideal—one aspect of the *split feminine* within the author. She seems a strangely prescient harbinger of the age of Romanticism with its pure and sacred ideal of the feminine, which can leave "a strange *split* in our feelings,"[10] as I quoted Robert Johnson earlier in Chapter Three. Charite simply lacks the strength to survive her lover's loss. She dies young.

The other side of the split in the wounded anima could be *Photis*, the sensual plaything of Apuleius' protagonist, Lucius. At the beginning of the tale, Photis, the slave-girl who served the dark sorceress, is the one who administered the magic potion that got him into all this (asinine) mess in the first place. Ironically, Photis' name means "light," as does the name of Lucius. Given that the Platonists depicted revelation often as a flash of blinding light emerging from the dark (like the lamp in Psyche's darkened bedchamber), perhaps Apuleius has intuited that illumination is present even in the dark. It remains unrealized, however, until the darkness is faced and lived through.

The hungry boy, Lucius, lives out his dark impulses by using Photis to meet his every erotic desire. He appears to have no genuine affection for her; she is a means to an end. As a slave to the witch, this anima figure is not free from the collective nature of the author's unconscious. This erotic anima could just as easily be languishing in some brothel in the shadowlands of his imagination, like a serving wench or prostitute. As we've seen in the Eros–Venus–Psyche triangle, the mother complex, unrenounced, lies at the heart of this split that contaminates a man's mature love of a woman. The mother's looming presence is directly proportional to the degree that the father's is missing, the vital link with him often severed or obstructed in early life for such a man. When the relationship to the affirming father figure stands between the child and the mother, the boy can develop a boundaried self and the necessary separation from the mother.

Returning to the earlier thread in the story, a deeper, transcendent form of love is revealed when Lucius encounters Charite in the robber's cave. As the two await an uncertain and terrifying fate, the beautiful girl evokes inexplicable new feelings in Lucius, loving feelings, feelings of loyalty and sympathy for her suffering. He is willing to save her at any cost, even at the risk of his own skin. Though these feelings are still only in embryonic form within Lucius, they signal the beginning of a change in him.

The meaning attached to Charite's name is highly significant here because it transcends the personal psychology of the author, Apuleius and evokes several associations to love. The "Charites" in Greek mythology were three daughters of Zeus later known as the Graces, their names meaning splendor, good cheer, and luxuriant beauty. They were special attendants to the love goddess, Aphrodite and served other deities as well, among them Eros. "Charity," stemming from the same root as "Charite," means love and kindness in Latin, the written language of Apuleius. Charity is often used in translation to convey the spiritual love that the early Christians appropriated from the Greek: *Agape*. This is a selfless, altruistic love. *The American Heritage Dictionary* defines "agape" as "God's Love for humanity." Agape was also the name for the original meal that early Christians ate in common. Hence agape is also communion, a receiving of divine love that feeds both body and soul.

The idea of agape was embraced by the early Christians. Saint Paul implored the Corinthians to turn away from their preoccupation with eros and to embrace agape, the Love of God. Given that *The Golden Ass* was written in the second century AD, Apuleius would certainly have had some familiarity with the concept of Christian love, despite the fact that he apparently had little use for that upstart Jewish sect. Apuleius' tale, one might argue, does exhibit a certain Neo-Platonic bias toward the privileging of the spiritual over the animal—the psychological Mary conquering the sensual Eve, if you will. As we recall, the architects of Christianity, Augustine among them, drew heavily upon the Platonic idea of detachment from the emotions and sensual desires.

Despite this apparent Neo-Platonic bias, Apuleius conveys an important lesson in his amusing cautionary tale—one that challenges our illusions to this very day: If arrogance and the unending thirst for pleasure and instant gratification become more important than human care and respect for the dignity of others, then we will remain slaves for eternity to the animal in our nature, through our will to power and our addictions.

On the other hand, we must take care not to slough off the animal skin too readily, as Lucius comes to realize. There are many painful lessons that Lucius learns while inhabiting the animal body, lessons that prepare him for his later life of spiritual service.

The animal is true and loyal to its own nature and lives to be only what it can be. For these qualities, Jung long considered the animal to be the most moral of all creatures. The animal in man, likewise, lives in the body and instincts and teaches us a kind of common *sense* and emotional knowing. When the nose gets a whiff that "something is rotten Denmark," or when the gut begins to twist with a bad feeling about some impending course of action, we disregard these kinds of knowing at our own peril.

A revisioning of the text of *The Golden Ass* affords us a third way of thinking about this problem that has consumed young Lucius, one that suggests neither amputation of sensual desires nor possession by them, but brings new meaning. Without a relationship to one's "animal soul" the feelings and instincts that make us human and connect us to others are jeopardized. This speaks to the meaning of the slave-girl *Photis' name*—"the light." By initiating Lucius into the ways of sensuous delights and witchcraft he descends into the darkness of his nature. There he is forced to endure the hardships and difficulties of life as a lowly beast of burden, but it is from these experiences that he gains compassion for the pain of others. The impact upon Lucius by *Charite*, whose name carries the meaning of God's love, speaks as well to an awakening of a selfless love where the needs of the suffering are placed before the personal desires of the individual. These sacrifices and acts of love and compassion inspired by Photis/eros and Charite/agape represent the third way emerging in the person of Lucius as he struggles between the animal and the spirit in his being.

## *Clinical Vignette*

Let us turn now to the case of a 39-year-old male patient whose mother had abruptly abandoned him and his sisters when he was just 6 years of age. He had come to realize that this had left him deeply wounded and fearful of trust and intimacy. His father, from whom my patient was now estranged, was left with the children but provided no understanding for his son's loss. Instead, this cold and critical man felt little but disdain for his sensitive child. My patient internalized his father's cruel name-calling: he was "a sap," and "wimpy," terms his father had also thrown at his ex-wife. Although his mother reentered his life when he was eight, several years after the divorce, my patient described her as a needy, infantile woman who looked to him to take care of her. When she returned his father wanted nothing to do with the boy and sent him to live with her. He described feeling trapped and suffocated by her dependency upon him. As soon as he could, he left home to get away from her. When he reached adulthood he spent years in lonely isolation. His occasional attempts at dating and romance always led either to rejection at the hands of "cold women" who thought he was too needy, or to his own withdrawal from caring women when he perceived them to be too needy. He was trapped in reenactments of the past that reflected his utter hopelessness about needing or receiving a mother's nurturance.

To cope with terrible depression and loneliness that would ensue after his failed attempts at relating, beginning in his early twenties my patient would attempt to restore his sense of self by frequenting prostitutes; later in his life he would attend strip bars, peepshows, and porn websites. Hearing of his many failed forays into the world of relationships, I wondered whether the real issue was his inability to tolerate the feelings of that inconsolable child within him that had been abandoned at so tender an age.

The ritual-like sequence of hopefulness followed by abandonment and then humiliation ensured his return each time to the safety and certainty of sexual enactment. This repeated cycle offered him a certain measure of control. The hope that he might one day find his dream girl could be seen as an attempt to manipulate the future through maintaining an idealistic, romantic fantasy, that he never expected to really come true. If he took a risk with a woman he saw as out of his league, it would inevitably lead to a terrible rejection and humiliation. By maintaining a romantic idealization and the pursuit of impossible relationships, ill-fated from the beginning, he could stay suspended in midair, all alone, yet safe within the pattern of what he had always known.

It seemed as though my patient was reenacting the pain of his mother's cold and abrupt abandonment on the one side, and the fear of closeness that might lead to smothering and loss of self on the other. He longed for the missing mother to ease his abject loneliness, to care for and regulate him, but this would mean submission to a horribly ravenous and needy mother who threatened to suck the life from him.

A year before beginning treatment with me he became critically ill, coming perilously close to death over the course of several surgeries. It was as if his body's own caregiving capacities were breaking down, mirroring the lack of love and care he had felt throughout his life. It was at this time that he had what we might consider a religious experience while awaiting yet another surgery in his hospital room early in the morning. He looked through his window and saw the beauty of nature, and he felt an indescribable sense of peace, for he knew he was in God's hands. With it came gratitude for the gift of life.

Some time after his recovery my patient converted to Catholicism. Its rich symbolic traditions, welcoming community, and practices of confession, communion, and fasting provided a powerful containment for him, which helped to curb his sexual acting-out. After bouts with his sexual addiction, often precipitated by narcissistic slights and unbearable loneliness, he would go to confession and find hope and solace through the forgiveness granted by his priest. He would feel massive shame and deep wells of sadness for his wrongdoings, but these would help, he felt, bring him back into the light and back on track. He gained strength from celibacy, and that helped him to develop a sense of separation from temptations he felt too weak to resist. Meanwhile, at times, I felt a duality in him when he tried to be too pure and good while denying what was human and earthy. The swings between willful submission to fantasies of sexual predation that "he just couldn't help," and the woeful shame and guilt that came in the aftermath had a clear sadomasochistic quality to them.

He was always on the hunt for a religious woman that he could marry. Somewhere in that urgency for marriage he believed that if someone could love him enough she could magically rescue his child self and undo the terrible past. In fact, he was still hoping for a fantasy woman who would save him from the feelings of his destitute child part. But this repetitive cycle had the opposite effect, for every failed love affair or rejection would re-cement the past's template onto his present existence, sealing out all hope for a future of new possibilities. When he recognized this, a deep despair arose within him. The alternatives in his life had been either to obliterate his vulnerable feelings by looking for a woman to rescue or be rescued by, or to turn to porn for the "quick cum"—that instant relief from the despair. But the terrible feelings that followed the latter course of action were pure hell for him—"complete separation from God," as he said. I encouraged him to locate the inconsolable child within him who had lost his mother when he was six years old, because I had a hunch that the inner child was the source of that despair. Perhaps if he could begin to relate to that destitute child's pain he could learn to tolerate and contain his pain and loneliness without the need to act out. In an active imagination, he described the feeling of "dying of loneliness," and of a "pained heart" from his derisive father.

The weekend that followed our session proved to be a tumultuous one. After this last session he felt an overwhelming sense of despair and loneliness, which he attributed to the dredging up of those unbearable feelings. During the weekend he couldn't bear it any longer and ran off to a strip bar and paid for a series of lap dances and back-room sex favors. Ironically just a week before, he had completed a long period of fasting between Ash Wednesday and Easter, and he had been celibate for the past four months. At our next session, on a Monday night, he shamefully confessed his slip. Attempting to bring into sharp relief the binary opposites he had been swinging between, I said, "This is all really weird. One week you're at Easter, fasting, receiving communion and all that, and then the next week you're going to strip joints and having lap dances with prostitutes! I don't know what to make of it."

In an attempt to try to get at the meaning behind his acting-out behavior, without the judgment he may have been expecting from me, I asked my patient to describe his experience with the woman at the strip bar. He spoke about something that he hadn't usually experienced with prostitutes before, something quite unexpected and new for him. He was drawn to a particular woman who showed kindness to him, someone he could imagine as a girlfriend rather than a porn star (two common sexual fantasies that men come to prostitutes to enact). "It was intimacy that I craved," he said. "It seemed like she wanted me to be happy. She didn't want to just use me to get my money and then get rid of me. She seemed to genuinely care about me." He recognized that he felt accepted by her; his sexuality could be affirmed. He could feel like a phallic man instead of a shameful little boy. More importantly, because of the "business arrangement," they could be sexually intimate, *without neediness*, coming from him or from her. There were natural boundaries between the two, without the sense of the devouring neediness that plagued his every relationship. I encouraged him to imagine in that moment how he felt being with her. In the fantasy he called her the "inner 'compassionate prostitute.'" With her he felt an atmosphere of warmth and kindness, he was relaxed, happy, authentic—he could be himself. He did not worry about being good or bad, he felt attractive, he was at ease with his sexuality, without inhibitions. This was a new experience for him.

Two parts of my patient's life had been at odds for many years, and he swung like a pendulum from one to the other. This turbulent episode gave rise to a new level of self acceptance in him. In the period following this experience, no grand realizations presented themselves in his work, only small steps that emerged over time. He gradually moved toward a new standpoint that opened up multiple meanings in each pole of the binary opposites that I call here by the names of Mary and Eve. As we traced the course of his fantasies, his psyche quite spontaneously presented him with the transcendent symbol of a kind, compassionate prostitute, an enigmatic other from whose face the divine could be intuited. He could care about her and feel cared for as well as affirmed by her, without the crippling neediness so reminiscent of his abandoning mother—a woman whom he could never depend on because of her own parasitic needs. In this emergent symbol, the compassion of Mary had been incorporated into the sexually vital eroticism of Eve. This experience was followed soon after by a "warm and erotic dream" that echoed the sentiments of the previous active imagination. In the dream he met a wonderful woman. She was "sexy and kind" and showed a genuine interest in him. He wondered where a dream like that could have come from. He felt "struck by the grace of God," and experienced a deep humility. These experiences became valuable resources that he could draw upon when painful regressions threatened to pull him back into old patterns of behavior.

In the aftermath of these events, my patient began to imagine, for the first time, a life by himself. There was a grounded, sober lucidity about him when he spoke about this. He was starting to question whether he would still be willing to "give everything up for a relationship." These words gave us a glimpse of an emerging autonomy within him, in which he would be capable of renouncing the old illusion that someone would come along who could simply love him enough to magically erase the memories of his terrible past. In this brief vignette we can observe the *third* or unknown thing—the "compassionate prostitute," as part of an emergent process that transcends the binary opposites and resolves their split.

To gain a greater understanding of the origins of my patient's split, it may be useful to revisit Laplanche's notion of the enigmatic signifier. Like all mothers with their babies, my patient's own mother was beset with deep insecurities, and emotional needs that flooded the unformed psyche of her child with enigmatic affects. As in the process Laplanche outlines, these aroused anxieties in the boy were too unbearable to cope with and were therefore repressed. The repeated erotic fantasies and enactments he engaged in from late adolescence on were often set off by rejections in love, or by retranslations of his mother's abandonment. These could be considered his way of compulsively maintaining what Laplanche would describe as the gap between the ego and these repressed affects. It is possible that his later anguish about his repeated failures of integrity immediately preceding the active imagination, produced an upwelling of these repressed, enigmatic affects. From the space of the transcendent function, a living symbol could then emerge—the compassionate prostitute. This symbol transcended his split and brought an opening for new possibilities.

In this movement we see signs of greater resiliency and cohesiveness in the self, enabling my patient to bear the uncertainties of his present life while relinquishing his compulsive need to fill his emptiness through the repetition of the past. Releasing the past gave him a chance to experience the present, opening into a future with undetermined possibilities. A year after this work my patient, who had never sustained a lasting relationship of any length before, became engaged to a woman whom he described as embodying a healthy balance of sensuality and earthiness with a compassionate heart and a religious passion. A year later they were married.

The next section continues with the theme of love's ambiguous nature.

### Eros the Sweetbitter

In Greek mythology *Chaos* was called the Great Abyss of the Infinite, the eternal and pre-existent emptiness of space from which all things arose. In some stories Eros, considered among the most ancient of deities, evolves from Chaos and the Divine Principle as a power of nature that harmonizes all things. Yet as kin to Chaos the primal Eros is shattering and enigmatic.

Eros is also considered one of the primary healing gods of ancient Greece. At the entrance to the Temple of Aesculapius in Epidaurus, where the sick came for healing, were paintings of Eros and *Methe* (drunkenness.) Love and drunkenness were seen as the great healing powers in nature, the latter being an intoxication that transcends the confines of the ego state and opens the self to the transformative and the eternal.[11]

Eros is sometimes depicted in Greek art holding a torch to a butterfly—the form in which Psyche is often depicted—and sadistically burning its wings. This signifies his capacity to both torture and yet purify the human soul through love.[12] Similarly, *Sappho*, the early Greek poet from the island of Lesbos, speaks of him this way, "Eros once again limb-loosener whirls/ me sweetbitter, impossible to fight off, creature stealing . . ."

Sappho continues, "I don't know what I should do, two states of mind in me."[13] The bittersweetness of Eros points to that instant of desire as simultaneously the meeting of pleasure and pain. Perhaps the ultimate pain and hopelessness arise from the *pathos of separation*. The annihilation of self into other, as depicted in the lovers' union, *occupies the same moment* as the pain of inevitable endings.

Through Eros and Psyche's ecstasy and suffering, the couple—ascended from earth, elevated, divine—give birth to *Voluptas*, her name paradoxically deriving from the state of pleasure-filled sensual delight. As the *third*, born of the two, Voluptas both connects and separates. Once sensual desire is realized and satiated in the lovers' union, there is no longer lack. When the sense of lack is filled there is a cessation of desire which brings about the separation of the two lovers. Yet the loss is excruciating, painful. Suffering ensues from separation.

As Levinas writes, "the pathos of *voluptuosity* is made of *duality*."[14] "Pathos" here describes the suffering of separation and loss that arises simultaneously with voluptuous passion. Simply put, suffering arises in passionate love due to the fact that the lovers are not a union of one, but rather two distinct others under an illusion of oneness that soon dissolves. By the word "duality," Levinas suggests that the other is not an object that becomes mine, nor do I become theirs. We are not the same. Rather, self and other are separate, *dual* subjects. The refusal to accept this distance between the two turns the ego back in on itself and into narcissism, reducing the lover to the same.

Levinas then tells us that "In voluptuosity the Other, the feminine, withdraws into its mystery. The relation with it is a relation with its absence . . ."[15] Here Levinas alludes to Love that desires to reach the Beloved but falls short because of the self-satisfying nature of eros. This could be described as Love abiding in a "vertigo," symbolically "above" voluptuous pleasures yet "below" the Other, which has withdrawn into the mystery of its infiniteness and is separated by distance and height.

Elsewhere Levinas speaks paradoxically of the Beloved as both voluptuous in body and naked and vulnerable in *face*. If we recall, it is the irreducible face in its nakedness, that may shatter the subject's narcissism and call him to his ethical responsibility to the other. It is by way of the human face, Levinas says, that an obscure light from beyond the face can filter through, coming from the mystery of "what *is not yet* . . . more remote than the possible." In this sense love goes beyond the beloved's intimate and knowing eyes to reveal perhaps a trace of God.[16]

Levinas is describing an enigma, a gap beyond our capacity to fathom, glimpsed in the paradox of desire for the Beloved which is also self-gratifying need, the ambivalence of love as transcendence and concupiscence (desirousness), passion and compassion. The Other that awakens the human to his egotism and resulting primordial shame may also open the possibility of *interpersonal* relationship—of loving relations of a different order. What then appears is a love that welcomes the lover's ineffable and distinct differences rather than one based on underlying romantic attitudes that tend to appropriate objects of desire.[17]

## *The Capacity to Love*

When the pain of love's losses or separation become too much for a man to bear, it is not unusual for destructive consequences to follow, since they provide a means of defense against some imagined ancient and annihilating fear. Many tales, both classic and modern, speak of these destructive defenses and the rare moments where love transcends them. To love again, despite the inevitable pain that will surely follow, is a grand human achievement.

## *High Fidelity*[18]

A rather obscure film adaptation of a Nick Hornsby novel, *High Fidelity* (2000), begins with the breakup of a couple, Laura and Rob (played by Iben Hjejle and John Cusack.) After he slams the door and yells obscenities at her as she drives away, this cynical and depressed man launches into five of his "most memorable," and humiliating breakups. Each is a re-translation of his first—a junior-high crush that was quickly extinguished when he caught the girl making out with another boy. Laura, as it turns out, has left Rob because he has been with another woman. However, this is just a symptom of deeper problems in the relationship. She could no longer reach him. He couldn't be counted on to commit to her, or to anything. By the time he had reached this point in the game of love a cynical patina had formed around a jaded heart incapable of risking deeper intimacy. Rather than risk the further pain that might result from closeness, he had succumbed to being seduced by fantasies that could take him away to anywhere but where he was. Of course, only when the "real thing" leaves does he painfully realize what he had and what he has lost.

The loss of Laura forces Rob to take stock of the failures and fears that have prevented him from moving on with his life. As fate would have it, Rob is given another chance when Laura comes back into his life. On the night of her father's funeral she simply cannot bear her grief alone, and she reaches out to Rob. After a few twists and turns in the plot they get back together, and soon after, he proposes marriage to her. When she stops laughing at him, she asks him why he wants to marry her, and this is what he says.

> "Other women, . . . I was thinking that they're just fantasies and they always seem really great because there are never any problems. And if there are they're cute problems . . . Then I come home and you and I have real problems . . . There's no lingerie –
>
> Laura breaks in, "I have lingerie!!!"
>
> "Yes, you do. You have great lingerie. You also have cotton underwear I've seen a thousand times that's hanging on the thing. And they have it too. I just don't

have to see it. Because it's not the fantasy. Don't you understand? I'm tired . .
. of the fantasy. Because it doesn't really exist. And there are never really any
surprises. It never really delivers. . . . And I'm tired of it, and I'm tired of everything else for that matter. . . . But I don't ever seem to get tired of you."

After so many failed relationships Rob has finally come to the point where he is weary
of the illusions, weary of the quick retreat when difficulties arise or when the ordinariness
of life becomes too oppressive. He seems to have recognized that his endless projections
onto the fantasied objects of desire were evasions of human intimacy, perhaps designed to
guard against the fear of becoming too vulnerable and getting hurt or rejected as a result.

Many people in long-term relationships have difficulty maintaining closeness, but rather than relieve the pressure by leaving the marriage or having an affair, they learn to tolerate more and more distance from each other. They pay a price for this arrangement. It is
a common belief that romantic passion is fragile and unreliable and that in these stable,
long-term relationships it slowly fades. On the contrary, in most romantic relationships
it may well be the deepening of intimacy that becomes increasingly more dangerous. To
counteract this threat of uncertainty, partners may so habitually focus on their needs for
stability and security that this eventually deadens their passion.[19]

Somehow Rob could stand in the present moment and bear the fear of an uncertain
future to be with Laura. He could see her just as she was, "good enough" in her human
ordinariness and limitations—just like him. In seeing her as she was and not as he wished
she'd be, he came to an amazing revelation. He would never grow weary of her! When you
love someone, the mystery of the other can never be fully known. For the beloved is always
changing and moving as new possibilities emerge in the discourse of relationship.


## *Scheherazade*

In the Persian tale of "One Thousand and One Nights" and in the beauty of Rimsky-Kor-
sakoff's melodies and dances, the heroine, Scheherazade, risks everything by reaching into
the darkness to bring back a soul on the edge of irreparable ruin. She is empowered by her
very nakedness and vulnerability to undertake this selfless act.

The story begins with a Persian king whose new bride has been unfaithful to him.
When he discovers her infidelity, he finds her betrayal unbearable and has her executed.
He decrees that henceforth *all* women are unfaithful. He then arranges for his vizier to
supply him every few days with a new virgin bride to marry, whom he will then execute
the morning after their wedding night. He kills one woman after another until there are
no virgins left in the kingdom. He has gone mad. Against the protests of her father, the
vizier's own daughter, Scheherazade, volunteers to marry the murderous king. On their
wedding night she weaves an entrancing tale that has the king's rapt attention; she stops

the story before its completion, however, and the king postpones her execution until he can hear the ending on the following night. On the next night, of course, the clever girl completes the tale and quickly begins a new story, again ending the storytelling session before completing the tale. She continues this process for one thousand and one nights, with each story providing a needed moral lesson for her deeply disturbed husband. His greatest healing comes, however, not from the wisdom of the stories, but rather from the ongoing human presence of Scheherazade, whose unrelenting courage and love have brought him back from the darkness. Upon the thousand and first night, the king has returned to his former self and he pardons his wife.

Here a deadly narcissism has enveloped an unbearable wound suffered by the king, brought about by his original wife's betrayal of his own innocence and trust. In violent retaliation he sets out to destroy everything virginal and vulnerable. Psychologically, he insulates himself against the threat of a human intimacy that might activate his original trauma and the loss that he cannot grieve. We can think of this as an attempt to evacuate his own wounded innocence and vulnerability into the abjected other.

In the violent compulsion that grips the king, each night of passion is followed the next morning by the closing down of his vulnerability. He cannot bear to stay open and related because the uncertainty evoked by these feelings is too threatening. His annihilation of the devalued object collapses these dimensions and maintains his control and certainty. But Scheherazade suspends the conclusions to each of her stories from one night to the next so that *they cannot be known* or resolved until the next night. In this way the king learns he can bear these uncertain endings and live through them. From Scheherazade's ongoing presence he learns he can endure the uncertain moments in intimacy and vulnerability, as well—that there is another way—one that transcends the trauma of betrayal of innocence.

In the role of the other—whose nakedness and fragility has somehow endowed her with a strange authority over his life—Scheherazade calls into question the unspeakable violence of her king. He in turn renounces his murderous decree and returns to his humanity and his responsibility. For it is the transcendent face of the other, vulnerable and bare, that appears before the awakened subject and commands him to murder no more. Through its unyielding presence and devotion, and regardless of the sacrifice, Love transcends deadly peril and bridges the greatest distance.

## *Eternal Sunshine of the Spotless Mind*[20]

On a cold and dreary Valentines Day, two people on the fringes of life are drawn to a small seaside town, where they meet. Seemingly opposites, Joel (Jim Carey) is withdrawn and tentative, while Clementine, (Kate Winslett) is exuberant, impulsive, and dysfunctional. Both are utterly human.

As the intersecting timelines of *Eternal Sunshine of the Spotless Mind* (2004) reveal, the two apparent strangers are not strangers at all. And somehow they have managed to find each other again. As we learn, their earlier two-year relationship had flamed out. In its final throes neither is able to stop it. "[I]n the heat-death of their togetherness," James Parker writes, the couple becomes disgusted and bored with each other and each undergoes a disreputable medical procedure that erases the entire relationship from their minds.[21] As the inventor of the procedure matter-of-factly explains to Joel, "Ms. Kruczinski was not happy and she wanted to move on. We provide that possibility. . . . She decided to erase you from her mind." Stunned and shaken at this revelation, Joel undergoes the process as well.

The premise of the film is the repugnant notion that when the pain of endings becomes too much to bear, we may simply take a pill of forgetfulness to eradicate what *seems* to be useless suffering. The metaphor arising from the film brings to mind the idea discussed above, that amnesia barriers may be erected around traumatic memories. These are a means of dissociation or self-protection against fears of psychic annihilation. The destruction of all links to internal states of mind, or to interpersonal relationships that might retraumatize the individual, can be viewed as a form of destructive narcissism. The name of the medical facility that does the procedures in the film reinforces this idea: the clinic is called *Lacuna*. The word refers to a cavity or a gap where something is missing. In psychoanalysis, it describes certain severe emotional states where a person's important and often painful or terrible memories are simply missing, or states in which the person may lack any affect in regard to them.

The film's title offers a profound historical insight into painful loss that is met with negation rather than grief. The phrase "Eternal sunshine of the spotless mind" is derived from Alexander Pope's Ovidian heroic epistle, "Eloisa to Abelard," written in 1717 and inspired by the twelfth-century tragic romance between Abelard and his beautiful young student, Eloisa.

The historical Eloisa's illicit love affair and secret marriage to the famed Parisian philosopher and teacher Abelard was met by her family with violence and brutality. They castrated him, and he entered a monastery, bidding her to do the same. She was tormented by their separation. Years later she read a book he had written in which he detailed his great misfortunes, and this reawakened her desire for him. Painfully, they began a written correspondence, exploring the nature of love, both human and divine.

Abelard had come to see his castration as a divine intervention that had mercifully freed him of the bonds of carnal love. His sacrifice had allowed him to find strength in the purity of the spirit. In Pope's poem, the anguished Eloisa begs for the veil of forgetfulness.

> No, fly me, fly me, far as pole from pole;

Rise Alps between us! And whole oceans roll!
Ah, come not, write not, think not once of me,
Nor share one pang of all I felt for thee.

How happy is the blameless vestal's lot!
The world forgetting, by the world forgot.
Eternal sunshine of the spotless mind!
Each pray'r accepted, and each wish resign'd . . .[22]

Abelard's apparent disdain for the impurities of the flesh and Eloisa's tortured longing for their lost love bring to mind the tales of fatal love sung by troubadours from the Courts of Love—stories, which were influenced by or arose in conjunction with the cult of the *Cathars.* In their Manichaean beliefs these "pure ones" pictured earth as the domain of Satan; only in Heaven, upon death, could mankind find God's eternal love. This idea reflects a dualistic viewpoint that splits the eroticism of Venus from the purity of Mary, Queen of Heaven. A similar idealization appears to be present in Abelard's thinking, raising the question to what extent his vows could be a form of repression of his traumatic wounding and loss—his own form of "spotless mind."

Similarly, Eloisa prays for the return of the blameless innocence of "eternal sunshine," for the slate to be wiped clean, and for her anguish to relent. Wishing that she had never ventured into the perilous oceans of love's endless suffering, she pleads for her memory to be "spotless," for the messy, oozing wound of tortured, unrequited love to be expunged.

An intrapsychic view illuminates the violence that underlies these fantasies of love and death. Abelard's castration reflects his terror of the inner fragmentation and death that could result from the merging of souls when love is consummated. His flight from this intolerable dread of annihilation leads to a total abjection of the love object as a means of restoring the self.

The medieval lovers handle the pain of lost love both through Abelard's devaluation and attempts to rise above it on the one hand, and Eloisa's fervent prayers that it be forgotten on the other. The years have added a patina of elegance and nobility to the plight of the tragic lovers in Pope's poem. Yet the trials Eloisa and Abelard suffered for love have been posed anew to the film's anonymous, postmodern couple, Joel and Clem, in hopes of a brighter outcome.

To return to the plot of the film, on the night of his process, a dreadful realization dawns upon Joel in his dream state, although it comes too late to do anything about it: he does not wish to lose his memories of Clementine—either the good ones or the bad ones. As the Lacuna technicians search the neural pathways of his mind to erase his memories, the "couple" attempts a frantic escape from the "erasers" by jumping in and out of countless dream-memories in Joel's psyche. To retain some semblance of his memory of her, they must try to throw the erasers off their trail. So they hide Clem in earlier memories in his life, from the time in which he had not yet met her—memories from his early childhood that arouse feelings that I imagine he has never come to terms with—fear, sadness, and humiliation, emotions that he must relive in the moment.

The lines of the old song that bears her name come to my mind. Like the deeply felt memories just mentioned, these words evoke feelings of contrition and regret for the loss of a loved one. "Oh my darling Clementine, you are lost and gone forever, *dreadful sorry*, Clementine" (my italics). *Clementine* and *clemency*—which means an instance of mercy— are derived from the same root source. Joel's memories represent the emotionally potent experiences that a man must bear—his earliest fears, shame, and humiliation, sorrow, loss, regret, contrition, and mercy. In bearing the truth of these things, he may discover the resilience needed to better hold the turbulent vicissitudes innate in human intimacy and its loss, and thereby overcome his tendency to retreat into narcissism.

Despite the dream-ego's late heroics, Joel cannot subvert the procedure he undergoes. It is completed and deemed a success. Yet somehow, something unexplainable and miraculous occurs. I will allow *The Atlantic*'s James Parker to describe the "reunion" of Joel and Clementine at the seaside town and the film's conclusion. His thoughtful reflections speak to the acceptance of our human imperfections and the courage to love in spite of the inevitable disappointments that life affords us, bringing to a close this endearing, most-human story.

> [A]s freshly minted strangers, they meet again; they are drawn to each other; they begin to fall in love again. Then the attempt at mutual erasure comes to light: they learn that they have been through all of this already. What to do? In an overlit, discolored hallway, they stare at each other, grim with foreknowledge—and decide to go for it all over again. How beautiful! Ghastly as they look under the fluorescent tubes, the lovers stand together in this instant on a scuffed little summit of human dignity: by embracing their situation (and each other), they have transcended it.[23]

## *Clinical Vignette*

Late in my work with a 52-year-old man, a dream appeared that spoke to the simple truths brought out in my discussion of "Eternal Sunshine of the Spotless Mind." His dream offered us a glimpse into the workings of an inner transcendent factor emerging in his life. One might think of this inner content as *Sapientia*—Wisdom—but this was not a grand but a lowly wisdom, quietly and slowly emerging in a modest subject. Its emergence, however, finally rendered pointless his lifelong process of projection-making, in this case onto erotic and idealized images of love—representations of *Helen*.

At the point when my patient began his psychotherapy, he had suffered numerous deflating wounds to the narcissistic illusions on which his ideas of romantic, ideal love were based. The erotic soul image of Helen had been faithfully attached to countless faces and forms throughout his extended adolescence. He then spent many years working through what von Franz has referred to as an "outstanding" mother complex. When he had this dream, many years later, the Father Principle that had been missing in his life owing to his personal father's absence was emerging within our intersubjective process, and the dream seems to reflect this. As a result of our work, he had suffered and come down to earth, and was learning what it meant to be a humble man. To a large degree he had ceased animating the world with his projections, or at least he had begun to come to his senses rather quickly, and, as the dream suggests, was coming to an acceptance of the inevitable human imperfections and limitations in life and love. As a result, his marriage was becoming a source of renewed meaning to him after many years of frustration and difficulty with intimacy.

The dream, occurring six years into the analysis, speaks powerfully to the patient's increasing acceptance of his life and his increasing capacity to bring a grounded, reflective presence to his relationships.

> I am in Ken's waiting room. I notice he has a toy mechanical cat. It's extraordinarily lifelike. I ask if it bites. Yes, it nips and scratches. He holds it, petting it. Then I am holding Ken, cradling him like a baby. I see flabs of skin from his belly that are exposed under his shirt. He is very old now. On his belly I glimpse a faded old red rose tattoo. His wife walks into the room and I say hello.

The patient identified the cat with the theme of the mechanical nature of his complexes, which take the form of his old splitting behavior and escapes into inflated, unreal ego states. We realize that this old behavior does cause pain on the surface of the skin. Then, the scene changes and I have become the baby being lovingly cradled, and he sees what he describes as my ugly flabby belly with a faded rose tattoo. This is very significant in the life of my patient, for it signifies a largely defensive (mechanical) aesthetic attitude giving way to loving in a more human, embodied, and accepting way. Early in his life he witnessed his father's cruelty toward his mother for becoming overweight after the birth of himself and his sisters. He in turn unconsciously adopted his father's preferences. A "fat belly" on a girl or woman had always been repulsive to him.[24] He admitted to sharing the same feeling about his mother.

My patient associated the rose with the culture's symbol of the transcendent heart of love and love's ideal of perfection.[25] You may recall that in the tale of *The Golden Ass* it is the sacred rose that is the long-awaited antidote Queen Isis provides for poor Lucius to ingest. Her radiant vision appears to him in a dream at the seashore the night after Lucius has escaped his captors, his escape prompted by their plans to subject him to a public act of bestiality with a convicted murderess. Ingesting the rose garland that the Priests of Isis have brought for him the following day, he sloughs off the beast's hide and becomes a man again. As a transformed human being he undergoes initiation into service to the goddess, bringing the saga of *The Golden Ass* to an end. In the symbolic language of psychology, the "mother-bound man" has liberated himself from the mother complex by bearing the terrible contents of his emerging shadow. In the conflict between our longing for instinctual desires and spirit, the opposites disappear, and something transcendent emerges; we see the possibility of Love in a new form.

Returning to my patient's dream, the rose was in the form of a tattoo. Tattoos are indelibly etched or fixed, again on the skin's surface—like the "everlasting indestructibility of the complex," as Hillman reminds us.[26] The "faded rose" tattoo is a stylized image and hints at the necessary rapprochement with the heart, free of the "fading" intellect's critical aestheticism. The rose has descended down to the belly. The round belly embodies the passion for being, biological, earthy necessity, and the embrace of an indwelling presence of life's fullness. The paunch of the full belly, the hearty belly laugh, and similar terms, bring to mind the carnivalesque excesses that Rabelais exalted.

The image of the analyst in the dream contains both the baby and the old father whom the patient embraces and cares for tenderly. His own association was to the belly of the Laughing Buddha, which signifies the Buddhist pilgrim's final stage, as he nears the wisdom of an enlightened state and a return to a childlike spirit. The multidimensional image of the baby/old man suggests the emergence, through the transference, of a new and living symbol, a third or unknown thing, shown in the patient's love and acceptance of the analyst/Other.

My patient's feeling for me in the dream, however, brought something shameful and unexpected into the present space and time. Our analytical work with the "loving of the belly" awoke in him the pain he had never acknowledged for the narcissistic violence he had perpetrated upon his mother and on every woman that he replaced her with through his perception of their aesthetic imperfections. The image of the baby/old man, my patient realized, was a symbol for his own mother, exposed and fragile, and he was ashamed. Without any words to describe the moment, he glimpsed in the face of his mother the Infiniteness of the (m)other who reveals itself in the most "vulnerable of all weakness," for, in the words of Levinas, "[a] human *face* has no defense."[27] His recognition of his mother's own utter defenselessness and innocence at the hands of such cruelty evoked a compassion and tenderness for her that he had not felt before. His welcoming of "my wife," who has entered the room in the dream, hints at this rapprochement.

Through these and other experiences over our years of work together, we could trace a progression that began with the melancholic longing in his imagination for union with *Helen*—a need that compelled him to desire what he lacked. The capacity to love, emerging from the collapse of that narcissistic defense, brought a relationality both grounded and transcendent into being. The transient awareness of the transcendent presence of *Sapientia* in the world of his involvements evoked a desire for wisdom in him, albeit a "lowly wisdom."

• • • • •

The final section of this book continues the theme of the transcendent *third*, which in analytical work signifies the resilience needed to bear the conflicts and vicissitudes of love and relationships. I am indebted here to Steven Mitchell's analysis of Nietzsche's profound metaphor of the "sandcastles on the shore," which I paraphrase in the pages that follow.[28] Nietzsche envisions two dimensions in which our lives are lived. In the world of illusions we create meanings and forms that are played out and soon discarded. He names this the *Apollonian* dimension, for Apollo was the god of illusions, dreams, art, and music. In Nietzsche's framework, the undoer of all illusions is Dionysus. In the *Dionysian* dimension we are part of a larger unity in which we are immersed, and even individual existence is illusory. The fullest embodiment of living Nietzsche calls *the tragic*, and it is situated, he tells us, in balance between the Apollonian and Dionysian worlds.

The tragic man can pursue Apollonian fantasies and illusions to his heart's content, yet renounce them in pure Dionysian fashion when the inevitable realities of our human limitations present themselves. The life of the tragic man is a series of works of art in progress, continually being created and destroyed, his individuality, as Mitchell says, "articulated, developed and relinquished."[29]

Nietzsche describes the Apollonian man building an elaborate sand castle on the shore at low tide. He imagines himself to be timeless, and therefore believes that his work of art will last forever as well. In the eternal moment of his illusion he cannot conceive of anything contrary. Oblivious to the inevitable reality of the oncoming tide, he is devastated and shocked when his creation is demolished by the waves.

The Dionysian man, on the contrary, never puts a shovel to the sand, because he knows all too well what is coming; as Mitchell writes, he knowingly stands back beyond the high water mark, secretly "tyrannized and depleted by reality."[30] He is overly aware of his life's impermanence and could not justify the work entailed in building something, unless he could be certain that his creation would last for an eternity. He doesn't suffer fools lightly and therefore holds no illusions about things lasting forever.

Nietzsche's *tragic man*, who stands poised between the *Apollonian man* and *Dionysian man*, observes the tides and knows full well the transitory nature of his creation. He sets about to build his "castle in the sand" despite the recognition that the pressing waters will one day wash away everything he has made. In Mitchell's words, "The inevitable limitations of reality do not dim the passion in which he builds his castles; in fact, the inexorable realities add a poignancy and sweetness to his passion. . . [This,] Nietzsche suggests, is the richest form of life . . ."[31]

We may courageously commit ourselves to loving another, fully and without restraint, ever knowing that eventually that person will leave us—in death or in some other devastating way. But not today, and probably not tomorrow. We will face that inevitable disappointment, bear it, even mourn it, as deeply as we love. But the disappointments we are prepared to confront will not dim the fires that inspire and transform us in love today. The building of our "sandcastles on the shore" is undertaken with the full knowledge that the tides of time and the vicissitudes of life will cover the shoreline and take away all we have built. The resilient man—whom Nietzsche calls the *tragic man*—knows this, yet does not turn away from the endeavor, despite the costs.

Joseph Campbell's prelude to an early thirteenth century troubadour's poem in honor of *Minn*, the Goddess of Love, describes the "world-transfiguring sentiment of love" as "an experience of that . . . *transcendent, immanent* ground of being, *beyond duality*."[32] (my italics.) Campbell's reference to Love as "transcendent" yet "immanent" speaks again to the paradoxical nature of eros' many faces. The poem to *Minn* by the German "minnesinger" or minstrel, Walther von der Vogelweide (1170–1230) will conclude this last section of the chapter.[33]

> Minne is neither male nor female,
> She has neither a soul nor a body,
> She resembles nothing imaginable.
> Her name is known; her self, however, ungrasped
> Yet nobody from her apart
> Merits the blessing of God's grace.
> She comes never to a false heart.[34]

## *Final Thoughts*

Narcissism results in an avoidance of being seen, being revealed through another's eyes, being unconcealed to oneself. It prevents the welcoming of the other in (her) differences and shared humanity, prevents a generous expansiveness that considers the other before oneself. The desperate clinging to control over what one *knows*—to keeping all people and things at bay, to making them the same as oneself—belies a fundamental lack, a terror felt about confronting gaps of uncertainty. These are echoes, I believe, of the infant's original trauma—the loss of the maternal body that in fantasy seems all containing—always already *there*, before memory or words.

All people are haunted by a sense of loss because they are moved by necessity to leave the maternal body to become human. In narcissism, however, fantasies of return mark a refusal to come into the world. They become a means of avoiding life. In a man embedded in narcissism, an undertone of melancholic longing for the ineffable, unmourned (M)other elicits endless repetitions of romantic dramas that are hollow to him and without substance. Sometimes a man is cast in the role of prey, enthralled by imaginary intimacies that always fail, leaving him feeling discarded and lost in utter despair, withdrawn from life. Sometimes he plays the predator who seeks to control the desired object, passing on to her his own pain and suffering; in the inevitable loss that follows he disavows the object as he disavows his own tenderness. These are the guises of narcissism, that spinner of illusion, the most primal and earliest defender against one's fears of loss and annihilation—a defender who readies a man to sacrifice the other to save himself.

In the midst of this seeming futility, can one ever hope to be delivered back to himself, to a renewed life, ungoverned by such an unseen defense? As these tales of love, drawn from life and art, have shown, an opportune moment in time may arise when a man is suddenly awakened and dislodged from his narcissism, perhaps by some unforeseen tragedy or trauma, perhaps by the stark, unbearable truth of the harm he has done in his life, a truth that—this time—he cannot escape. Sometimes the encounter is not so shattering but takes instead the form of a slow erosion of the false self, as in the analytic encounter. But in every case, he stands revealed before the gaze of the Other, glimpsed in the faces of those most naked, whose vulnerability stirs his torment and responsibility for them. His false self falls away, useless, as he feels the shame of his own violence.

The original suffering, humiliation, and shame, born of disavowed loss, are now agonizingly present in all their enigmatic traces. They can be endured by a resilience brought into being in the name of the Father—the kind of man the individual hoped he would become. The hope that the enigmas of life can somehow be resolved, however, or that he may finally be freed of their burden, tempts a man to maintain a fearful stance with respect to life. In truth these enigmas are unfathomable. Jung's words about honoring the uncertainties of life speak to this. "Anyone who takes the sure road is as good as dead."[35] Yet through ongoing engagement with life's difficulties and uncertainties one can come to a plain acceptance of their underlying mystery, and a recognition that there are no guarantees for a future that is forever unwritten. It is through this surrender that one can, paradoxically, transcend one's endless repetitions of the narcissistic patterns.

Throughout our history of love, in all the ambiguities of immanent passion and desire for the Beloved, eros mirrors both the need for sameness and a desire for the Infinite that lies beyond our reach. Passion suspends the twins, Eros and Psyche, above life, until a fateful reckoning born of loss ushers forth love's descent from the heights. From the acceptance of love and its inevitable uncertainty and loss, what I have called a transcendent relationality may come to live in the space between the two. In the embrace of the lover as human, separate, and finite, we paradoxically glimpse what is infinite, interpenetrating, and enduring in love.

In conclusion I will quote from Jung, who writes of love as an experience of something more than ourselves, a love that

> is not transference and not friendship in the usual sense, not sympathy either. It is more primitive, more primordial, and more spiritual than anything we are capable of describing. The upper story is no longer you or I, it is the many of which you yourself are a part, and everyone is part of it whose heart you touch. There differentness does not prevail, but rather immediate presence. It is an eternal mystery; how could I ever explain it?[36]

## *Notes*

1  Donna M. Orange, *Thinking For Clinicians* (New York: Routledge, 2010), 91.

2  Adriaan T. Peperzak, and Emmanuel Levinas. *To the Other: An Introduction to the Philosophy of Emmanuel Levinas* (West Lafayette, IN: Purdue University Press, 1993), 193–94.

3  Emmanuel Levinas, *Totality and Infinity*, translated by Alphonso Lingis (Pittsburgh, PA: Duquesne University Press, 1969), 254.

4  "Four stages of eroticism were known in the late classical period. Hawwah (Eve), Helen (of Troy), the Virgin Mary, and Sophia. The series is repeated in Goethe's *Faust* in the figures of Gretchen as the personification of a purely instinctual relationship (Eve); Helen as an anima figure; Mary as the personification of the 'heavenly', ie Christian or religious, relationship; and the 'eternal feminine' as an expression of the alchemical *Sapientia*." *C.W.* 16, 174.

5  The later Gnostic and alchemical writings, and the Canticles of the Spanish mystics depicting Wisdom as the Beloved, Sophia, and *Sapientia*, can be traced back to the *Song of Songs*, 6:3: "I am my Beloved's and my Beloved is mine," and to Proverbs 8:22, 27: "The Lord created me as the beginning of his way, the first of his works of old.... When he established the heavens, I was there..." Wisdom is present, alongside the Creator, from the beginning. In Proverbs 9:1–2, Wisdom is alluded to as a feminine personification. "Wisdom has built her house, she has hewn out her seven pillars." Rabbi A. J. Rosenberg, *The Books of Esther, Song of Songs, Ruth* (New York: Judaica Press, 1992), 72; Rabbi A. J. Rosenberg, *The Book of Proverbs* (New York: Judaica Press, 1993), 806, 807.

6  Here I run the risk of appearing to classify these four dimensions of a man's eros as if they were absolutes and could fit nicely and distinctly into four slots in a theory, but that would ultimately deaden them. These are cultural and historical signifiers that have been defined by their place in time. Therefore what they have come to signify is constructed and not necessarily universally held. Symbols can signify many things. Once we put them on a pedestal they stop growing and become iconic.

7  *C.W.* 14, 523–24.

8  Historians tell us of Apuleius' happy marriage to a woman twenty years his senior. One can only imagine, without any certainty, of course, that their enduring love probably lacked the kind of fiery blaze that consumes young and foolish lovers.

9  Let us not, however lose sight of the *symbolic* meaning of sacrifice and death as *initiation* that brings new life and cohesion to disparate parts of the psyche.

10  Robert Johnson, *We* (New York: HarperCollins, 1983), 71.

11  Marie-Louise von Franz, *The Golden Ass of Apuleius* (Boston: Shambhala, 1970), 83, 84.

12  von Franz, *The Golden Ass*, 82.

13  Anne Carson, *Eros the Bittersweet* (Normal, IL: Dalkey Archive Press, 1998), 3.

14  Levinas, *Totality and Infinity*, (my italics), 276.

15  Levinas, *Totality and Infinity*, 276–77.

16  Levinas, *Totality and Infinity*, 254–55.

17  Peperzak, *To the Other*, 176.

18  *High Fidelity.* 2000. Screenplay by D.V. DeVincentis, Steve Pink, John Cusack, and Scott Rosenberg, based upon Nick Hornby, *High Fidelity* (New York, NY: Riverhead Books 1995), Directed by Stephen Fears.

19  Stephen A. Mitchell, *Can Love Last?* (New York: Norton, 2002), 27, 28, 45.

20  *Eternal Sunshine of the Spotless Mind.* 2004. Screenplay by Charlie Kaufman. Directed by Michel Gondry.

21  James Parker, "The Existential Clown," *The Atlantic Online* at http://www.theatlantic.com/doc/print/200812/jimcarey, 2 (accessed 1/13/2009).

22  Alexander Pope, "Eloisa to Abelard" at http://en.wikipedia.org/wiki/Eloisa_to_Abelard, 1 (accessed 1/26/10).

23  Parker, "Existential Clown," 2.

24  This is typical in the Dorian Gray type of narcissistic personality; see Chapter Five.

25  The rose has reached the end of its adaptation and is therefore "perfect."

26  James Hillman, *Senex and Puer: An Aspect of the Historical and Psychological Present* (Zurich: Rhein-Verlag, 1968), an offprint from *Eranos-Jahrbuch* XXXVI / 1967, 323.

27  Peperzak, *To the Other*, 64.

28  Stephen A. Mitchell, "The Wings of Icarus: Illusion and the Problem of Narcissism," at http://www.wawhite.org/Journal/mitchell_art5.htm, 7 (accessed 12/29/2008). see also: http://www.wawhite.org/uploads/PDF/SMitchell-WingsofIcarus.pdf

29  Mitchell, "The Wings of Icarus: Illusion and the Problem of Narcissism," 7.

30  Mitchell, "The Wings of Icarus: Illusion and the Problem of Narcissism," 7.

31  Mitchell, "The Wings of Icarus: Illusion and the Problem of Narcissism," 7.

32  Joseph Campbell, *The Masks of God: Creative Mythology* (New York: Viking Press, 1968), 181.

33  See the section on *Parzival* in Chapter Five of this book.

34  Campbell, *Masks of God*, 181–182 (my italics); From Carl von Krause, Carl. *Die Gedichte Walthers von der Vogelweide*. (Berlin: Walter de Griyter & Company, 1962), 11.

35  C. G. Jung, *Memories, Dreams, Reflections* (New York: Vintage Books, 1965), 297.

36  C. G. Jung, letter of April 18, 1941, in *Letters*, vol. I . Selected and edited by Gerhard Adler, in collaboration with Aniela Jaffé. Translations from the German by R. F. C. Hull (Princeton, NJ: Princeton University Press, 1973), Bollingen Series 95, 373.

# GLOSSARY

**active imagination.** A method Jung developed in order to induce an active dialogue with the unconscious while in a waking state. In a relaxed, trancelike state, one holds in mind an image (e.g., from a dream) and inquires of the image its origins, meaning, and so on, as if it were another person. "Glossary," in Polly Young-Eisendrath and Terence Dawson, eds., *The Cambridge Companion to Jung,* 1997.

**alterity.** The quality of "being other" than the subject. Alterity differs from Otherness in that alterity suggests difference but also entails the capacity to think about and develop relations to the other, whereas the Other can never be known, only glimpsed.

**amnesia barrier.** A barrier that is the product of a "destructive, dismembering activity . . . involving aggression in service of dissociation," and that surrounds the mechanisms of the *self-care system.* The amnesia barrier is erected around "split compartments of the mind" so as to dissociate bad internal parts of the psyche containing traumatic memories from the good ones. Kalsched, "Daimonic Elements in Early Trauma." *Journal of Analytical Psychology* 48(2) (2003): 148.

**anima.** The essence of the person that transcends the psyche's complexes. In the classical sense, it means soul or "breath of life." *Anima* is originally contra-sexual because it is usually discovered through the force of *eros* in projection or relationship. Because the mother is the first love of our lives, the *anima* is initially contaminated by elements of the mother complex, so when a negative *anima* mood captures a man we could consider that the *anima* has been possessed by the mother complex. When he develops a relationship to his inner feminine, the *anima* takes on distinct functions in the psyche that differentiate her from the mother complex, such as relatedness, creativity, and spiritual dimensions. She may be personified in dreams, imagination, myth, and fairy tale as the perfect woman, as seductress, as femme fatal, as soul guide—as woman in all forms. If a man is overly identified with his *anima* he may be besieged by all varieties of emotions, including bad moods, touchiness, oversensitivity, and jealousy. If *anima* remains unconscious, we may feel compelled to look for her in concrete form in the external world through projections, which lead to the enactment of repetitive patterns in relationships; however, these are illusions, for she already exists within.

**archetypal defenses of the self-care system.** Kalsched's conception of a defensive and primitive psychic structure, formed as a consequence to early life trauma. A young, innocent, vulnerable internal child-object must be preserved at all costs by an archetypal protecting and persecuting caretaking system that serves as an encapsulating defense against further trauma, inevitably insulating the individual from new life. Donald Kalsched, *The Inner World of Trauma: Archetypal Defenses of the Personal Spirit*, (London: Routledge, 1996), 12.

**autoeroticism.** An early narcissistic state in which one's own person is taken as the sexual object, and erotic feelings are generated without outer stimulation.

**capacity for concern.** A concept described by D. W. Winnicott in "The Capacity for Concern," *Bulletin of the Menninger Clinic* (1962), 74–78. Winnicott theorizes that the capacity for concern and whole-object relations occurs through emotional development that enables the baby to experience loving, "erotic and aggressive drives toward the same object at the same time" (74). He postulates the coming together in the mind of the infant of the "object-mother," the one who "may satisfy the infant's urgent needs," and the "environment-mother," the one who "provides care in handling and in general management." When it can be demonstrated that mother can survive the baby's ruthless and destructive usage of the object (as in breast-feeding), the infant begins to develop a greater inner stability and independence (75–76). Meanwhile, the baby's relationship to the environment-mother will engender feelings of protection for the mother that inhibit the baby's aggression. The baby then turns away from the breast, which leads to the weaning process. In this ambivalent situation, the infant's anxiety arises over the threat of losing the mother should the baby consume her. The anxiety becomes bearable through the baby's "growing confidence" that it can contribute and make reparations to the environment-mother. The anxiety then "becomes a sense of guilt" (76–77). It is through the "achievement" of guilt that anxiety is linked to ambivalence. This ambivalence infers the development of an integrated ego that can hold the good object along with the knowledge that you can destroy it. Concern is more integrated still and speaks to the sense of responsibility toward the object.

**cohesion.** According to the *Webster New World Dictionary*, a term that derives from the Latin *cohaerere*, or cohere, meaning "to stick together as parts of a mass"; also, "to become or stay united in action; be in accord." Psychologically, cohesion refers to a quality of the ego when it is dislodged or differentiates from the complexes. Obstruction to this differentiation process may occur because the ego is over-identified with "ego-syntonic complexes" (those complexes that are so close to consciousness that they seem to be a part of the ego personality and therefore regulate life in an isolating and deadening repetition); it may also occur from the ego's unconscious "possession" by the complexes' largely negative affects, or in the projection of those affects generated by the complexes onto others. In place of these labile emotional reactions that cause the ego to swing back and forth between fractious psychic parts, cohesion is marked by a sense of flow and continuum between the different self-states. Unlike "wholeness," which infers completion, cohesion suggests an ongoing, lifelong process of unfolding.

**colonizing.** A term, according to the *American Heritage Dictionary*, describing the occupation of a distant land by a group that remains subject to or ultimately connected with the parent country that maintains control or jurisdiction over the colony. Psychologically, "colonizing" refers to the narcissistic person's need to appropriate or maintain control over another person by treating them like an object or a "colony" that is subject to the needs and expectations of the narcissistic person.

**complex.** Jung's concept of the complexes refers to emotionally charged groups of images or ideas that are relatively autonomous, splinter identities in the unconscious. (The exception is the **ego complex**, which is the seat of consciousness.) Complexes may appear to take possession of consciousness, causing disturbances in intention and will.

These complexes were defined as the sum of ideas magnetically gathered about a particular feeling-toned event or experience . . . there was postulated a "core nuclear element" in the complex that consisted of an image. The dynamism of the complex . . . was an affective tone, which could range through an emotion of varying intensity. That gave it the energic power and purposeful intention that could lead to action. C. Jess Groesbeck, "Carl Jung," in *Comprehensive Textbook of Psychiatry*, H. I. Kaplan and B. J. Sadock, eds. (New York: Williams & Wilkins, 1985), 433.

In the **binary complex**, usually one pole is more identified with ego-consciousness, while the opposite is found in shadow form or through projection onto another person. The **mother complex** refers to a group of feeling-toned ideas connected with the image and experience of mother, initially informed by the experience with the personal mother. "Mother" refers to the symbol of everything that functions as a mother to the individual, both negatively and positively. Pertinent to our discussion of the negative aspects of narcissism, if the ego is identified too strongly with the mother, as in the case of a "mama's boy," then the mother complex might show itself in overly nurturing forms that encourage infantile and insufficient modes of adapting to the world. This may appear reversed in dream images of being devoured or castrated. The mother complex in its negative form may also show itself in womanizing, where no one woman will ever do. When a man is caught in the negative mother complex, he can be split-off, cold, and uncaring in his emotional life. If the ego is more differentiated from the mother complex, then the male may have a closer connection to his feelings and a larger capacity for relatedness. These are a sampling of the many varied forms the complexes can take.

*coniunctio.* "The factors which come together in the coniunctio are conceived as opposites, either confronting one another in enmity or attracting one another in love." C. G. Jung, *The Collected Works of C. G. Jung* (Princeton, NJ: Princeton University Press, 1970), 14, 3. The coniunctio was referred to by a late medieval philosopher as the "uniting of separated qualities or an equalizing of principles" (Sir George Ripley, as cited by *C.W.* 14, 3). The coniunctio is a medieval Latin term, coined by alchemists who conducted quasi-chemical experiments; by combining basic physical, binary elements, a "third thing" would emerge from their chemical conjunction. The philosophers' own psychic contents and cultural constructions—religious, mythological, philosophical, astrological, or mystical—would invariably be projected onto the physical elements, their thinly veiled allusions in fact pointing to transformation and transcendence of baser, shadow-like elements in the psyche, as well as the union of the earthly soul with the heavenly spirit in man.

**death *coniunctio*.** A Latin term that describes the compulsion to dissolve in the fantasy of oneness, as in the lovers' fusion of ecstasy and suffering (which is actually a form of Freud's death drive). This addictive pull toward the romantic illusion of paradise may be a compensatory refusal to live or to bear life's difficulties. It may also be seen as a submission to the death mother, and thus reflect a weak and immature ego's lack of internal boundaries and need for immersion in the mother complex—either in its negative or positive aspects.

**death drive.** Part of early Freudian "drive theory" that has been re-visioned by contemporary psychoanalysis. It is hypothesized that in the death drive external disturbances create pressure and the urge to return to a previous, undifferentiated state. The regression to fantasies of a preanimate existence is an attempt to obliterate or disavow painful or unbearable memories and affects, and to restore the original idyllic state of inorganic life, free from the pain and difficulties of life. At the heart of the death drive is the process of repetition compulsion. The recapitulation of loss and annihilation lies at the core of symptoms we feel compelled to repeat, such as traumatic loss, self-destructiveness, sadomasochism, and other psychopathology. By paradoxically returning to an earlier state of inorganic life, death itself becomes the dialectic "origin and aim of life." For Sigmund Freud's "Remembering, Repeating, and Working Through," 1915/1958, 39, see Jon Mills, "Reflections on the Death Drive," *Psychoanalytic Psychology*, 23(2) (2006): 373–82; Freud's quote is at page 378. Through the repetition of trauma that will bring dissolution we may begin again. Death gives way to satisfaction and the restoration of life.

**ego.** The complex at the center of consciousness that transforms the energies of the self, which Jung considered both the regulating center and totality of the psyche—both conscious and unconscious. The ego is the "I" from which we perceive the world, our orientation to reality; it is a "lens" that may be distorted by the ego's narrow, one-sided, inflated, or fixed perceptions of the world. The ego's orientation to the world is broadened, corrected, or enriched by the assimilation of unconscious contents, a process enhancing its cohesiveness and capacities for conscious reflection. In this way the ego may become the personal incarnation of the self.

**emergence.** A term, according to the *Oxford English Dictionary*, derived from the Latin and defined as "the rising (of a submerged body) out of the water," and "to rise from (under the surface of) the earth." According to Cambray,

Creation myths involving imagery of emergence, . . . have been noted throughout history and across cultures . . . [t]hese stories and their associated imagery can be seen to manifest a transcultural pattern, archetypal in appeal, symbolic of birth or rebirth, and forming the deep background to . . . the concept of emergence. Joe Cambray, "Towards the Feeling of Emergence," *Journal of Analytical Psychology* 51(1) (2006): 2.

**enantiodromia.** As defined by the Greek philosopher Heraclitus, this occurs "[w]here the deepest point of saturation with darkness gives birth to a rapidly expanding point of light." The forces striving for wholeness and union manifest often at the time of greatest need.

**encapsulation.** A state of enclosure; the *Oxford English Dictionary* describes this as a process: "to enclose in a capsule, to summarize or isolate as if in a capsule." Frances Tustin (1972) defines encapsulation "as a defense against annihilation anxiety through which a person attempts to enclose, encase and to seal-off the sensations, affects and representations associated with it." Tustin's definition is cited in Earl Hopper,

"Encapsulation as a Defense Against the Fear of Annihilation," *International Journal of Psychoanalysis* 72 (1991): 607.

**enigmatic signifier.** Laplanche's term for unconscious messages from the mother, often filled with sexual meaning, that bathe the helpless infant in a sea of unfathomable affects and signs. They cannot be meaningfully deciphered or translated by the infant because it has no psychic framework to metabolize them. Out of the infant's fear and dread of these enigmatic contents they become repressed, sinking into the unconsciousness to become the core of the infant's subjectivity. A gap forms between consciousness and unconsciousness and powerful, enigmatic fantasies are created and emerge from this core of being. These enigmatic signifiers appear throughout our lives, in ways that are disruptive and challenging to the ego's orientation. Our development of consciousness may come as a result of our engagement with them, and our attempts to respond to them or translate them.

**Enlightenment.** In its broadest definition, a philosophy of reason, arising in the late seventeenth or eighteenth centuries from a broad response to the Church and European monarchs, which maintained control over the bodies and minds of their subjects by demanding absolute obedience and blind faith. The philosopher Immanuel Kant spoke of the Enlightenment as giving people the ability to think for themselves, and the freedom and courage to use their own intellect. Freedom and equality were two of its slogans. These rebellious ideas were expressed in the face of Church beliefs in such antiquated practices as exorcisms and witchhunts, which were thought to root out the devil in the unfaithful—superstitions going back to the Dark Ages. Enlightened, scientific thinking became the authoritative medium though which to ascertain the truth. The momentous social, intellectual, technological, political, and scientific breakthroughs that followed, typified for example by the advent of the industrial revolution and freemasonry, are products of the Enlightenment.

Later, social and ethical problems—compensating mechanisms—arose in response to the Enlightenment's belief that the quest for knowledge and reason in all things is a pure virtue that casts no shadow. Contemporary thought still invokes the Enlightenment's original ideals, though it has largely departed from them, as seen in the alienating processes that produced such horrors as World Wars I and II and the Holocaust. In 1944, in the face of the Holocaust, Theodore Adorno and Max Horkheimer, eminent German philosophers, wrote *Dialectic of Enlightenment*. Its first lines state: "In the most general sense of progressive thought, the Enlightenment has always aimed at liberating men from fear and establishing their sovereignty. Yet the fully enlightened earth radiates disaster triumphant." Max Horkheimer and Theodore Adorno, *Dialectic of Enlightenment*, translated by John Cumming (New York: Continuum, 1973), 3. In their view, the Enlightenment transformed reason into a dangerous and irrational force that came to dominate both the natural order and humanity, as seen in the rise of fascism.

**eschatology.** The study of religious beliefs surrounding death.

**intersubjectivity.** An expanding and complex area of investigation in contemporary psychoanalysis. The term refers to what occurs when patient and analyst, as subject and object, share a psychic field between them, like that of an infant and mother, and where the process is understood as a transformative engagement of the two people. Another way to imagine intersubjectivity is through the idea that the self becomes itself only in relation to another. This is in contrast to traditional, intrapsychic views of an inner center of the individual that guides the development of the subject, and where his psychic contents unfold that another (the analyst) interprets in a neutral and objective way. Intersubjectively, self reflection, and intention combine with dependency upon the other, and where each may impact the other emotionally. Stephen A. Mitchell, *Relationality: From Attachment to Intersubjectivity* (Hillsdale, NJ: The Analytic Press, 2000, 64). Meaning is constructed in the discourse of patient and analyst and emerges in the relational space between subject and object, as opposed to an object (analyst) who holds privileged knowledge that he bestows upon the subject (patient), bringing meaning to the subject. With intersubjectivity, the subjectivity of the patient may affect the analyst through the countertransference and the analyst may, in turn, give voice to the subjectivity within him that expresses this shared subjectivity, now *inter*subjectivity. Early on, Jung described this as the "shared field" of consciousness and unconsciousness in the transference and countertransference of patient and analyst.

*jouissance.* A French term that defies translation, but refers to a paradoxical pleasure that expresses the qualities of both ecstasy and death. Jouissance produces an almost intolerable degree of excitement, derived in part from desire's transgression of what is forbidden.

**Kabbalah and the Tree of Life.** Kabbalah is the Jewish mystical tradition which for centuries flourished in Spain. A kabbalist from Spanish Castille, Rabbi Joseph Gikatalia, (1248–1323), wrote a meditational guide for spiritual ascension entitled "The Gates of Light." It was considered the key to Jewish mystical teachings. In it was contained a diagram of the Tree of Life. The wisdom of the kabbalah speaks of the Tree as a ladder to heaven, a metaphor for the ten divine emanations, or *Sefirot*, that are the basis for all levels of physical, emotional, and spiritual life. See Areh Kaplan, *Meditation and Kabbalah* (York Beach, ME: Samuel Weiser, 1982), 125–27. Six of these "forces and forms" are seated in dynamic tension to one another on the Tree on either side of an axis or center pillar of "Grace" containing four additional *Sefirot*. Each of the ten places has a corresponding archangel that dwells there. See Z'ev ben Shimon Halevi, *Kabbalah Tradition of Hidden Knowledge* (London: Thames & Hudson, 1980), 7. Many of the greatest sages and kabbalistic teachers of Spain were exiled in 1492. They later came to settle in what was to become the vital center for all kabbalistic learning—*Safed*, in the Holy Land.

**love.** *Webster's New World Dictionary* defines love as "a deep and tender feeling of affection for or attachment or devotion to a person." An important distinction must be drawn between a more passive receiving or being loved and the more active capacity to love. In this book the active capacity is privileged and described as the task of giving *to* another for their sake, as opposed to the expectation of being given to or being stroked by another; it is considered an achievement in the transcendence of narcissism.

**mana-personality.** A term describing inflation of the ego caused by the invasion of autonomous unconscious contents, leading to the ego's identification with such archetypal personifications as "great man," hero, healer, guru, or gifted artist, as examples.

**Manichaeanism.** A dualistic form of Gnosticism originating in Persia that views evil as deriving from the dark power of matter—referred to as the *Demiurge*, the ruler of an inherently corrupt material world where God holds no sway. The light power of God dwelling in Heaven engages in the eternal struggle with the Demiurge over human souls corrupted by their earthly existence. Saint Augustine's Christian neoplatonism was a rejection of his youthful Manichaean beliefs, which he supplanted with the notion that everything, even the corporeal world, is part of God's creation.

**narcissism.** The many "pathological" forms of narcissism can be thought about as a form of life at the surface demanding the maintenance of sameness; it is caused by early, traumatic loss or interruption of maternal containment. The narcissistic individual fears or hates *alterity* and uncertainty, all qualities presenting difference, as well as those that cannot be controlled. In the story of "Narcissus and Echo," Narcissus' mother is told by a soothsayer that her son would live to a ripe old age, so long as he *not know himself*. Narcissists are thus terrified of the unknown, including their inner depths, out of which could arise contents they fear might annihilate them or evoke their original trauma of abandonment. In a similar way, Narcissus spurned all would-be lovers, vowing that "they would have no power over him." From this we can surmise that narcissists encapsulate themselves against feelings of vulnerability and intimacy that *mutual* relationships—without guarantees—could produce. Hence, grandiose and omnipotent defenses insulate the narcissist against threats of retraumatization. Others are things to be used to meet their needs, often as erotic objects to fuse with, to idealize, and then to devalue when they cease to maintain the narcissist's illusions of grandeur. In destructive forms of narcissism, some individuals seek to annihilate any human contact. Other people may become targets for attack when the narcissist's superiority feels threatened, or when they are slighted or offended. These are defenses that compensate for hidden, thin-skinned oversensitivities, inferiorities, and vulnerabilities. (The narcissist is actually both "the god and the worm," as Neville Symington refers to him.)

For the purpose of this book, the idea of narcissism in its healthy or normal conformations is not a central area of emphasis, but I define it below in the glossary term for "primary narcissism."

Also, Lacan's ontological conception of narcissism is described more fully on Page One of the Introduction. Briefly, narcissistic fantasies develop in the pre-verbal child, that identifies its image in the mirror as one of deceptive coherence and flawlessness. This narcissistic illusion attempts to negate the child's sense of lack and fragmentation that is innate to its human existence.

**ontological:** A term relating to the essence or nature of being.

**Other.** A term originally derived from Hegel and incorporated into the postmodern, Jewish philosophy of Emmanuel Levinas which defies understanding or category. The Other is unknowable, ineffable, enigmatic, infinite, irreducible, sacred, and tormenting. Its mere trace can be glimpsed *intersubjectively* or interpersonally—that is, as other than what we would think of as psychic processes or the "interior" subjectivity of being. It is experienced in the "face of the other," as Levinas would say. The Other is already there, before subject or object exist, and the awareness of our subjectivity, our psychic development, comes through the impact of the primacy of the Other. The Other stands in contrast to the ego's *sameness*, which requires certainty and attempts to appropriate those who are different from itself by reducing the other to the known, or *sameness*. Sameness is observed, for example, when complexes and their habitual, repetitive patterns become reactivated. To Levinas, the egotistical need for the other to be the same is the origin of all violence. In the traumatic destabilizing and shattering of the ego by the Other, the subject awakens to his endless responsibility to the other, who is revealed in (her) vulnerability, sacredness, and nakedness, through "the *face* of the other." Before all ethics lies our responsibility for the other; placing them before ourselves.

**post-traumatic stress disorder**. In PTSD unbearable terror and anxiety originating in an original trauma is reenacted whenever there is a threat to one's security that recalls the earlier incident. Extreme measures are learned to avoid any breakdown in the protective boundaries that keep the anxiety and fear at bay.

**primary** and **secondary narcissism.** Early concepts developed in Freud's thinking that describe the original stages of narcissism. In infancy, the process he called primary narcissism proves to be vitally necessary in the formation of an infant's nuclear self. This comes about when the infant can internalize the parental ideal, which Kohut calls the "self-object," and the parents in turn can mirror back a sense of omniscience and power. When there is a lack of separateness between the mother and infant, the baby identifies with the omnipotence of the idealized parents. Later in development when the child's adaptation to the world fails, it was thought to initiate the state of "secondary narcissism," where the child seeks a return to the infantile state of fusion between mother and baby through regressive behaviors.

**psychic "thin skin."** Psychologically, thin skin refers to a primitive mental state experienced as an insufficient psychic protective insulation, easily punctured. In the extreme cases it could lead to fantasies of falling into endless space. Thin skin is in binary opposition to the thicker, second skin that serves to provide an autistic-like encapsulation that allows nothing to penetrate the defenses. In the narcissist, these describe polarities of the complex whose defensive properties are maintained by repeated swings between the two.

**puer-senex bipolar complex.** Latin terms that describe the binary opposition of archetypal images (the representations of primordial, universal images) within the male psyche, in this case of the eternal youth and the old man. From ancient myth we see the *puer aeternus* as the young god who is son/lover to the Great Mother, and the *senex* as Saturn, Cronus, or Old Father Time. Psychologically, they are two poles of the masculine archetype. When the bi-polar complex is in balance in the psyche, the puer is seen in a positive light as the spirit of youth, and the youthful, creative spirit in a man, whereas the positive aspects of the senex include wisdom, groundedness, responsibility, maturity, and so on. When the two are split, a man identified with the puer side of the complex may act adolescent, immature, fearful of commitments, oversensitive, provisional, and ungrounded. The negative aspects of the senex side of the complex may be reflected in a man who is dried up and cynical, leaden, emotionally removed, and rigid.

**Romanticism.** The antagonistic counter-movement following the Enlightenment; it originated in the last half of the eighteenth century and attained prominence in Europe between 1800 and 1830. The Romantics turned away from the conviction that reason and order prevailed in all things. For them, spirit was reflected as invisible nature and nature was seen as visible spirit. Thus one could not hope to explain everything in nature in a scientific, rational way, as the thinkers of the Enlightenment proposed. The influential ideas of the eighteenth-century philosopher Immanuel Kant bridged the end of the Enlightenment with the dawning age of Romanticism. He proposed that the world could not be known, that our claims to knowledge were limited by our senses. He divided the universe into the "numinous" and the "phenomenal." The numinous realm was the source of "a priori" knowing, ungraspable to our phenomenological experience. Romanticism was characterized by the privileging of feeling over knowing, and intuition and emotion over rationality, as well as the valuing of aesthetic ideals in relation to love of beauty, tastes, and art; sensual and aesthetic experience of the sublime and untamed nature; and adherence to classical traditions (especially those of the Greeks). Inner experience, the irrational, the mystical, and the numinous were the leading principles that gave form to the rich philosophical and artistic innovations of the Romantic era.

**self.** A term encompassing the "principle of coherence, structure, organization that governs balance and integration of psychic contents." It is conceptualized by Jung as the "innermost nucleus of the psyche." Marie-Louise von Franz, "The Process of Individuation," from *Man and His Symbols*, edited by C. G. Jung (London: Aldus Books, 1964), 196. The self thus corresponds to the unconscious regulating center of the psyche from which consciousness develops.

The self appears in dreams, myths, and fairytales . . . in the form of a totality symbol, such as the circle, square . . . cross, etc. When it represents a *complexio oppositorum*, a union of opposites, it can also appear as a united duality . . . *yang* and *yin*, . . . etc. Empirically, therefore, the self appears as a play of light and shadow, although conceived as a totality and unity in which the opposites are united. [*C.W.* 6, "Definitions," par. 790.]

Therefore, the archetypal images of the self appear as symbols of wholeness and possess a numinous, transcendent power that invests life with meaning. See Polly Young-Eisendrath and Terence Dawson, eds., *The Cambridge Companion to Jung* (Cambridge, UK: Cambridge University Press, 1997), 318–19. As the various definitions suggest, the self appears paradoxically in images that depict the totality of the psyche and its core. Most importantly for this writing, I distinguish between the lower case (s)elf and the capitalized (S)elf, which has another set of meanings.

**Self.** Jung alludes at times to a rarer meaning that he applies to the use of the word "Self," which has more religious or philosophical undertones, one that could be related to what Levinas may have had in mind with his concept of the "Other" that transcends the psyche altogether. The Self, too, is conceived of as unknowable, unrepresentable, an infinite mystery that maintains its transcendence from the *totality* of the psyche. In Jung's psychology, even the Collective Unconscious is part of the totality of psyche and is therefore contained within psyche's finiteness. The Self's destruction of the ego's fixed constructions, in service to development of greater psychic cohesion, may be experienced through its emerging shadow contents—its traces. See Lucy Huskinson, "The Self as Violent Other," *Journal of Analytical Psychology* 47(3) (2002), 437. *Intersubjectively*, we locate traces of the Self in the relational field between subject and object (for example, patient and analyst.) In this field new and transcendent contents emerge into consciousness through the discourse that dislodges the ego from its narcissistic orientation. In my view, when the Self shatters the fixity of the ego, self structures become more fluid and cohesive, giving rise to new contents that emerge into consciousness.

**shadow.** Term describing an aspect of the psyche that lies in direct, compensatory relation to the ego, in that the ego's projection onto outer objects of its own shadow contents contains hidden, repressed, feared, hated, or unacceptable aspects of its own unconscious personality. However, when an ego complex is too fixed or diminished, the contents of the shadow that are brought to awareness may confront the ego's attitudes and thereby reinvigorate the psyche with a new orientation. The ego's capacity for openness to the endless, ongoing manifestations of the shadow, through subjection to such deflations, leads to greater resilience and cohesion in the psyche. In this sense, the shadow is the servant of the Self.

**Shekhinah.** The name *Shekhinah* comes from the Hebrew verb *shakhan* in its *feminine* form, which means "to dwell within." It comprises the energy of manifestation and is the feminine aspect of the light closest to our physical realm (Rabbi Ted Falcon, personal communication). In speaking of Shekhinah and her placement among the ten *Sefirot* on the Kabbalistic Tree of Life, Gershom Scholem says,

> [Shekhinah] becomes the last attribute [*Malchut*, manifestation or "the kingdom"] through which the Creator acts in the lower world. It is the "end of thought." From its source at the "beginning of thought" in *Hokhmah* ["wisdom",] the thought of creation pursues its task through all the worlds . . .

We see that Shekhinah is identified with Wisdom, the "highest" *Sefirah* on the Tree and with the "lowest" manifestation. Scholem continues,

> The emphasis placed on the female principle in the symbolism of the last *Sefirah* heightens the mythical language of these descriptions. Appearing from above as "the end of thought," the last *Sefirah* is for man the door or gate through which he can begin the ascent up the ladder of perception of the Divine mystery. Gershom Scholem, *Kabbalah* (Jerusalem: Keter Publishing House, 1974), 112.

**splitting.** Although the term derives from British Object Relations theory it can be applied in many contexts. In early object relations, splitting is an often normal primal response of infant to mother, prior to its development of capacities to hold the mother as ambivalent—both good and bad. The "good" mother who feeds, soothes, and contains the baby's anxieties cannot possibly be the same "bad" mother who isn't always attuned to the baby's fears, unmet needs, and anguish, and who may herself, at times, become overwhelmed by or unresponsive to the baby's needs. When this occurs, the infant cannot "safely feed" and thrive, because it cannot tolerate the anxiety associated with the bad mother. Therefore the splitting process protects that most fundamental bond necessary for survival. There is no sense of history or continuity when the infant splits off the bad from the good mother. The infant retreats to what is called the "paranoid-schizoid position" until the time when "whole object relations" and a "depressive position" can be achieved. Here the maturing baby can experience past, present, and future with its mother. It learns that it can bear the mother's loss when she leaves, not as a hopeless and irreparable destruction of the good, but rather as a sad but tolerable absence, mixed with hope of return and reunion of mother with baby. Splitting and retreat to the paranoid-schizoid position is similar to what happens, in Jungian terms, when one is being activated by a complex, a process that can be set off at any time throughout life. This understanding of splitting as a primal process underlies my use of the term in various contexts throughout the book.

**substance.** As defined in the *American Heritage Dictionary*, this term refers to the essential nature of anything; that which is solid or real; it can also be a solid or substantial quality or characteristic, as in a man of substance.

**transcendent function.** A term that refers to "[m]aking conscious what was unconscious . . . whereby the repetitive symbolism of the unconscious is transformed into the specificity of consciousness." Joseph Henderson, "Reflections on the History and Practice of Jungian Analysis," in *Jungian Analysis* (London: Open Court Publishing, 1982), 19. Through the conflict between the conscious and the unconscious a third or new content emerges from the conflict of the opposites. "The confrontation of the two positions generates a tension charged with energy and creates a living, third thing . . . a living birth that leads to a new level of being, a new situation." *C.W.* 8, 90.

**transitional space.** Winnicott described a transitional space between the baby and mother in which the baby's omnipotent phantasies evolve into the creative use of outer objects in service to the ego's development. This transition occurs when the empathic mother is able to create an outer reality that is close enough to fit the baby's omnipotent needs. This allows the baby to gradually modify its omnipotent phantasies in favor of an intermediate area between phantasy and reality. D. W. Winnicott, "Ego Distortion in Terms of True and False Self" (1960), in *The Maturational Processes and the Facilitating Environment* (Madison, CT: International Universities Press, 1965), 146

# BIBLIOGRAPHY

Adams, Henry. *Mont-Saint-Michel and Chartres*. New York: The Heritage Press, 1933.

Alexander, Richard. "Some Notes on the Origin of Despair and Its Relationship to Destructive Envy." *Journal of Melanie Klein and Object Relations* 15(3) (1997): 417–40.

Almond, Barbara R. "Monstrous Infants and Vampyric Mothers in Bram Stoker's *Dracula*." *International Journal of Psychoanalysis* 88 (2007): 219–35.

Andreas-Salomé, Lou. "The Dual Orientation of Narcissism." *Psychoanalytic Quarterly* 31 (1922): 1–30.

Apuleius. *The Transformations of Lucius otherwise known as The Golden Ass*. Translated by Robert Graves. NY: Noonday Press, 1951.

Augustine, Saint, Bishop of Hippo. *Confessions*, *Great Books of the Western World*, Volume XVIII. Chicago: Encyclopedia Britannica, 1952.

Bair, Deirdre. *Jung: A Biography*. Boston: Little, Brown, 2003.

Bakhtin, M. M. *Rabelais and His World*. Bloomington, IN: Indiana University Press, 1984.

Barnard, Suzanne. "Diachrony, *Tuche*, and the Ethical Subject in Levinas and Lacan." In *Psychology for the Other*, edited by Edwin E. Gant & Richard N. Williams. Pittsburg: Duquesne University Press, 2002.

Becker, Brian W. "Self as Other? A Levinasian Analysis of Carl Jung's Concept of the Self-Ego Relation." Paper presented at Psychology for the Other Seminar, Seattle University, Seattle, Washington, 10/16/2006.

Beebe, John. *Integrity in Depth*. New York: Fromm International Publishing, 1995.

Begg, Ean. "Evidence for Continuity for the Black Virgin Tradition." In *The Cult of the Black Virgin*, pp. 5–28. London: Penguin Books, 1985.

Bennet, E. A. *What Jung Really Said*. London: Macdonald, 1966.

Berg, Rav P. S. *The Essential Zohar*. New York: Bell Tower, 2002.

Britton, Ronald. "Narcissism and Narcissistic Disorders." Paper presented at Northwest Psychoanalytic Society, EBOR Conference, Seattle, September 30, 2005.

Bruno, Anthony. "Torquemada and the Spanish Inquisition." At http://www.trutv.com/library/crime/notoriousmurders/mass/torquemada/2.html (accessed 12/26/09).

Bulfinch, Thomas. "The Story of Lancelot: The Lady of Shalott." In *Bulfinch's Mythology*: *The Age of Fable, The Age of Chivalry, Legends of Charlemagne*, foreword by Alberto Manguel, 365–69. New York: Modern Library, 2004. [First publication in *The Age of Chivalry* (1858).]

Cambray, Joe. "Towards the Feeling of Emergence," *Journal of Analytical Psychology* 51(1) (2006): 1–20.

Campbell, Joseph. *The Masks of God: Creative Mythology*. New York: Viking Press, 1968.

Carotenuto, Aldo. *A Secret Symmetry: Sabina Spielrein between Jung and Freud*. New York: Pantheon Books, 1984.

Carson, Anne. *Eros the Bittersweet*. Normal, IL: Dalkey Archive Press, 1998.

Cavicchioli, Sonia. *The Tale of Cupid and Psyche: An Illustrated History*. New York: George Braziller, 2002.

Cotterell, Arthur, and Rachel Storm. *The Ultimate Encyclopedia of Mythology*. London: Hermes House, 1999.

Critchley, Simon. *Ethics–Politics–Subjectivity: Essays on Derrida, Levinas, and Contemporary French Thought*. Brooklyn, NY: Verso, 1999.

———. "Introduction." In *The Cambridge Companion to Levinas*, edited by Simon Critchley and Robert Bernasconi, 1–32. Cambridge, UK: Cambridge University Press, 2002.

Dickinson, Emily. "A death-blow is a life-blow to some." At http://www.bartleby.com/113/4046.html (accessed 3/5/2011).

Dorpat, Theo. L. *Wounded Monster: Hitler's Path from Trauma to Malevolence*. Lanham, MD: University Press of America, 2002.

Edinger, Edward. *Ego and Archetype*. Baltimore, MD: Penguin Books, 1972.

———. *The Mysterium Lectures*. Toronto: Inner City Books, 1995.

Eigen, Michael. "On the Significance of the Face," *Psychoanalytic Review* 67 (1980-81): 425-439.

Ellenberger, Henri F. *The Discovery of the Unconscious*. New York: Basic Books, 1970.

"Exodus." In *The Jerusalem Bible,* English text revised and edited by H. Fisch, 62–114. Jerusalem: Koren Publishers, 1992.

*Ezekiel*. Translation and commentary by Rabbi Moshe Eisemann. Brooklyn, NY: Mesorah Publications, 1988.

Fauriel, Claude. *Histoire de la poésie provençale*. Vol. I. Paris: J. Labitte, 1846.

Freud, Sigmund. "Remembering, Repeating, and Working Through." *Standard Edition* 12: 145–56. London: Hogarth Press, 1914.

Frosh, Stephen. "Melancholy Without the Other." *Studies in Gender and Sexuality* 7(4) (2006): 363–78.

Gambini, Roberto. *Soul and Culture*. College Station, TX: Texas A&M University Press, 2003.

Gediman, Helen. *Fantasies of Love and Death in Life and Art*. New York: New York University Press, 1995.

Ghent, Emmanuel. "Masochism, Submission, Surrender." *Contemporary Psychoanalysis* 26(1) (1990): 211–42.

Giddings, Robert, ed. *John Keats, Selected Letters*. Oxford, UK: Oxford University Press, 2002.

Goethe, Johann Wolfgang von. *West-Eastern Divan,* "II. Book of Hafis: The Unlimited." At http://www.archive.org/stream/westeasterndivan00goetuoft/westeasterndivan00go-etuoft_djvu.txt (accessed 2/22/2007). Translated by Edward Dowden. London: J.M. Deny & Sons LTD, 1914. [Original publication date 1819.]

———. *Faust: A Tragedy in Two Parts*. Translated by John R. Williams. London: Wordsworth Editions Limited, 1999. [Original publication dates: Part I, 1828–1829; Part II, 1832].

Gottlieb, R. M. "The Legend of the European Vampire: Object Loss and Corporeal Preservation." *Psychoanalytic Study of the Child* (49) (1994): 465–80.

Green, Andre. *Life Narcissism Death Narcissism*, translated by Andrew Weller. London: Free Association Books, 2001.

Groesbeck, C. Jess. "Carl Jung." In *Comprehensive Textbook of Psychiatry*, H. I. Kaplan and B. J. Sadock, eds., 433-440. 4th ed. Baltimore, MD: Wilkins & Wilkins, 1985.

Guggenbuhl-Craig, Adolf. *Eros on Crutches*. Irving, TX: Spring Publications, 1980.

Halevi, Z'ev ben Shimon. *Kabbalah: Tradition of Hidden Knowledge*. New York: Thames & Hudson, 1979.

Hauke, Christopher. "Psychology and the Postmodern." Paper presented at the Northwest Alliance for Psychoanalytic Study, Seattle, Washington, May 8, 2003.

Haule, John. *Divine Madness: Archetypes of Romantic Love*. Carmel: Fisher King Press, 2010.

Hay, Daisy. *Young Romantics: The Tangled Lives of English Poetry's Greatest Generation*. New York, NY: Farrar, Straus and Giroux, 2010.

Hayman, Ronald. *A Life of Jung*. London: Bloomsbury Publishing, 1999.

Henderson, Joseph. "Reflections on the History and Practice of Jungian Analysis." In *Jungian Analysis*, edited by Murray Stein, 3–26. London: Open Court Publishing, 1982.

Henderson, Joseph, and Maude Oakes. *The Wisdom of the Serpent*. Toronto, ON: The Macmillan Company, 1963.

Hillman, James. *The Myth of Analysis*. Evanston, IL: Northwestern University Press, 1972.

———. *Senex and Puer: An Aspect of the Historical and Psychological Present*. Zurich: Rhein-Verlag, 1968, an offprint from *Eranos-Jahrbuch* XXXVI / 1967.

———. *A Blue Fire: Selected Writings by James Hillman*, "Father: Saturn and Senex", Introduced and edited by Thomas Moore, 208-216. NY: Harper & Row, 1989. Originally published "On Senex Consciousness," *Spring* (1976): 146-165.

Hinton, Alex. "The Poetics of Genocidal Practice: Life Under the Khmer Rouge." In *Violence*, edited by Neil Whitehead, 160–70. Santa Fe, NM: School of American Research, 2004.

Hinton, Ladson. "Fools, Foolishness, and Feeling Foolish." *Psychological Perspectives* 12(1) (1981): 43–51.

———. "Shame as a Teacher: 'Lowly Wisdom' at the Millennium." In *Proceedings of the 14th International Congress for Analytical Psychology*, edited by M. Mattoon, 15–16. Einsiedeln: Daimon Verlag, 1998.

———. "Narcissism, the Unknown, and the Passion for Being." Paper presented to the Jungian Psychotherapy Association, Seattle, Washington, September 22, 2001.

———. "How Did We Become 'Modern'?" Paper presented during training at the North Pacific Institute for Analytical Psychology, Seattle, Washington, October October 4, 2002.

———. "The Fool." Presentation to the North Pacific Institute for Analytical Psychology, Seattle, Washington, October 31, 2003.

———. "The Enigmatic Signifier and the Decentred Subject." *Journal of Analytical Psychology* 54(5) (2009): 637–57.

Hopper, Earl. "Encapsulation as a Defense Against the Fear of Annihilation." *International Journal of Psychoanalysis* 72 (1991): 607–24.

Huskinson, Lucy. "The Self as Violent Other: The Problem of Defining the Self." *Journal of Analytical Psychology* 47(3) (2002): 437–58.

Horkheimer, Max, and Adorno, Theodore. *Dialectic of Enlightenment*, translated by John Cumming. New York: Continuum, 1973.

Jacoby, Mario. *Individuation and Narcissism: The Psychology of Self in Jung and Kohut*. London: Routledge, 1985.

Johnson, Robert. *We: Understanding the Psychology of Romantic Love*. San Francisco: HarperSanFrancisco, 1983.

Joseph, Steven M. "Jung and Kabbalah: Imaginal and Noetic Aspects." *Journal of Analytical Psychology* 52(3) (2007): 321–41.

Jung, C. G. *Memories, Dreams, Reflections*. New York: Vintage Books, 1965.

———. *The Collected Works of C. G. Jung*. Vols 1–20, Suppl. A. Princeton, NJ: Princeton University Press, 1970.

———. *Letters*, Vol. 1. Selected and edited by Gerhard Adler, in collaboration with Aniela Jaffé. Translations from the German by R. F. C. Hull. Princeton, NJ: Princeton University Press, 1973; Olten, Switzerland: Walter Verlag, 1973. Bollingen Series 95.1.

———. *Nietzsche's Zarathustra Seminar: Notes of the Seminar Given in 1934–1939*, vols. I and II, ed. J. L. Jarrett. London: Routledge, 1989.

———. *The Red Book: Liber Novus*, edited by Sonu Shamdasani, translated by Mark Kyburz, John Peck, and Sonu Shamdasani. New York: W.W. Norton & Company, 2009.

Jung, Emma, and Marie-Louise von Franz. *The Grail Legend*. Princeton, NJ: Princeton University Press, 1960.

Kahane, Henry, and Renée Kahane. "Proto-Perceval und Proto-Parzival." In Emma Jung and Marie-Louise von Franz, *The Grail Legend*, Princeton, NJ: Princeton University Press, 1960.

Kalsched, Donald. *The Inner World of Trauma: Archetypal Defenses of the Personal Spirit*. London: Routledge, 1996.

———. "Daimonic Elements in Early Trauma." *Journal of Analytical Psychology* 48(2) (2003): 145–69.

———. "Trauma and Daimonic Reality in Ferenczi's Later Work." *Journal of Analytical Psychology* 48(4) (2003): 479–89.[13]

Kaplan, Areh. *Meditation and Kabbalah*. York Beach, ME: Samuel Weiser, 1982.

———. *Inner Space*. Jerusalem: Moznaim Publishing, 1990.

Kavaler-Adler, Susan. *The Creative Mystique: From Red Shoes Frenzy to Love and Creativity*. New York: Routledge, 1996.

Kearney, Richard. *Poetics of Imagining: Modern and Post-Modern*. Edinburgh: Edinburgh University Press, 1998. Perspectives in Continental Philosophy, 6.

———. *Strangers, Gods and Monsters: Interpreting Otherness*. New York: Routledge, 2003.

"Keats, John." In *Encyclopedia Britannica*. Chicago: University of Chicago Press, 1991, vol. 6, 780-781.

Knox, Jean. "The Fear of Love: The Denial of Self in Relationship." *Journal of Analytical Psychology* 52(5) (2007): 543–63.

Kohut, Hans. "Forms and Transformations of Narcissism." *Journal of the American Psychoanalytic Association* 14 (1966): 243–72.

Kristeva, Julia. *Powers of Horror: An Essay on Abjection*. New York: Columbia University Press, 1982.

———. *Black Sun: Depression and Melancholia*. New York: Columbia University Press, 1989.

———. "On Melancholy Imagination." In *Postmodernism and Continental Philosophy*, edited by Hugh Silverman and and Donn Welton, 12–25. Albany NY: State University of New York Press, 1989. Studies in Phenomenology and Existentialism 13.

Lacan, Jacques. "The Mirror Stage as Formative of the *I* Function." In *Ecrits*, translated by Bruce Fink, 75–81. New York: Norton, 2006.

Laplanche, Jean. *New Foundations for Psychoanalysis*. Oxford, UK: Blackwell, 1989.

———. *Essays on Otherness*, edited by John Fletcher. New York: Routledge, 1999. Warwick Studies in European Philosophy.

Levinas, Emmanuel. *Totality and Infinity*, translated by Alphonso Lingis. Pittsburgh, PA: Duquesne University Press, 1969.

———. *The Levinas Reader*, edited and translated by Sean Hand. Oxford, UK: Basil Blackwell, 1989.

———. *Difficult Freedom: Essays on Judaism*, translated by Sean Hand. Baltimore: Johns Hopkins University Press, 1990.

———. *Entre Nous*, translated by Michael B. Smith and Barbara Harshav. New York: Columbia University Press, 1998.

———. *Otherwise Than Being: Or, Beyond Essence*, translated by Alphonso Lingis. Pittsburgh, PA: Duquesne University Press, 1998.

———. *Is It Righteous To Be: Interviews with Emmanuel Levinas*, edited by Jill Robbins. Stanford, CA: Stanford University Press, 2001.

Longhurst, John Edward. *The Age of Torquemada*. Lawrence, KS: Coronado Press, 1964, at http://vlib.iue.it/carrie_books/longhurst2/07.html (accessed 12/26/2009).

Mann, Thomas. *Joseph and His Brothers*. London: Vintage Random House, 1999. [New York: Knopf, 1938.]

Maraniss, David. *First in His Class*. New York: Touchstone/Simon and Shuster, 1995.

Marshall, Karol. "Eros the Sweetbitter." Paper presented at the Forum of the Northwest Alliance for Psychoanalytic Study, Seattle, Washington, May 8,1999.

Melville, Herman. *Moby-Dick*. New York: Signet Classic, 1998. [New York: Harper, 1851.]

Miller, Alice. *Prisoners of Childhood*. New York: Basic Books, Inc., 1981.

Mills, Jon. "Reflections on the Death Drive." *Psychoanalytic Psychology* 23(2) (2006): 373–82.

Milton, John. *Paradise Lost*. Indianapolis: Bobbs-Merrill, 1962. [Edinburgh: A. Donaldson, 1767.]

Mitchell, Stephen A. *Relationality: From Attachment to Intersubjectivity*. Hillsdale, NJ: Analytic Press, 2000.

———. *Can Love Last?* New York: Norton, 2002.

———. "The Wings of Icarus: Illusion and the Problem of Narcissism." At http://www.wawhite.org/Journal/mitchell_art5.htm (accessed 12/29/2008).

Montaigne, Michel de. "Apology." In *Oeuvres completes*, edited by Albert Thibaudet and Maurice Rat. Paris: Gallimard, 1962. Biblioteque de la Pleiade.

Mudd, Peter. "Jung and the Split Feminine." *Round Table Review* 6(1) (1998): 1, 4–9.

Munk, Rabbi Elie. *The Call of the Torah*. Brooklyn, NY: Menorah Publications, 1994.

*The Nag Hammadi Scriptures: The Revised and Updated Translation of Sacred Gnostic Texts,* Edited and translated by Marvin Meyer, "The Gospel of Thomas" #22. NY: HarperCollins, 2007, 133-156.

Neumann, Erich. *Amor and Psyche*. Princeton, NJ: Princeton University Press, 1956.

———. *The Origins and History of Consciousness*. Princeton, NJ: Princeton University Press, 1970.

———. *The Child*. Boston, MA: Shambhala Publications, 1973.

Nietzsche, Friedrich. *Beyond Good & Evil: Prelude to a Philosophy of the Future*, translated by Walter Kaufmann. New York: Vintage Books, 1966.

———. "The Birth of Tragedy." In *The Birth of Tragedy and Genealogy of Morals*, translated by Francis Golffing, 1-146. Garden City, NY: Doubleday/Anchor, 1956.

Oelsner, Robert. "Introduction to the Work of Ron Britton." Pre-lecture paper presented at the Inter-Institute Guest Lecture Series, Seattle, Washington, March 19, 2008.

Ogden, Thomas H. "Analyzing the Matrix of Transference." In *Master Clinicians on Treating the Regressed Patient*, edited by L. Bryce Boyer and Peter Giovacchini, 593–606. Northvale, NJ: Jason Aronson, 1990.

Orange, Donna M. *Thinking for Clinicians*. New York: Routledge, 2010.

Ovid. "The Legend of Narcissus and Echo." In *Ovidius Metamorphoses*, translated into the German by Hermann von Breitenbach. Zurich: Artemis-Verlag, 1958.

Papadopoulos, Renos K. "Jung and the Concept of the Other." In *Jung in Modern Perspective*, edited by Renos K. Papadopoulos and Graham S. Saayman, 54-88. Bridgeport, UK: Prism Press, 1991.

Parker, James. "The Existential Clown." In *The Atlantic Online* at http://www.theatlantic.com/doc/print/200812/jimcarey (accessed 1/13/2009).

Peperzak, Adriaan T., and Emmanuel Levinas. *To the Other: An Introduction to the Philosophy of Emmanuel Levinas*. West Lafayette, IN: Purdue University Press, 1993. Purdue Series in the History of Philosophy.

Plato. "Phaedo." In *Great Dialogues of Plato*, translated by W.H.D. Rouse, pp. 460–521. New York: Mentor, 1956.

Plato. *Timaeus and Critias*. Translated by Desmond Lee. New York: Penguin, 1977.

Pope, Alexander. "Eloisa to Abelard." At http://en.wikipedia.org/wiki/Eloisa_to_Abelard (accessed 1/26/2010).

Putnam, Hilary. "Levinas and Judaism." In *The Cambridge Companion to Levinas*, edited by Simon Critchley and Robert Berasconi, 33–62. Cambridge, UK: Cambridge University Press, 2002.

Rafeeq, Hasan. *Aporia: Divining the Divine: The Role of God in Levinasian Ethics*. At http://humanities.byu.edu/philosophy/aporia/volume/vol.112/hasanto.html (accessed 3/23/05).

Raff, Jeffrey. *Jung and the Alchemical Imagination*. York Beach, ME: Nicholas-Hays, 2000.

Rahn, Otto. *Crusade Against the Grail*. Rochester, VT: Inner Traditions, 2006.

Raubolt, Richard. "Book Review: Wounded Monster," review of *Wounded Monster: Hitler's Path from Trauma to Malevolence*, by Theo. L. Dorpat, *Journal of Trauma Practice* 3(3), 2004; at http://raubolt.blogspot.com/2007/11/book-review-wounded-monster.html (accessed 1/22/10).

Rosenberg, Rabbi A. J. *The Book of Proverbs*. New York: Judaica Press, 1993.

———. *The Books of Esther, Song of Songs, Ruth*. New York: Judaica Press, 1992.

Rosenfels, Paul. *Love and Power: The Psychology of Interpersonal Creativity*. New York: Libra Publishers, 1966.

Rougemont, Denis de. *Love in the Western World*, translated by Montgomery Belgion. Princeton, NJ: Princeton University Press, 1983: [London: Faber and Faber, 1940.]

———. *Passion and Society*, translated by Montgomery Belgion. London: Faber and Faber, 1956.

Ruether, Rosemary Radford. *Gaia and God: An Ecofeminist Theology of Earth Healing*. New York: HarperCollins, 1992.

Saint John of the Cross. "Spiritual Canticle." In *The Complete Works of Saint John of the Cross, Doctor of the Church*, translated and edited by E. Allison Peers from the critical edition of P. Silverio de Santa Teresa. Westminster, MD: Newman Press, 1964, vol. 2.

Samuels, Andrew, *The Plural Psyche*. London: Routledge, 1989.

Sattinover, Jeffrey. "Puer Aeternus: The Narcissistic Relation to the Self." *Quadrant* 13(2) (1980): 75–108.

Scholem, Gershom Gerhard. *Kabbalah*. Jerusalem: Keter Publishing House, 1974.

Sebillot, Paul. *Le Folk-Lore de France*. Vol. III. Paris: Guilmoto, 1906.

Seidler, Gunter H. *In Others' Eyes: An Analysis of Shame*, translated by Andrew Jenkins. Madison, CT: International Universities Press, 2000.

Severson, Randolf. "Puer's Wounded Wing: Reflections on the Psychology of Skin Disease." In *Puer Papers*, edited by James Hillman, 129–51. Irving, TX: Spring Publications, 1979.

Shattuck, Roger. *Forbidden Knowledge*. New York: Harcourt Brace, 1996.

Stein, Ruth, "Why perversion? 'False love' and the perverse pact." *International Journal of Psychoanalysis* 86 (2005): 775–99.

Symington, Neville. "Phantasy Effects that which It Represents." *International Journal of Psychoanalysis* 66 (1985): 349–57.

———. *Narcissism: A New Theory*. London: Karnac Books, 1993.

———. *A Pattern of Madness*. London: Karnac Books, 2002.

Taylor, Mark C. *Altarity*. Chicago: University of Chicago Press, 1987.

Teresa of Avila. *The Life of Saint Teresa of Avila by Herself*, translated by J.M. Cohen. London: Penguin Books, 1957. [written before 1567.]

———. *Interior Castle*, translated and edited by E. Allison Peers. Garden City, NY: Double-day Image Books, 1961. [written 1577.]

Tressider, Jack. *Dictionary of Symbols*. San Francisco: Chronicle Books, 2005.

von Eschenbach, Wolfram. *Parzival*, translation and introduction by Helen M. Mustard and Charles E. Passage. New York: Vintage Books, 1961.

von Franz, Marie-Louise. "The Process of Individuation." In C. G. Jung, ed., *Man and His Symbols*. London: Aldus Books, 1964.

———. *The Golden Ass of Apuleius*. Boston: Shambhala, 1970.

———. *The Problem of the Puer Aeternus*. New York: Spring Publications, 1970.

———. *Alchemy: An Introduction*. Toronto: Inner City Books, 1980.

Von Krause, Carl. *Die Gedichte Walthers von der Vogelweide*. Berlin: Walter de Griyter & Company, 1962.

Waldenfels, Bernhard. "Levinas and the Face of the Other." In *The Cambridge Companion to Levinas*, edited by Simon Critchley and Robert Berasconi, 63–81. Cambridge, UK: Cambridge University Press, 2002.

Wilde, Oscar. *The Picture of Dorian Gray*. New York: Dover Publications, 1993.

Wilson, Bee. "Mein Diat: Adolf Hitler's diet," *New Statesman* (London) 127(4406): 40ff (October 9, 1998), at http://web.archive.org/web/20050321091219/http://www.findarticles.com/p/articles/mi_m0FQP/is_n4406_v127/ai_21238666 (accessed 1/7/2010).

Winnicott, Donald W. "Mind and Its Relation to the Psyche-Soma" (1949). In *Through Paediatrics to Psychoanalysis*, 243–54. New York: Basic Books, 1975.

———. "Ego Distortion in Terms of True and False Self" (1960). In *The Maturational Processes and the Facilitating Environment*, 140–52. Madison, CT: International Universities Press, 1965.

———. "The Capacity for Concern." *Bulletin of the Menninger Clinic* (1962): 74–78. See also "The Development of the Capacity for Concern" (1963). In *The Maturational Processes and the Facilitating Environment*, 73–82. Madison, CT: International Universities Press, 1965.

Wolff, Toni. *Structural Forms of the Feminine Psyche*, translated by Gela Jacobson. *Psychological Perspectives* 31 (1995): 77–90.

Young-Eisendrath, Polly, and Terence Dawson, eds. *Cambridge Companion to Jung*. Cambridge, UK: Cambridge University Press, 1997.

Ward, Aileen. *John Keats: The Making of a Poet*. New York: Viking, 1963.

Zimmer, Heinrich Robert. *The King and the Corpse*, edited by Joseph Campbell. Princeton, NJ: Princeton University Press, 1948.

*The Zohar*, translation and commentary by Daniel C. Matt. Stanford, CA: Stanford University Press, 2004.

# FILM REFERENCES

*Bram Stoker's Dracula*. 1992. Screenplay by James V. Hart, based upon Bram Stoker, 1897, 1965. New York: Signet Classic. Directed by Francis Ford Coppola.

*Dr. Jekyll and Mr. Hyde*. 1941. Screenplay by John Lee Mahin, Percy Heath and Samuel Hoffenstein, based upon Robert Louis Stevenson, *The Strange Case of Dr. Jekyll and Mr. Hyde*. 1886. London: Longmans, Green & Co. Directed by Victor Fleming.

*Eternal Sunshine of the Spotless Mind*. 2004. Screenplay by Charlie Kaufman. Directed by Michel Gondry.

*Family Man*. 2000. Screenplay by David Diamond and David Weissman. Directed by Brett Ratner.

*High Fidelity*. 2000. Screenplay by D.V. DeVincentis, Steve Pink, John Cusack, and Scott Rosenberg, based upon Nick Hornby, *High Fidelity*. 1995. New York: Riverhead Books. Directed by Stephen Fears.

*Reign Over Me*. 2007. Screenplay by Mike Binder. Directed by Mike Binder.

*The Curse of the Cat People*. 1944. Screenplay by DeWitt Bodeen. Directed by Gunther von Fritsch and Robert Wise.

*The Graduate*. 1967. Screenplay by Calder Willingham and Buck Henry, based upon Charles Webb, *The Graduate*. 1963. New York: Washington Square Press. Directed by Mike Nichols.

*The Natural*. 1985. Screenplay by Roger Towne and Phil Dusenberry, based upon Bernard Malamud, *The Natural*. 1952. New York: Farrar, Strauss and Cudahy. Directed by Barry Levinson.

# INDEX

*You might also enjoy reading these Jungian publications*

**The Creative Soul** *by Lawrence Staples*
ISBN 978-0-9810344-4-7

**Guilt with a Twist** *by Lawrence Staples*
ISBN 978-0-9776076-4-8

**Enemy, Cripple, Beggar** *by Erel Shalit*
ISBN 978-0-9776076-7-9

**Divine Madness** *by John R. Haule*
ISBN 978-1-926715-04-9

**Farming Soul** *by Patricia Damery*
ISBN 978-1-926715-01-8

**The Motherline** *by Naomi Ruth Lowinsky*
ISBN 978-0-9810344-6-1

**The Sister From Below** *by Naomi Ruth Lowinsky*
ISBN 978-0-9810344-2-3

**Like Gold Through Fire** *by Bud & Massimilla Harris*
ISBN 978-0-9810344-5-4

**The Art of Love: The Craft of Relationship**
*by Bud & Massimilla Harris*
ISBN 978-1-926715-02-5

**Resurrecting the Unicorn** *by Bud Harris*
ISBN 978-0-9810344-0-9

**The Father Quest** *by Bud Harris*
ISBN 978-0-9810344-9-2

*Phone Orders Welcomed*
*Credit Cards Accepted*
*In Canada & the U.S. call  1-800-228-9316*
*International call  +1-831-238-7799*
*www.fisherkingpress.com*

35125950R00174

Made in the USA
San Bernardino, CA
18 June 2016